**Keep this book. You will need it and use it throughout your career.**

## About the American Hotel & Lodging Association (AH&LA)

Founded in 1910, AH&LA is the trade association representing the lodging industry in the United States. AH&LA is a federation of state lodging associations throughout the United States with 11,000 lodging properties worldwide as members. The association offers its members assistance with governmental affairs representation, communications, marketing, hospitality operations, training and education, technology issues, and more. For information, call 202-289-3100.

*LODGING*, the management magazine of AH&LA, is a "living textbook" for hospitality students that provides timely features, industry news, and vital lodging information.

## About the Educational Institute of AH&LA (EI)

An affiliate of AH&LA, the Educational Institute is the world's largest source of quality training and educational materials for the lodging industry. EI develops textbooks and courses that are used in more than 1,200 colleges and universities worldwide, and also offers courses to individuals through its Distance Learning program. Hotels worldwide rely on EI for training resources that focus on every aspect of lodging operations. Industry-tested videos, CD-ROMs, seminars, and skills guides prepare employees at every skill level. EI also offers professional certification for the industry's top performers. For information about EI's products and services, call 800-349-0299 or 407-999-8100.

## About the American Hotel & Lodging Educational Foundation (AH&LEF)

An affiliate of AH&LA, the American Hotel & Lodging Educational Foundation provides financial support that enhances the stability, prosperity, and growth of the lodging industry through educational and research programs. AH&LEF has awarded hundreds of thousands of dollars in scholarship funds for students pursuing higher education in hospitality management. AH&LEF has also funded research projects on topics important to the industry, including occupational safety and health, turnover and diversity, and best practices in the U.S. lodging industry. For information, call 202-289-3180.

# MANAGING TECHNOLOGY in the HOSPITALITY INDUSTRY

# Educational Institute Books

UNIFORM SYSTEM OF ACCOUNTS FOR THE LODGING
INDUSTRY
*Ninth Revised Edition*

RESORT DEVELOPMENT AND MANAGEMENT
*Second Edition*
*Chuck Y. Gee*

PLANNING AND CONTROL FOR FOOD AND BEVERAGE
OPERATIONS
*Fifth Edition*
*Jack D. Ninemeier*

TRAINING FOR THE HOSPITALITY INDUSTRY
*Second Edition*
*Lewis C. Forrest, Jr.*

UNDERSTANDING HOSPITALITY LAW
*Fourth Edition*
*Jack P. Jefferies/Banks Brown*

SUPERVISION IN THE HOSPITALITY INDUSTRY
*Third Edition*
*Raphael R. Kavanaugh/Jack D. Ninemeier*

ENERGY AND WATER RESOURCE MANAGEMENT
*Second Edition*
*Robert E. Aulbach*

MANAGEMENT OF FOOD AND BEVERAGE OPERATIONS
*Third Edition*
*Jack D. Ninemeier*

MANAGING FRONT OFFICE OPERATIONS
*Sixth Edition*
*Michael L. Kasavana/Richard M. Brooks*

STRATEGIC HOTEL/MOTEL MARKETING
*Revised Edition*
*Christopher W. L. Hart/David A. Troy*

MANAGING SERVICE IN FOOD AND BEVERAGE
OPERATIONS
*Second Edition*
*Ronald F. Cichy/Paul E. Wise*

THE LODGING AND FOOD SERVICE INDUSTRY
*Fifth Edition*
*Gerald W. Lattin*

SECURITY AND LOSS PREVENTION MANAGEMENT
*Second Edition*
*Raymond C. Ellis, Jr./David M. Stipanuk*

HOSPITALITY INDUSTRY MANAGERIAL ACCOUNTING
*Fifth Edition*
*Raymond S. Schmidgall*

PURCHASING FOR HOSPITALITY OPERATIONS
*William B. Virts*

THE ART AND SCIENCE OF HOSPITALITY MANAGEMENT
*Jerome J. Vallen/James R. Abbey*

MANAGING TECHNOLOGY IN THE HOSPITALITY
INDUSTRY
*Fourth Edition*
*Michael L. Kasavana/John J. Cahill*

MANAGING HOSPITALITY ENGINEERING SYSTEMS
*Michael H. Redlin/David M. Stipanuk*

BASIC HOTEL AND RESTAURANT ACCOUNTING
*Fifth Edition*
*Raymond Cote*

ACCOUNTING FOR HOSPITALITY MANAGERS
*Fourth Edition*
*Raymond Cote*

CONVENTION MANAGEMENT AND SERVICE
*Sixth Edition*
*Milton T. Astroff/James R. Abbey*

HOSPITALITY SALES AND MARKETING
*Fourth Edition*
*James R. Abbey*

MANAGING HOUSEKEEPING OPERATIONS
*Second Edition*
*Margaret M. Kappa/Aleta Nitschke/Patricia B. Schappert*

DIMENSIONS OF TOURISM
*Joseph D. Fridgen*

HOSPITALITY TODAY: AN INTRODUCTION
*Fourth Edition*
*Rocco M. Angelo/Andrew N. Vladimir*

MANAGING BAR AND BEVERAGE OPERATIONS
*Lendal H. Kotschevar/Mary L. Tanke*

ETHICS IN HOSPITALITY MANAGEMENT: A BOOK OF
READINGS
*Edited by Stephen S. J. Hall*

HOSPITALITY FACILITIES MANAGEMENT AND DESIGN
*Second Edition*
*David M. Stipanuk*

MANAGING HOSPITALITY HUMAN RESOURCES
*Third Edition*
*Robert H. Woods*

FINANCIAL MANAGEMENT FOR THE HOSPITALITY
INDUSTRY
*William P. Andrew/Raymond S. Schmidgall*

HOSPITALITY INDUSTRY FINANCIAL ACCOUNTING
*Second Edition*
*Raymond S. Schmidgall/James W. Damitio*

INTERNATIONAL HOTEL MANAGEMENT
*Chuck Y. Gee*

QUALITY SANITATION MANAGEMENT
*Ronald F. Cichy*

HOTEL INVESTMENTS: ISSUES & PERSPECTIVES
*Third Edition*
*Edited by Lori E. Raleigh and Rachel J. Roginsky*

LEADERSHIP AND MANAGEMENT IN THE HOSPITALITY
INDUSTRY
*Second Edition*
*Robert H. Woods/Judy Z. King*

MARKETING IN THE HOSPITALITY INDUSTRY
*Fourth Edition*
*Ronald A. Nykiel*

CONTEMPORARY HOSPITALITY MARKETING
*William Lazer/Roger Layton*

UNIFORM SYSTEM OF ACCOUNTS FOR THE HEALTH,
RACQUET AND SPORTSCLUB INDUSTRY

CONTEMPORARY CLUB MANAGEMENT
*Edited by Joe Perdue for the Club Managers Association of America*

RESORT CONDOMINIUM AND VACATION OWNERSHIP
MANAGEMENT: A HOSPITALITY PERSPECTIVE
*Robert A. Gentry/Pedro Mandoki/Jack Rush*

ACCOUNTING FOR CLUB OPERATIONS
*Raymond S. Schmidgall/James W. Damitio*

TRAINING AND DEVELOPMENT FOR THE
HOSPITALITY INDUSTRY
*Debra F. Cannon/Catherine M. Gustafson*

# MANAGING TECHNOLOGY in the HOSPITALITY INDUSTRY

**Fourth Edition**

**Michael L. Kasavana, Ph.D., CHTP**
**John J. Cahill, CHA, CHTP**

EDUCATIONAL INSTITUTE
American Hotel & Lodging Association

# Disclaimer

This publication is designed to provide accurate and authoritative information in regard to the subject matter covered. It is sold with the understanding that the publisher is not engaged in rendering legal, accounting, or other professional service. If legal advice or other expert assistance is required, the services of a competent professional person should be sought.
  —*From the Declaration of Principles jointly adopted by the American Bar Association and a Committee of Publishers and Associations*

The authors, Michael L. Kasavana and John J. Cahill, are solely responsible for the contents of this publication. All views expressed herein are solely those of the authors and do not necessarily reflect the views of the Educational Institute of the American Hotel & Lodging Association (the Institute) or the American Hotel & Lodging Association (AH&LA).

Nothing contained in this publication shall constitute a standard, an endorsement, or a recommendation of the Institute or AH&LA. The Institute and AH&LA disclaim any liability with respect to the use of any information, procedure, or product, or reliance thereon by any member of the hospitality industry.

# Contents

# Acknowledgments

The Educational Institute appreciates the significant contributions (both direct and indirect) of three committees to this fourth edition of *Managing Technology in the Hospitality Industry:* the Technology Committee and the E-Business Committee of the American Hotel & Lodging Association and the CHTP Advisory Council of Hospitality Financial and Technology Professionals.

## American Hotel & Lodging Association Technology Committee

Robert S. Bennett
SVP Systems Property and Services
Pegasus Solutions, Inc.

Carol Beggs
Vice President Technology
Sonesta International Hotels
Corporation

Kathleen Pearl Brewer, Ph.D.
Associate Dean for Academic Affairs
University of Nevada Las Vegas

Brian P. Garavuso
Chief Technology Officer
MeriStar Hotels & Resorts

Mark Haley, CHTP
Principal
The Prism Partnership

Danny Hudson
White Plains, NY

Jon Inge
President
Jon Inge & Associates

Richard J. Jackson
AH&LA Staff Liaison
Vice President/Chief Information
 Officer
American Hotel & Lodging
Association

Sherry Marek
Vice President of Marketing
Datavision Technologies

Joseph Martino
IDeaS, Inc.

Gary Mesich
VP IR Business Services
Marriott International

Francis J. Nardozza
REH Capital Partners

Kirby D. Payne, CHA
President
American Hospitality Management
Company

Darrin Pinkham, CHTP
Director of Technology
Boca Resorts, Inc.

Richard Siegel
President & Publisher
Hospitality Upgrade

David Sjolander
Vice President Hotel Information
Systems
Carlson Hospitality Corporation

Victor L Vesnaver
Product Marketing
V2

## American Hotel & Lodging Association
## E-Business Committee

Scott Anderson
President & CEO
Swan, Inc.

Robert S. Bennett
Technology Committee Liaison
SVP Systems Property and Services

William Brown
Assistant Vice President E-Commerce
Interval International

Cihan Cobanoglu
Assistant Professor
University of Delaware

D. Lee Davis
Director, Electronic
Business-Hospitality Practice
Unisys Corporation

Clay Dickinson
Principal
IBM Global Services, Travel and
Transportation

Tim Durant
Executive Vice President
Passkey.com, Inc.

Christopher Eastman
Chief Information Officer
MeriStar Hotels & Resorts

Richard J. Jackson
AH&LA Staff Liaison
Vice President/Chief Information
Officer

Michael L. Kasavana
Professor
Michigan State University

Peter Klebanoff
V. P., Industry Relations
LodgeNet Entertainment

Francis J. Nardozza
REH Capital Partners

Michael D. Olsen, Ph.D.
Professor
Virginia Tech Department of
Hospitality & Tourism Management

Kirby D. Payne, CHA
AH&LA Officer Liaison
President

Daniel Rothfeld
SVP, E-Commerce
Choice Hotels

Andrew Sherry
Director, Online Ventures
USA Today

Barry Shuler
SVP, Information Resource
Marriott International

Jules Sieburgh
SVP & CTO
Host Marriott Corporation

Donald Smith
Vice President of Sales
WorldRes, Inc.

Maryam T. Wehe
Executive Vice President, Business
Strategy and Development
Marriott International

Alan E. Young
V.P. Hotel & Systems Integration
Newtrade Technologies Inc.

## Hospitality Financial and Technology Professionals
## CHTP Advisory Council

Brian P. Garavuso, CHTP
Chief Technology Officer
Interstate Hotels and Resorts

Scott T. Barter, CHAE, CHTP
Director of Finance
Fontainebleau Hilton Resort

Mark Bigalke, CHTP
MIS Director
Grand Teton Lodge Co.

Brian J. Brady, CHTP
Info. Systems Director
Crown American Hotels

Pamela Burke, CHTP
Consultant
O'Neal/GAJ Inc.

John J. Cahill, CHTP, CHA
Chief Information Officer
Manhattan East Suite Hotels

Cihan Cobanoglu, Ph.D., CHTP
Asst. Professor, Hosp. IT &
E-Commerce
University Of Delaware-HRIM

Stephen P. D'Erasmo, CHTP
Manager, Information Systems
Walt Disney World

Mark Hamilton, CHE, CHTP, MHM
Director, Hospitality Technology
Evans & Chastain, L.L.P.

Darrin R. Pinkham, CHTP
Chief Technology Officer
Loews Hotels At Universal Orlando

Clifton J. Rath, CHTP
IS Manager
RLK & Company

Jeremy Rock, CHTP
RockIT Group

Thomas M. Steinberg, CPA, CHTP,
CHAE
President & CEO
Stonehill Systems Inc.

Lenora Streitfeld, CHAE, CHTP
Controller
Seawane Club

Lucinda Hart
Director of Executive Services
Hospitality Financial and Technology
Professionals

Frank I. Wolfe, CAE
Executive Vice President/CEO
Hospitality Financial and Technology
Professionals

# Chapter 1 Outline

Property Management Systems
    Reservations Module
    Rooms Management Module
    Guest Accounting Module
PMS Interfaces
Point-of-Sale Systems
Sales and Catering Systems
Hospitality Accounting Systems
E-Commerce
    E-Distribution
    Enterprise Systems
    Web Site Development

# Competencies

1. Describe the basic functions common to property management systems. (pp. 3–9)

2. Identify stand-alone technology systems that may interface with property management systems. (pp. 9–13)

3. Describe the basic functions of a point-of-sale system. (pp. 13–15)

4. Describe the basic functions of a sales and catering system. (pp. 15–17)

5. Identify hospitality accounting modules typically provided by back-office software packages. (pp. 17–19)

6. Explain the impact of e-commerce on hospitality organizations. (pp. 20–26)

# 1

# Hospitality Technology Systems

$\mathbf{H}$OW MUCH DOES a manager need to know about technology to operate a technology system? About as much as a motorist needs to know about auto mechanics to drive a car. A motorist does not need to master the mechanical wonders of the internal-combustion engine to drive a car. A driver simply needs to learn how to instruct the machine—how to turn the ignition key, push the gas pedal, apply the brake, and so on. Sparks jump, cylinders explode, pistons pump, and gears turn, regardless of the driver's knowledge of mechanical engineering. However, if a motorist has some understanding of auto mechanics as well as basic auto maintenance skills, the car should perform even better and meet his or her transportation needs for a longer period of time.

Similarly, in order to use technology, a manager does not need to learn the intricacies of electronic circuitry etched on silicon chips. The manager simply needs to learn the commands by which to instruct the system to carry out the desired functions. However, if a manager also has some basic knowledge about the essential operations of a system, he or she will be better equipped to use technology as an effective tool in managing information needs. A basic knowledge of the way systems operate enables managers to select technology applications which best meet the information needs of their operations, or to enhance and expand their present systems. Some knowledge of technology can be extremely helpful in identifying the functions desired from a system and in understanding the functioning of the system itself.

Despite the increasing number of functions being built into modern hospitality applications, no one system is likely to cover all areas a property may need to manage.[1] At a minimum, a property management system (PMS) and an accounting system will be needed. If there is a bar or restaurant, a point-of-sale (POS) system will also be needed. For operations with several function rooms and strong group meeting or wedding/banquet business, a sales and catering system is essential. Those with extensive food and beverage operations will also gain much from the cost controls provided by inventory and purchasing systems.

Apart from these, there are a host of sub-systems that manage such functions as telephone call accounting and charging, voice mail, electronic door locks for the guestrooms, energy management, pay-per-view movies, mini-bars, bookings for spa/tennis/golf, and so on. These systems are produced primarily by specialists (not the main PMS vendor) and interact with the PMS through interfaces of varying

3

degrees of complexity and capability. Getting the best out of these multiple systems at one location depends, to a large degree, on the ease and extent of data exchanges between them.

## Property Management Systems

An automated lodging information system is commonly called a **property management system (PMS).** Although the components of a PMS may vary, the term "PMS" is generally used to describe the set of application programs that directly relate to front office and back office activities. "Application software" is the term for programs that instruct the hardware of a technology system in what to do, when to do it, and how to do it.

A PMS does not actually manage a property in the commercial real estate sense; it helps manage virtually every aspect of a guest's visit to a property. Primary functions performed by a PMS include:

- Allowing for the creation of a wide range of room rates, covering different rooms, dates, and company/association discounts.

- Tracking the availability of all guestrooms and rates for at least the next 12 months.

- Tracking the details of each guest's reservation, whether as an individual or as part of a group.

- Helping select an appropriate room for the guest either on or before arrival.

- Facilitating the check-in process.

- Keeping an up-to-the-minute record of all the expenses guests charge to their room during their stay, either directly or through an interface to one of the many sub-systems managing other aspects of the property, such as bar/restaurant point-of-sale charges.

- Accepting full or partial payment when guests check out.

- Following through on any resulting accounts receivable if part of the payment is charged to an outside account, such as the guests' company.

Front office PMS applications consist of a series of programs (or modules) including reservations, rooms management, and guest accounting functions. A variety of stand-alone applications may also be interfaced with an installed property management system. Popular interfaces include point-of-sale systems, call accounting systems, electronic locking systems, energy management systems, auxiliary guest service devices, guest-operated devices, and others. Back office applications typically included in PMS packages contain modules covering accounting and internal-control functions. The following sections briefly describe some of the basic features of PMS front office applications, as outlined in Exhibit 1.

### Reservations Module

A **reservations module** enables a hotel to rapidly process room requests and generate timely and accurate rooms, revenue, and forecasting reports. Exhibit 2 shows

**Exhibit 1    PMS Front Office Applications**

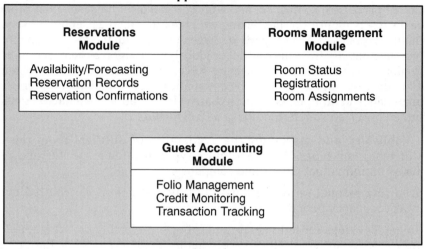

**Reservations Module**

Availability/Forecasting
Reservation Records
Reservation Confirmations

**Rooms Management Module**

Room Status
Registration
Room Assignments

**Guest Accounting Module**

Folio Management
Credit Monitoring
Transaction Tracking

**Exhibit 2    Sample PMS Reservations Screen**

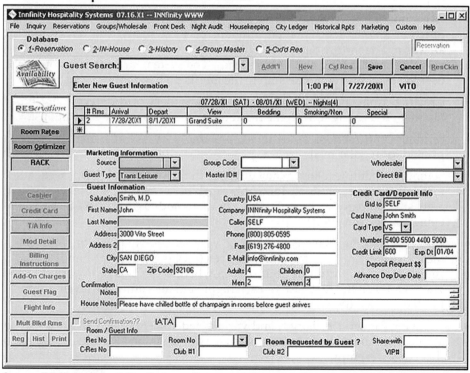

Source: INNfinity Hospitality Systems. For more information, browse the company's Web site at http://www.innhs.com

a sample PMS reservations screen. Reservations received at a central reservations site can be processed, confirmed, and communicated to the destination property before the reservationist finishes talking with the caller on the telephone. When the destination property uses a property management system, the reservation module receives data directly from the central (or global) reservation system, and in-house reservations records, files, and revenue forecasts are immediately updated. In addition, the reservations data can be automatically reformatted into preregistration materials and an updated expected-arrivals list can be generated. Functions performed by a reservations module of a PMS include:

- Establishing and displaying the availability of different room rates for different room types, dates, and guest types, including specific rates negotiated for individual groups and companies.

- Allowing manual setting of length-of-stay restrictions as required during peak occupancy periods.

- Taking bookings for individuals and groups, preferably checking guest history records automatically to see whether they've stayed at the property before.

- Blocking specific room numbers for guests, when appropriate (VIP, specific request from the guest, etc.).

- Accommodating requests to share rooms. Guests should be able to be from different market segments, on different package plans, and have different arrival and departure dates. The only thing they need to have in common is at least one overlapping night of their stay. The system should also prompt the user to adjust the room rate among the guests on overlapping days.

- Creating group bookings with differing numbers of different room types blocked on each night, with the rapid entry of names from a rooming list.

- Sending confirmations as required, preferably by fax or e-mail, as well as printed for regular mail.

- Setting up multiple folios for any guest, with the system posting charges automatically to the appropriate folio (this capability is used to handle cases where a guest's company will reimburse only room and tax, with all other charges being paid by the guest).

- Creating package plans consisting of various combinations of room rates, meal charges, and fees for other services (parking, spa, etc.) bundled into a single charge, with full flexibility as to whether the charge is posted to the guest's folio on the first, last, or each night, and allocating the revenue appropriately to each department.

- Allowing for service charges and various federal, state, and city taxes to be applied automatically to appropriate charges, tracking all guests and groups that are tax-exempt.

- Tracking at least one travel agent for each reservation, and reporting on the commission payable after check-out.

- Recording the payment of advance deposits, applying them to the correct guest records, or tracking their return/forfeiture in the event of cancellation, in accordance with hotel policy.

## Rooms Management Module

A **rooms management module** maintains up-to-date information regarding the status of rooms, assists in the assignment of rooms during registration, and helps coordinate many guest services. Since this module replaces most traditional front office equipment, it often becomes a major determinant in the selection of one PMS over another. This module alerts front desk employees of each room's status. The front desk employee simply enters the room's number at a keyboard and the current status of the room appears immediately on a display screen. Once the room becomes clean and ready for occupancy, housekeeping changes the room's status through a terminal in the housekeeping work area, and the information is immediately communicated to the front desk. Functions performed by a rooms management module of a PMS include:

### Check-In

- Retrieving the guest's reservation, preferably by swiping his/her credit card through a magnetic-card reader on the workstation.

- Presenting a list of available rooms that match the guest's requirements from which the front desk agent can select (or automatically select the first one) and check in the guest, overriding a room's housekeeping status manually if necessary.

- Providing for the one-step check-in of groups after verifying guest names, room types, and sharing arrangements.

### Housekeeping

- Automatically setting the status of all occupied rooms to "dirty" each night.

- Allowing the grouping of dirty rooms into housekeeping sections and assigning them to specific attendants and supervisors, using different levels of cleaning difficulty for different room types.

- Updating each room's status as cleaning progresses, either manually on a PMS workstation or automatically through the attendants' dialing into the system from the guestroom phone.

- Tracking discrepancies between each room's occupancy status as recorded by the front desk and as reported by housekeeping, to identify possible "skips" (i.e., should be occupied, housekeeping reports it as vacant) or "sleeps"(i.e., should be vacant, reported as occupied).

- Changing any room's status to "out of order" to allow for correction of engineering or maintenance issues, preferably also issuing engineering work orders.

PBX Operators

- Providing instant access to the guest list for the current day, including arrivals and guests already checked out.

- Providing on-demand access to the guest list for any future or past date.

- Taking messages for guests and track their delivery.

## Guest Accounting Module

A **guest accounting module** increases the hotel's control over guest accounts and significantly modifies the night audit routine. Guest accounts are maintained electronically, thereby eliminating the need for folio cards, trays, or posting machinery. The guest accounting module monitors predetermined guest-credit limits and provides flexibility through multiple folio formats. When revenue centers are connected to the PMS, remote point-of-sale terminals communicate with the front desk, and guest charges are automatically posted to the appropriate folios. At check-out, outstanding account balances are transferred automatically to the city ledger (accounts receivable) for collection. Exhibit 3 shows a sample guest folio. Functions performed by a guest accounting module of a PMS include:

Charge Posting

- Allowing cashiers to post charges for multiple departments directly to guest folios.

- Allowing for the automatic posting of charges to guest folios from sub-systems such as point-of-sale systems, call accounting systems, and so on.

- Transferring charges from one folio to another.

- Allowing corrections to the current day's postings and adjustments to those from previous days. Corrections may be kept on the folio record for display on the workstation, but are not printed on the folio.

- Keeping an audit of all postings and changes to them.

- Tracking credit limits for each guest and report when a limit is exceeded. If a credit card authorization interface is used, it should automatically dial out for increased authorization amounts as necessary.

Check-Out

- Posting credits to guests' folio(s) in the form of cash, checks, credit card payments, or transfers to other folios, both for in-house guests and for authorized direct-billing accounts.

- Providing for a simple, one-step check-out process for groups, after appropriate action on any outstanding folio balances.

End-of-Day

- Running a series of reports to help the front office audit staff close out the day's operations, including cashiers' shift balances, room rate discrepancies from rack rate, over-credit guests, and so on.

**Exhibit 3    Sample PMS Guest Folio**

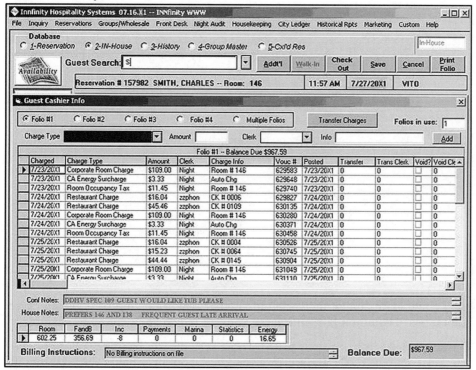

Source: INNfinity Hospitality Systems. For more information, browse the company's Web site at
http://www.innhs.com

- Running a full data back-up for the day's operations.

- Changing the accounting date in the system.

- Setting all occupied rooms to a housekeeping status of "dirty."

- Running various sets of standard operations reports for distribution to managers.

# PMS Interfaces

Whether to automate the room-charge posting from the many other systems at the property or to increase the effectiveness of the staff using different systems, every PMS needs a range of interfaces. An **interface** is the connection and interaction between hardware, software, and the user. Hardware interfaces are plugs, sockets, wires, and the electrical pulses that travel through them. Software interfaces are the programming languages, codes, and messages that programs use to communicate with each other and to the hardware. User interfaces are the keyboards, mice, commands, and menus that are used to communicate with the hardware and software system. **PMS interfaces** are the formats and languages that define data that

**Exhibit 4    Common PMS Interfaces**

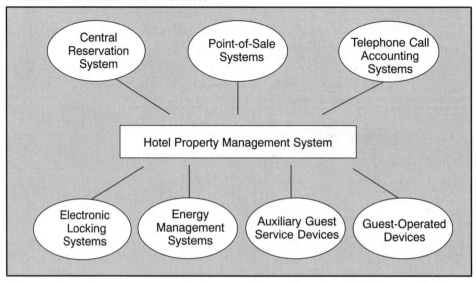

one system is capable of delivering to another. The following sections offer brief summaries of common PMS interfaces, some of which are identified in Exhibit 4.

**Central Reservations System (CRS).** These systems can be one-way or two-way interfaces. A one-way interface receives guest bookings made through the airlines/travel agencies or through the hotel chain's own centralized booking office. Bookings are merged automatically into the PMS reservations module, with certain exceptions (e.g., requests for suites) held for manual review. With a two-way interface, in addition to receiving bookings, the system automatically adjusts the room and rate inventory held in the CRS for the property to reflect changes in the PMS. For hotel companies that collect centralized guest history data from each property, this interface also transmits stay details for the guest to the central system upon check-out.

**Internet.** Increasingly common, this interface allows visitors to the property's own Web site to book reservations directly in the PMS. The PMS should allow the property to restrict the room and rate types made available to this channel. More sophisticated versions allow group coordinators to access the PMS through the Web site to manage their own group bookings, enter rooming lists, and so on, and allow individuals to enter a group or corporate code to book at the negotiated rates. In addition, many properties offer **high-speed Internet access (HSIA)** wired directly into the guestroom. Sometimes this is provided at no charge as an amenity; in other installations, a charge is made for each 24 hours of use. The choice is largely based on the property's guest mix and local demand for access. A city-center, business-oriented property might well attract more guests by offering free Internet access, whereas a resort might not see the same benefit. Both HSIA types require an access server to issue temporary Internet addresses to the users' PCs.

The charged systems also require detection facilities to identify which room is using the service and to post a charge to the guest folio.

**Sales and Catering.** This interface passes PMS guestroom availability to the sales and catering system to give sales managers a complete picture of property availability, including function rooms and guestrooms. The interface also receives details of group blocks made in the sales and catering system to establish a group master and folio in the PMS.

**Point-of-Sale.** This interface receives and responds to requests from the point-of-sale (POS) system to display the guest names registered in a specific guestroom, then accepts the POS charge against the selected guest's folio. The trend is to pass increasing levels of POS check data to the PMS (often as many as sixteen sub-totals) to reduce the number of POS charges disputed at check-out. PMS/POS interfaces have been developed, which allow the PMS to:

- Retrieve full details of the POS check from the guest's PMS folio.

- Recognize when a POS check has been opened for a particular guest in a food and beverage outlet and set a corresponding location flag on the PBX operator's guest list.

- Alert the POS cashier that the guest settling his or her check has a message entered in the PMS.

- Enable the guest to check out of the PMS from a POS terminal, for example, after breakfast.

Some interfaces also pass revenue sub-totals for all POS settlement types (not just room charges) to the PMS at end of day, which can make it easier to prepare nightly operational reports.

**Credit Card Processing.** At check-in, this interface automatically dials out to verify the validity of the card and authorize appropriate funds for the guest's stay, usually calculated as the total room charge for the number of days plus a hotel-set level of incidental expenditure per day. During the guest's stay, if the guest's PMS credit limit is exceeded, the interface automatically dials out during the end-of-day procedures to increase the authorized amount. At check-out, the interface dials out to collect the funds due and, at end of day, processes the transaction batch. Originally, it was necessary to have one credit card interface for each system needing to handle this payment type (e.g., PMS, POS, spa bookings, etc.), but vendors are now combining all requests through a single connection.

**Revenue Management.** This interface constantly passes current levels of reservations booking activity in the PMS to a separate revenue management system. This system then analyzes it against pre-set goals and historical trends, and suggests changes in the PMS rates and length-of-stay restrictions.

**Back Office Accounting.** Because accounts receivable (City Ledger) is almost invariably part of the PMS, this interface typically transfers a journal, reflecting end-of-day operational totals to the general ledger.

**Call Accounting.** A **call accounting system (CAS)** enables a hotel to take control over local and long-distance telephone services and to apply a markup to switchboard operations. A call accounting system can place and price outgoing calls. This interface receives phone charges from a call accounting system attached to the PBX and posts them to the guest's folio, with details of the phone number called.

**Electronic Locks.** Many types of electronic locking systems are available today. Often, these systems interface with a PMS, thereby enabling management to exercise important key control measures. One kind of electronic locking system (ELS) functions through a terminal at the front desk. The terminal selects a code that will permit entry and then produces a card for the guest to use. Once a code is entered and a card produced, all previous codes for that lock are canceled, and cards issued to previous guests no longer function.

**Energy Management.** This interface sends a message to the EMS at check-in to change the guestroom thermostat to its predefined "occupied" setting and at check-out to set it back to the "vacant" setting. Interfacing energy management systems with a PMS links guestroom energy controls with the front office rooms management module. An **energy management system (EMS)** electronically monitors guestroom temperatures. This may lead to significant reductions in energy consumption and lower energy costs. For example, in the cold winter months, an unoccupied room may be maintained at a temperature of 60° F (15.6° C). When a guest checks in and is assigned a guestroom, the computer can automatically adjust the room's temperature to a more comfortable 70° F (21.1° C). By the time the guest reaches the room, the temperature will be acceptable, and the hotel's energy costs will have been reduced.

**Auxiliary Guest Service Devices.** Automation has simplified many auxiliary guest services, such as the placement of wake-up calls and voice messaging for guests. These functions are often performed by auxiliary guest service devices (such as electronic message-waiting systems and voice mail systems) that are marketed as stand-alone systems but can be interfaced with the rooms management module of a PMS. A PBX (telephone switch) interface unblocks the guestroom phone for long-distance calls upon check-in and blocks it again at check-out. The interface sends signals to the PBX to turn on a light on the guestroom phone when a message is left for a guest and to turn it off again when the message has been delivered. The interface also receives codes dialed into the PBX by housekeeping staff from the guestroom to update the room's cleaning status. Sometimes combined with the PBX interface, a voice mail system creates a new voice mailbox when a guest checks in and clears it at check-out. The interface receives a signal when a message is left in the voice mailbox to turn on the message-waiting flag in the PMS, and clears it when the guest retrieves the message. This alerts the front desk cashier to the presence of any messages still in the guest's mailbox at check-out.

**Guest-Operated Devices.** Guest-operated devices can be located in a public area of the hotel or in private guestrooms. In-room guest-operated devices (such as vending machines, movies, and video games) are designed to be user-friendly systems. An assortment of devices provide concierge-level service with in-room

**Exhibit 5  POS Server Touch Screen**

| Prev. Client | Table | Next Client | Tbl Name | Firm | GENERAL MENU | Screen |
|---|---|---|---|---|---|---|
| Hold | CMD | Redistribu | Course #1 | Course #2 Course #3 | Quantity | Item rank |

PETER    TABLE    9 Custom 1    

Appetizer    13-taco

| | | |
|---|---|---|
| 1 NEW YORK STEAK | 20.95 | |
| 1=> MEDIUM | $0.00 | |
| 1=> FRENCH FRIES | $0.00 | |
| 1 BTLE MUSCADET | 22.00 | |

Grill    Burger    Brkfast

CHICKEN    Sdwich    Fries

Pizzas    Sea food    PASTA    Dessert

Coffee    BEER

**TOTAL $48.95**    WINES

Soft drink    Cocktail    **BAR**

| Up | Split | Reorder |
|---|---|---|

| Down | Status | Void | Send | Print | Close | Next | Exit |
|---|---|---|---|---|---|---|---|

Source: Maitre'D POS. For more information browse the company's Web site at http://www.maitred pos.com

convenience. Pay-per-view movie interfaces can be one-way or two-way systems. A one-way interface receives charges from the pay-per-view (PPV) movie management system to post to the guest's folio. A two-way interface receives and responds to requests from the pay-per-view system to display the guest's folio on the guest-room TV and processes folio settlement and guest check-out actions entered into the system by the guest. Vending and mini-bar interfaces receive charges and post them to the guest's folio.

## Point-of-Sale Systems

A point-of-sale system is as much the technology core system for restaurants, (and other food and beverage operations) as the PMS is for lodging operations. A **point-of-sale (POS) system** captures data at the time and place of sale. These systems use terminals that are combined with cash registers, bar code readers, optical scanners, and magnetic stripe readers for instantly capturing sales transactions. In restaurants, these systems manage the ordering and delivery of all menu items in one or more restaurants and/or bars. As such, it must be capable of handling different menus and different pricing at different times of the day. Exhibit 5 shows a sample POS server touch screen.

Orders are typically entered on the system's workstations in the main seating area and are automatically routed to printers in the hot or cold preparation areas or in the service bar, as appropriate. Several systems allow all items on an order to be entered at once, with some, usually the main course, held back to be printed and prepared at a later time to suit the pace of the guests' meal. Guest checks are printed on demand.

Most systems can track the hours that employees work through simple sign-on/sign-off routines; several also offer inventory/purchasing functions and recipe analysis. However, more specialized time and attendance and inventory/ purchasing systems are commonly used in these areas. The main functions performed by a POS system include:

Order Entry

- Creating menu items that can be sold at different prices at different times in different outlets (restaurant, cafeteria, bar, room service, etc.).

- Creating modifiers that can (or must) be applied to individual menu items.

- Allowing menu items to be grouped together into combinations with a single price.

- Defining a default kitchen/bar printer where orders for each menu item will be routed, plus a secondary printer in case the first is unavailable.

- Allowing some ordered items to be held back for printing in the kitchen at a later time, either automatically after a pre-determined interval or manually when the server judges that the timing is right.

- Maintaining and displaying to all servers a current total of significant menu items in short supply, such as daily specials, counting down the number available as they are ordered.

- Providing for the simple, rapid entry of quick-service items such as coffee or bar drinks.

- Providing a simple way to re-order a round of drinks.

- Allowing for the ordering of off-menu items, with preparation instructions.

Settlement

- Allowing for the straightforward splitting of charges on a check among the guests at a table, including dividing the cost of individual items or the whole check between two or more guests, in varying proportions.

- Allowing checks to be transferred from one server to another.

- Combining checks for different tables and/or servers.

- Automatically adding a pre-set gratuity percentage and/or service fee for parties exceeding a certain size or for deliveries such as room service.

- Providing full reporting of tips.

- Recording the settlement of checks to cash, check, charge card, and to a guest's room folio.

- Tracking all check item voids, corrections, and adjustments.

- Providing a full set of operating reports, including cashiers' shift balances, menu item popularity/profitability, server productivity, and so on.

In addition to a hotel PMS interface, POS systems may interface with a food and beverage inventory/purchasing (IP) system. This interface sends details of menu items sold to the IP system, which breaks down the items into their standard ingredient quantities and notes, in decrements, the theoretical inventory levels on hand. Sometimes, this interface also receives current ingredient costs from the purchasing system to allow for checks against the POS menu prices.

## Sales and Catering Systems

To control the number of rooms sold at discounted rates, properties usually allocate a certain number of guestrooms for sale to groups (usually defined as any booking for ten or more guestrooms) and corporations, leaving the remainder to be sold through the reservations office. The sales and catering system handles the property's group sales efforts, as well as the booking of function rooms for meetings, banquets, weddings, conferences, and other events.

Sales and catering systems have traditionally been stand-alone systems, relying on the front office staff to enter changes in guestroom availability either manually or through a PMS interface. Often, the final invoice for a banquet function is generated in the PMS as part of the group folio. Recently, the capabilities of these interfaces have been increasing, as more PMS vendors incorporate sales and catering functions into their base product. Both approaches aim to provide a more complete picture of group bookings than the separate systems do. The main functions performed by a sales and catering system include:

Group Sales

- Creating group/company master records, similar to guest profile records but also including links between companies (to allow simple consolidation of booking information across a parent company's multiple divisions) and multiple contacts per group/company.

- Facilitating contact management, including assignment of contacts to sales managers, tracking all interactions with each contact with follow-up "tickler" reminders. Ticklers should preferably be both free-form and available in predefined sequences of actions, depending on the type of business being booked. Exhibit 6 shows a sample sales call information screen.

- Displaying availability of function rooms and guestrooms, showing for the latter both the number set aside for group business and the total available in the hotel for each day.

- Creating and tracking group bookings on both a tentative and definite basis, each booking set at a specified group rate, and for specified function rooms and blocks of guestrooms, all of which can vary by day.

**Exhibit 6   Sample Sales Call Information Screen**

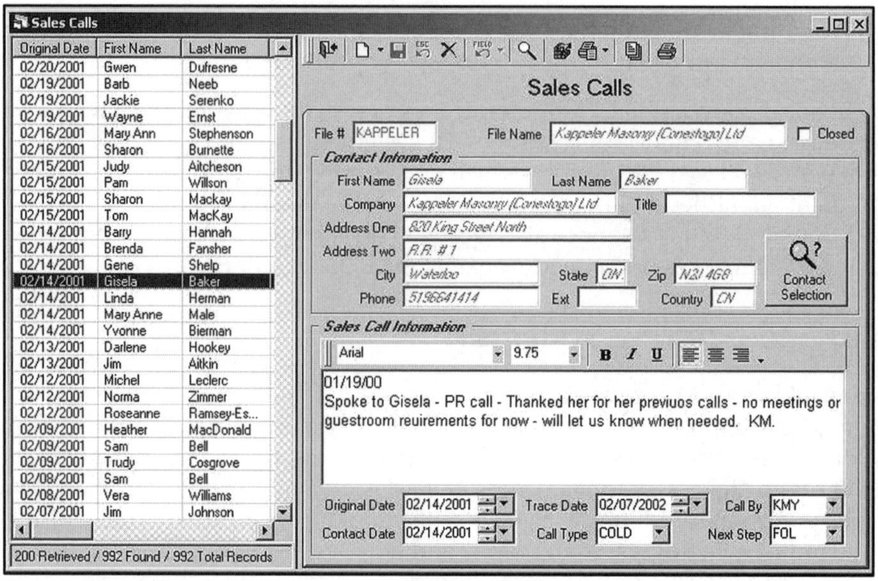

Source: Visual One Systems. For more information, browse the company's Web site at
http://www.visualonesystems.com

- Allowing the entry of a "wash" percentage, which will adjust the contracted number of rooms/guests to an "expected" level based on prior experience with this group/company or type of business.

Function Rooms

- Creating function room records defining their size, capacity in various configurations (ballroom, conference, schoolroom, etc.), and ability to be subdivided through movable walls. Preferably incorporating photos (either still or panoramic) of each room in typical configurations.

- Displaying availability of function rooms graphically, showing the period each is booked and for which client.

- Creating and tracking room bookings, allowing for the unavailability of subdividable spaces if one such division is booked, and including flags to indicate noisy events and "do not move" requests if a specific room is needed.

- Allowing for the simple relocation of an event from one room to another. Creating pick-lists of standard-priced menus that can be used as the basis for any event's food and beverage needs.

- Managing lists of audio-visual and other equipment and furniture available for rent.

- Creating event contracts for client signatures, and banquet event orders (BEOs) that list all details of each event on each day. The latter should include the room(s) booked by date and time, set-up configurations required, all menus, audio-visual equipment, and any other special items, with prices.

A sales and catering system commonly interfaces with a property management system, a room layout drawing system, and event/meeting announcement boards. The sales and catering system may also send details of an individual event (number of guests, set-up configuration, furniture required, etc.) to a separate software package, which then generates a drawing of the room with all appropriate furniture and equipment in place. The system also may send details of all events taking place on the current day to display systems (TV-based or custom display panels) in appropriate locations in the public areas and/or outside the meeting rooms.

Catering-specific software monitors and controls the activities associated with each stage of catering service. In addition to containing data on all purchased food and beverage products, catering files include data on such nonfood items as labor, serving utensils, production equipment, rental equipment, disposable items, and entertainment options. The more complete this file, the easier it becomes for the caterer to assemble an entire catering service package.

## Hospitality Accounting Systems

The number of accounting modules provided by a back office software package may vary widely. A back office system may contain application software designed to monitor and process accounts receivable and accounts payable transactions, payroll accounting, and financial reporting. Additional back office programs include inventory control and valuation, purchasing, budgeting, and fixed asset accounting. Exhibit 7 summarizes typical hospitality accounting applications. The primary functions performed by an accounting system include:

- Creating a chart of accounts according to standard hospitality accounting practices and guidelines.

- Handling 12- or 13-period accounting years, according to the property's preference.

- Permitting full individual and batch posting transactions and adjustments, with audit trail.

- Maintaining transaction details, including audit trails, for at least a full fiscal year.

- Facilitating the creation and tracking of budgets and forecasts.

At the lodging property level, an accounting system may be restricted to financial reporting and accounts payable functions, because accounts receivable is almost always incorporated into a PMS. Payroll is often contracted out to a service company, although some properties include it within their accounting functions. Fixed asset accounting is rarely implemented at the property level. Many properties use general accounting packages either at the property or, more commonly, in multi-property groups on a central server accessed remotely by users at the properties.

The following sections present an overview of the applications that may be included in a back office package.

**Exhibit 7   Hospitality Accounting Applications**

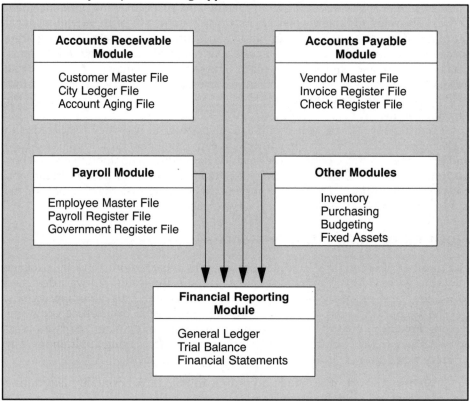

**Accounts Receivable.** An **accounts receivable module** monitors outstanding balances of guest accounts. An account receivable is a dollar amount representing charged purchases made by a guest who has deferred payment for the products and services rendered by the hotel. Accounts receivable balances can be automatically transferred from front office software applications, or they can be manually posted directly into an accounts receivable program. Once entered into the back office system, account collection begins. Account billings and the aging of accounts receivable can also be monitored by back office software.

**Accounts Payable.** The **accounts payable module** tracks purchases, creditor positions, and the hotel's banking status. Accounts payable activities normally consist of posting purveyor invoices, determining amounts due, and printing checks for payment. Three major files maintained by an accounts payable module are the:

- Vendor master file

- Invoice register file

- Check register file

The vendor master file contains an index of vendor names, addresses, telephone numbers and vendor code numbers, standard discount terms (time and percentage), and space for additional information. An invoice register file is a complete list of outstanding invoices cataloged by vendor, invoice date, invoice number, or invoice due date. This file becomes especially important when management wishes to take advantage of vendor discount rates. The calculation and printing of bank checks for payment to vendors is monitored through the check register file. Check production and distribution is summarized into a payables report and reconciled with bank statements.

**Payroll Accounting.** A **payroll accounting module** is a complex part of a back office package because of the variables involved in properly processing time and attendance records, unique employee benefits, pay rates, withholdings, deductions, and required payroll reports. The payroll accounting module must be capable of handling job codes, employee meals, uniform credits, tips, taxes, and other data that affect the net pay of employees. The unique nature of payroll data dictates that special care be taken to maintain an accurate payroll register, to closely control the issuing of payroll checks, and to protect the confidentiality and propriety of payroll data.

**Inventory.** A back office **inventory module** automates several internal control and accounting functions. Internal control is essential to efficient hospitality industry operations. By accessing inventory data maintained by an inventory master file, a back office inventory module is generally able to address three of the most common inventory concerns: inventory status, inventory variance, and inventory valuation. "Inventory status" refers to an account of how much of each item is in storage; "inventory variance" refers to differences between a physical count of an item and the balance maintained by the perpetual inventory system; and "inventory valuation" refers to the monetary or dollar value of items in inventory.

**Purchasing.** A back office **purchasing module** maintains a purchase order file and a bid specification file. This module enhances management's control over purchasing, ordering, and receiving practices. Using minimum/maximum inventory-level data transferred from the inventory module, the purchasing module generates purchase orders based on an order point established through usage rate and lead-time factors. A purchasing module may also use a zero-based inventory system and generate purchase orders based on projected sales volume.

**Financial Reporting.** The use of a **financial reporting module**, also called a general ledger module, involves the specification of a chart of accounts (a list of financial statement accounts and their account numbers) and a systematic approach to recording transactions. The design of the general ledger module is often crucial to an effective back office system. The financial reporting module is generally capable of tracking accounts receivable, accounts payable, cash, and adjusting entries. In addition, most financial reporting modules are capable of accessing data from front office and back office modules to prepare financial statements, which include the balance sheet, the statement of income (and supporting departmental schedules), and a variety of reports for use by management.

# E-Commerce

As the discipline has matured in other industries, **e-commerce** has come to include all aspects of business and market processes enabled by the Internet and Web-based technologies.[2]

The **Internet** is a large and complex series of electronic networks designed to provide universal access to information and communication services around the world. Often referred to as the "information superhighway," the Internet resembles the intricate traffic patterns of local and county roads with connections to state and interstate highways. The Internet was initially conceived at about the same time as the development of interstate highways. The design of the interstate highway system, linking major cities across the country, was based upon the need to maintain a continuous flow of supplies throughout the country. The roadways were designed with sufficient alternate routing so that a steady flow of materials to all parts of the nation could be ensured.

Similar ideas were important in the creation of the Internet. Using the interstate highway system as a model, the government turned its attention to similarly securing its intelligence system. The focus shifted from protecting vehicular traffic patterns to ensuring a continuous movement of data between mainframe computers at various strategic locations from coast to coast. Internet planners sought to create a myriad of alternate communication routes across a wide range of computer platforms.

The Internet has created a communications and information explosion with the potential to affect virtually every aspect of the hospitality industry. In an office environment, most networks connect individual desktop computers to a separate computer, called a **server**. The server controls the flow of information along the network. It can also be used to establish a gateway to other networks beyond the office environment. The Internet takes the concept of networks to its fullest application by seamlessly connecting large numbers of very complex networks. The Internet is an affiliation of tens of thousands of private, commercial, educational, and government-supported networks around the world. When a user connects to the Internet, data and information can be shared with millions of other users.

The **World Wide Web (www)**, also known simply as the Web, is only one of the many different parts of the Internet. It is the best-known part because its user-friendly features have attracted millions of users. Unlike text-only sites found on much of the Internet, the Web offers an incredibly rich combination of text, images, sound, animation, and video. The graphic and video options of the Web and the surging numbers of "surfers" have enticed thousands of businesses, organizations, educational institutions, government agencies, and individuals to create their own Web pages and participate in the dissemination of information along the Web.

Much of the user-friendly nature of the Web stems from the **HyperText Transfer Protocol (http)** that structures information on the Web. This protocol is a set of file download commands embedded within the hypertext markup language (html) used to place text, graphics, video, and other information displays on the

Web. The "http" indicates that the Web page can handle nonsequential links to other hypertext pages—a trait characteristic of all Web pages.

A **Uniform Resource Locator (URL)** designates the Internet address of a site, usually the site's homepage. A site's homepage is the first screen or Web page presented when a destination site is located. URLs are usually built into the hypertext of a Web document, enabling users to jump from site to site along the Web. The URL for an organization, hotel, restaurant, club, or individual consists of a series of letters and punctuation marks. Each grouping of letters represents a section of the path that leads to a desired site.

The best way to find a Web site when you don't know its address is to use a search engine. A **search engine** is a software program that reads indexed Web sites and creates lists and links to sites that match a user's inquiry. Most search engines provide tips on how to efficiently search for information. Generally, the more specific your query, the more relevant will be the list of sites your query generates. However, even if the resulting list is long, you can usually scroll or page through the list and decide which sites are worth a look. Then it's simply a matter of clicking on the link or URL to go directly to the Web document.

E-commerce, like traditional commerce, involves the buying and selling of goods and services. In e-commerce, however, transactions are supported by the use of the Internet or another electronic medium. A company's e-commerce offering may be as simple as an electronic brochure describing the company and its products and services or as sophisticated as an online catalog, featuring thousands of products. E-commerce offers instant access to information and, if warranted, the ability to quickly compare products, make choices, purchase items, and complete a transaction. The Internet and e-commerce are having a dramatic effect on the supply chain in most industries, and hospitality is already a prominent participant.

The initial implementation of e-commerce in hospitality dates back to when the first electronic hotel reservation was taken by a travel agent and delivered to a hotel via telex or fax. Due to the vast amount of product and rate information that already exists in an electronic form, the implementation of e-commerce in the hospitality industry has been primarily focused on the front-end distribution of hotel rooms.

Well beyond the sale of hotel rooms, e-commerce will have far-reaching implications for the hospitality industry. As industry consolidation continues, and operators and suppliers become more sophisticated in their business practices, an increasing number of routine tasks and transactions will take place online. E-commerce does not end with the development of a slick Web site or the ability to accept electronic reservations. It will also find its way into interactions with suppliers, accountants, payment services, government agencies, and even competitors. This online community will demand changes in the way we do business from production to consumption and will even affect those companies and hotels that might otherwise not be part of the electronic economy beyond accepting online reservations.

What is driving the e-commerce revolution? Computers and networking options such as **electronic data interchange (EDI)** standards have existed for some time, but the Internet is the first ubiquitous two-way data communications platform that operates on a set of common standards. The wide availability and inexpensive nature of the medium have led to the development of business applications and supporting transaction standards that enable previously stand-alone systems to communicate easily with one another. This reduces the cost of integrating systems, allowing free exchange of information while eliminating duplicate data entry and redundant manual processes.

## E-Distribution

The travel industry is uniquely poised to take advantage of the continuing growth and acceptance of consumer-based e-commerce. Unlike many industries, hospitality has been leveraging electronic forms of distribution for many years, regularly digitizing product information and making inventory available online.

Long before the current popularity of the Internet and consumer access to online services, the hospitality industry was an active participant in e-distribution. From the first booking made by a travel agent via an airline reservation terminal, the hospitality and broader travel industries have been e-commerce pioneers. As the term suggests, **e-distribution** is the means by which hotels make their products and services available via electronic channels, including travel agents, wholesalers, consolidators, and consumers. Such channels are widely viewed as more convenient for those constituents that have online access and are often a less expensive source of bookings than traditional telephone channels. E-distribution includes the following two major categories:

- Global distribution systems
- Internet distribution systems

**Global distribution systems (GDSs)** are principally used by members of the travel industry to book airline, hotel, car, and cruise reservations worldwide. Unfortunately, most of these systems were principally designed to sell airline reservations and, as such, are not easily adapted to offer the many different products and services available from the hospitality industry. Various industry groups have been working hard to help drive the direction of these systems to better serve the industry.

According to the **Hotel Electronic Distribution Network Association (HEDNA)**, booking volume through the GDSs continues to grow. The ability to affect the volume of business that comes through this channel is largely based on the amount of attention paid to associated marketing efforts. Most of the major chains and representation companies can help member properties understand how best to position their products and services in these systems.

As use of the Internet increases, various consumer-oriented booking systems have become available. From the large, popular sites that are related to, or rely on, GDSs, to Internet-specific and "boutique" solutions, **Internet distribution systems (IDSs)** have become one of the fastest growing segments of Internet-based e-commerce. Unlike GDSs, these systems are typically used by consumers to book airline, hotel, car, and cruise ship reservations for themselves. The wealth of information available to consumers has never been greater, and consumers expect and shop hard to find lower prices online. As a consequence, the environment has become very competitive. A well-thought-out e-commerce strategy includes a property-specific Web presence.

Another valuable IDS is the electronic clearance center for distressed inventory. "Name your own price" sites and last-minute Internet-based bargain notifications have provided an effective way for hotels to dispose of distressed or otherwise underutilized inventory. The management of such channels will continue to be a critical factor in a property's e-distribution strategy. The sheer number of focused users of these systems suggests that diligent management of inventory will reap great rewards. Hotel managers should leverage this and all electronic channels to broaden their market reach for motivated customers. Gone are the days when hotel managers should keep rooms open for unexpected, late-arriving customers. Particularly during high occupancy periods, hotels should leverage broad-reaching e-distribution mechanisms to the fullest extent possible.

## Enterprise Systems

Property management systems, point-of-sale systems, and other technology systems discussed earlier in this chapter are, for most part, property-based systems. An **enterprise system** addresses the technology needs of multi-property hospitality organizations, such as hotel and restaurant chains as well as management companies. An enterprise system often uses intranet- or Web-based technology to eliminate the labor-intensive efforts of central offices in manually updating property-level databases one at a time. The system accesses data in real time (or at selected intervals) directly from individual property systems. Property-level data are consolidated and analyzed, enabling the corporate office to compare properties, generate timely reports, and provide feedback to individual properties, groups of properties, or all properties within the organization.

For restaurant chains, enterprise systems enable individual units to focus on operations and guest service—leaving the database administration tasks to the corporate office. These systems offer the corporate office an immediate channel and great flexibility when implementing changes that affect such areas as:

- Menu items
- New promotions
- Pricing
- Recipes
- Inventory items
- Tax tables

For lodging companies, enterprise systems may include a central reservations application fully synchronizing room inventories and rate plans. This application may integrate with GDS and IDS providers. Enterprise systems for lodging companies also provide detailed status reports based on real-time operational statistics. The reports can be consolidated by division, by location, by property type, or by other categories designated by the lodging company. These systems also offer the central office the capability to adjust revenue management strategies based on key performance data such as:

- Average daily rate

- Length of stay

- Occupancy percentage

- RevPAR (revenue per available room)

- Rooms revenue

Lodging companies can also monitor budget performance and provide feedback to properties that compares budgeted figures to actual results with variances noted. Exhibit 8 shows a sample corporate consolidation report.

Enterprise systems go beyond simple database management and consolidation of financial information. Since the systems may directly access the technology systems at each property level, the central office can produce extensive individual guest histories (including current and past spending patterns) and group business reports (booking pace, spending pattern, billing information, etc.). These guest histories and group reports become available to managers at properties company-wide.

## Web Site Development

Web sites may be the best thing to happen to collateral and marketing material since Guttenberg's invention of the printing press. Aside from word of mouth, there has never been a more cost-effective way to distribute information and provide services. The challenge lies in creating and managing Web sites that take advantage of sophisticated electronic capabilities and fully meet users' expectations.

Compared to traditional advertising or printed collateral, Web sites are available to viewers anytime they want to see them, and content is relatively inexpensive to change. However, because consumers demand current, correct information and expect Web sites to use cutting-edge technologies, sites require constant review, change, improvement, and creativity. The only interaction many guests may have with a property is what they see on its Web site. This virtual relationship should be nurtured just as carefully as if the guest were at the front desk asking questions. Managers should be cautious as they select a firm or consultant to develop a site. Many inexperienced, under-skilled companies advertise themselves as Web developers. Their products can be disappointing.

A logical extension of a marketing Web site is an internal **intranet** designed to facilitate communication among staff. An intranet can provide staff members with timely access to important company information.

In addition, some hospitality companies create a specialized portion of their outward-facing Web site that is available only to their best guests or suppliers. This **extranet** can enable a company to transact business, share information with trading partners, and improve efficiency. While the required technology and applications can be more complex and expensive than those needed for the more

**Exhibit 8   Sample Corporate Consolidation Report**

Microsoft Excel - Sample Corp Flash - Overview.xls

File  Edit  View  Insert  Format  Tools  Data  Window  TM1  Help

R17

| | SAMPLE CORPORATE FLASH | | | | | Forecast | | | | | | | |
|---|---|---|---|---|---|---|---|---|---|---|---|---|---|
| | | | | | | Jan | 21 | | | | | | |

**Current Day**

| Rooms | Rate | Revenue | RevPar | Occ % | | Rooms | Rate | Revenue | RevPar | Occ % |
|---|---|---|---|---|---|---|---|---|---|---|
| 158 | $ 76.37 | $ 12,065.95 | $ 60.33 | 79% | Comfort Inn & Suites | 2,970 | $ 74.94 | $ 222,584.25 | $ 53.00 | 71% |
| 71 | $ 80.84 | $ 5,739.76 | $ 45.55 | 56% | Comfort Suites | 1,581 | $ 86.83 | $ 137,279.75 | $ 51.88 | 60% |
| 184 | $ 75.68 | $ 13,925.98 | $ 44.07 | 58% | Holiday Inn | 3,387 | $ 79.29 | $ 268,566.69 | $ 40.47 | 51% |
| 154 | $ 50.14 | $ 7,721.23 | $ 35.42 | 71% | Hotel Circle | 3,618 | $ 50.82 | $ 183,859.14 | $ 40.16 | 79% |
| 147 | $ 78.50 | $ 11,539.55 | $ 53.18 | 68% | Regency Plaza | 2,544 | $ 75.78 | $ 192,790.09 | $ 42.31 | 56% |
| 714 | $ 71.42 | $ 50,992.47 | $ 47.35 | 66% | West Coast | 14,100 | $ 71.28 | $1,005,079.92 | $ 44.44 | 62% |
| 93 | $ 65.67 | $ 6,107.00 | $ 48.47 | 74% | Barnabey's Resort | 1,998 | $ 76.40 | $ 152,654.90 | $ 57.69 | 76% |
| 100 | $ 74.05 | $ 7,404.76 | $ 41.60 | 56% | Holiday Inn | 1,928 | $ 72.29 | $ 139,375.51 | $ 37.29 | 52% |
| 17 | $ 58.31 | $ 991.30 | $ 17.09 | 29% | Jolly Roger | 692 | $ 75.18 | $ 52,023.38 | $ 42.71 | 57% |
| 44 | $ 82.29 | $ 3,620.64 | $ 19.06 | 23% | Seaside Inn | 2,307 | $111.21 | $ 256,559.73 | $ 64.30 | 58% |
| 121 | $141.13 | $ 17,076.20 | $ 90.83 | 64% | Watergate | 3,246 | $141.25 | $ 458,503.20 | $116.14 | 82% |
| 417 | $ 91.95 | $ 38,343.00 | $ 46.87 | 51% | East Coast | 11,172 | $103.20 | $1,152,908.33 | $ 67.12 | 65% |
| 1,131 | $ 78.99 | $ 89,335.47 | $ 37.68 | 48% | Total | 29,326 | $ 91.23 | $2,675,402.39 | $ 53.73 | 59% |

**Variance to Forecast**

| | | | | | | | | | | |
|---|---|---|---|---|---|---|---|---|---|---|
| 11 | $(11.01) | $ (778.05) | $ (3.89) | 6% | Comfort Inn & Suites | -27 | $ (5.86) | $ (19,599.75) | $ (4.67) | -1% |
| -42 | $ (7.31) | $ (4,221.24) | $(33.50) | -33% | Comfort Suites | -295 | $ (4.00) | $ (33,115.25) | $(12.52) | -11% |
| -18 | $ (3.54) | $ (2,078.02) | $ (6.58) | -6% | Holiday Inn | -522 | $ (2.26) | $ (50,221.31) | $ (7.57) | -8% |
| 31 | $ (3.55) | $ 1,117.28 | $ 5.13 | 14% | Hotel Circle | 660 | $ (4.20) | $ 21,111.54 | $ 4.61 | 14% |
| -15 | $(12.02) | $ (3,125.45) | $(14.40) | -7% | Regency Plaza | 247 | $ (5.89) | $ 5,180.09 | $ 1.14 | 5% |
| -33 | $ (9.01) | $ (9,085.48) | $ (8.44) | -3% | West Coast | 63 | $ (5.78) | $ (76,644.68) | $ (3.39) | 0% |
| -8 | $(15.37) | $ (2,078.00) | $(16.49) | -6% | Barnabey's Resort | 125 | $ (0.23) | $ 9,111.90 | $ 3.44 | 5% |
| -24 | $ 1.31 | $ (1,614.24) | $ (9.07) | -13% | Holiday Inn | -382 | $ (2.84) | $ (34,165.49) | $ (9.14) | -10% |
| -13 | $(30.32) | $ (1,667.70) | $(28.75) | -22% | Jolly Roger | -140 | $ 0.51 | $ (10,101.62) | $ (8.29) | -11% |
| -36 | $(10.48) | $ (3,800.94) | $(20.00) | -19% | Portofino Inn | -460 | $ 5.06 | $ (37,149.35) | $ (9.31) | -12% |
| 1 | $(18.65) | $ (2,096.80) | $(11.15) | 1% | Watergate | 209 | $ 4.02 | $ 41,744.20 | $ 10.57 | 5% |
| -71 | $ (9.19) | $ (11,011.58) | $(13.46) | -9% | East Coast | -617 | $ 2.56 | $ (33,484.75) | $ (1.95) | -4% |
| -387 | $(22.95) | $ (65,413.06) | $(27.59) | -16% | Total | -795 | $ (1.91) | $ (129,974.29) | $ (2.61) | -2% |

Source: Datavision Technologies. For more information, browse the company's Web site at http://www.datavisiontech.com

generalized marketing area of a site, the true value of e-commerce technology lies in the improvement of standard business processes. Extranets are the next big step in the development of Web sites and e-commerce.

The following suggestions can start managers thinking about how best to incorporate Web sites in their operations:

- New and interesting information should be readily available on the Web site so that guests know what is going on at the property.

- Seasonal changes in business should be highlighted to take advantage of buying patterns and the interests of guests. In year-round resorts, the winter backdrop and features of the site may be very different from those used during summer months.

- As new technologies become available and cost effective, look for ways to integrate them into the site. Online reservations, maps, and activity scheduling have all evolved since the first person typed "www" in a Web browser.

- Look for new ways to leverage the benefits of technology. Guests would like nothing better than to be more efficient in doing business. The Web site can be a portal for guests to communicate, retrieve information, and provide input on things they like and dislike. If the property caters to large meetings or tour groups, there may be a way to share billing and payment information online.

- Incorporate technology into the operation wherever possible. Take advantage of the Internet to communicate with employees. Schedules, newsletters, suggestions, evaluations, praise, benefit administration, daily updates, and computer-based training programs can be included on an intranet site.

When taking advantage of a Web presence, managers should attend to the timeliness of the information, the services supported, and ways to differentiate the "electronic brochure," or storefront, from competitors. Managers will need to dedicate enough human and financial resources to ensure that the desired results are achieved. The amount of effort put into the development and ongoing maintenance of the site has a direct impact on its success.

# Endnotes

1. Portions of this chapter have been adapted from *An Introduction to Hotel Systems: Fundamentals & Glossary*, written by Jon Inge and produced by the Technology Committee of the American Hotel & Lodging Association with a grant from the American Hotel & Lodging Foundation.

2. Portions of this chapter have been adapted from *e-Commerce: Frequently Asked Questions*, written by Victor L. Vesnaver, Principal, V2 Consultants, with an editorial review by David Sjolander, Carlson Hospitality Corporation, and produced by the Technology Committee of the American Hotel & Lodging Association with a grant from the American Hotel & Lodging Foundation.

 # Key Terms

*Property Management Systems and Interfaces*

**accounts payable module**—Tracks purchases, creditor positions, and the hotel's banking status.

**accounts receivable module**—Monitors outstanding balances of guest accounts.

**call accounting system (CAS)**—A property management system interface that enables a hotel to take control over local and long-distance telephone services and to apply a markup to switchboard operations.

Chris Barron

814-443-6526

AAA

**electronic locking system (ELS)**—Interfaces with a property management system and allows the front desk to control the locking of rooms electronically.

**energy management system (EMS)**—Electronically monitors guestroom temperatures.

**financial reporting module**—Tracks accounts receivable, accounts payable, cash, and adjusting entries.

**guest accounting module**—Front office application software that maintains guest accounts electronically. The guest accounting module increases the hotel's control over guest accounts and significantly modifies the night audit routine.

**interface**—Connection and interaction between hardware, software, and the user.

**inventory module**—Automates several internal control and accounting functions.

**payroll accounting module**—Handles job codes, employee meals, uniform credits, tips, taxes, and other data that affect the net pay of employees.

**point-of-sale (POS) system**—Network of terminals that are combined with cash registers, bar code readers, optical scanners, and magnetic stripe readers for instantly capturing sales transactions. In restaurants, these systems manage the ordering and delivery of all menu items in one or more restaurants and/or bars.

**property management system (PMS)**—Set of computer programs that directly relate to a hotel's front office and back office activities.

**property management system (PMS) interfaces**—Stand-alone technology systems that may be linked to a hotel's property management system; the formats and languages that define data that one system is capable of delivering to another.

**purchasing module**—Enhances management's control over purchasing, ordering, and receiving practices.

**reservation module**—Front office application software that enables a hotel to rapidly process room requests and generate timely and accurate rooms, revenue, and forecasting reports.

**rooms management module**—Front office application software that maintains up-to-date information regarding the status of rooms, assists in the assignment of rooms during registration, and helps coordinate many guest services.

## E-Commerce

**e-commerce**—All aspects of business and market processes enabled by the Internet and Web-based technologies.

**e-distribution**—Selling products or services over the Internet or some other electronic medium. Hospitality e-distribution includes the GDS and Internet-based sales channels.

**electronic data interchange (EDI)**—Transfer of data between different companies using networks such as the Internet. As more and more companies are connected to the Internet, EDI is an increasingly important mechanism for companies to buy, sell, and trade information.

**enterprise system**—Addresses the technology needs of multi-property hospitality organizations, such as hotel and restaurant chains as well as management companies.

**extranet**—External Web site that gives a company's customers and partners access to certain documents and other data. An extranet administrator invites the customers and partners and sets site permissions for what documents, discussions, and other areas can be viewed.

**global distribution system (GDS)**—Electronic networks used by travel agents and some Internet-based distribution channels to make airline, hotel, car rental, and cruise ship reservations.

**high-speed Internet access (HSIA)**—Any one of a variety of services that provide fast access to the Internet. The most common and cost-effective types of HSIA include DSL and cable modem services. Cable modem services are generally provided by a local cable TV provider and utilize cable facilities to provide fast Internet access. Other forms of HSIA include satellite, private data line, and frame relay services.

**Hotel Electronic Distribution Network Association (HEDNA)**—The prominent trade association supporting the industry's use of electronic distribution channels: www.hedna.org.

**HyperText Transfer Protocol (http)**—Set of file download commands embedded within the hypertext markup language used to place text, graphics, video, and other information displays on the World Wide Web.

**Internet**—Interconnected system of networks that share standards and protocols connecting computers around the world.

**Internet distribution system (IDS)**—Internet-based services providing consumers the ability to book airline, hotel, car rental, and cruise ship reservations.

**intranet**—An internal Web site for a company's employees or workgroups. This private, secure site is usually accessible via the Web and can be used to share documents, calendars, and event information. An Intranet site is an ideal online communication tool for businesses, departments, groups, and organizations and can be used to centralize important company information, post documents, create group schedules, and announce events.

**search engine**—Software that reads indexed Web sites and creates lists and links to sites that match a user's inquiry.

**server**—Controls the flow of information along a network and establishes a gateway to other computer networks.

**Uniform Resource Locator (URL)**—Designates the Internet address of a site, usually the site's homepage.

**World Wide Web (www)**—A user-friendly part of the Internet that offers an incredibly rich combination of text, images, sound, animation, and video.

# Review Questions

1. What are the basic functions performed by a reservations module of a property management system?

2. What are the basic functions performed by a rooms management module of a property management system?

3. What are the basic functions performed by a guest accounting module of a property management system?

4. Why are property management system interfaces necessary?

5. What are the basic functions performed by a point-of-sale system?

6. What are the basic functions performed by a sales and catering system?

7. What are the basic functions performed by a hospitality accounting system?

8. How have hospitality businesses been affected by e-commerce?

9. How do enterprise systems interact with property management systems?

10. What advice concerning Web site development would you give to hospitality managers?

# Internet Sites

For more information, visit the following Internet sites. Remember that Internet addresses can change without notice. If the site is no longer there, you can use a search engine to look for additional sites.

## Hospitality Associations

American Hotel & Lodging Association
http://www.ahla.com

Club Managers Association of America
http://www.cmaa.org

Educational Foundation of the National Restaurant Association
http://www.foodtrain.org

Educational Institute of the American Hotel & Lodging Association
http://www.ei-ahla.org

Hospitality Industry Technology Exposition and Conference
http://www.hitecshow.org

Hospitality Finance and Technology Professionals (HFTP)
http://www.hftp.org

Hotel Electronic Distribution Network Association (HEDNA)
http://hedna.org

National Restaurant Association
http://www.restaurant.org

## Hotels and Restaurants

Affinia Hospitality
http://www.affinia.com

Best Western International
http://www.bestwestern.com

Cendant Corporation
http://www.cendant.com

Choice Hotels International
http://www.hotelchoice.com

Fairmont Hotels and Resorts
http://fairmont.com

Darden Corporation
http://www.darden.com

Hard Rock Café International, Inc.
http://www.hardrock.com

Hilton Hotels Corporation
http://www.hilton.com

Hyatt Hotels and Resorts
http://www.hyatt.com

InterContinental Hotels Group
http://www.ihgplc.com

Interstate Hotels & Resorts
http://www.ihrco.com

McDonald's Corporation
http://www.mcdonalds.com

Marriott International, Inc.
http://www.marriott.com

Radisson Hotels & Resorts
http://www.radisson.com

Spaghetti Warehouse
http://www.meatballs.com

Starwood Hotels & Resorts
Worldwide, Inc.
http://www.starwood.com

TGI Friday's Incorporated
http://www.tgifridays.com

Walt Disney World Resorts
http://www.disney.go.com

Westin Hotels and Resorts
http://www.westin.com

***Links to Hospitality Technology Companies***

Opus Resources Ltd.
http://www.ehotelier.com

Siegel Communications, Inc.
http://www.hospitalityupgrade.com

# Chapter 2 Outline

Input/Output Components
    Keyboards
    Touch-Screen Terminals
    Other Input Components
    Monitors
    Printers
    Common Hospitality I/O Components
The Central Processing Unit
    Read-Only Memory (ROM)
    Random Access Memory (RAM)
External Storage Devices
    Magnetic Tapes
    Magnetic Disks
    Hard Disks
    CD Technology
Anatomy of a Computer
    Microprocessor Characteristics
    CPU Speed
    Bus System
    System Architecture
    Computer Add-Ons
Software
The Operating System
Networks
Internet Hardware Components

# Competencies

1. Identify and describe system input components. (pp. 33–35)

2. Identify and describe system output components. (pp. 35–38)

3. Explain the function of a system's central processing unit and distinguish read only memory from random access memory. (pp. 39–41)

4. Identify and describe common external storage devices. (pp. 41–43)

5. Explain how the processing capability and speed of a system are measured. (pp. 43–46)

6. Identify and describe components or devices commonly added on to a system. (pp. 46–47)

7. Explain the function of an operating system. (pp. 48–50)

8. Identify and describe hardware components fundamental to Internet operations. (pp. 51–52)

# 2

# Hospitality Technology Components

THE PHYSICAL EQUIPMENT of a computer system is called hardware. Computer hardware is visible, movable, and easy to identify. In order to have a computer system, three hardware components are required: an input/output (I/O) component, a central processing unit (CPU), and an external storage device.

Input/output components allow users to interact with the system. For example, users can input data through a keyboard and receive output on a monitor (also called a display screen) and/or on paper through a printer.

The central processing unit (CPU) is the control center of the system. Inside are the circuits and mechanisms that process and store information and send instructions to the other components of the system. The system is said to *read* when it takes data in for processing and to *write* when it sends processed data out as information. All input entering the system is processed by the CPU before it is sent to the internal memory or to an output device. Similarly, all output (sent to a monitor, printer, or other device) has first been processed by the CPU. There is no direct link between input and output devices. Whenever information moves within the computer system, it passes through the CPU.

External storage devices retain data and/or programs that the CPU can access. Data and programs can be permanently stored on such external devices as magnetic tapes, magnetic disks, hard disks, and optical disks.

This chapter examines these types of technology components, including processing systems, operating systems, networks, and Internet hardware components.

## Input/Output Components

Keyboards and touch-screen terminals are common input units. Display monitors and printers are common output units. For most data processing, the computer system needs a keyboard for input and a monitor for output. For a paper record of the processed data, a printer is also needed. Disk drives are also input/output devices; they are capable of sending stored data in either direction—for input to the central processing unit, or for output to a monitor or printer.

### Keyboards

A keyboard is the most common input device. While specialty keyboards can be uniquely configured, the number, positioning, and function of keys are relatively standard. Common groupings of keys are:

- Function keys
- Alphabet keys
- Cursor control keys
- Numeric keys

**Function Keys.** Function keys are usually spread across the top of a keyboard and are numbered F1 through F12. These keys perform different operations when used in conjunction with different software applications. That is, the operation performed by the F3 key in one software application may be entirely different from the operation the F3 key performs in another software application.

**Alphabet Keys.** These keys normally function like the keys on a typewriter. Since electronic word processing normally performs several functions automatically, the "enter" key is used to force a break in the automatic line return (such as at the end of paragraphs).

**Cursor Control Keys.** A set of arrow keys is used in conjunction with the display screen. The cursor is a marker on a display screen that indicates where the next character to be entered will appear. The cursor control keys are marked by arrows. When one of these keys is pressed, the cursor moves in the direction of the arrow indicated on the key. Cursor movement is often determined by the particular software application that is being run on the computer system. Individual software applications may have specifically defined instructions for the cursor control keys.

**Numeric Keys.** When the "Num Lock" key is on, the keys that make up the cursor control keypad are converted to a numeric keypad and perform much like the keys of an adding machine or calculator.

## Touch-Screen Terminals

Manufacturers have developed terminals that enable the user to enter data without having to type a command from a keyboard. One such device is the touch-screen terminal. A **touch-screen terminal** is a cathode ray tube (CRT) with a grid of tiny beams of light over its glass screen. When the screen is touched in a sensitized area, the light beam is broken. This causes a signal to be transmitted to the computer. The touch-screen terminal is especially appealing to those who cannot type well or those interested in simplified input procedures. Since touch-sensitive screens can move large quantities of data easily, they are especially effective as order entry devices in food service operations and are useful for many graphic business applications (such as charts, graphs, and so on).

## Other Input Components

Other common input components include computer mice, scanners, voice recognition systems, and various types of handheld devices. A computer **mouse** is a small pointing device designed to fit comfortably under a user's hand. The mouse is connected to the CPU by a long cord or a wireless infrared sensor. A mouse is used in place of, or in combination with, a computer keyboard. With it, a user is capable of choosing commands, moving text and icons, and performing a number of operations. Moving the mouse across a flat surface moves a pointer, which is equivalent to a traditional cursor. The pointer is a small graphic symbol that shows users where the next entered character will appear.

A **scanner** is an input device capable of translating a page of text into a machine-readable format. A scanner is used to input text or graphic images into the computer. Scanners convert the text and images on a page into digitized information that can be recognized by the computer.

Voice recognition input involves instructions spoken by human voice. This input component converts spoken data directly into electronic form suitable for system entry. Experimentation with voice recognition technology is of special interest to the hospitality industry. A hotel reservations program may generate a series of prompts or cues to which a potential guest responds by pushing designated buttons on the telephone and/or by speaking into the mouthpiece of the headset. The computer acknowledges the user's input and may generate an additional series of prompts. The impact of voice recognition in the hospitality industry could be significant.

Handheld devices are similar to personal digital assistants (PDAs). A PDA is a handheld computer that serves as an organizer for personal information. It generally includes a name and address database, to-do list, and note taker. Most PDAs are pen-based and use a stylus to tap selections on menus and to enter printed characters. The unit may also include a small on-screen keyboard that is tapped with the pen. Data from the PDA can be transferred to a desktop computer system through a cable connection or wireless transmission. Housekeeping status and inventory control applications enable users to input data while working throughout their areas. Once the task or shift ends, the data can be transferred to the larger system.

## Monitors

A **monitor** (also called a display unit or screen) is the most common output unit. The type of monitor selected often depends on the kind of system used and the needs of the individual user. In addition to traditional designs, flat-screen terminals and large screen units are available. Exhibit 1 shows sample traditional and flat-screen monitors. Monitors typically are purchased as high-resolution units. High-resolution displays enable impressive graphics with various foreground and background color combinations while operating a variety of software applications. Types of monitors include:

- CGA (color graphics adapter); low-end color screen also referred to as RGB (red, green, and blue).
- EGA (enhanced graphics adapter); a step-up from CGA in screen resolution and clarity (uses digital signals).
- VGA (video graphics array); best for desktop publishing and computer-aided design software (uses analog signals).
- SVGA (super video graphics array); popular option among a variety of monitor units (uses digital and analog signals).

**Exhibit 1    Traditional and Flat-Screen Monitors**

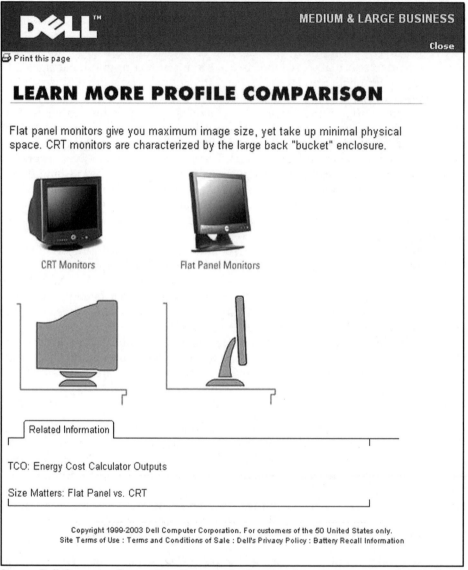

Source: Dell Computer Corporation. For more inofrmation, browse the company's Web site at http://www.dell.com

- LCD (liquid crystal display); blue or black letters on grayish white background (typically found on handheld units).

- GP (gas plasma); orange letters on a black screen (normally limited to handheld units).

# Printers

Printers are considered output devices and part of the hardware of a system. They can be classified in relation to how they actually go about printing processed data. Printer speed is generally measured in characters per second (cps), lines per minute (lpm), or pages per minute (ppm).

An **impact printer** depends on the movement of a print head or paper-feeding mechanisms to place data on the page. The simplest printers, such as dot matrix printers, place characters in a row one after another, then return the carrier to the left margin as the paper is moved up to another line. A line-printing terminal (LPT) is an impact printer that prints one line of type at a time.

Some allow for bidirectional printing in which the print head goes from left to right only on every other line. On the alternating lines it reverses itself and prints right to left, saving time. Otherwise the time the print head takes to go from the right margin back to the left would be wasted.

A dot matrix printer is inexpensive and, for impact printers, is relatively fast. The text and graphic material it produces is of fair print quality.

Dot matrix printers form characters by firing a vertical line of pins through an inked ribbon onto the paper. Each time a pin is fired, it strikes the inked ribbon and presses it against the paper to produce a dot. In the case of some dot matrix printers, the dot is about 1/72nd of an inch in diameter. The size varies slightly depending upon the age of the ribbon and the type of paper used. As the print head moves horizontally across the page, pins are fired in different patterns to produce letters, numbers, symbols, or graphics.

For example, to print a capital "T," the print head fires the top pin, moves 1/60th of an inch, fires the top pin again, moves 1/60th of an inch, fires seven pins, moves 1/60th of an inch, fires the top pin, moves another 1/60th of an inch, and fires the top pin once more to finish the letter. All this happens in only 1/100th of a second.

All impact printers rely on the durability of their mechanical parts for accurate print positioning, and all are in some degree limited as to the type of data they can print and their ability to move around the page. A **nonimpact printer,** on the other hand, achieves accurate print positioning electronically and has the capability of using a greater range of type styles more quickly and efficiently than impact printers. Nonimpact printers include thermal, ink jet, and laser printers.

**Thermal Printers.** A thermal printer, also referred to as an electrothermal printer, works by burning a protective layer off specially treated paper to reveal ink. Thermal (heat-sensitive) paper has a paper base covered with a layer of ink and a coating of aluminum. The printer forms characters by passing high voltage through printing wires for a fraction of a second. This high voltage burns away the aluminum coating to reveal the ink beneath. Thermal printers are quiet and reliable because they have few moving parts. However, because they require special heat-sensitive paper, their operating costs may be higher than those of other types of printers.

**Ink Jet Printers.** An ink jet printer works by spraying a minute and finely controlled jet of ink onto paper. The printer establishes a high voltage between its paper roller and an ink rod. The ink rod is composed of carbon grains encased in a glass tube. A spark jumps between the paper roller and the ink rod carrying enough carbon from the nozzle to make a dot on the paper. The ink (carbon) is electrically charged as it is sprayed onto the paper. Once charged, the ink can be moved around by electric fields in much the same way an electron beam is used to produce a picture on a television set. Ink jet printers are extremely versatile because they can produce a wide range of characters and high-quality graphics.

**Laser Printers.** A laser printer is relatively quiet, highly efficient, and somewhat expensive. Many laser printers are similar in appearance to desktop photocopying machines. While other printers print one character at a time, laser technology enables these devices to print an entire page all at once. Given this speed of output, many laser printers come equipped with collating capabilities. In addition, optional font (print style) packages and advanced graphics and color capabilities are available.

## Common Hospitality I/O Components

The most common I/O unit used in the hospitality industry is the CRT unit ("CRT" is an acronym for cathode-ray tube). The CRT unit is composed of a television-like video screen and a keyboard that is similar to a typewriter keyboard. Data entered through the keyboard can be displayed on the screen. The CRT operator can edit and verify the on-screen input before sending it for processing. Businesses are implementing touch-screen and hand-held units at an unprecedented rate. Ease of data entry and portability of data entry devices contribute to their increased application.

Other types of I/O equipment common in the hospitality industry include keyboard-and-display units such as electronic cash registers, point-of-sale devices, kitchen monitors, and line-printing terminals. Electronic cash registers and point-of-sale (POS) devices are designed to record transactions and monitor account balances. With hotel property management systems, restaurant charges can be captured by a point-of-sale unit in the restaurant and transmitted to the front office where guest folios are automatically updated with the charges.

One important difference among I/O units is the type of output they produce. A CRT unit displays output on a monitor for the user to examine; this type of output is referred to as **soft copy** because it cannot be handled by the operator or taken from the system. Printers, however, generate a paper copy of the output called a **hard copy**. Most systems are designed so that they can produce both types of output. For example, a hotel's front desk terminal might have a CRT unit that the employee uses to view a soft copy of a guest's folio during the guest's stay and at check-out. However, when the guest checks out, a hard copy of the folio will be generated from a printer so that the guest will be provided a printed record of account. Obviously, output displayed on a screen is much more temporary and its use more constricted than output printed on paper. Generally, hospitality managers obtain essential reports in hard copy form, allowing storage outside the computer and providing a base for information backup.

**Exhibit 2    System Hardware Components**

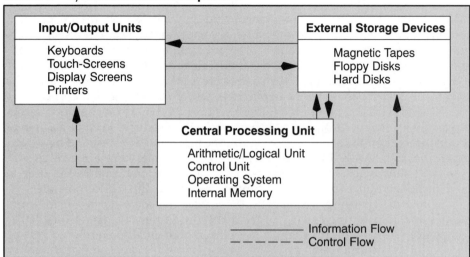

## The Central Processing Unit ————————————————

The **central processing unit** (CPU) is typically the most important and most expensive hardware component found within a computer system. It is the "brain" of the system and is responsible for controlling all other system components. As shown in Exhibit 2, the CPU is composed of four subunits.

The first subunit is the arithmetic and logical unit (ALU), which performs all the mathematical, sorting, ranking, and processing functions.

The second subunit is the control unit, which is responsible for determining which units in the computer system can be accessed by the CPU. If a unit is capable of interacting directly with the CPU, it is said to be "online;" "off-line" refers to the condition in which there is no direct connection between a system unit and the CPU. It is important to realize that although computer units may be switched on (powered-up), they are not necessarily online. For example, when a printer is connected to a CPU and its power switch is turned on, only the operating system or the application software can switch the printer to an online status. The printer will respond to commands from the CPU only when it is online.

The third subunit of the CPU houses a portion of the operating system. The **operating system** is responsible for orchestrating the hardware and the software within the computer system. It establishes the system's priorities and directs its resources to accomplish desired tasks. Operating systems are discussed in greater detail elsewhere in this chapter. The final subunit of the CPU is the system's internal (or primary) memory, which is housed in a set of specialized circuits. One part of internal memory, called **read-only memory** (ROM), holds a permanent record of information that the computer needs to use each time it is turned on. Another part of internal memory, called **random access memory** (RAM), holds a temporary version of the programs and/or data that users are processing.

## Read-Only Memory (ROM)

ROM (also known as PROM—permanent read-only memory) stores a permanent control program entered by the computer developer and may also house the computer's operating system. The control program contains specific sets of commands and instructions that guide the most fundamental routines carried out by the computer system. For example, the control program contains instructions for the conversion of keyboard entries into binary codes for processing by the CPU.

Since ROM is composed of a limited syntax (vocabulary), a computer recognizes only its own preprogrammed commands. If a user tries to enter a different command, the computer will not recognize the input and may respond by reporting that a "SYNTAX ERROR" has occurred. For example, some application software will start when the user types "GO"; another may require the user to double-click an icon. Different ROM contents recognize different commands.

Storing the control program in ROM enables the computer to "read" commands and instructions that program the fundamental operations of the computer system while preventing users from accidentally altering or erasing portions of the control program. Users cannot "write" or save information to the ROM area of the computer's internal memory. In fact, with many systems, users are prohibited from accessing, referencing, or reviewing any of the programs that are stored in ROM.

The ROM area of the computer's internal memory does not require a constant power supply to retain the commands, instructions, or routines that the manufacturer includes as part of the control program. ROM is described as nonvolatile memory because programs stored in ROM are not lost when the computer is turned off or otherwise loses electrical power.

## Random Access Memory (RAM)

All data that a user enters into the system are temporarily stored in the random access memory (RAM) area of the computer's internal memory. Since data stored in RAM can be accessed and/or altered by the user, RAM is often described as **read/write** memory: the user can both "read" from RAM (retrieve data), and "write" to RAM (store data).

Since all user operations are carried out in RAM, it is important that the amount of RAM supported by a particular computer system be sufficient to meet the user's needs. RAM size is typically designated in terms of the number of megabytes that RAM is able to temporarily store. A 256Mb machine has enough RAM capacity to temporarily store up to 256 megabytes of data; a 512Mb machine has enough RAM capacity to temporarily store up to 512 megabytes of data; and so on. How does storage capacity translate into typed pages?

A single 8 $\frac{1}{2}$- by 11-inch page of double-spaced type contains approximately 2K (2,000) characters. Therefore, a rough conversion of memory capacity to printed pages would be two to one. In other words, 256Mb converts to approximately 128,000 pages.

Because software application programs vary in the amount of RAM they require, RAM capacity is an important consideration in selecting a computer system. Many users who purchased personal computers just a few years ago have found it necessary to upgrade the RAM capacities of their machines in order to accommodate more sophisticated software packages.

When the computer loses electrical power, or is turned off, all user data stored in RAM is lost. For this reason, RAM is referred to as **volatile memory**. In order to save data held in RAM for future use, the user must save it on some type of external storage device.

# External Storage Devices

An external storage device is the system component that retains data and/or programs that can be accessed by the CPU. Data and programs can be permanently saved on a variety of external storage devices.

An important factor in selecting the kind of external storage device for a particular system is the kind of access that users need to have to the stored data. User access to stored data will be addressed in the following sections, which discuss some of the more common external storage devices: magnetic tapes, magnetic disks, hard disks, and optical discs.

## Magnetic Tapes

A magnetic tape is an external storage device that is made from a polyester base material coated with an oxide compound. It is this compound which gives the tape its durability and electromagnetic properties. Magnetic tape units are referred to as a **sequential access medium** because they store data in chronological sequence.

The way a user accesses data stored on magnetic tape is similar to the way in which anyone searches for a portion of a recording stored on a cassette tape recorder—the user must wind and rewind the tape until the desired portion of data is found. Because this can be a cumbersome process, magnetic tape is not a feasible storage device for many hospitality operations. However, using magnetic tapes to store back-up data may represent a significant cost advantage. Therefore, in some situations, magnetic tape may serve as a backup system on which to store data that are not required on a regular basis. However, if tapes are stored for very long periods of time, they must be periodically recopied or the tightly coiled magnetic surfaces may contaminate each other. Magnetic tape is classified as **nonvolatile memory**—memory that holds its content without power.

## Magnetic Disks

A **magnetic disk** (also called a "diskette" or a "floppy" disk) is a popular, inexpensive external storage device and is frequently used for transporting data and programs from one location to another. It is made of a hard-plastic outer jacket and a thin, flexible-plastic inner disk. The inner disk is coated with a magnetized oxide compound designed to hold electronic information. The size and density of the disk depend on the type of disk drive used. Exhibit 3 diagrams the basic features of magnetic disks.

The surface of a disk is divided into tracks, which are invisible concentric rings of magnetic zones. Each track contains a number of sectors. The tracks and

**Exhibit 3    Diagram of a Magnetic Disk**

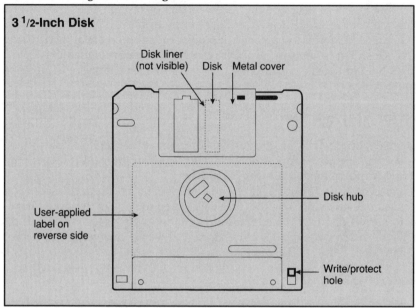

sectors are numbered, enabling the computer to store information on the disk at specific locations (e.g., sector 7 of track 3, sector 4 of track 23, etc.). The number of tracks and sectors on a disk is largely determined by the computer operating system through a process known as formatting (also called initializing). **Formatting** creates the tracks and sectors on which the system is able to read and write information. Once formatted, high-density 3 1/2" disks are capable of storing approximately 1,440,000 bytes (1.44Mb) of data.

Magnetic disks are a form of nonvolatile memory and are often referred to as a **random access medium** because data can be stored in any available location on the disk. Since the tracks and sectors of the disk are numbered, the system records where data is stored and allows a user to access stored data quickly and easily. For example, when a disk is inserted in the appropriate disk drive slot, the disk drive holds the jacket of the disk still and spins the inner disk, reading information from (or writing information to) the disk surface through an opening in the jacket called a head slot.

When a user instructs the computer to store information on a disk, the information is stored in an area of unused disk space. A user can also instruct the system to write over information that is already stored on the disk. This can be convenient for updating inventory records, personnel files, and so on. However, if information is written over old information, the old information will be erased, and it will not be able to be retrieved again.

A special form of magnetic disk is the **zip disk**. This disk compresses data to conserve storage and requires its own zip drive. Zip disks are usually available in three capacities: 100Mb, 250Mb, and 1 Gb.

## Hard Disks

**Hard disks** (also called fixed or rigid disks) are external storage devices that are much faster to use and store far greater amounts of information than magnetic disks. Hard disks are permanently online to the computer system.

Hard disk devices are manufactured in a dust-free environment and hermetically (heat) sealed to protect against foreign matter. The sealed hard disk device is mounted on a chassis that spins the disk at high speed. The hard disk drive has two recording heads, one below and one above the disk. Both recording heads are used to read and write to the disk's surfaces. The access time of a hard disk device is dependent upon the mechanism used to move the recording heads across the disk.

Data stored on a hard disk are classified as nonvolatile. Users should copy the contents of a hard disk onto magnetic disks or other storage devices for protection and security. Since hard disks are capable of holding so much more data than magnetic disks, copying their contents may require numerous disks and could be very time consuming. It is for these reasons that large capacity optical discs become popular information back-up options. A removable hard disk may also be a feasible back-up option.

## CD Technology

Common forms of optical disc storage are CD-R, CD-RW, and DVD. A CD-R, which stands for Compact Disc-Read, is a high-capacity disc that can be written only once. A CD-R stores data in a form that can be read quickly. Two important characteristics of a CD-R drive are access speed and data transfer rate. The access speed is the elapsed time required to locate and retrieve stored data. The data transfer rate is the time it takes the system to display the retrieved data. The higher the CD-R drive speed, the faster the system can access data from the disk. CD-R discs are used to distribute large amounts of data to a small number of recipients and also to archive data. CD-RW stands for Compact Disc-ReWritable. While CD-R is read-only, CD-RW drives can both read and record (or write) information onto a compact disc and create separate files similar to those on a hard disk. A DVD is an optical storage device that operates similarly to a CD-RW, except that its capacity is significantly larger. DVD originally stood for Digital VideoDisc, but today stands for Digital Versatile Disc. For the most part, the technology is referred to simply as DVD.

# Anatomy of a Computer

The technical descriptions contained in this section closely parallel the operations and equivalent components often found in both small minicomputers and large mainframe computers. Exhibit 4 diagrams a workstation computer system.

## Microprocessor Characteristics

The microprocessor is the central processing unit of a computer. The number assigned to a microprocessor chip refers to the complexity of its CPU. The microprocessor is the chip that processes instructions and carries out system commands.

**Exhibit 4  Sample Workstation**

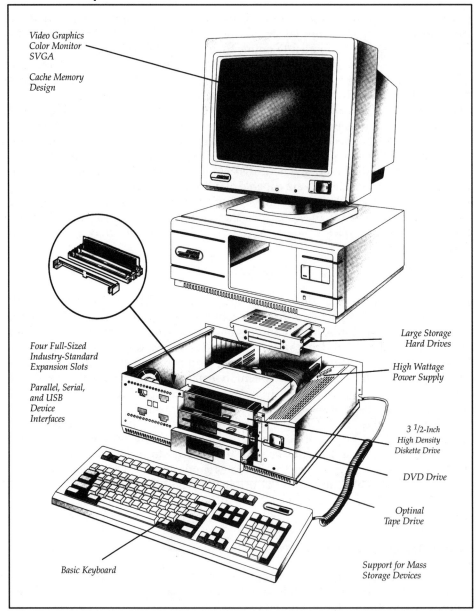

Video Graphics
Color Monitor
SVGA

Cache Memory
Design

Four Full-Sized
Industry-Standard
Expansion Slots

Parallel, Serial,
and USB
Device
Interfaces

Large Storage
Hard Drives

High Wattage
Power Supply

3 1/2-Inch
High Density
Diskette Drive

DVD Drive

Optinal
Tape Drive

Basic Keyboard

Support for Mass
Storage Devices

Central processing units vary in the amount of information they can process. Older microprocessors process significantly fewer bytes of data at a time. A byte of data is eight bits, or the amount of information contained in one character (a letter or numeral). The more information a computer can process at one time, the faster it operates. The difference between an 8-bit, 16-bit, 32-bit, and 64-bit CPU is akin to the difference between a 2-lane, 4-lane, 8-lane, and 16-lane highway. Surely the 16-lane road moves more traffic faster.

## CPU Speed

In addition to processing capability of a CPU, speed is also an important factor. The speed of a central processing unit is termed its "clock rate" or "clock speed." Clock speed can be measured in **megahertz (MHz)** or in **gigahertz (GHz)**. One MHz is equivalent to one million cycles per second; a gigahertz is equivalent to one billion cycles per second. A 1 GHz computer, for example, will operate slower than a 3 GHz computer. Just as CPU processing ability can be compared to the lanes on a highway, the CPU clock speed can be related to the highway speed limit. The higher the clock speed, the faster the CPU can process data.

Personal computers are most often identified by the model number or name of the microprocessor contained in the system unit. The introduction of each new microcomputer means an increase in microprocessor clock speed. Until the introduction of Pentium processors, vendors described the microcomputer by a modified version of the microprocessor's model number. For example, the Intel Corporation's pre-Pentium processors were referenced without the "80" prefix in the product's microprocessor identification number. Hence, the 80486 processor is referred to as a 486 processor. The Pentium, Pentium 2, Pentium 3, and Pentium 4 shifted Intel's product line to words and away from product numbers. Pentium 3, abbreviated as P3, and Pentium 4, abbreviated as P4, are popular CPU models.

## Bus System

Inside a computer there are channels through which signals travel. A bus system is defined as the electronic circuitry over which power, data, address, and other signals travel. Signals need to get from one location to another, and the system's bus architecture facilitates such movements.

There are three buses within a computer system; together they make up the computer's input/output (I/O) bus system. One transports data (data bus), another directs operations (address bus), and another transmits instructions (control bus). A data bus is the electrical pathway over which data travels between the CPU, disk drives, and peripherals. The address bus is responsible for finding the specific address that contains the requested data, and the control bus transports instruction on what to do with addresses and data. Assume the CPU needs to send two instructions such as "start reading data at address abc" and "stop reading data at address xyz." The messages "start reading data" and "stop reading data" will be carried on the control bus. The proper location of data elements would be accessed by the address bus. The requested data would be sent to the CPU through the data bus.

A computer's BIOS is important since it transports signals among the different input and output devices and the computer's microprocessor. The BIOS is basically a platform into which peripheral devices (serial ports, parallel ports, or network cards) are inserted. Add-ons to PCs are typically connected to the system's BIOS.

## System Architecture

Advancements in input/output (I/O) architecture are changing the way in which computers process data. The capabilities of the I/O bus should match the number of bits a microprocessor can process at once. A bus's clock speed is not the same as a CPU clock speed. Since bus speed is measured in nanoseconds (billionths of a second) and CPU speed is clocked in GHz (billions of cycles per second), I/O bus speed and CPU clock speed typically do not match exactly. Some variance in speeds is tolerable. Similar to differing speeds among motorists on merging high-ways, major imbalances between I/O bus and CPU speed may lead to traffic jams. Computer traffic jams are termed bottlenecks.

Historically, most computers were built using Industry Standard Architecture (ISA) in which I/O buses have fixed bit or byte widths (referred to as bandwidth). Given the increased capability of microprocessors, ISA is often too slow for CPUs with newer microprocessors that manage large amounts of data at a time. Extended Industry Standard Architecture (EISA) and Micro Channel Architecture (MCA) were developed in response to the need for a bus that is compatible with developing microprocessors that process larger quantities of data more quickly and efficiently. These systems are designed to more easily handle the workload created by faster, more powerful microprocessors.

## Computer Add-Ons

Add-ons are components or devices that are added to a computer system to increase its storage capacity, modify its architecture, or upgrade its performance. An add-on generally requires the insertion of a special circuit board inside the computer unit. Before expanding the capabilities of a computer system, the user must recognize the limitations placed on add-on components by the computer's power supply. The power supply unit provides electrical current to the computer. Power supply is expressed in watts. The more watts, the more internal add-on components a computer will be able to support.

While there are many peripheral devices that may be connected to a computer system and/or microcomputer, the most popular add-on components are expanded memory, extended memory, internal modems, fax boards, and interface boards.

**Expanded Memory.** The additional memory that resides outside the computer's basic memory and that can be accessed in revolving blocks is referred to as **expanded memory.** Since expanded memory was developed in response to some limited microprocessor capabilities, it historically has been available through add-on boards. These boards are inserted into one of the computer's expansion slots. Expanded memory takes advantage of unused reserved memory that the computer believes is in use when, in reality, it is not. For example, the computer system may reserve several Mbs of space for the system monitor. Should the system monitor require only half of the reserved space, expanded memory can be used to take advantage of this opening. Expanded memory swaps blocks of memory located outside the computer for unused memory located within the computer. The borrowing of this available memory is commonly referred to as "bank switching." Some computer operating systems work better with expanded memory than others. Expanded memory is additional memory that enables large programs to use memory beyond conventional limitations. Expanded memory is slower than extended memory, but it is compatible with more software. Computers with extended memory can also take advantage of expanded memory, but the opposite is not true.

**Extended Memory.** The linear memory that reaches beyond a system's basic limits is referred to as **extended memory**. Extended memory often comes built into the system board of some microprocessing units or can be purchased as an add-on. Unlike expanded memory, which swaps unused computer memory within the system's limits, extended memory begins to provide memory outside the system limits. Extended memory is usually required for advanced multitasking (running several applications simultaneously). Extended memory operates faster than expanded memory, but is compatible with fewer types of software.

**Internal Modem.** A modem is a telecommunications device that is used to transmit digital data over analog telephone lines linking one computer to another. A modem board is installed on the computer's main board and enables the computer to place and receive data calls. Once a number is dialed and the modem detects a proper answer, data file transfer begins. At the end of the session, the telephone connection is broken.

**Fax Board.** "Fax" is an abbreviation of "facsimile." A fax board allows a computer user to send and/or receive electronic documents. These documents can vary from text copy to pictures, diagrams, and maps. Fax boards prepare data files for transmission and then, using an internal modem, place a telephone call to the destination computer for transmission. Once connected, the fax board transmits the document.

**Interface Boards.** Peripheral devices often need more than a cable to communicate with a computer. Some peripherals need both a cable and an interface board. An interface board (also referred to as an interface card) is a series of microchips on a printed circuit board containing an input/output port. The interface board connects to the CPU and allows communications between the CPU and an input/output device. It is the circuitry of the chips and board that allows the peripheral to understand information it receives from the computer. An interface board is placed into an available expansion slot inside the computer. The input/output port (plug point) of the interface board protrudes outside the computer for cable connections or for antenna attachment (in the case of wireless transmission).

**Network Interface Card.** A Network Interface Card (NIC), also referred to as a "network adapter card," enables the computer to communicate on a network. The NIC basically performs two functions: it sends data and receives data. Some NICs contain a memory chip and are capable of storing incoming and outgoing data. NICs must be compatible with the network cabling used to establish the physical connections within the network.

**Exhibit 5  Mediating Role of the Operating System**

```
                          O
                          P
                          E
                          R
                          A
                          T
  Hardware Components      I     Application Software
                          N
  Input/Output Units      G     Word Processing
  Central Processing Units       Electronic Spreadsheets
  External Storage Devices  S    Database Management
                          Y     Communications
                          S
                          T
                          E
                          M
```

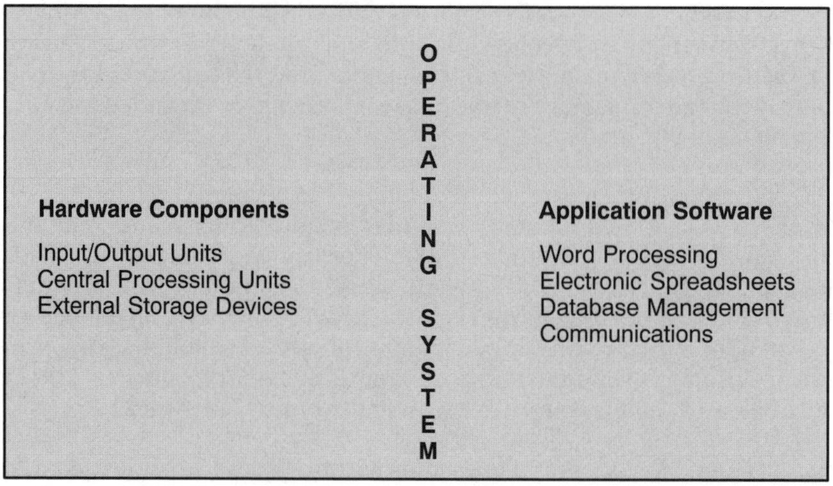

# Software

The hardware of a computer system does nothing by itself. In order for hardware components to operate, there must be a set of instructions to follow. Instructions that command a computer system to perform useful tasks are called computer programs. A set of programs that instructs or controls the operation of the hardware components of a computer system is called **software**. Software programs direct data processing through hardware operations.

Many people's first exposure to the power of computers is through generic application software such as word processing packages, electronic spreadsheet programs, or database management systems.

Experienced system users are familiar with systems software, which must be present for application software to establish a connection with computer hardware components. The discussion of systems software in this chapter focuses primarily on operating systems.

# The Operating System

A portion of systems software is the operating system. Like other types of systems software, the **operating system** controls interactions between hardware components of a computer system and application software programs. An operating system is necessary for a computer system to be able to carry out instructions generated by application software programs. The operating system manages routine computer functions while maintaining system priorities. The operating system controls how the system receives, transfers, and outputs information at the most fundamental levels. The computer cannot function without an operating system. Exhibit 5 illustrates the role of the operating system in mediating application software and hardware components of a computer system.

A computer system must have a control mechanism if it is to run application software programs without constant intervention from the user. When a user directs the system to save a program or data to an external storage device, something must happen within the system so that the entered command successfully initiates the proper sequence of operations for storing the program or data. The management of such routine functions is handled by the computer's operating system.

In simplest terms, the operating system is the program that controls the execution of other programs. Think of the operating system as the traffic controller of a busy metropolis, directing the flow of traffic by controlling the signals at every street corner. Like the traffic controller, the operating system is at the center of computer activity, directing the flow of data and instructions from application software programs to the various hardware components of the computer system.

Common types of operating systems include Windows (Windows 2000, Windows XP, Windows NT), UNIX, and OS/2. The following sections briefly examine each of these operating systems.

**Windows Operating System.** Windows is a graphical user interface (GUI) that contains several user-friendly files. A GUI allows a mouse (or other pointer device) to interact with computer screens containing icons (small pictorial representations) and drop-down and pull-down menus. To select a program, the user merely moves the cursor to the appropriate icon or menu item and clicks the mouse. Unlike a character user interface (CUI), which requires the user to enter text commands, a graphical user interface relies upon cursor control and icon selection. GUI was one of the original aspects of Windows that helped distinguish it from other operating systems.

An important characteristic of Windows is the fact that multiple programs and files can be open and used simultaneously. In addition, Windows incorporates a standardization of design among compatible programs. By learning the basics of one Windows-based application the user becomes familiar with other Windows applications.

Newer versions of Windows support several different user interfaces, including the traditional Windows interface and network-enabled (and Internet-enabled) interfaces. A network-enabled Windows interface combines the functionality of Windows with an Internet browser-like screen in which icons function like hyperlinks on the World Wide Web of the Internet.

**UNIX Operating System.** The UNIX operating system is modular and hierarchical in nature. It starts at a single point called the root directory and branches out into subdirectories, eventually reaching the level of individual program, text, and data files. In UNIX, everything is stored in a file.

UNIX is a powerful multi-user system composed of three levels of programs: the kernel, the shell, and the user environment. The kernel contains the basic operating system. It is the software that is closest to the hardware. The kernel controls access to the resources among users and maintains the file system. The user never interacts directly with the kernel.

The shell is a software program with which the user most commonly interacts. The shell serves as a connection between the user and the kernel, interpreting keyboard input into language the kernel can understand and execute. The shell may also function as a programming language.

The user environment consists of a file system and UNIX utilities or commands. Such commands as copying or removing files, text editing, software development, and the like reside in the user environment section of UNIX. UNIX is a CUI operating system.

**OS/2 Operating System.** A characteristic of OS/2 is its capacity for multitasking. OS/2 is credited with being the first operating system to make working with several applications at once an efficient process.

The OS/2 operating system, originally designed to be a multi-user system, presents the user with a main menu called the program selector. Because it is network-oriented, this approach differs from that of the other operating systems. The program selector is divided into three areas: *start a program, update,* and *switch to a running program.* Selecting START A PROGRAM leads to a second menu containing all available OS/2 programs. UPDATE, as its name implies, offers all the tools necessary to edit the list of OS/2 programs available through the START A PROGRAM option. SWITCH TO A RUNNING PROGRAM allows the user to leave the program selector and to move to an application already in process.

The two terms commonly used to describe OS/2 are multitasking and memory-handling. Multitasking refers to the execution of more than one program simultaneously. Memory-handling is directed at the advantages gained by users of large software applications. Compared to UNIX, OS/2 requires a lot of internal computer memory. Once installed, the OS/2 operating system overcomes most of the memory limitations associated with running large application software programs under other operating systems. Similar to Windows, OS/2 is a GUI operating system.

Regardless of which operating system a user selects, there are several common functions available through operating system commands. Some of the more useful operating system commands include utilities (operations) such as the following:

- Formatting magnetic disks and optical discs

- Displaying the content of storage media

- Copying files from one source medium to another

- Comparing the contents of copied files to verify that they are identical

- Deleting files from storage media

The user's manuals produced by the manufacturers of operating system software give detailed instructions on how to carry out these commands. Users must enter the commands exactly as their manuals instruct. Key substitutions that may work on typewriters (such as typing the numerals 1 and 0 by using the lower case "L" or the upper case "o" letter keys) do not work on computers.

# Networks

A **network** is a configuration of workstations that enables users to share data, programs, and peripheral devices (such as printers). Data sharing allows systemwide communications, and program sharing enables users to access infrequently used programs without the loss of speed or memory capacity that would result if those programs were installed at each desktop unit (referred to as a "client"). From an economic perspective, device sharing is an important benefit derived from networking. Expensive peripheral devices, such as high-capacity storage devices and color laser printers, can be made available to all clients cabled to a server.

A network environment can be configured as client-server (c/s) or peer-to-peer (p/p). A client-server environment links a powerful computer (the file server, or simply the server) to several (a handful, dozens, or even hundreds) of other, less powerful computers (the clients). Clients may access a variety of programs stored on the server and draw upon the server's processing power to perform tasks more quickly and more efficiently than if they operated in a stand-alone mode.

An advantage of the client-server environment is that the server can handle multiple client requests simultaneously. Client-server networks also improve system performance by managing communications (e-mail) and providing network administration (monitoring and security).

Unlike the client-server network, in a peer-to-peer network, each workstation functions as both a client and a server. Since any client can be a server and any server can be a client, the devices are considered to have equal, or peer, status. Peer-to-peer networks, like client-server networks, support communications, database management, and file sharing. Unlike client-server networks, peer-to-peer networks may achieve lower levels of performance and be more prone to security and access control problems.

# Internet Hardware Components

The Internet is a collection of diverse networks. Data transmitted on the Internet will likely travel between several types of networks, computers, and communication lines before reaching a final destination. Special hardware components of the Internet are designed to move data from network to network in a seamless operation. Such devices as bridges, gateways, and routers are essential to effective Internet operations.

A **bridge** connects two or more networks that use the same data transfer protocol (the same address format). A bridge makes attached networks appear to operate as a single network. The purposes of a bridge are to extend network capabilities and to isolate network traffic.

A **gateway** provides a means for two incompatible networks to communicate. A gateway simply converts the sending computer's request into a format that the receiving computer can understand.

Internet host computers are connected to **routers** that direct messages between different areas of the Internet. A router interprets the protocol used in a data packet (a group of data being sent over the Internet) and translates between sending and receiving protocols. Routers therefore can be used to connect networks that use different protocols.

Internet technology applied within a company and whose use is restricted to company employees is referred to as an **intranet**. Most companies construct a firewall around their intranets. A firewall is a combination of hardware and software that allows only authorized individuals to access the intranet for specific purposes. Employees can use the firm's intranet to access Internet resources, but a firewall prevents those on the Internet from interacting with the intranet.

## Key Terms

*Input/Output*

**cursor**—A flashing marker on a display screen that indicates where the next character to be entered will appear.

**hard copy**—A printed paper copy of system-processed information.

**impact printer**—An electronic printer, such as a dot matrix printer, that prints character by character and line by line.

**ink jet printer**—An electronic nonimpact printer that works by spraying a minute and finely controlled jet of ink onto paper. The ink (carbon) is electrically charged as it is sprayed onto the paper. Once charged, the jet of ink can be moved around by electric fields in much the same way that an electron beam is used to produce a picture on a television set.

**laser printer**—A high-speed electronic nonimpact printer similar in appearance to desktop photocopying machines. While other printers print one character at a time, laser technology enables these devices to print an entire page all at once.

**monitor**—A system output device that is usually capable of displaying both text and graphics (e.g., graphs, pie charts, etc.) in soft copy. Also, these output units may be programmed to various foreground and background color combinations while operating many software applications.

**mouse**—A small manual input unit used in place of, or with, a keyboard. Designed to fit comfortably under a user's hand, it controls the cursor or pointer on the display screen. It can also be used to choose commands, move text and icons, and perform a number of operations.

**nonimpact printer**—A category of electronic printers that includes thermal, ink jet, and laser printers.

**scanner**—A system input device capable of translating a page of text into a machine-readable format by converting the images on a page into digitized information that the system can recognize.

**soft copy**—Output on a monitor that cannot be handled by the operator or be removed from the system.

**touch-screen terminal**—A terminal that contains a unique adaptation of a cathode ray tube (CRT) screen and a special microprocessor to control it. The self-contained microprocessor displays data on areas of the screen that are sensitive to touch.

Touching one of the sensitized areas produces an electronic charge that is translated into digital signals telling what area was touched for transmission to the microprocessor. This signal also instructs the microprocessor to display the next screen.

*System Components*

**central processing unit (CPU)**—The control center of a system. Inside are the circuits and mechanisms that process and store information and send instructions to the other system components.

**expanded memory**—The additional memory capacity that resides outside the system's basic memory. It can be accessed in revolving blocks, and is available as add-on boards that are inserted into one of the system's expansion slots.

**extended memory**—Memory that reaches beyond a system's basic limits; usually required for advanced multitasking (running several applications simultaneously).

**hardware**—A systems term referring to the physical equipment of a system. Hardware is visible, movable, and easy to identify. In order to have a system, three hardware components are required: an input/output (I/O) component, a central processing unit (CPU), and an external storage device.

**gigahertz (GHz)**—A unit of electrical frequency equal to one billion cycles per second; used to measure the speed of a system's central processing unit.

**megahertz (MHz)**—A unit of electrical frequency equal to one million cycles per second; used to measure the speed of a system's central processing unit.

**nonvolatile memory**—Memory that holds its content without power. A term describing ROM (Read Only Memory); programs stored in ROM are not lost when the system is turned off or otherwise loses electrical power.

**operating system**—Responsible for orchestrating the hardware and the software within the system. It establishes the system's priorities and directs its resources to accomplish desired tasks.

**random access memory (RAM)**—Often abbreviated as RAM, a portion of a system's internal memory that holds a temporary version of the programs or data that users are processing.

**read-only memory (ROM)**—Often abbreviated as ROM, a portion of the internal memory of a system that holds a permanent record of information that the system needs to use each time it is turned on.

**read/write**—A system is said to "read" when it takes data in for processing and "write" when it sends processed data out as information. RAM is often described as read/write memory; the user can both read from RAM (retrieve data) and write to RAM (store data).

**software**—A systems term referring to a set of programs that instructs or controls the operation of the system's hardware components. Software programs tell the system what to do, how to do it, and when to do it.

**volatile memory**—A systems term used to describe random access memory (RAM); when the system loses electrical power, or is deliberately turned off, all user data stored in RAM is lost. In order to save data stored in RAM for future use, the user must instruct the system to save it on some type of external storage device.

*External Storage*

**formatting**—A process that creates the tracks and sectors of a disk on which the system is able to read and write information.

**hard disks**—External storage devices that are much faster to use and store far greater amounts of information than magnetic disks. Hard disks are permanently online to the system.

**magnetic disks**—External storage media, also called diskettes or floppies, frequently used for shipping data and programs from one location to another. They are made of thin, flexible plastic protected by a jacket. The plastic is coated with a magnetized oxide compound designed to hold electronic information. The size of the disk (eight-inch, five-and-one-quarter inch, or three-and-one-half inch) depends on the type of system used.

**random access medium**—A characteristic of an external storage medium (such as magnetic disks) permitting data to be stored in any available location on the disk. Since the tracks and sectors of the disk are numbered, the system allows a user to access stored data quickly and easily.

**sequential access medium**—A systems term referring to an external storage medium, such as a magnetic tape, which stores data in chronological sequence.

**zip disk**—Compresses data to conserve storage and requires its own zip drive; usually available in three capacities: 100Mb, 250Mb, and 1 Gb.

*Internet Hardware*

**bridge**—A hardware component of the Internet that connects two or more networks that use the same data transfer protocol. A bridge makes attached networks appear to operate as a single network. The purposes of a bridge are to extend network capabilities and to isolate network traffic.

**gateway**—A hardware component of the Internet that provides a means for two incompatible networks to communicate. A gateway simply converts the sending system's request into a format that the receiving system can understand.

**intranet**—Internet technology applied within a company to create a private network that forms a single company-wide information system. The use of the intranet is restricted to company employees.

**network**—A configuration of workstations that enables users to share data, programs, and output devices (such as printers).

**router**—A hardware component of the Internet that directs messages between different areas of the Internet.

## Review Questions

1. What does the term "hardware" mean? Identify the three hardware components necessary for a computer system, and describe their functions.

2. What are the various types of keys typically found on a system's keyboard?

3. What is the difference between an impact printer and a nonimpact printer? Give examples of each type of printer.

4. What is the difference between RAM and ROM?

5. What terms do the following abbreviations represent: I/O, CPU, CRT, CD-R, CD-RW, DVDE?

6. What is meant by the term "software"?

7. What are the various functions performed by most operating systems?

8. What is the difference between a sequential access medium and a random access medium?

9. What are examples of external storage devices?

10. Identify three hardware components essential to effective Internet operations, and describe their functions.

## Internet Sites

For more information, visit the following Internet sites. Remember that Internet addresses can change without notice. If the site is no longer there, you can use a search engine to look for additional sites.

Apple Computer, Incorporated
http://www.apple.com

Compaq Computer Corporation
http://www.compaq.com

Dell Computer Corporation
http://www.dell.com

Digital Equipment Corporation
http://www.digital.com

Elo TouchSystems
http://www.elotouch.com

Gateway 2000 Incorporated
http://www.gw2k.com

Intel Corporation
http://www.intel.com

International Business Machines, Inc.
http://www.us.pc.ibm.com

NEC Corporation
http://www.nec.com

Maitre'D Point of Sale Touch-Screen Systems
http://www.maitredpos.com/mdpos.html

Sony Electronics, Incorporated
http://www.sony.com

## Chapter 3 Outline

E-Distribution Systems
    Global Distribution Systems
    Internet Distribution Systems
Intersell Agencies
Central Reservation Systems
    Affiliate and Non-Affiliate Systems
    CRS Functions
    Additional Services
Property-Level Reservation Systems
    Reservation Inquiry
    Determination of Availability
    Creation of the Reservation Record
    Confirmation of the Reservation
    Maintenance of the Reservation Record
    Generation of Reports
    New Developments
Reservations Through the Internet

## Competencies

1. Distinguish global distribution systems from Internet distribution systems. (pp. 57–61)

2. Distinguish affiliate from non-affiliate central reservation systems. (pp. 61–63)

3. Identify the basic functions and services performed by a central reservation system. (pp. 63–66)

4. Describe the functions and features of the reservation module of a property management system. (pp. 66–71)

5. Describe the management reports typically generated by a reservation module of a property management system. (pp. 71–72)

# 3

# Reservation Systems

**W**HILE MANY INDUSTRIES computerized during the 1960s, the hotel industry did not actively pursue the possibilities of automation until the early 1970s. This relatively late start enabled the hotel industry to benefit from advances in technology. When other industries were struggling to upgrade their existing systems, hoteliers received greater value for dollars spent on newer hardware components and easier-to-operate software packages. This is especially true in regard to the first generation of reservation systems. However, these reservation systems became less efficient as technological advances linked reservations directly to comprehensive property management systems, central reservation systems, and global distribution systems. Soon, second generation systems matured and were pushed to their processing capabilities. The implementation of next generation reservation systems included Internet distribution systems and a myriad of intermediary and referral networks. These worldwide reservation systems more effectively link hotel reservations to systems developed for airlines, car rental agencies, travel agencies, cruise lines, and other travel-related businesses.

The proper handling of reservation information is critical to the success of hotel companies and individual properties. Reservations can be made for individuals, groups, tours, or conventions. Each request for accommodations creates a need for an accurate response in relation to the room types and rates available at a given point in time—making it critical that all distribution channels have access to current availability information.

This chapter examines computer-based reservations management systems involving global distribution systems, Internet distribution systems, central reservation systems, intersell agencies, and property-direct reservation systems. Exhibit 1 lists the various types of reservation channels.

## E-Distribution Systems

**E-distribution** is the means by which hotels make their products and services available via electronic channels, including travel agents, wholesalers, consolidators, and consumers. Such channels are widely viewed as more convenient for those constituents that have online access and are often a less expensive source of bookings than traditional telephone channels. E-distribution includes the following two major categories:

- Global distribution systems
- Internet distribution systems

**Exhibit 1   Reservation Channels**

```
Global Distribution Systems
        SABRE
        Galileo International
        Amadeus
        WorldSpan

Internet Distribution Systems

Central Reservation System
        Affiliate Reservation Network (Hotel Chains)
        Non-Affiliate Reservation Networks
                Leading Hotels of the World
                Preferred Hotels
                Distinguished Hotels

Intersell Agencies

Property Direct (PMS Reservations Module)

Internet
```

Competing hotel companies may participate in the same global or Internet distribution systems. Therefore, e-distribution systems must provide a security system that protects the proprietary nature of room and rate availability data. Security is usually maintained through passwords, data encryption, firewalls, and other security methods. Users of a system may be issued passwords that restrict access to proprietary data. Although passwords may need to be changed frequently, they can offer effective measures of security.

## Global Distribution Systems

**Global distribution systems (GDSs)** are often formed as joint ventures linking a number of diverse businesses. By directly linking the reservation systems of hotel, airline, car rental, and travel agency companies on a worldwide basis, global distribution systems provide access to travel and tourism inventories around the world. A global distribution system can represent a significant portion of reservations business for many airport and resort properties.

Most central reservation systems connect with one of the global distribution systems. The largest and best known GDSs include SABRE, Galileo International, Amadeus, Sahara, and WorldSpan. Each GDS is owned by an airline or consortium of airlines. GDSs provide worldwide distribution of hotel reservation information and allow selling of hotel reservations around the world. GDSs also provide distribution of airline tickets, automobile rentals, and other services required by travelers. Exhibit 2 presents the home Web page for SABRE's Travelocity site.

Selling hotel rooms is usually accomplished by connecting the hotel company reservation system with the GDSs. Most travel agents around the world have terminals connected to one or more of the many airline reservation systems to book

**Exhibit 2   Sample GDS—SABRE's Travelocity**

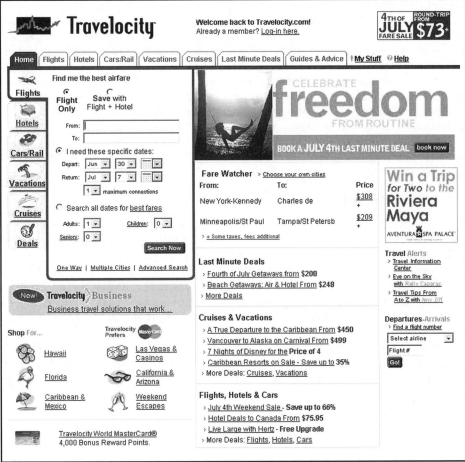

Source: Travelocity (http://www.travelocity.com) is the Internet extension of the SABRE Group, Inc., an airline reservation system providing a global distribution system for hotels, car rental companies, bed and breakfast options, and cruise lines.

airline travel. By having hotel accommodations and automobile rentals available in the computer system at the same time, most GDSs provide single-source access to most of the travel agent's selling requirements. In one transaction, a travel agent can sell an airline ticket, hotel room, and automobile rental.

Although many global distribution systems perform similar functions, each maintains unique internal system formats in relation to room rate; room type; and availability, confirmation, and settlement information. A key to the success of distribution systems is the **smart switch**. This switch translates reservations transactions into as many unique formats as required by diverse network interconnections, thereby allowing users to share data from different reservation systems without having to deal with complex formats, files, and operating systems. The smart switch can access reservation system files and convert the data into easy-to-use formats and files.

Travel agents were once reluctant to book hotel rooms through GDSs because room availability and rates were not always accurate and the confirmation process to the hotel was not always foolproof. Within the past ten years, hotel companies have linked their central reservation systems to GDSs, which allows travel agents to book reservations directly into hotel systems and verify room availability and rates. This is called **seamless connectivity**. Confirmations come from the hotel companies' systems, eliminating the concern about the inaccuracy of data or the unreliability of the confirmation process.

Since most airlines have leisure travel departments, airline reservations agents can also sell hotel rooms. With over 200,000 terminals around the world, GDSs have become a powerful force in hotel reservations.

## Internet Distribution Systems

**Internet distribution systems (IDSs)** are consumer-oriented reservation systems which have become one of the fastest growing e-distribution channels. Unlike GDSs, these systems are typically used by consumers to book airline, hotel, car, and cruise ship reservations for themselves. The wealth of information available to consumers has never been greater, and consumers expect and shop hard to find lower prices online. As a consequence, the environment has become very competitive. "Name your own price" sites and last-minute Internet-based bargain notifications have provided an effective way for hotels to dispose of distressed or otherwise under-utilized inventory.

Typically, IDSs are operated by independent Web site sponsors that develop an online hotel reservation booking engine. IDS sites can connect to a hotel property in at least three ways:

1. Connection to the hotel company's central reservation system

2. Connection to a switching company that connects to the hotel's central reservation system

3. Connection to a GDS that connects to the hotel's central reservation system

# Intersell Agencies

Domestic competition for hotel reservation commissions is intense since other segments of the travel industry (consolidators, wholesalers, booking agencies, etc.) may also operate reservation systems. Airline carriers, travel agencies, car rental companies, and chain hotels offer stiff competition to independent central reservation systems entering the reservations marketplace.

The term **intersell agency** refers to a reservation network that handles more than one product line. Intersell agencies typically handle reservations for airline flights, car rentals, and hotel rooms. The spirit of an intersell promotion is captured by the expression "one call does it all." Although intersell agencies may channel their reservation requests directly to individual hotels, some elect to communicate with central reservation systems or electronic distribution channels.

It is important to note that a local, regional, or national intersell arrangement does not preclude a hotel property from participating in a GDS or IDS or from processing reservations directly with a front office reservation PMS module.

Although there are a variety of options for interconnecting various intersell agencies with individual properties, the goal of integrating operations is to minimize suspense time. Suspense time refers to the elapsed time from system inquiry to response. Minimal suspense time results when, instead of communicating with participating individual properties, intersell agencies are able to automatically share reservation system information (rate and room availability). Information sharing provides intersell reservation agents with a simplified method for booking a guest's complete travel requirements, and also provides participating hotels with a way to simultaneously update the central reservation system (CRS). Intersell systems enhance product distribution while providing a basis for cost-effective CRS operations. The CRS simply increases its exposure while reducing its operating expenses.

# Central Reservation Systems

Since the early 1970s, the hospitality industry has seen many independent central reservation systems enter and leave the marketplace. The problems encountered by these systems are not related to difficulties in generating demand for their services. Rather, they are related to servicing demand at an acceptable level of profitability. Expensive equipment (hardware components and communication devices), high overhead, and extensive operating costs have made it difficult for independent central reservation systems to succeed. The staff required to process individual reservation requests and maintain diverse reservation records for a multitude of hotel properties can lead to dwindling revenues and soaring operating costs.

Increased on-line interaction between hotel property management systems, central reservation systems, and e-distribution systems decentralizes the reservation function but centralizes marketing and sales efforts in relation to the reservations process. This results in greater control of reservations handling at the property level and increased sales efforts at various distribution channels on behalf of the participating properties.

## Affiliate and Non-Affiliate Systems

There are two types of **central reservation systems (CRSs)**: affiliate and non-affiliate systems. An **affiliate reservation system** refers to a hotel chain's central reservation system in which all participating properties are contractually related. Each property is represented in the computer system database and is required to provide room availability and inventory data to the central reservation office on a timely basis. Chain hotels link their operations in order to streamline reservations processing and reduce total system costs. Exhibit 3 presents a sample central reservation system. Typically, a central reservation office of an affiliate system performs the following functions:

**Exhibit 3    Sample Central Reservation System**

### Brilliant CRS

This special version of Brilliant was developed to seamlessly integrate with the Cendant Corporation Central Reservation System. The technology behind this solution is our renowned Property Management System, Brilliant Front Office. The Brilliant-CRS product will help you in your daily work and make things easier using a 2-way interface to the Cendant CRS.

**I have a Cendant Hotel; tell me how it works!**
All reservations created in the CRS by agents, websites, or travel agents are automatically sent to Brilliant-CRS. Additionally, the reservations that are made in the hotel are sent automatically to the CRS. This ensures the inventories on CRS and your PM System at the hotel always balance. The interface also opens and closes inventory in the PM System, providing current rates and room availability. This helps to maximize your occupancy at the optimal rate!

**Functionality Highlights**

- **Reservations**
  Reservations created locally are automatically sent to CRS. All updates are automatically received from the CRS on a predetermined schedule.
- **Rates**
  Individual rates are published on the CRS and these rates are managed through the system.
- **Invoicing**
  Multiple invoices, invoice splitting, multi currency
- **Front Office**
  Walk In, Check In /Out, Guest Messaging
- **Reporting**
  Over 175 standard reports included. Integrated Report writer based on SQL statements for custom and ad-hoc reporting
- **Integration**
  Integrate with Microsoft Office
- **Interfaces**
  We interface to all major vendors. Please contact our Sales Team for specific questions.

Datasheet (PDF)
Other products

Source: Brilliant Hotelsoftware Ltd. For more information, browse the company's Web site at http://www.mybrilliant.net

- Deals directly with the public

- Advertises a central telephone number and/or Web site address

- Provides participating properties with necessary technology

- Communicates room availability and inventory data to e-distribution channels and non-affiliate reservation systems based on information supplied by individual properties

- Performs data entry services for remotely located or non-automated properties

- Delivers reservations and related information to properties quickly and cost-effectively

- Maintains statistical information on the volume of calls, talk time, conversion rates, denial rates, and other statistics (talk time refers to the number of minutes reservationists spend on a call; conversion rate is the ratio of booked business to total number of inquiries; and denial rate refers to reservation requests that were turned away)

- Performs customer relations management functions for corporate-sponsored guest recognition and loyalty programs

- Maintains a property profile of demographic information about callers requesting reservations

- Bills properties for handling reservations

Some affiliate systems enter into agreements with non-chain properties, allowing them to join the system as overrun facilities. An **overrun facility** is a property selected to receive reservation requests after chain properties have exhausted room availabilities in a geographic region.

A **non-affiliate reservation system** refers to a subscription system linking independent properties. A hotel subscribes to the system's services and takes responsibility for updating the system with accurate room availability data. Examples of non-affiliate reservation systems are Leading Hotels of the World, Preferred Hotels, and Distinguished Hotels. Non-affiliate systems generally provide the same services as affiliate systems, thus enabling independent hotel operators to gain benefits otherwise available only to chain operators. However, many non-affiliate systems process reservations solely on the basis of the availability of room types. With this method, room types are classified as either "open" or "closed." Most affiliate systems process reservations on the basis of a declining inventory of both room types and room rates. This method helps participating properties to maximize revenue potential and occupancy.

Affiliate and non-affiliate central reservation systems often provide a variety of services in addition to managing reservations processing and communications. A CRS may also serve as an inter-property communications network, an accounting transfer system, or a destination information center. For instance, a CRS is used as an accounting transfer system when a chain hotel communicates operating data to company headquarters for processing. When a CRS communicates reports on local weather, special events, and seasonal room rates, it serves as a destination information center.

## CRS Functions

Central reservation services are provided by the central reservation office (CRO). The CRO receives room rate and availability information from participating properties. Non-automated properties may send this information in the form of hard copy and the CRO manually enters the information into the CRS database. Information from connected properties is typically sent over communication lines and enters the database directly. In a CRS network configuration, the responsibility and control of room and rate information lies at the property level. The key to successful central reservation management is that the individual properties and the central system have access to the same room and rate availability information in real time. When this is the case, reservationists at the CRO can directly confirm room rates and availability at the time of reservation.

The timely delivery of reservation confirmations from a CRS to individual properties is vital. Many chain systems provide multiple delivery alternatives to ensure that properties receive all new reservations, modifications, or cancellations. For example, most central reservation systems relay processed transactions to member properties through on-line interfaces. Although on-line interfacing between central reservation offices and property-level systems is fast and effective, some networks may also e-mail or fax the information to properties to ensure successful completion of the reservation process.

The goals of a CRS are to improve guest service while enhancing profitability and operating efficiency. A CRS accomplishes these goals by:

- Providing access to special room rates and promotional packages

- Instantly confirming reservations

- Communicating with major airline, travel, and car rental agencies

- Creating comprehensive guest files

Basic services provided by most central reservation systems include automatic room availability updating and corporate-wide marketing.

**Automatic Room Availability Updating.** As a room is sold, whether through an e-distribution channel, a CRS, an individual property, or a remote intersell agency, the inventory of rooms available for sale is simultaneously updated for all reservation sources. Having current, synchronized room availability information for each participating distribution channel provides the ability to automatically close out room types without obtaining direct property approval. The advantage of an effective distribution system is that reservationists (at any distribution channel) can directly confirm room rates and availability at the time reservations are made.

In the past, a CRS primarily was provided intermittent room availability data from participating properties at regularly scheduled intervals. This meant that when a property booked its own reservations, there would be no immediate record sent to the CRS; updating waited until the next scheduled reporting period. As the CRS booked reservations for a property, messages were sent to the property and printed on dedicated reservation printing devices. The property was often required to enter these printed transactions into its in-house reservation system so that accurate room availability data could be recalculated. In turn, this recalculated data was sent back to the CRS as an update on room availability. Today, advances in technology allow for real-time updating.

**Corporate-Wide Marketing.** A CRS can function as a powerful marketing resource. The CRS normally contains important marketing data on individual guests and may provide participating properties with profiles of groups holding reservations. New central reservation systems technology allows hotels to vary room rates for each room type on a daily basis. Varying conditions of supply and demand enable the room rates to slide within the ranges prescribed by each individual property. This approach is called revenue management (also yield management). Revenue management can be very effective in balancing room sales and room rates to optimize room revenue.

Guest history data can be extremely helpful in processing reservations for returning guests. These data also serve as the basis for determining demographic and geographic patterns of guests staying at participating hotel properties. Repeat guests may qualify for special frequent traveler or other loyalty program rewards offered by a hotel chain or individual property. By accessing guest history data, central reservation systems are usually able to direct and support a variety of marketing-oriented programs. Guest profile data may include:

- Guest identification number

- Full name and preferred salutation

- Level of membership in the program

- Home and business address and telephone numbers

- Type of guestroom preferred

- Amenities, such as king-size bed, non-smoking room, or newspaper preference

- Preferred form of account settlement

For each guest's stay, the system may track the guest's arrival and departure dates, number of room nights by room type, and a revenue breakdown by rooms, food and beverage, and other categories. In addition, special promotions, packages, and/or recreational activities may be noted.

## Additional Services

In addition to maintaining up-to-date information about room availability and rates, a comprehensive CRS may maintain such data as:

- Room types
- Room rates
- Room decor
- Room location
- Promotional packages
- Travel agent discounts
- Alternative booking locations
- Guest recognition programs
- Special amenities
- Weather conditions and news reports
- Currency exchange rates
- Connectivity to affiliate Web sites
- Connectivity to the company's guest history file

In addition to processing reservations, a CRS may perform a variety of other services. A reservation system may serve as an administrative network for inter-property communications. The reservation system may also be used as the preferred platform to transfer accounting data from individual properties for processing at company headquarters. In addition, the system may operate as a destination information center by serving as a communications channel for local weather, news, and reports on special hotel features. Central reservation systems can report:

- Travel or airline agent performance statistics
- Effectiveness of special promotional packages
- Sales forecasting information

Newer systems enable the participating hotels to build in specific rules and procedures for each of the hotel's promotional packages or products. Some central reservation systems expand their basic services to include such functions as:

- Revenue management (yield management)
- Centralized commission reporting
- Links to intersell agencies
- Deposit/refund accounting
- Links to e-distribution systems

**Revenue management,** also called yield management, is a set of demand forecasting techniques used to develop pricing strategies that will maximize rooms revenue for a lodging property. Centralized commission reporting details the amounts payable to travel agencies (and others) booking commissionable business with a hotel through the hotel's CRS. Hotel companies that require advance deposits to ensure reservations may find the CRS helpful in maintaining accounting records. Records can be kept of deposits made with reservation requests and of amounts refunded to individuals or groups who cancel reservations within the allotted time and procedures specified by management.

# Property-Level Reservation Systems

Property-level reservation systems are specifically designed to meet the particular needs of the lodging industry. A property management system (PMS) typically supports a reservation module designed to streamline reservations handling and channel distribution management. The specific needs and requirements of individual properties determine whether stand-alone reservation management software is purchased and operated separately or as a part of an overall PMS.

A PMS reservation module enables a reservationist to respond quickly and accurately to callers requesting future accommodations. This module also connects to a CRS for seamless reservation processing. The module significantly reduces paperwork, physical filing, and other clerical procedures, providing the reservationist with more time for giving personal attention to callers and for marketing the various services the hotel offers. Stored information can be accessed quickly, and many of the procedures for processing requests, updating information, and generating confirmations are simplified.

The reservationist's initial inquiry procedures create a **reservation record** that initiates the hotel guest cycle. Reservation records identify guests and their needs before their arrival at the property and enable the hotel to personalize guest service and appropriately schedule needed personnel and resources. In addition, reservation modules can generate a number of important reports for management's use. The following sections describe typical activities associated with the use of a PMS reservation module. These activities also apply to a majority of the booking engines used in e-distribution channels. These activities include:

- Reservation inquiry

- Determination of availability

- Creation of the reservation record

- Confirmation of the reservation

- Maintenance of the reservation record

- Generation of reports

## Reservation Inquiry

A reservation request can be received in person; over the telephone; via postal delivery, facsimile, or electronic mail; or through an interface with an external reservation distribution channel. Regardless of its origin, the reservation request is formulated into a **reservation inquiry** by the reservationist or automatically by the software application. This inquiry typically contains the following data:

- Date of arrival

- Type and number of rooms requested

- Number of room nights

- Room rate code (standard, special, package, etc.)

- Number of persons in party

The reservationist enters the data through a software template according to rigidly defined inquiry procedures. Simultaneous processing involves a **real time capability**. This means that the reservationist receives the necessary feedback from the system in order to respond to a caller's requests during the telephone call. The real time capability of many reservation modules is designed to provide quick responses (less than three seconds) and, therefore, enables the reservationist to edit, alter, or amend the inquiry while the caller is still available for comment. Once the inquiry is matched with rooms availability data, the PMS assigns and blocks a room, thus removing it from the room availability database.

**Exhibit 4   Sample Room Availability Search Screen**

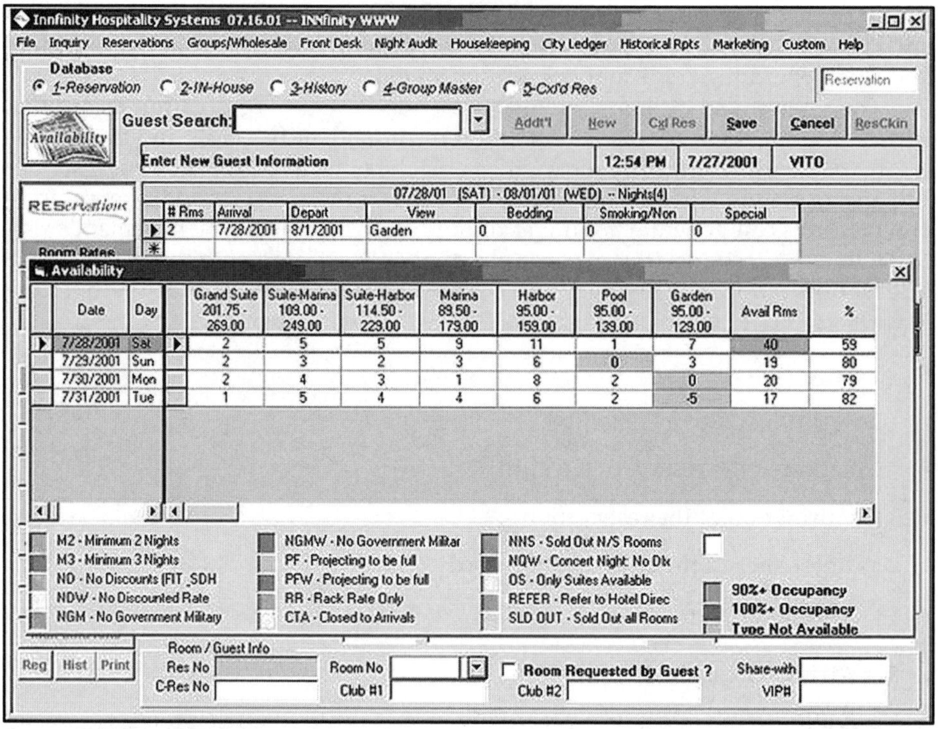

Source: INNfinity Hospitality Systems. For more information, browse the company's Web site at http://www.innhs.com

## Determination of Availability

Once entered, the reservation inquiry is compared to rooms availability data according to a predetermined system algorithm. The algorithm is a computer-based formula designed to sell rooms in a specified pattern (by zone, floor, block, etc.). Processing a reservation request may result in one of several system-generated responses that appear on the reservationist's display screen:

- Acceptance or rejection of the reservation request
- Suggestions of alternative room types or rates
- Suggestions of alternative hotel properties

Exhibit 4 presents a sample room availability search screen.

## Creation of the Reservation Record

Once the reservation request has been processed and the room blocked, the system requires that the reservationist complete the reservation record by collecting and entering necessary data, such as:

**Exhibit 5   Sample Reservation Record Screen**

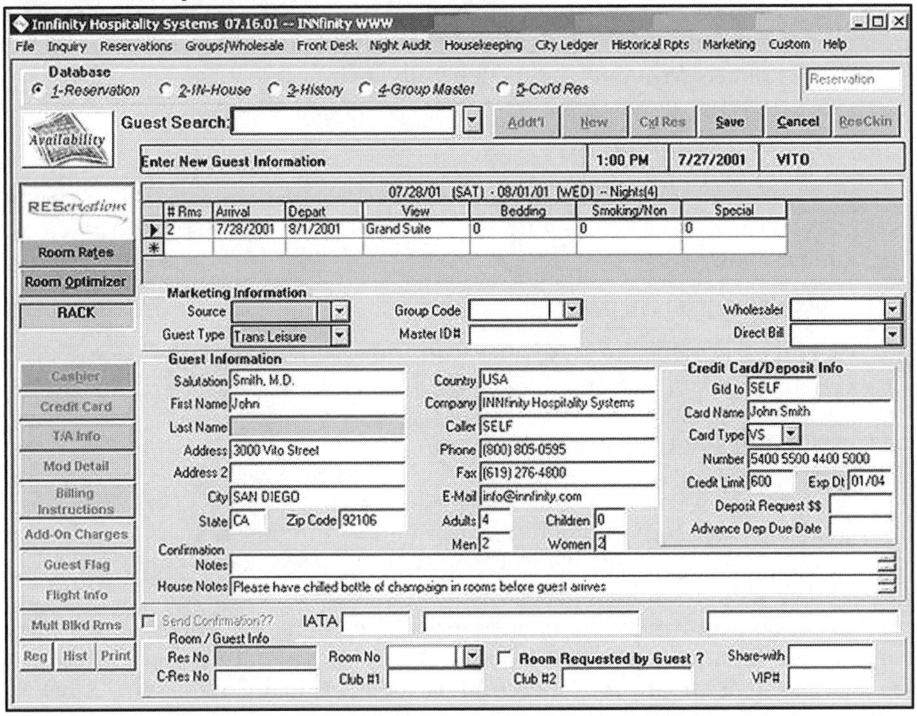

Source: INNfinity Hospitality Systems. For more information, browse the company's Web site at http://www.innhs.com

- Guest's contact data (name, address, e-mail address, and telephone number)
- Time of arrival
- Reservation classification (advance, confirmed, guaranteed)
- Confirmation number
- Caller data (agency or secretary)
- Special requirements (handicapper, crib, no smoking, etc.)

Exhibit 5 presents a sample reservation record.

A major benefit of automated processing is the streamlining of the initial inquiry and the collection of secondary reservation record data. This often proves to be more efficient to callers and property personnel. For example, if all data were collected at the outset and the system denied the reservation request, the reservationist and the caller would have spent a lot of time exchanging information that turned out to be of little use.

## Confirmation of the Reservation

Property management systems can automatically generate letters of confirmation at the time a reservation request is processed. Information can be retrieved from the reservation record and printed on a specially designed hotel form or into an electronic format for e-mail or fax distribution. While there are probably as many formats and styles of confirmation letters as there are automated hotels, acknowledgments within confirmation letters generally include:

- Guest's name and address

- Date and time of arrival

- Type, number, and rates of rooms

- Number of nights

- Number of persons in party

- Reservation classification (advance, confirmed, guaranteed)

- Special services requested by the guest

- Confirmation number

- Request for deposit or prepayment

- Update of original reservation (reconfirmation, modification, or cancellation)

- Cancellation policy

Reservation confirmations may be printed or e-mailed immediately. However, they are normally generated as part of the stream of output produced during the time of system update. A **system update** performs many of the same functions as those performed by the night audit routine in non-automated properties. System updates are run daily to allow for report production, system file reorganization, system maintenance, and to provide an end-of-day time frame.

## Maintenance of the Reservation Record

Reservation records are stored in an electronic file and commonly segmented by date of arrival (year, month, day), group name, and guest name. File organization and the method of file retrieval are critical to an effective reservation module because callers frequently update, alter, cancel, or reconfirm their reservations. For example, should a caller request a cancellation, the reservationist must be able to quickly access the correct reservation record, verify its contents, and process the cancellation. In turn, the reservationist provides the caller a system generated cancellation code number.

Data from reservation records may be used to generate preregistration forms. Reservation records can also serve as preregistration folios for pre-sale guest cycle transactions. Prepayments, advance deposits, and cash payouts are examples of transactions that can be posted to the reservation record and later transferred to the guest's in-house folio.

In addition, the reservation module has the ability to interface with other front office functions. Reservation record data can be:

- Printed onto preregistration cards to facilitate faster check-in procedures.

- Used as the basis for creating electronic guest folios and information lists (alphabetical listings or sequential room number listings).

- Transferred to commission agent files for later processing.

- Formatted for eventual inclusion in a guest history file.

## Generation of Reports

Similar to many PMS applications, the number and type of reports available through a reservation module are functions of the user's needs, software capability, and database contents. A PMS reservation module is designed to maximize room sales by accurately monitoring room availabilities and providing a detailed forecast of rooms revenue. A computer-generated **rooms availability report** lists, by room type, the number of rooms available each day (net remaining rooms in each category). A **revenue forecast report** projects future revenue by multiplying predicted occupancies by current house rates. A PMS reservation module can also automatically compile and generate:

- Reservation transaction records

- Expected arrival and departure lists

- Commission agent reports

- Turnaway statistics

A **reservation transaction record** provides a daily summary of reservation records that were created, modified, or canceled. Reservation modules may also generate supplemental summaries of specialized activities, such as cancellation reports, blocked room reports, and no-show reports. **Expected arrivals lists** and **expected departures lists** are daily reports showing the number of guests expected to arrive and depart, the number of stay-overs (the difference between arrivals and departures), and the names of guests associated with each transaction. **Commission agent reports** delineate reservation transactions and commissions payable, by agent. Agents having contractual agreements with a hotel may earn commissions for the business they book at the property. A **turnaway report**, also called a refusal report, tracks the number of room nights refused because rooms were not available for sale. This report may be especially helpful to hotels that experience peak demand periods.

## New Developments

Since reservations management was the first functional area of hotels to be computerized, it has received a great deal of vendor research and development. Additionally, the airline industry has spent millions of dollars developing its own reservation techniques, many of which have been adapted to the needs of hotels. One of the more interesting developments in reservations technology is experimentation with automated speech recognition (ASR).

Currently available are interactive multi-media and virtual reality presentations for independent travelers, meeting planners, and travel agents. The addition of voice input/output seems the next step as lodging companies continue to develop panoramic photography and full-motion property tours through their Internet sites.

Experimentation with verbal recognition/synthesis technology (spoken commands) is promising and may significantly affect hotel reservation modules in the near future. Research is presently being conducted that requires users to possess a microphone or headset and display screen. The reservations program generates a series of cues and questions on the screen to which the potential guest responds orally by speaking into the mouthpiece of the headset or microphone. The system acknowledges the user's input and may generate an additional series of cues and questions. Although these systems presently use and understand only a limited vocabulary, the future looks bright for this application.

## Reservations Through the Internet

Vacation travelers, business travelers, corporate travel offices, international visitors—all are able to use the World Wide Web to arrange for their own travel and accommodation needs. The variety of potential guests accessing Internet sites to place reservations has prompted travel and hospitality companies to develop simple, user-friendly reservation procedures.

Large and small hotels alike have a presence on the Internet. Chains often have a web site focusing first on the brand and its features, then on the individual properties. Most chain Internet sites allow visitors to the site to book reservations. Independent hotels are also experimenting with web sites. While they may not be as sophisticated as chain sites, usually due to the cost of operating such sites, they normally provide similar information and allow visitors to make reservations, if only by e-mail.

Exhibit 6 presents a series of screens that walk prospective guests through the process of reserving rooms at the Internet site of the Holiday Inn hotel chain. In this particular reservation process, users first identify the area of the world relevant to their travel needs and then narrow down their destination, first by country and then by city. The city screen provides a listing and description of hotels. After selecting a hotel, users input the necessary reservation information. They can guarantee their reservations by providing personal or corporate credit card data.

The degree of privacy and security of financial transactions over the Internet has prompted concern, and, in many cases, this concern has limited the volume of Internet commerce. Security procedures exist today and will become even more sophisticated in the future. When users access online reservation systems, web browsers generally provide a security alert.

In addition to providing a user-friendly reservations process and securing transactions, online systems also perform important marketing functions for the hospitality company. Reservation features of many Internet sites enable users to access detailed pictures of individual hotels. Some enable users to download multimedia presentations of the features and benefits of the hotel chain and of individual hotels—complete with a "walk through" of the property and a virtual tour inside the various rooms and services offered.

**Exhibit 6   Sample Internet Reservation Screens**

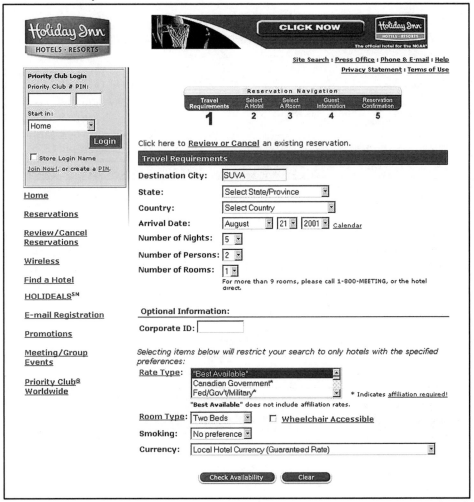

*(continued)*

## 🔑 Key Terms

**affiliate reservation system**—A hotel chain's reservation system in which all participating properties are contractually related. Each property is represented in the computer system database and is required to provide room availability data to the reservations center on a timely basis.

**central reservation office**—Typically deals directly with the public, advertises a central telephone number, provides participating properties with necessary communications equipment, and bills properties for handling reservations.

**Exhibit 6** *(continued)*

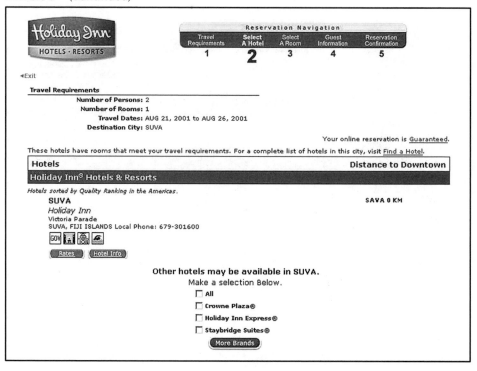

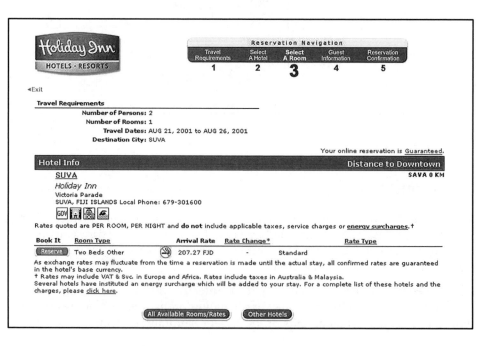

**Exhibit 6**  *(continued)*

---

**Holiday Inn**
HOTELS · RESORTS

| Reservation Navigation | | | | |
|---|---|---|---|---|
| Travel Requirements | Select A Hotel | Select A Room | Guest Information | Reservation Confirmation |
| 1 | 2 | 3 | **4** | 5 |

◄Exit

Your online reservation is Guaranteed.

### Reservation Information

**Your Itinerary**

| | |
|---|---|
| **Hotel:** | **SUVA** |
| | *Holiday Inn* |
| | Victoria Parade |
| | SUVA FIJI ISLANDS |
| **Phone:** | Local Phone: 679-301600 |
| **Arrival Date:** | AUG 21, 2001 |
| **Number of Nights:** | 5 |
| **Number of Rooms:** | 1 |
| **Number of Persons:** | 2 |
| **Room Type:** | Two Beds Other Non-Smoking |
| **Rate Type:** | Standard |
| **Rate:** | 207.27 FJD **, per room, per night, plus tax***, services charges and energy charges. |
| **Cancel By:** | 6PM local hotel time on **AUG 21, 2001** or your credit card will be billed for a minimum of **1 night.** |

### Guest Information

Making reservations is fast and easy for Priority Club members. Members earn valuable points or miles for every stay. If you are a member, login now to pre-populate the fields below with your member information. If you're not a member, join today! (Don't worry, we'll take you right back here when you're done.)

**Priority Club Number:** [     ]  **Pin:** [     ]

[ Login ]

-OR-

**If you are not Priority Club member, please enter your information below:**
* Indicates required fields.
Privacy Statement

| | |
|---|---|
| **Name:** | *First [          ] |
| | *Last [          ] |
| ***Telephone:** | [          ] |
| ***E-mail:** | [          ] |
| ***E-mail Verify:** | [          ] |
| ***Mailing Address:** | [          ] |
| | [          ] |
| | [          ] |
| | *City [          ] |
| | State/Province [          ▼] |
| | ZIP/Postal Code [     ] |
| | *Country [ UNITED STATES ▼] |

**Guarantee Information**
* Indicates required fields.
Your Credit Card is Safe.

| | |
|---|---|
| ***Card Type:** | [          ▼] |
| ***Credit Card Number:** | [          ]  (EX: 123456789) |
| ***Exp. Date:** | [  ▼] [  ▼] |

**Special Information**
We will forward any special information that you would like sent with your reservation. Requests **cannot be guaranteed** and are based on availability and on a first-come-first-served basis.

**Comments:** [          ]

[ Confirm ]  [ Cancel ]  [ Clear ]

It may take a few moments before your confirmation is complete.

---

Source: Holiday Inn Hotels and Resorts. For more information, browse the company's Web site at http://www.ichotelsgroup.com

**central reservation system**—An external reservation network. *See also* affiliate reservation system *and* non-affiliate reservation system.

**commission agent report**—Delineates reservation transactions and commissions payable, by agent.

**e-distribution**—The selling of products or services over the Internet or some other electronic medium. Hospitality e-distribution includes the GDS and Internet-based sales channels.

**expected arrivals list**—A daily report showing the number of guests and the names of guests expected to arrive with reservations.

**expected departures list**—A daily report showing the number of guests expected to depart, the number of stay-overs (the difference between arrivals and departures), and the names of guests associated with each transaction.

**global distribution system (GDS)**—Electronic networks used by travel agents and some Internet-based distribution channels to make airline, hotel, car rental, and cruise ship reservations.

**Hotel Electronic Distribution Network Association (HEDNA)**—The prominent trade association supporting the industry's use of electronic distribution channel (www.hedna.org).

**Internet distribution system (IDS)**—Internet-based services providing consumers the ability to book airline, hotel, car rental, and cruise ship reservations.

**intersell agency**—A reservation network that handles more than one product line. Intersell agencies typically handle reservations for airline flights, car rentals, and hotel rooms.

**non-affiliate reservation system**—A subscription system linking independent properties. A hotel subscribes to the system's services and takes responsibility for updating the system with accurate room availability data.

**overrun facility**—A hotel property selected to receive reservation requests after chain properties have exhausted room availabilities in a geographic region.

**real time capability**—Refers to simultaneous processing. For example, real time capability enables a reservationist to receive necessary feedback from the system immediately in order to respond to a caller's requests during a telephone call.

**reservation inquiry**—A reservation request is formulated into a reservation inquiry by the reservationist. This inquiry typically collects the following data: date of arrival, type and number of rooms requested, number of room nights, room rate code (standard, special, package, etc.), and number of persons in party.

**reservation record**—The reservationist's initial inquiry procedures create a reservation record that initiates the hotel guest cycle. Reservation records identify guests and their needs before guests arrive at the property; such records enable the hotel to personalize guest service and appropriately schedule needed personnel.

**reservation transaction record**—Provides a daily summary of reservation records that were created, modified, or canceled.

**revenue forecast report**—Projects future revenue by multiplying predicted occupancies by current house rates.

**rooms availability report**—Lists, by room type, the number of rooms that are available each day (net remaining rooms in each category).

**seamless connectivity**—The ability of travel agencies to book reservations directly into hotel reservation systems, as well as verify room availability and rates.

**smart switch**—Translates reservations transactions into as many unique formats as required by diverse network interconnections, thereby allowing users to share data from different reservation systems without having to deal with complex formats, files, and operating systems. The smart switch can access reservation system files and convert the data into easy-to-use formats and files.

**system update**—Performs many of the same functions performed by the night audit routine in non-automated properties. System updates are run daily to allow for report production, system file reorganization, and system maintenance, and to provide an end-of-day time frame.

**turnaway report**—Also called a refusal report, tracks the number of room nights refused because rooms were not available for sale. This report is especially helpful to hotels with expansion plans.

**yield management**—A set of demand forecasting techniques used to develop pricing strategies that will maximize rooms revenue for a lodging property.

# Review Questions

1. What role might the Internet play in a global distribution system?
2. How do affiliate reservation systems differ from non-affiliate reservation systems?
3. What services are provided by a central reservation system?
4. What does the term "intersell agency" mean?
5. Why is data security a concern of global distribution systems?
6. What are the typical activities associated with the use of a PMS reservation module?
7. What data are collected through reservation inquiry procedures?
8. What data are generally included in confirmation letters produced by property-level reservation systems?
9. How can a property use data maintained by reservation records?
10. What kinds of reports can be produced by PMS reservation modules?

# Internet Sites

For more information, visit the following Internet sites. Remember that Internet addresses can change without notice. If the site is no longer there, you can use a search engine to look for additional sites.

### Internet Reservation Sites

Business Travel Net
http://www.business-travel-net.com

Hotel and Travel on the Net
http://www.hoteltravel.com

HotelsOnline
http://www.hotelsonline.net

Internet Travel Network
http://www.itn.net

Resorts Online
http://www.resortsonline.com

Travelocity
http://www.travelocity.com

TravelWeb
http://www.travelweb.com

### Technology Sites

Brilliant Hotelsoftware Ltd.
http://www.mybrilliant.net

CSS Hotel Systems
http://www.csshotelsystems.com

Execu/Tech Systems Inc.
http://www.execu-tech.com

Fidelio Products
http://www.micros.com

Hospitality Industry Technology
Exposition and Conference
http://www.hitec.org

Hospitality Industry Technology
Integration Standards
http://www.hitis.org

HOST International
http://www.hostgroup.com

Hotellinx Systems Ltd.
http://www.hotellinx.com

INNfinity Hospitality Systems
http://www.innhs.com

Newmarket International, Inc.
http://www.newmarketinc.com

# Chapter 4 Outline

Rooms Management Module
    Room Status
    Room and Rate Assignment
    In-House Guest Information Functions
    Housekeeping Functions
    Generation of Reports
Guest Accounting Module
    Types of Accounts
    Posting to Accounts
    Front Office Audit
    Account Settlement
    System Update and Reports

# Competencies

1. Identify features and functions of the rooms management module of a hotel property management system. (pp. 81–87)

2. Define room status terms and explain the importance of eliminating room status discrepancies in hotel operations. (pp. 82–85)

3. Explain how managers can use various reports commonly generated by the rooms management module of a hotel property management system. (pp. 87–88)

4. Identify features and functions of the guest accounting module of a hotel property management system. (pp. 88–96)

5. Describe the different types of folios that a guest accounting module may use to monitor transactions. (pp. 89–92)

6. Explain how managers can use various reports commonly generated by the guest accounting module of a hotel property management system. (pp. 96–97)

# 4

# Rooms Management and Guest Accounting Applications

A̲N AUTOMATED PROPERTY MANAGEMENT SYSTEM monitors and controls a number of front office and back office functions while supporting a variety of ancillary application software that relate to front office and back office activities. While not all property management systems (PMS) operate identically, a rooms management module is always an essential component of front office software.

A rooms management module maintains current information on the status of rooms, assists in the assignment of rooms during registration, and helps coordinate many guest services. A guest accounting module processes and monitors financial transactions that occur between guests and the hotel. When remote point-of-sale devices, situated at various revenue centers throughout the hotel, are interfaced with a guest accounting module, guest charges are communicated to the front desk and automatically posted to the appropriate electronic guest folios.

## Rooms Management Module

The rooms management module is an important information and communications branch within a property management system. It is primarily designed to strengthen the communication links between the front office and the housekeeping department. Most rooms management modules perform the following functions:

- Identify current room status.

- Assist in assigning rooms to guests at check-in.

- Provide in-house guest information.

- Organize housekeeping activities.

- Provide auxiliary services.

- Generate timely reports for management.

A rooms management module alerts front desk employees of the status of each room, just as, in the past, room racks did in nonautomated operations. A front desk employee simply enters the room's number, and the current status of the room is displayed immediately on the terminal's screen. Once a room

**Exhibit 1    Sample Rooms Status Report**

```
ROOM STATUS REPORT — KELLOGG CENTER
05/19      18:56
RU-PAGE 1                                        FLOOR(S) 2, 3, 4, 5, 6, 7
     201  OOO   202  O/D   203  CO    204  V/C   205  V/C   206  O/C
     207  V/C   208  V/C   209  V/C   215  O/C   216  V/C   217  V/C
     219  OOO   220  V/C   222  O/D   223  OOO   224  OOO   225  OOO
     227  V/C   230  OOO   231  V/C   232  V/C   233  O/C   301  V/C
     302  O/D   303  O/D   304  O/D   305  O/D   306  O/D   307  O/C
     308  O/C   309  O/D   311  O/C   312  O/D   313  O/C   314  V/C
     316  V/D   317  O/D   319  OOO   320  V/C   322  V/C   323  V/C
     325  OOO   327  V/C   328  V/C   329  O/D   330  O/D   331  O/D
     332  O/D   333  O/D   401  V/C   402  V/C   403  V/C   404  V/C
```

```
     715  V/C   716  V/C   717  V/C   719  V/C   720  V/C   722  V/C


     77  V/C   2  V/D   18  OOO   54  OCC   5  CO
```

Courtesy of Kellogg Center, Michigan State University, East Lansing, Michigan

becomes clean and ready for occupancy, housekeeping staff change the room's status through a desktop terminal in their work area, or a guestroom touchtone phone, or a wireless hand-held device. The updated room status information is immediately communicated to the front desk. Rooms status reports may also be generated at any time for use by management. Exhibit 1 illustrates one type of **rooms status report**.

Rooms management modules are also capable of automatic room and rate assignments at the time of check-in. In addition, their ability to display guest data on screens at the front desk, switchboard, concierge station, and other remote locations eliminates the need for traditional front office equipment, such as room racks and information racks. A rooms management module also enables management to efficiently schedule needed housekeeping staff and to review detailed housekeeping productivity reports. In addition, automated wake-up systems and message-waiting systems can be interfaced with the rooms management module to provide greater control over these auxiliary guest services. Exhibit 2 summarizes functions performed by a rooms management module.

## Room Status

Before assigning rooms to guests, front desk employees must have access to current, accurate information on the status of rooms in the property. The current status of a room can be affected by information about future availability (determined

**Exhibit 2    Functions of a Rooms Management Module**

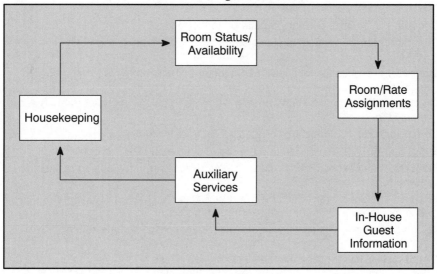

through reservations data) and information about current availability (determined through housekeeping data).

Information about future availability is important because it may affect the length of stay of in-house guests. Access to rooms availability data that extend several days into the future gives front desk employees reliable **room status** information and enhances their ability to satisfy the needs of guests while maximizing occupancy. Consider the following example.

Mr. Gregory checks in on Thursday for a one-night stay. However, during the course of his work on Friday, he finds it necessary to stay over through the weekend. The front desk employee may be inclined to approve this extension based on the fact that Friday night's business is light. Later, upon checking reservations data, the employee learns that although the hotel has a low occupancy forecasted for Friday evening, all rooms are reserved on Saturday night. This obviously poses a problem that needs to be resolved according to hotel policy, but it is better for the problem to surface Friday than on Saturday night when the house is full.

The housekeeping description of the current status of a room is crucial to the immediate, short-run selling position of that room. Common room status definitions are presented in Exhibit 3.

Information about current availability is absolutely essential in order for front desk employees to properly assign rooms to guests at the time of check-in. In the past, non-automated front office systems often experienced problems because of a breakdown in communication between housekeeping staff and front desk employees. Automated front office applications, on the other hand, ensure timely communications by converting data input by front desk employees, housekeepers, or guest services personnel into messages that are available at several locations throughout the lodging operation.

**Exhibit 3    Room Status Definitions**

**Occupied:** A guest is currently registered to the room.

**Complimentary:** The room is occupied, but the guest is assessed no charge for its use.

**Stayover:** The guest is not checking out today and will remain at least one more night.

**On-change:** The guest has departed, but the room has not yet been cleaned and readied for resale.

**Do not disturb:** The guest has requested not to be disturbed.

**Sleep-out:** A guest is registered to the room, but the bed has not been used.

**Skipper:** The guest has left the hotel without making arrangements to settle his/her account.

**Sleeper:** The guest has settled his/her account and left the hotel, but the front office staff has failed to properly update the room's status.

**Vacant and ready:** The room has been cleaned and inspected and is ready for an arriving guest.

**Out-of-order:** The room cannot be assigned to a guest. A room may be out-of-order for a variety of reasons, including the need for maintenance, refurbishing, and extensive cleaning.

**Lock-out:** The room has been locked so that the guest cannot re-enter until he/she is cleared by a hotel official.

**DNCO (did not check out):** The guest made arrangements to settle his or her account (and thus is not a skipper) but has left without informing the front office.

**Due out:** The room is expected to become vacant after the following day's check-out time.

**Check-out:** The guest has settled his or her account, returned the room keys, and left the hotel.

**Late check-out:** The guest has requested and is being allowed to check out later than the hotel's standard check-out time.

The hotel property management system routes data through the rooms management module and, thereby, helps coordinate the sale of rooms. Hotel technology is capable of instantly updating the housekeeping status of rooms, which enables front desk employees to make quick and accurate room assignments to guests at the time of check-in. For example, when a housekeeping attendant informs the property management system that a room's status has been changed from on-change to vacant and ready, a notice is automatically relayed to the front desk.

**Room status discrepancy** is a term that refers to situations in which the housekeeping department's description of a room's status differs from the room status information that guides front desk employees in assigning rooms to guests. These discrepancies can seriously affect a property's ability to satisfy guests and maximize rooms revenue. Nonautomated properties experience room status discrepancies not only because of time delays in communicating room status information from the housekeeping department to the front desk, but also because of the cumbersome nature of comparing housekeeping and front desk room status information. Consider the following scenario.

Mr. Gregory checks out of a nonautomated hotel and the desk clerk forgets to change his room's status in the room rack—giving the impression that Mr. Gregory remains an in-house guest. When housekeeping attendants clean the room, they may notice that Mr. Gregory's luggage and belongings have been removed (since the room has been vacated). However, if the housekeeping report does not indicate that Mr. Gregory is a check-out and not a stayover, the actual status of the room may go undetected. As long as this room status discrepancy exists, the hotel will not sell Mr. Gregory's vacated room because the room rack at the front desk will erroneously continue to indicate that the room is occupied. Unfortunately, this situation, termed a **sleeper**, arises all too often in nonautomated hotels. Why is it called a sleeper? Since the guest's card remains undisturbed in the room rack, it is described as being asleep. It remains so until corrected (awakened).

An automated property management system operates without a room rack. Instead, the rooms management module generates a **rooms discrepancy report** that signals to management the specific rooms whose status must be investigated to resolve discrepencies. The report notes any variances between front desk and housekeeping room status updates. This is an important dimension of the rooms management module and provides an aspect of control that may otherwise be difficult to achieve.

## Room and Rate Assignment

Rooms management modules may be programmed to assist front desk employees in assigning rooms and rates to guests at the time of check-in. Modules may make automatic assignments or require front desk personnel to input data to initiate room assignments.

Automatic room and rate assignments are made according to parameters specified by hotel management. Rooms may be selected according to predetermined floor zones (similar to the way in which guests are seated in a dining room) or according to an index of room usage and depreciation schedules. The system may track room histories (frequency of use) and rank rooms according to usage data. The system may then use this information to assign rooms on a basis that evenly distributes occupancy loads across the full inventory of rooms.

Interactive room and rate assignments are popular programs in the lodging industry. These programs give front desk personnel direction in decision-making situations while increasing control over actual room assignments. For example, in a property with 800 rooms, a front desk employee can narrow the search routine by clarifying the guest's needs through a series of room and rate category queries. In addition, the front desk employee may use the rooms management module to display an abbreviated list of available rooms selected by type and rate. This abbreviated list enables the front desk employee to quickly suggest a room to a guest at check-in. This ensures a faster check-in process than would a less directed search through the rooms availability database.

To accommodate guest preferences and to ensure smooth check-in procedures, rooms management modules typically feature an override function that front desk employees can use to bypass the room or rate assignments automatically generated by the system. An override function is often a useful feature since guest preferences may be difficult to anticipate. For example, most automatic room-and-rate-assignment programs will assign guests only to rooms whose status is "clean and available for occupancy." However, many times it may be necessary to assign a particular guest to a room whose status is on-change. For example, a guest may arrive for check-in and have to leave immediately to attend an afternoon meeting. An override function permits the front desk employee to complete the necessary check-in procedures while informing the guest that the room won't be available for occupancy until some time later in the day.

## In-House Guest Information Functions

The rooms management module is also designed to provide a limited review of guest data. Guest data can be displayed on terminal screens, handheld devices, or other media, enabling a guest services coordinator, switchboard operator, concierge, or front desk employee to quickly identify the name, room number, and telephone extension of a particular guest. This function of the rooms management module also contributes to the elimination of such traditional information sources as information racks, room racks, and telephone lists. Terminals may also be located at room service order stations, garage outlets, and other high-guest-contact areas to enhance employees' recognition of guests, thereby creating opportunities to personalize the services provided.

Guest data may also be transferred from a rooms management module to a point-of-sale (POS) area to expedite the verification and authorization of charge purchases guests make. When a point-of-sale terminal in a dining area is interfaced with the hotel's property management system, guest data can be reviewed before charges are accepted. This capability allows cashiers to verify that a particular room is occupied and that the correct guest name is on the room folio. Access to this data minimizes the likelihood of charges being accepted for the wrong guest folios, for guests who have vacated their rooms, or for guests who have been denied charge privileges.

## Housekeeping Functions

Important housekeeping functions performed by the rooms management module include:

- Forecasting the number of rooms to be cleaned.
- Scheduling room attendants.
- Assigning workloads.
- Measuring productivity.

A rooms management module forecasts the number of rooms that will require cleaning by processing current house counts and the expected number of arrivals.

After determining the number of rooms that will require cleaning, most modules can generate schedules for individual room attendants and assign a specific number of rooms to each attendant on the basis of property-defined standards.

Upon first entering a room to clean it, a room attendant may use the room's telephone interface to the PMS to enter his or her identification code, room number (not always necessary), and the code identifying the room's current status. The system may automatically log the time of the call. When a room is clean and ready for inspection, the room attendant again uses the room's telephone interface to notify the inspector's station, and the system once again records the time of the call. The log of room attendants' times in and out enables the rooms management module to determine productivity rates. Productivity rates are determined by calculating the average length of time an attendant spends in a room and the number of rooms attended to during a shift. Productivity reports keep management apprised of potential inefficiencies while also tracking the location of housekeeping personnel throughout a shift.

## Generation of Reports

The number and types of reports that can be generated by a rooms management module are functions of the property's needs, software capacity, and the contents of the rooms management database. A wide variety of reports are possible because the rooms management module overlaps several key areas, such as the rooms department, the housekeeping department, and auxiliary services. Most rooms management modules are designed to generate reports that focus primarily on room availability, room status, and room forecasting. These reports are designed to assist management in scheduling staff and distributing workloads.

A **rooms allotment report** summarizes rooms committed (booked or blocked), by future date. One type of **expected arrival/departure report** is shown in Exhibit 4. A **registration progress report** provides the rooms department with a summary of current house information. The report may list present check-ins, the number of occupied rooms, names of guests with reservations who have not yet registered, and the number of rooms available for sale. A registration progress report may also profile room status, rooms revenue, and average room rate. Exhibit 5 shows one type of registration progress report. A **rooms activity forecast** provides information on anticipated arrivals, departures, stayovers, and vacancies. This report assists managers in staffing front desk and housekeeping areas. An **actual departures report** lists the names of guests who have checked out and their room numbers, billing addresses, and folio numbers.

A **housekeeper assignment report** is used to assign floor and room numbers to room attendants and to list room status. This report may also provide space for special messages from the housekeeping department. System-generated **housekeeper productivity reports** provide productivity information for each housekeeper by listing the number of rooms cleaned and the amount of time taken to clean each room.

At the end of each month, quarter, and year, rooms management modules are capable of generating **rooms productivity reports** that rank room types by percentage of occupancy and/or by percentage of total rooms revenue. Rooms

**Exhibit 4   Sample Expected Arrival/Departure Report**

ARRIVALS, STAYOVERS, DEPARTURES FOR KELLOGG CENTER
DA-PAGE 001
05/13   8:40

| DATE | ARRIVE | STAYON | DEPART | GUESTS | SOLD | UNSOLD | REVENUE |
|------|--------|--------|--------|--------|------|--------|---------|
| 05/13 | 27 | 112 | 23 | 143 | 139 | 7 | 6,435.00 |
| 05/14 | 27 | 117 | 22 | 151 | 144 | 2 | 6,593.00 |
| 05/15 | 20 | 126 | 18 | 162 | 146 | 0 | 6,806.00 |
| 05/16 | 72 | 21 | 125 | 143 | 93 | 53 | 4,907.00 |
| 05/17 | 35 | 16 | 77 | 62 | 51 | 95 | 2,460.00 |
| 05/18 | 43 | 41 | 10 | 100 | 84 | 62 | 3,995.00 |
| 05/19 | 27 | 33 | 51 | 72 | 60 | 86 | 2,837.00 |
| 05/20 | 53 | 21 | 39 | 86 | 74 | 72 | 3,874.34 |
| 05/21 | 14 | 26 | 48 | 49 | 40 | 106 | 2,002.00 |

Courtesy of Kellogg Center, Michigan State University, East Lansing, Michigan

management modules may also produce a **rooms history report** depicting the revenue history and use of each room by room type. This report is especially useful to those properties using an automatic room-assignment function based on a rotational usage of rooms.

# Guest Accounting Module

The most critical component of a hotel front office system is the guest accounting module. The creation of electronic folios enables remote point-of-sale terminals to post charges directly to guest and non-guest accounts. The guest accounting module gives management considerable control over financial aspects of the hotel guest cycle. This front office module is primarily responsible for online charge postings, automatic file updating (auditing) and maintenance, and folio display/printing upon demand. In addition, guest accounting modules may provide electronic controls over such areas as folio handling, account balances, cashier reconciliation, food and beverage guest-check control, account auditing, and accounts receivable. Exhibit 6 diagrams the sequence of activities involved in the process of guest accounting. The following sections discuss guest accounting modules in relation to:

*   Types of accounts (also referred to as folios).
*   Posting to accounts.
*   Front office audit.
*   Account settlement.
*   System update and reports.

**Exhibit 5   Sample Registration Progress Report**

```
                    HOUSE COUNT DISPLAY        COMPLEX      1
                          03/28             15:20:02

VACANT/READY ROOMS            144      ROOMS RESERVED              23
OCCUPIED ROOMS                  4      BLOCKS RESERVED             23
VACANT ROOMS ON CHANGE          0      DAY RNTL RESVD               0
     MAINT    0                        ROOMS STAYING OVER           6
     CLEAN    0                        ROOMS DEPARTING              0
     DIRTY    0                        DAY RNTL DEPT                0
ROOMS DUE ON MAINTENANCE        0
DISCREPANT ROOMS                2      CURRENT ROOMS TO SELL      121
                                       CURRENT OCCUPANCY PERCENT    4
    --GUEST STATISTICS--                PROJECTED ROOMS TO SELL    121
GUEST ACCTS TO CHECK-IN         0      PROJECTED ROOMS OCCUPIED    29
GUEST ACCTS TO CHECK-OUT        0      PROJECTED OCCUPANCY PERCENT 19
   GUESTS TO ARRIVE      0
   GUESTS ARRIVED        0                   --ROOMS RESERVED--
   GUESTS TO DEPART      0
   GUESTS DEPARTED       0              C     0        6        0
CURRENT # OF GUESTS             4       1     0        7        0
                                        2     0        8        0
                                        3     0        9        0
WALK-INS  0     EARLY DEPT      0       4     0        B       23
                                        5     0       ALL      23
```

Source: Lodgistix, Wichita, Kansas.

## Types of Accounts

An automated property management system ensures that preregistration folios are prepared for guests arriving with reservations. Preregistration folios are typically produced by the PMS reservations module when a reservation record is created. When guests arrive without reservations, front desk employees capture and enter the necessary data into the guest accounting module at check-in. Data elements needed to create a folio are referred to as header information. Common header elements include:

- Guest name.
- Street address.
- E-mail address.
- Room number.
- Folio number.

If self-check-in terminals are available at the property, guests may enter the necessary data themselves by responding to system-generated cues. Header

**Exhibit 6    Guest Accounting Activities**

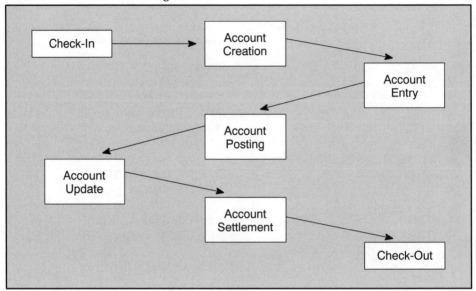

information collected by these terminals can be transmitted to the PMS and used in folio creation.

While not all hotel guest accounting modules offer the same folio formats, common types of automated system folios include:

- Individual folios.
- Master folios.
- Non-guest folios (city accounts).
- Employee folios.
- Control folios.
- Semipermanent folios.
- Permanent folios.

**Individual folios** (also referred to as "room folios" or "guest folios") are assigned to in-house guests for the purpose of charting their financial transactions with the hotel. Exhibit 7 presents a sample guest folio. **Master folios** (also referred to as "group folios") generally apply to more than one guest or room and contain a record of transactions that are not posted to individual folios. Master folios are commonly created to provide the kind of billing service required by most groups and conventions. For example, consider the needs of the International Gymnastics Conference. While attendees at this conference are responsible for their own food and beverage expenses, the sponsoring organization has agreed to pay all associated room charges. As participants dine at various food and beverage outlets in the hotel, their deferred payments are posted to their individual folios. Each night's

**Exhibit 7    Sample Guest Folio**

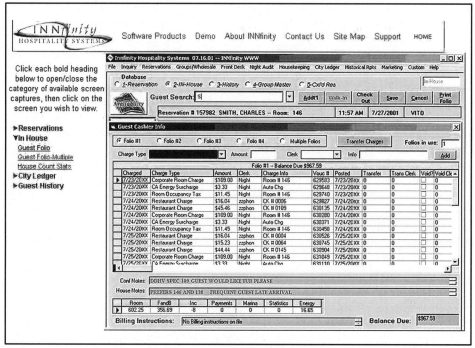

Courtesy of INNfinity Hospitality Systems (www.innhs.com)

room charges, however, are posted to the group's master folio. At check-out, each guest receives a folio documenting only the charges for which he or she is responsible. The conference administrator is responsible for settling the master folio containing the room charges.

**Non-guest folios** are created for individuals who have in-house charge privileges but are not registered guests in the hotel. These individuals may include health club members, corporate clients, special club members, political leaders, or local celebrities. Non-guest account numbers are assigned at the time that the accounts are created and may be printed (or imprinted) on specially prepared account cards. When purchases are charged to non-guest accounts, cashiers may request to see the account card as a verification that a valid posting status exists.

Procedures for posting transactions to non-guest folios are similar to those required for online posting of transactions to individual folios. Instead of inputting a room number, the cashier, front desk employee, or auditor inputs the designated account number. The use of a unique billing number alerts the guest accounting module to the type of account being processed. For example, a six-digit account number may signal a non-guest account, while a four-digit number may signal an in-house guest account. The major difference between accounting for non-guest and in-house guest transactions is in the area of account settlement. Individual folios are settled at check-out; terms for settlement of non-guest accounts are usually defined at the time these accounts are created. The term "settlement" refers to bringing an active folio to a zero balance by posting cash received, or by transferring the folio balance to the city ledger or credit card company account for eventual settlement.

When properties offer charge privileges to employees, transactions may be processed in a manner similar to non-guest accounts. **Employee folios** can be used to record employee purchases, compute discounts, register expense account activity, and separate authorized business charges from personal expenditures.

The efficiency of a guest accounting module in carrying out continuous posting and auditing procedures often depends upon the existence of control folios. **Control folios** may be constructed for each revenue center and used to track all transactions posted to other folios (individual, master, non-guest, or employee). Control folios provide a basis for double-entry accounting and for cross-checking the balances of all electronic folios. For example, as an in-house guest charges a purchase at the hotel's restaurant, the amount is posted (debited) to the appropriate individual folio, and the same amount is simultaneously posted (credited) as a deferred payment to the control folio of the food and beverage outlet. Control folios serve as powerful internal-control documents and greatly simplify ongoing auditing functions.

A **semipermanent folio** is used to track "bill to" accounts receivable. A guest who establishes credit privileges prior to check-in may be allowed to settle his or her folio balance by billing a sponsoring organization or individual. The front desk agent then transfers the guest's folio balance to a semipermanent folio to enable the back office to track the billing and subsequent collection of payment from the approved third party (bill-to agency). Once the outstanding balance is paid, the semipermanent folio is closed.

A **permanent folio** can be used to track guest folio balances that are settled to a credit card company. A permanent folio is established for each entity with which the hotel has a contractual payment program. For example, a hotel could establish a permanent folio for American Express, Discover, Visa, Diner's Club, and MasterCard. When the guest charges a folio balance to an acceptable credit card account, the guest accounting module transfers the balance to the appropriate permanent folio. A permanent folio enables the tracking of receivables beyond the guest's stay. Permanent folios exist as long as the hotel continues to maintain a business relationship with the entity.

## Posting to Accounts

Account entries can be made from terminals at the front desk or from remote POS terminals that interface with the PMS guest accounting module. Account entries can also be made internally—that is, from within the guest accounting module itself. For example, during the system update routine, room charges and taxes may automatically be posted to all active guest folios. Although guest accounting modules vary in the specifics of their operation, most modules rely on specific data entry requirements in order to ensure that amounts are properly posted to the appropriate folios. Data entry requirements may consist of the following sequence:

- Room number (or account number for non-guest transactions).
- Identification code.
- Reference code.
- Charge total.

After a room number (or account number) is entered, a guest accounting module may require that an identification code be entered as well. This is generally done by inputting the first few letters of the guest's last name. An **identification code** enables the guest accounting module to post a charge to the correct folio when multiple accounts exist under the same room number. In these situations, simply inputting a room number does not guarantee that the correct folio is retrieved and held ready to accept a transactional posting. To assist proper posting, a guest identification code is part of the required data entry sequence.

Before a charge can be posted to a folio, the guest accounting module may also require that a **reference code** be entered. This is typically done by inputting the serial number of a departmental source document or a unique departmental identifier. Departmental **source documents** are usually serially numbered for internal-control purposes. This numbering system helps the guest accounting module conduct investigative searches and analyze account entries made by individual employees through POS terminals within the property.

The final data entry requirement is to input the amount of the charge. However, before accepting a charge and posting it to a folio, the guest accounting module initiates a **credit monitoring routine**. This routine compares the current folio balance with a predetermined credit limit (also called a **house limit**) that is determined by management. Although most guest accounting modules allow managers to specify a single house limit, some provide for further options based on guest history information, such as whether the guest is a repeat customer or a known business associate. Other options may include setting a house limit on the basis of the type of reservation or the credit authorization limits established by individual credit card companies.

Regardless of how a guest's credit limit is established, an attempt to post a charge to an account initiates a credit monitoring routine, thus ensuring that the outstanding balances during a guest's stay do not exceed the account's credit limit. When hotel policy dictates that a line of credit is not to be extended to a guest, a folio can be set at a no-post status. The guest accounting module will not permit charges to be posted to a folio with a no-post status.

When in-house guests make charge purchases during their stay at the hotel, they are typically asked to present their room keycard as verification that a valid posting status exists for their individual folios. When guestroom doors are controlled by a locking system with electronic keycards, the system may be interfaced with a PMS guest accounting module. The interface enables the keycard to be used to authorize the posting of charges to the guest's folio from remote POS terminals. If a guest presents a keycard for an unoccupied room (an account with a no-post status) or a guest account that already has been closed (settled), the system will not permit the cashier to post the charge. Entering the guest's identification code (the first few letters of the purchaser's last name) may provide further evidence that the person making the charge is not a currently authorized guest at the hotel.

## Front Office Audit

Front office modules of a property management system enable several audit functions to be performed continuously throughout the guest cycle. Automated systems enable the front office auditor to spend more time auditing transactions and analyzing front office activities and less time performing postings and bookkeeping entries as with prior nonautomated systems. Monitoring account balances and verifying account postings require a simplified procedure that compares guest ledger and non-guest ledger audit data with the front office daily report for balancing. When these documents are out of balance, there is usually an internal computational problem or an unusual data processing error. For example, the interface between the point-of-sale system may have been inoperative for a short time during the day. The point-of-sale system may show the total number and amount of the day's transfers to the front desk system, but the front desk system may have different totals due to the system problem. The front office auditor must reconcile the differences and post the adjusting entries to the guest ledger to bring the two systems in balance.

An automated guest accounting application may retain previous balance information for guest and non-guest accounts, along with appropriate transactional details in an electronic database. Whereas previous balances were necessary in manual and semi-automated systems, automated guest accounting applications can calculate current balances very quickly and do not need a previous balance to act as a starting point for each additional transaction posted. Front office staff are guided through a series of procedures and may need to input various data elements in response to system-generated directives or commands relative to the front office audit routine.

The guest accounting application performs numerous mathematical verifications to ensure postings are correct. For example, a range check will recognize postings of unusual size, such as a $15 charge being posted as $1,500. Since most guest accounting applications are capable of tracking each posting by time, shift, employee, folio number, and revenue center, they are capable of maintaining a detailed audit trail of transactional activity. Exhibit 8 shows a sample page from a daily transaction report listing local telephone calls produced by a guest accounting application.

Guest accounting applications also offer rapid access to information, thereby enabling front office management to more knowledgeably manage operations. Reports detailing revenue data, occupancy statistics, advance deposits, arrivals, no-shows, room status, and other operational information can be generated on request, or as part of the regular system update routine. Exhibit 9 presents a sample revenue center report.

## Account Settlement

The ability to print clear, itemized guest statements (with reference code detail) may significantly reduce guest disputes about folio charges. For example, assume

**Exhibit 8    Sample Local Telephone Transactions Report**

```
LODGISTIX RESORT & CONFERENCE CENTER (90003)                          PAGE    1
                                                                      JUL12
Department Audit Report - JUL12 - All Employees  - LO LOCAL           14:25:03

Folio Room Time Dept  Refer    Chrg/Pymt       Correct     Adjust   Comm Ded   ID

00241  210 0811  LO                .50+                                        PS
00127  105 0813  LO                .50+                                        PS
00152  112 0813  LO                .50+                                        PS
00152  112 0813  LO                .50+                                        PS
00127  105 0814  LO                .50+                                        PS
00171  201 0814  LO                .50+                                        PS
00234  207 0815  LO                .50+                                        PS
00234  207 0816  LO                .50+                                        PS
00243  223 0816  LO                .50+T                                       PS
00243  223 0816  LO                .50+                                        PS
00002  126 0817  LO                .50+                                        PS
00002  126 0817  LO                .50+                                        PS
00226 1000 0817  LO                .50+                                        PS
00226 1000 0818  LO                .50+                                        PS
00237  215 0818  LO                .50+                                        PS
00237  215 0818  LO                .50+                                        PS
00253  240 0819  LO                .50+                                        PS
00234  223 0823  LO                .50+                                        PS
00243  223 0823  LO                .50-T                                       PS
00085  230 0825  LO  2334                                 .50-A               PS
00012  107 0826  LO  34455                                .50-A               PS
00022  109 0827  LO                .50-T                                       PS
00023  109 0827  LO                .50+                                        PS
00001  111 0851  LO                            50.00-C                         JS
00001  111 0851  LO                            50.00+C                         JS
00001  111 0852  LO                .50+                                        JS
00022  109 0852  LO                .50+T                                       JS
00166  106 0852  LO                .50+                                        JS
00253  102 1814  LO                6.00+                                       MD

Total LOCAL                       16.00+          .00       1.00-      .00

End of report
```

that at check-out time Ms. Nessy has found what she believes to be a discrepancy in regard to a long-distance telephone charge appearing on her folio. The hotel cashier uses the reference code number on the folio to locate the proper telephone call record. The cashier then verifies the source (room number) from which the call was placed and the telephone number that was called. This procedure enables the hotel to quickly, objectively, and efficiently resolve disputes regarding amounts posted to individual folios.

System update routines can be programmed to generate preprinted folios (usually by 7:00 A.M.) for guests expected to check out that day. Preprinting folios significantly speeds up the check-out process and minimizes guest discrepancies. When additional charges are posted to folios that have already been preprinted, the preprinted folios are simply discarded and updated folios, with the correct account balances, are printed at the time of check-out.

Online, instantaneous posting of all charges leads to a major victory in the hotel's battle against late charges and charges made under false pretenses. **Late charges** are charged purchases made by guests that are posted to folios after guests have settled their accounts. Electronic folios are closed at the time of settlement.

**Exhibit 9    Sample Revenue Report**

| Lodgistix Resort & Conference Center (90003) | | | |
|---|---|---|---|
| Daily Report—July 12—Charges | | | |
| **Dept** | **Net** | **Gross** | **Adjust** |
| Room | 2301.00+ | 2301.00+ | .00 |
| City Tax | 42.68+ | 42.68+ | .00 |
| Occ Tax | 85.50+ | 85.50+ | .00 |
| Tax | 116.60+ | 116.60+ | .00 |
| Gift Shop | .00 | .00 | .00 |
| Health Club | .00 | .00 | .00 |
| Long Distance | 38.36+ | 38.36+ | .00 |
| Local | 15.00+ | 16.00+ | 1.00- |
| Parking | 5.00+ | 5.00+ | .00 |
| Paidout | .00 | .00 | .00 |
| Deli Food | 10.00+ | 10.00+ | .00 |
| Lounge Food | .00 | .00 | .00 |
| Pool Food | .00 | .00 | .00 |
| Restuarant Food | 301.31+ | 301.31+ | .00 |
| Deli Beverage | .00 | .00 | .00 |
| Lounge Beverage | 21.62+ | 21.62+ | .00 |
| Pool Beverage | .00 | .00 | .00 |
| Restaurant Beverage | .00 | .00 | .00 |
| Grand Total | 2937.07+ | 2938.07+ | 1.00- |

Courtesy of Sulcus, Phoenix, Arizona

Accounts that are accidentally closed can easily be reopened. Check-out, however, triggers a communication to housekeeping and internally sets the account to a no-post status. Because the guest accounting module can be interfaced with other front office modules, better communications among staff members are possible and more comprehensive reports are available for use by management.

## System Update and Reports

A system update in a guest accounting application accomplishes many of the functions in the audit routine. System updates are performed daily to enable system file reorganization, system maintenance, and report production, and to provide an end-of-day closure.

Since guest accounting applications systems continuously audit transactional postings as they occur, there may be little need for the auditor to perform account postings. The auditor should routinely review interface procedures to ensure the proper handling of automatically posted transactions from revenue outlets. In the case of guaranteed reservation no-shows, for example, postings may be programmed to flow automatically to a billing file. If a transaction needs to be independently posted, the guest's electronic folio can be displayed on a terminal screen for posting. Once complete, the folio can be placed back into electronic storage and printed on demand.

In some applications, the balancing of front office and department accounts is continuously monitored through an online accounting system. As a charge purchase is entered at a remote point-of-sale terminal, for example, the charge may be instantaneously posted to an electronic guest folio and an electronic departmental control folio. An electronic departmental control folio is an online internal accounting file that supports account postings originating from an operating department. To balance departments, the system tests all non-control folio entries against individual control folio transactions. An imbalance is just as likely to identify a problem in automatic posting techniques as a shortcoming in front office accounting procedures. Detailed departmental reports can be generated and checked against account postings to prove account entries at any time during the day.

Guest accounting modules are capable of producing a myriad of formatted statements and reports summarizing financial transactions that occur between guests and the hotel, activities within revenue centers, and audit findings. The analytical capacity of this module has simplified traditional hotel auditing procedures while providing increased control over guest accounting procedures. The ability to print guest and non-guest folios at any time during the guest cycle provides management with important accounting information on a timely basis. Room statistics and revenue reports, detailing occupancy loads and revenue generated by room night, give managers such essential information as occupancy percentages, average rate (per-room and per-guest), and departmental revenue summaries.

**Ledger summary reports** present guest, non-guest, and credit card activity by beginning balance, cumulative charges, and credits. **Revenue center reports** show cash, charge, and paid-out totals by department and serve as a macro-analysis of departmental transactions. **Guest check control reports** compare guest checks used in revenue outlets, such as in food and beverage outlets, with source documents to identify discrepancies. Transfers to non-guest (city) ledgers from guest accounts are automatically logged onto a **transfer report,** along with the printing of an initial dunning letter. A dunning letter is a request for payment of an outstanding balance (account receivable) owed by a guest or non-guest to the hotel.

Some system vendors provide an optional output format that enables the transfer of guest accounting data onto microfilm or microfiche. This increases the system's capacity to store information on minimal active file space.

# Key Terms

*Rooms Management Module*

**actual departures report**—Lists the names of guests who have checked out and their room numbers, billing addresses, and folio numbers.

**expected arrival/departure report**—A daily report showing the number and names of guests expected to arrive with reservations, as well as the number and names of guests expected to depart.

**housekeeper assignment report**—Used to assign floor and room numbers to room attendants and to list room status. This report may also provide space for special messages from the housekeeping department.

**housekeeper productivity report**—Provides a relative-productivity index for each housekeeper by listing the number of rooms cleaned and the amount of time taken to clean each room.

**registration progress report**—Provides the rooms department with a summary of current house information; may list present check-ins, number of occupied rooms, names of guests who have reservations but are not yet registered, and the number of rooms available for sale; may also profile room status, rooms revenue, and average room rate.

**room status**—Information about current availability is absolutely essential in order for front desk employees to properly assign rooms to guests at the time of check-in. Housekeeping's description of the current status of a room is crucial to the immediate, short-run selling position of that room. Common housekeeping descriptions of a room's status include on-change, out-of-order, and clean and ready for inspection.

**room status discrepancy**—A situation in which the housekeeping department's description of a room's status differs from the room status information that guides front desk employees in assigning rooms to guests. Discrepancies can seriously affect a property's ability to satisfy guests and maximize rooms revenue.

**rooms activity forecast**—Provides information on anticipated arrivals, departures, stayovers, and vacancies. This report assists managers in staffing front desk and housekeeping areas.

**rooms allotment report**—Summarizes rooms committed (booked or blocked), by future date.

**rooms discrepancy report**—Signals to management the specific rooms whose status must be investigated to avoid sleepers. The report notes any variances between front desk and housekeeping room status updates.

**rooms history report**—Depicts the revenue history and use of each room by room type. This report is especially useful to those properties employing an automatic room assignment function.

**rooms productivity report**—Ranks room types by percentage of occupancy and/or by percentage of total rooms revenue.

**rooms status report**—Indicates the current status of rooms according to housekeeping designations, such as on-change, out-of-order, and clean and ready for inspection.

**sleeper**—A vacant room that is believed to be occupied because the room rack slip or registration card was not removed from the rack when the guest departed.

### Guest Accounting Module

**control folio**—Constructed for each revenue center and used to track all transactions posted to other folios (individual, master, non-guest, or employee). Control folios provide a basis for double entry accounting and for cross-checking the balances of all electronic folios.

**credit monitoring routine**—Compares a guest's current folio balance with a credit limit (also called a house limit) that is predetermined by management officials.

**employee folio**—Used to track employee purchases, compute discounts, monitor expense account activity, and separate authorized business charges from personal expenditures.

**guest check control report**—Compares guest checks used in revenue outlets, such as in food and beverage outlets, with source documents to identify discrepancies.

**house limit**—A credit limit predetermined by management officials.

**identification code**—Generally, the first few letters of a guest's last name. An identification code enables the guest accounting module to process a charge to the correct folio when two separate accounts exist under the same room number.

**individual folio**—Assigned to an in-house guest for the purpose of charting the guest's financial transactions with the hotel.

**late charges**—Charged purchases made by guests that are posted to folios after guests have settled their accounts.

**ledger summary report**—Presents guest, non-guest, and credit card activity by beginning balance, cumulative charges, and credits.

**master folio**—Generally applies to more than one guest or room and contains a record of transactions that are not posted to individual folios. Master folios are commonly created to provide the kind of billing service required by most groups and conventions.

**non-guest folio**—Created for an individual who has in-house charge privileges but is not registered as a guest in the hotel. Individuals with non-guest folios may include health club members, corporate clients, special club members, political leaders, or local celebrities.

**permanent folio**—Used to track guest folio balances that are settled to a credit card company.

**reference code**—Generally, the serial number of a departmental source document.

**revenue center report**—Shows cash, charge, and paid-out totals by department and serves as a macro-analysis of departmental transactions.

**room variance report**—A report listing any discrepancies between front desk and housekeeping room statuses.

**semipermanent folio**—Used to track "bill to" accounts receivable.

**source document**—A printed voucher, usually serially numbered for internal-control purposes, from a revenue-producing department showing an amount that is charged to a folio.

**transfer report**—Shows transfers to non-guest (city) ledgers from guest accounts.

## Review Questions

1.  What primary functions does a rooms management module perform?

2.  How does a rooms management module help reduce room status discrepancies?

3.  How does a rooms management module automatically perform room and rate assignments? Explain how an override option may be useful to management.

4.  How can a rooms management module be used to schedule housekeeping staff and measure the productivity of room attendants?

5.  What are some of the reports that a rooms management module can generate?

6.  What are the primary functions a guest accounting module performs?

7.  What types of folios might a guest accounting module use? Give brief descriptions of each.

8.  Why are identification codes and reference codes important to online posting procedures?

9.  What are some of the advantages of the system update routine performed by a guest accounting module?

10. How are account settlement procedures influenced by a guest accounting application?

## Internet Sites

For more information, visit the following Internet sites. Remember that Internet addresses can change without notice. If the site is no longer there, you can use a search engine to look for additional sites.

### Hotel Property Management Systems

CMS Hospitality
http://www.cmshosp.com.au/

Micros Systems Inc.
http://www.micros.com

INNfinity Hospitality Systems
www.innhs.com

HOST Group
http://www.hostgroup.com

Hotel Information Systems
http://www.maisystems.com/

Remco Software Inc.
http://www.remcosoftware.com/

Springer-Miller Systems
www.springermiller.com

# Chapter 5 Outline

System Interface Issues
Point-of-Sale Systems
Call Accounting Systems
    HOBIC System Interface
    Features of Call Accounting Systems
    CAS/PMS Interfacing
Electronic Locking Systems
    Hard-Wired Locks
    Micro-Fitted Locks
    ELS Features
    ELS Reports
Energy Management Systems
Auxiliary Guest Services
Guest-Operated Devices
    Self-Check-In/Self-Check-Out
        Systems
    In-Room Entertainment Systems
    In-Room Vending Systems
    Guest Information Services

# Competencies

1. Describe the features and benefits of interfacing a point-of-sale system with a hotel property management system. (pp. 103–107)

2. Identify issues that managers should assess when interfacing a point-of-sale system with a hotel property management system. (pp. 103–107)

3. Describe the features and functions of a telephone call accounting system. (pp. 107–113)

4. Distinguish between hard-wired and micro-fitted electronic locking systems. (pp. 113–118)

5. Identify the features and functions of an energy management system. (pp. 118–119)

6. Identify automated services that hotels provide for guests and describe guest-operated devices that may interface with a hotel property management system. (pp. 119–124)

# Property Management System Interfaces

A FULLY INTEGRATED property management system (PMS) provides management with an effective means with which to monitor and control many front office and back office activities. Other areas of a lodging operation may also benefit from automation. Rather than function as part of a property management system design, some automated systems may perform more effectively as independent, stand-alone devices that can be interfaced with the property management system. Interfacing permits the property management system to access data and information processed by stand-alone systems, without affecting the primary structure of the property management system.

This chapter presents a detailed discussion of property management system interfaces. Important interfaces for hotel operations include:

- Point-of-sale systems

- Call accounting systems

- Electronic locking systems

- Energy management systems

- Auxiliary guest services

- Guest-operated devices

Some hotels have gone beyond installing basic property management systems by offering a variety of automated guest-operated devices. These devices are described in the final sections of this chapter. As the world's traveling public becomes more familiar with and skilled in using technology, there will be additional growth in this area of lodging services.

## System Interface Issues

While it may seem logical to interconnect all hospitality technology applications at a property, a number of questions arise:

- Which applications should be interfaced?

- How will the operation benefit from the interface?

- Which of the system and application vendors should perform the interface?

- How will management be sure that the interface is working properly?
- Will the interface maintain the integrity of the data?
- Could vendor support be compromised by the interface?

Connecting separate applications to a property management system is not without risk. If unsuccessful, data may be lost, application capabilities may be compromised, functionality may be slowed or lost, and overall confidence in the system may be shaken. Connecting two hardware components is not as troubling as software and networking issues. Running a serial cable (or establishing a wireless connection) is relatively easy; getting the devices to share information is more complex. The following five C's of interfacing may help managers minimize risks of interfacing hospitality technology:

- Confidence—test each system separately.
- Contracts—analyze existing provisions.
- Communications—determine the "what, when, and how" of information exchange.
- Comparisons—contact users who succeeded with the same interface.
- Contingencies—develop procedures for downtime.

**Confidence.** Before interconnecting two stand-alone applications (for example, a point-of-sale system and a property management system) be sure to test each system separately. There should be a high level of confidence in each system's operational capabilities before attempting to link them together. If there should be an interface problem and the components were not tested prior to connectivity, trouble shooting the problem is always more difficult.

**Contracts.** Before attempting to connect separate systems, management should commission a legal review of all involved product vendor contracts. There may be contractual interface restrictions requiring direct involvement of the original product vendor when attempting an interface. By analyzing existing contract provisions, management will be better informed as to the correct interface course of action.

**Communications.** When contemplating an interface, it is important to determine what information is to be exchanged, how frequently, and in what format. In addition, there is the question of whether a copy of transmitted data should remain at the original source system or whether it should be permanently moved to the receiving system. Knowing what, when, and how interfaced data streaming is to occur is important to effective interface design. For example, in the case of POS interfacing, how much order entry detail should be transmitted to the property management system? The details of order entry are really of importance to the food and beverage department, not the accounts receivable module of a back office accounting system. Hence, perhaps only total revenue amounts from the food and beverage outlet should be exchanged. When should the POS data be sent to the PMS? Well, since the property is going to bill its guests during service, there is probably no need to transmit POS data as it occurs (real time). Instead it will make more sense to wait until a guest check is closed, or, if feasible, consider batching the POS data until at the end of the meal period, or some later time. What about data format? A workable data transmission format will be dictated by the requirements of the receiving system in the interface.

**Comparisons.** One of the biggest mistakes hospitality managers can make is not contacting current users to determine the best means by which to accomplish an interface. Product vendors normally have a detailed list of installed users and tend to be aware of successful (and failed) interfaces to and from their product line. By contacting properties of a similar size and scope, managers can gain invaluable insight into interface solutions. For example, when considering interfacing a point-of-sale system with a property management system, the most efficient approach would be to inquire with the hospitality system vendor as to which of its installed users currently have successful POS interfaces.

**Contingencies.** Managers must be sure that staff members are trained to operate the enterprise efficiently should the interface fail during the data processing cycle. For example, when interfacing a POS system to a PMS, there needs to be a set of provisions governing backup procedures so that proper processing can be accomplished even if the interface is not operational. In addition, the operation should consider maintaining an inventory of spare parts, should any be required by the interface.

The decision to interface stand-alone hospitality system applications requires planning. While the technical aspects of the interface warrant careful management review and active participation, there are additional considerations. Remember the three "nevers" of interfacing:

1. Never be the first user of an interface.

2. Never be the largest user of an interface.

3. Never be the last user of an interface.

## Point-of-Sale Systems

A point-of-sale (POS) system is made up of a number of POS terminals that interface with a remote central processing unit. A **point-of-sale terminal** is normally configured as an independent, stand-alone computer system. This device contains all the necessary components of an automated system: an input/output device, a central processing unit, and storage (memory) capacity. Some POS terminals may not have central processing units. In these cases, in order for POS transactions to be processed, the terminals must be connected to a centralized, remote CPU.

Newer POS system designs link terminals within a local area network. Each terminal is networked to form an integrated POS system that functions without a large, remote CPU. This system architecture is referred to as a **PC-based register system**.

When the main processor of a POS system interfaces with a property management system, data can be directly transferred from the POS system to various front office and back office PMS modules for further processing. This interface accomplishes the basic objectives of electronic data processing. The amount of time required to post transactions to guest folios is significantly reduced, and the number of times various pieces of data must be handled is minimized. Relaying data collected by POS terminals to the property management system also significantly reduces the number of posting errors and minimizes the possibility of late charges.

The number and location of POS terminals or registers throughout a property is a function of a variety of factors, such as:

- Size and type of operation
- Physical design limitations
- Communication requirements
- Security considerations

For example, a large resort hotel may place one or more terminals at every revenue collection area, including:

- Restaurants
- Bar and lounge areas
- Room service stations
- Concession stands
- Gift shops
- Pool and spa areas
- Pro shops

Although a POS/PMS interface offers lodging properties significant advantages, there are also important concerns to address. Interface problems that may arise include these:

- Data transferred from the POS system may not meet the specific needs or data format of the property management system.
- POS system data may be lost, or misapplied, during the property management system update routine.
- General limitations and downtime situations of interface technology may interfere with effective system operations.

The amount and type of data communicated from a POS system to a property management system vary in relation to the particular type of POS system and property management system design. Problems may arise when the type of data needed by front office or back office property management system modules cannot be easily collected, extracted, or transferred from the POS system. For example, a POS system may not be able to:

- Divide revenues from the total amount of a guest check into separate food and beverage amounts.

- Transfer data relating to special hotel meal plans and promotions.

- Track taxes and tips.

Management officials may also have to address questions such as these:

- Will individual transactions or consolidated transactions be transmitted?

- Will data be transmitted as it is collected or batched and sent at a later time?

- How much data will be stored in property management system files and how much will be retained by the POS system?

- How and when will settlement affect stored transaction data?

- What audit procedures will be followed to ensure proper posting and monitoring of transactions?

- Will data be carried forward indefinitely?

- What contingency plans will be executed should an interface failure occur?

A hotel's property management system undergoes a system update routine on a daily (or more frequent) basis. The update generally occurs sometime during the slower evening hours. While the system is being updated, the POS interface may be inoperable. Careful planning must ensure that the interruption of data flow along the interface channel does not result in lost transactions or bottlenecks at either the POS or PMS end. For this reason, many properties schedule the property management system update when food and beverage outlets and other revenue-producing centers are closed, or during their slack business hours. In the case of a system or interface failure, non-automated procedures may have to be implemented at revenue outlets for the duration of the failure.

Before interfacing a POS system to a PMS, management may have to resolve problems related to interface technology. For example, a POS system may be dependent upon a unique set of application software unrelated to the needs of the hotel's property management system. Should this be the case, the primary application software of the POS system may need to be enhanced before the system is interfaced or synchronized with the property management system.

## Call Accounting Systems

Since 1981, it has been legal for lodging properties to resell telephone service to guests. This resale capability has enabled the hotel's telephone department, traditionally a loss leader, to become a potential profit center. A call accounting system (CAS) enhances management's control of expenses relating to local and long-distance telephone services.

While a CAS may operate as a stand-alone system, it is typically interfaced with a hotel's property management system. Generally, a CAS is able to handle direct-distance dialing, distribute calls through a least-cost routing network, and price outgoing calls. When a CAS is interfaced to a PMS front office guest accounting module, telephone charges can be posted immediately to the proper folio.

Call accounting systems conserve valuable space and often reduce maintenance and labor costs associated with traditional telephone systems. CAS hardware takes up much less space and requires less maintenance than the bulky switchboard equipment it often replaces. Labor costs decrease since a telephone operator is not involved in CAS call placement and distribution functions. Similarly, the automatic pricing of calls eliminates the need for manually calculating and posting telephone charges.

Calls are channeled through the CAS. As a backup system, calls may be routed to the hotel's HOBIC interface. **HOBIC** is an acronym for Hotel Billing Information Center. A CAS typically includes such features as:

- Automatic identification of outward dialing (AIOD)

- Automatic route selection (ARS)

- Least-cost routing (LCR)

- Call rating program (CRP)

- HOBIC system interface

Exhibit 1 diagrams a CAS designed to monitor administrative (non-guest) and guest telephone traffic. The hotel's PBX system serves as a primary control device for the entire call accounting system. The PBX usually contains a station message detail record (SMDR) that takes responsibility for charting and monitoring telephone traffic.

The following sections examine CAS features. The HOBIC interface is addressed first because some properties continue to back up telephone traffic management through this system.

## HOBIC System Interface

Before 1981, lodging properties used the HOBIC system to provide telephone service to guests. This system remains in use today, primarily as a backup system for installed call accounting systems.

The HOBIC system is a service supplied by a telephone company that records time and charges on each long-distance call made from a guestroom phone. Guest calls are placed on special telephone lines called HOBIC lines. When a guest places a call over these lines, the telephone company operator intervenes and asks the guest for his or her room number. Upon receiving the room number, the operator allows the call to go through. After completion of the call, the hotel receives the "time and charges" either from an operator calling the property or through a telephone company transmission received at a front desk fax machine.

Before January 1983, hotels received a commission from the telephone company for collecting charges from guests. The commission was a 15 percent discount on the property's telephone bill. However, due to the cost of installing and operating telephone system equipment and problems associated with the HOBIC system, hotel telephone departments were barely able to break even financially. Originally, HOBIC operators had no way of verifying the room number given by a guest, and time delays (between when a guest completed a call and when the property

**Exhibit 1   Overview of a Call Accounting System**

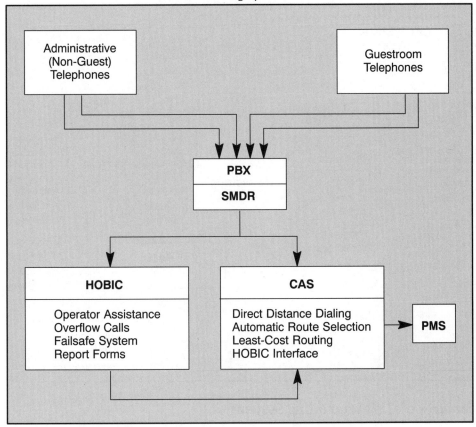

received the time and charges related to the call) often resulted in uncollectible late charges.

Despite its drawbacks, the HOBIC system is often interfaced with a CAS to perform the following functions:

- Supervise all operator-assisted calls.

- Process overflow telephone service from the CAS.

- Serve as a fail-safe telephone service.

For example, if a direct-dial call is placed and all available CAS lines are busy, the HOBIC lines may automatically become engaged to complete the call. When the HOBIC system is used to process overflow calls, the calls are communicated to the CAS for final pricing, recording, and reporting. Also, if the CAS becomes inoperable, the HOBIC system serves as a fail-safe mechanism by processing calls in a manner similar to properties without call accounting systems. This ensures continuous telephone service for guests.

**Exhibit 2    Simplified Flowchart of a CAS Operation**

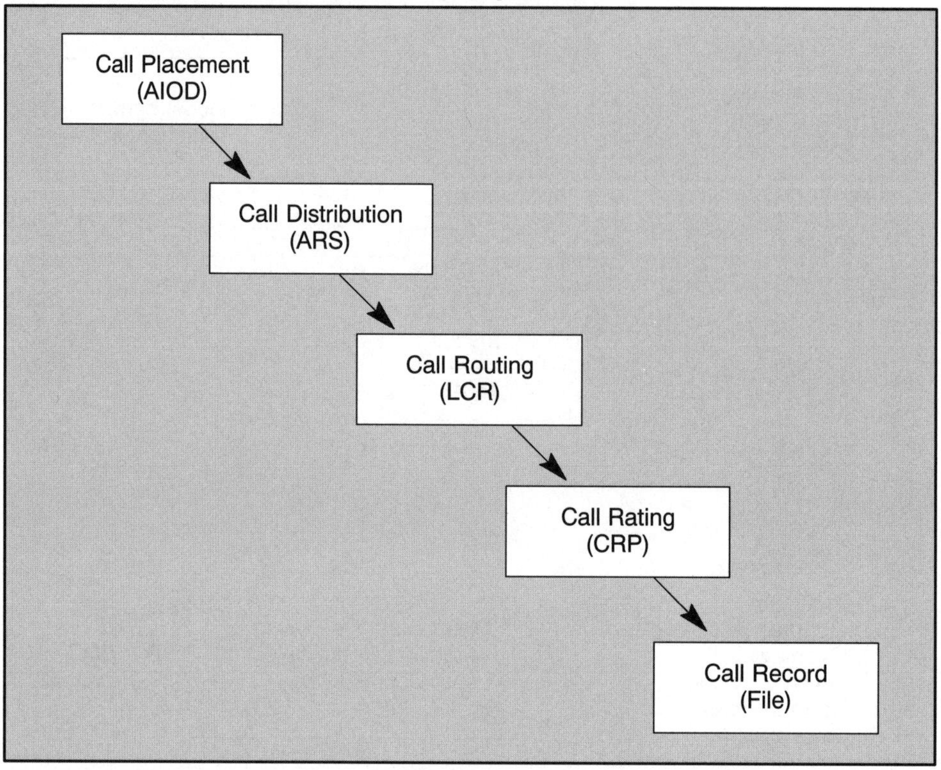

## Features of Call Accounting Systems

Exhibit 2 presents a simplified flowchart of the operation of a call accounting system. Functions that may be performed by a CAS include:

- Call placement
- Call distribution
- Call routing
- Call rating
- Call record

Call accounting systems have significantly simplified the sequence involved in call placement. Guests can direct-distance dial, eliminating operator intervention. With the HOBIC system, an operator intercepts outgoing calls to identify the guest's room number. This is not the case with a CAS. The **automatic identification of outward dialing** (AIOD) feature of a CAS immediately identifies the extension from which a call is placed.

As an outgoing call is placed, the CAS's call distribution equipment is engaged. How and where a specific call is routed are essential in determining its cost. With a **passive call accounting system**, there are no options available to the call distribution network. Selection of a route is based on convenience rather than on minimizing expense. An **active call accounting system**, on the other hand, employs an automatic route selection (ARS) switch with a least-cost routing (LCR) device. The **automatic route selection** (ARS) feature has become an essential CAS component and is usually capable of connecting with a variety of common carriers. A **common carrier** is any recognized entity that transmits messages or other communication for general use at accepted rates. The **least-cost routing** (LCR) capability directs calls over the least-cost available line, regardless of carrier. When the least-cost line is busy, the LCR automatically prompts the CAS to seek the next least expensive line. This search procedure is performed at high speed and with remarkable precision.

The manner by which a call is priced or rated will vary in relation to vendors, equipment packages, and electronic switches. A **station message detail record** (SMDR) is used to chart and monitor telephone traffic. The data collected by the SMDR is used to rate calls. Some systems base calls on a ringback mechanism; others incorporate a timeout feature. With a **ringback mechanism** or auto-answer detection software, the guest is charged only for calls that are answered. With a **timeout feature**, callers begin paying for calls after a predetermined amount of placement time. After a call is rated, it is entered into a call record file.

A call record is used to monitor details regarding calls processed by the CAS. This file may include:

- Date
- Guestroom extension number
- Telephone number dialed
- Time call was placed
- Duration of call
- Cost of call (per carrier charges)
- Tax and markup charges
- Amounts posted to guest folio

Most call rating systems calculate the price and tax of a call and automatically post the necessary data to appropriate call records. A **call record** is electronic or hard copy documentation containing essential transactional support data for individually placed and rated telephone calls. Call records are referenced on a guest folio and provide a means for resolving guest discrepancies relating to telephone charges.

Call records are automatically logged in a traffic transaction file. The **traffic transaction file** maintains data necessary for generating reports for management. Typically, records are organized by time of call placement (chronological file) or room extension number (sorted file). The extent of report detail is a function of management needs.

Telephone activity reports can be generated by date and/or time covering the entire company, a specific division, an individual property, a particular revenue

**Exhibit 3    Sample Report Listing Recent Calls**

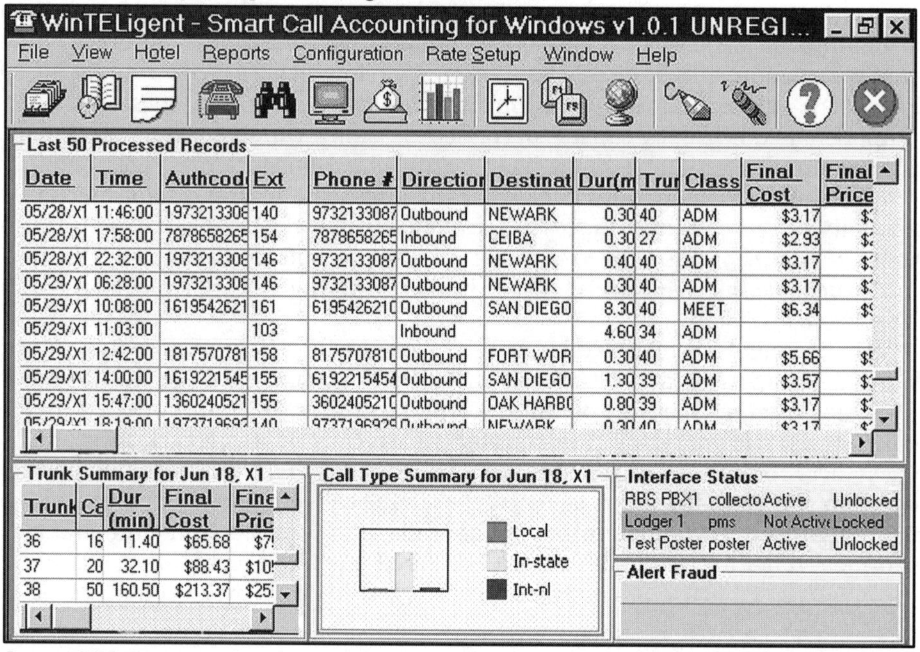

Source: RBS Computer Corporation. For more information, browse the company's Web site at http://www.rbscc.com

center, or even individual extensions or specific call destinations. Exhibit 3 is a sample report showing details for the most recently processed calls.

Call details can be seen in order of extension, date and/or time, phone number called, etc. Exhibit 4 shows some of the detail that can be accessed regarding a specific call placed through a CAS. In addition, statistical reports and "real time" alerts (by pager or e-mail) can inform managers to potential abuses with the phone system by indicating most expensive calls, longest calls, most frequently called numbers, etc.

## CAS/PMS Interfacing

A CAS/PMS interface offers lodging properties a number of significant advantages, such as:

- Enhanced guest services and guest satisfaction
- Improved communications networking
- Improved call pricing methods
- Minimized telephone traffic expenses
- Automatic charge posting to guest folios
- Automatic call detail records
- Detailed daily reports of telephone transactions

**Exhibit 4   Sample Call Detail**

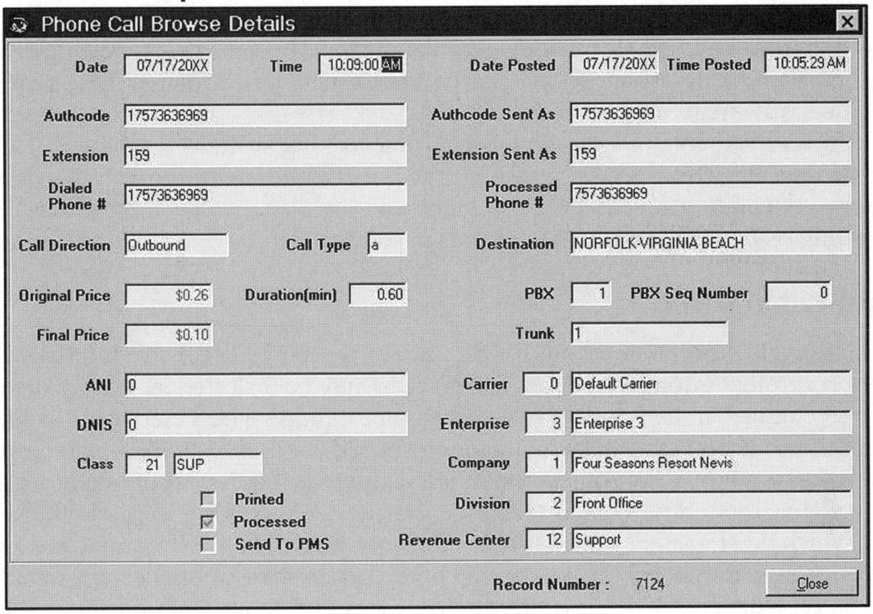

Source: RBS Computer Corporation. For more information, browse the company's Web site at http://www.rbscc.com

Since the CAS reduces operator intervention, the hotel telephone department can become more efficient with less labor. Eliminating telephone meter readings and reducing guest telephone charge discrepancies can also contribute to faster check-out times and more effective front desk operations.

Contingency backup procedures are a major concern when a call accounting system is interfaced with a property management system, even though the CAS is backed up by the HOBIC call system. Various problems can still arise. Energy backup concerns for the CAS usually mandate access to an uninterruptible power supply.

Another important CAS concern is the storage and distribution capacity of the system. Before purchasing and installing a CAS, management must be sure that telephone traffic throughout the hotel has been properly evaluated so that the proposed CAS will have adequate storage and distribution capacity for processing and storing telephone traffic data. Management may also wish to ensure that the proposed system is able to distinguish administrative (non-guest) calls from guest calls. Other important concerns focus on system maintenance, service, and vendor support. In many cases, management officials may need to initiate new telephone maintenance programs.

# Electronic Locking Systems

An electronic locking system (ELS) replaces traditional brass keys and mechanical locks with sophisticated guestroom access devices. Installing electronic locks on existing guestroom doors may be a minor job or it could involve a major recon-struction effort. Some systems require only the drilling of a small hole for wires to pass from the outside to the inside portion of the lock. In some cases, existing dead-bolt and latch hardware are retained as part of the new lock. Other systems require all-new hardware or even new doors.

Currently, there are a variety of electronic locking systems available to lodg-ing properties. These systems are either hard-wired or micro-fitted locking systems, depending on the property's age and/or management preference. The following sections describe these systems in some detail.

## Hard-Wired Locks

Hard-wired locks operate through a centralized master code console interfaced to every controlled guestroom door. The console may be a slotted switching device centrally located at the front desk. With this type of **hard-wired electronic locking system**, a front desk employee follows a prescribed check-in procedure and creates a new keycard. The console immediately transmits the keycard's code to the remote guestroom door lock. By the time the guest leaves the front desk, the key-card which he or she has been issued is the only workable guestroom access key. Keycards issued to previous guests who occupied the same room become invalid.

Since, with a hard-wired configuration, every controlled door must be cabled to the master console, hard-wired systems present both a challenge (expensive design) and an opportunity (improved security). Before such a system is installed, management should identify emergency procedures and energy backup sources. Hard-wired locking systems use AC (house current) as their primary energy source, with DC (battery pack) serving as emergency backup. Management must also determine when keycards are to be created (initially encoded) and how they are to be created, re-issued, recycled, and maintained.

## Micro-Fitted Locks

Micro-fitted locks operate as individually configured stand-alone units, thus avoiding the complex dedicated circuitry required by hard-wired locking systems. Each door has its own microprocessor that contains a unique, predetermined sequence of codes. A terminal at the front desk contains a database of code sequences for each door and is connected to a key encoding device. With a **micro-fitted electronic locking system**, the front desk employee completes guest check-in by encoding a keycard with the next code in the predetermined sequence of codes for an assigned room.

With hard-wired systems, codes are directly communicated from the master code console to the controlled doors. Micro-fitted systems do not possess this kind of communications capability. The front desk terminal and the microprocessors of controlled doors are separate units. What connects them is the predetermined sequence of codes. This means not only that the front desk terminal must be pro-grammed with the same predetermined sequence of codes that is contained within each door's microprocessor, but also that the terminal and each microprocessor must agree on which code in the sequence is currently valid. If the units are out of synchronization, the locking mechanism will need to be reset.

For example, assume that at check-in a family requests two rooms with a connecting door. The parents plan to stay in one of the rooms while their children stay in the other. Upon reaching the rooms, the family enters the first room and finds the connecting door to the other room already open. The next morning, the family checks out of both rooms, having never used the second room's keycard. The locking mechanism in the second room's door will not advance to the next code in the predetermined sequence because the keycard was never used. The terminal at the front desk, however, will automatically advance to the next code in the sequence when another guest checks into that room because it assumes that the last issued keycard has been used. Should this happen, the new guest (receiving the next keycard) will find that the keycard he or she has been issued fails to activate the lock. A front desk employee must then use a specially designed keycard to reprogram the room door's microprocessor so that the current code synchronizes with the front desk control console.

An important energy feature of micro-fitted electronic locking systems is that the microchips in each door are powered by battery packs and therefore do not require wiring to an external energy source. Some systems employ penlight size batteries, some D-size cells, while others use special battery units.

## ELS Features

Electronic locking systems may produce various levels of master keys. Most systems provide several distinct levels of security. One level may be established for housekeeping personnel, another for hotel security officers, and yet another for property management officials.

Some ELS designs provide a "do not disturb" option for guests. This option typically employs an indicator that displays a notice when the guest wants privacy. The notice is often given by a flashing red light located within the locking mechanism. This indicator may be triggered when a room attendant inserts a keycard into the locking mechanism. No longer must the housekeeping staff knock on the door or test the door's chain to realize that the guest is still in the room!

A safety feature built into some electronic locking systems prevents the door from opening while the keycard remains in the lock. This prevents a guest from entering a guestroom while forgetting to take the keycard from the lock. One system permits entry without keycard removal; however, it tracks the length of time the keycard is in the door. If the keycard remains in the locking mechanism beyond a predetermined time interval, the system destroys the keycard by scrambling its code. The reason for scrambling a keycard's code relates to guestroom security. A keycard that remains in a lock may be taken by someone other than the room's occupant. To avoid problems, hotel staff must inform guests that failure to promptly remove the keycard will cause it to become invalid.

Electronic locking systems have become an essential hotel feature. Exhibit 5 presents features of a sophisticated ELS system employing a touch-screen terminal. Exhibit 6 presents a more basic, stand-alone ELS system and explains how

**Exhibit 5   Components of an Interfacing Electronic Locking System**

# VISION SYSTEM

A wide range of hardware options exist for installing VISION software and integrating it with your hotel's PMS and IT system. In order to keep the cost of computer hardware and maintenance to a minimum, VingCard's VISION software and hardware utilizes global standards, such as Windows 95/98/2000/NT and LAN networking.

## Server and workstation

VISION offers a range of possibilities to choose from for your server and workstation needs. You may choose to integrate VISION onto your existing PMS workstations and server, or select a workstation offered by VingCard.

The VISION touchscreen workstation is specifically designed for busy check-in areas. The workstation offers the optimum in check-in efficiency, with an industry-leading combination of powerful hardware, outstanding ergonomics, and modern, aesthetic design.

If budget is a concern, you may choose to use off-the-shelf Pentium PCs to run your VISION system. You'll get all the benefits of VISION software (without the touchscreen ergonomics) at the lowest possible cost.

## LockLink™

The VISION system utilizes a dedicated portable Windows Pocket PC lock interrogator and programming unit.

Simply plug the LockLink™ into any lock in the hotel to program it, view and download the lock events from the entry log audit trail, or to see who has entered the door at what time.

## Software

VISION's hotel security software easily integrates with most property management and IT systems through shared hardware and magnetic stripe cards. The software is implemented in object-oriented coding, optimized for Windows 98/2000/NT.

## Card encoders

Automatic motor driven units allow rapid card encoding and verification of both magnetic- and smart card.

Any numbers of encoders can be connected in the LAN network directly, using TCP/IP or the PC serial port.

An optional multi-track encoder writes additional guest and billing data on tracks 1 and 2 for use by POS terminals.

## Electronic lock

All VingCard locks are designed and built specifically for hotel industry use, with rugged, solid steel construction, proven by over 20 years of use in thousands of properties throughout the world.

## Magnetic- or smart cards

High quality magnetic stripe cards may be custom imprinted to create a unique identity for your property.

Source: Vincard Vision System. For more information, browse the company's Web site at http://www.vingcard.com

**Exhibit 6  Components of a Stand-Alone Electronic Locking System**

# How it works...

2100 PLUS is as simple to set up as it is to use. No complex PC or network integration is required...and no time-consuming staff training is necessary. The self-explanatory, menu driven software makes installation easy and quick. In no time at all, your staff and guests can begin enjoying the benefits of the 2100 PLUS system, with its ideal combination of convenience, security and efficiency. And you will enjoy the peace of mind and strength that comes from working with the world's leading card lock company.

## Checking in

Upon greeting a new guest, the front desk staff asks for a few details and preferences, enters a few keystrokes in the standardized menus and simply swipes a blank keycard through the built-in encoder slot. In seconds, the guests are headed to their rooms with a personalized key. Nothing could be easier.

## Staff master access

Guests are not the only ones who need room access. Staff access is also necessary for cleaning and maintenance. With 2100 PLUS, you can build a powerful, individualized access system for your staff that provides an added measure of security for your guests.

Housekeepers, supervisors, hotel managers and other employees can be granted varying levels of access privileges. Employee keycards can be limited to specific hours of the day for additional guest protection. With personalized staff keycards, individual employees can be easily removed from the system without affecting other staff members.

## Reading the locks

Simply by lifting the handset out of the system controller base, you can create a portable device that allows you to easily program and read each individual lock. This LockLink serves a dual purpose by initially programming the locks during installation and subsequently downloading an audit trail of past events recorded in the lock. Since each keycard issued has its own unique code, you can see a detailed account of who has accessed a given room within a given period of time.

## Setting up the system

You are in total control. From the small, stand-alone system controller, you can effectively manage your entire locking system. Just insert your master memory card, and in a few keystrokes, you can create and maintain a customized locking plan for your property.

Source: Vingcard 2100 Plus System. For more information, browse the company's Web site at http://www.vingcard.com

managers can remove the system controller's handset to download an audit trail of access to individual rooms and guestrooms.

Another type of electronic locking does not require guests to possess keys or keycards at all. With this system, guests set the locking mechanism by programming their own four-digit code number. This system has not been widely adopted and guest acceptance may be an overwhelming factor in determining the future success of the system.

Some electronic locking system vendors provide additional technology that enables guests to use their personal credit cards for room entry. At the time of check-in, the guest's credit card is swiped through a magnetic strip reader. The reader captures and encodes the information contained on the card's magnetic strip and sends it as the access code for the appropriate guestroom door. When the guest arrives at the assigned room, the credit card operates as the room key.

## ELS Reports

One of the most significant advantages of an electronic locking system is that management can find out which keycards opened which doors, by date and time. Communicating this ELS capability to hotel staff and guests may help reduce the number of guestroom incidents.

An ELS typically maintains an audit trail of all activities involving the use of system-issued keycards. Some systems print reports detailing activities in chronological sequence. A system that records events as they occur generally does so because of limited memory, not because the resulting printouts are intrinsically more useful or effective. Other systems record and store activity data that can be formatted to provide printed reports on demand. The creation of reports, as well as other system functions, should be controlled by operator identification and password security codes.

## Energy Management Systems

Heating, lighting, ventilating, and air-conditioning equipment are essential to a hotel's existence. The greater the efficiency of this equipment, the better the hotel serves the needs of guests. Energy management systems may conserve energy, contain energy costs, and tighten operational controls over guestroom and public space environments. An important feature of these systems is their ability to minimize the building's energy needs while not significantly affecting the hotel's comfort conditions.

An energy management system may be a central feature of the rooms management module or operate as a stand-alone application. Historically, these systems were marketed as stand-alone systems and connectivity to the rooms management module was not very common.

An energy management system (EMS) is an automated system designed to manage the operation of mechanical equipment in a lodging property. The programming of this system enables management to determine when equipment is to be turned on or off or otherwise regulated. For example, if the meeting rooms of a property will be used from 10:00 A.M. to 2:00 P.M., the system controller can be programmed to automatically conserve energy during the hours the rooms will not be in use, while ensuring that by 10:00 A.M. the rooms reach a satisfactory comfort level for guests. This programming technique can usually be applied to equipment affecting various spaces throughout the property.

Although actual operating features of energy management systems vary, common energy control designs include:

- Demand control
- Duty cycling
- Room occupancy sensors

**Demand control** maintains usage levels below a given limit by shedding energy loads in an orderly fashion. Equipment units assigned to demand control programs are those that can be turned off for varying periods without adversely affecting environmental comfort conditions. Unfortunately, hotels and motels do not have very many equipment units that can be shed without adversely affecting the overall operation of the property and the comfort of its guests.

**Duty cycling** turns off equipment sequentially for a predetermined period of time each work cycle. Heating, ventilating, and air conditioning systems may be duty-cycled to reduce energy consumption while maintaining space comfort conditions. However, duty cycling is not normally applied to large horsepower motors that cannot be stopped and started on a frequent basis without overheating.

**Room occupancy sensors** use either infrared light or ultrasonic waves to register the physical occupancy of a room or zone. Whenever a guest enters a monitored space, sensors turn on whatever devices are under their control, such as lights, air conditioning equipment, heating equipment, and so on. When a guest leaves a monitored room, sensors react and, after a short delay, turn off or dim the lights and/or automatically reset the temperature.

An EMS/PMS interface offers a number of opportunities for energy control. For example, assume that, on a particular night, a 50 percent occupancy is forecasted for a 300-room property. Minimizing the hotel's energy consumption on this night becomes a factor in determining which rooms to sell. One approach would be to assign guests only to the lower floors of the property and significantly reduce the energy demands of rooms on the upper floors. By interfacing an energy management system to a front office rooms management module, it is possible to automatically control room assignments and achieve desired energy cost savings. In many cases, energy cost savings are tracked through specially created databases or electronic spreadsheets.

Comfort conditions in guestrooms, meeting and function rooms, public spaces, administrative offices, and other EMS-monitored areas can be controlled through a centralized system console. Energy management systems typically provide rapid access to heat, ventilating, and air conditioning (HVAC) levels at remote locations and display these readings on the console screen.

No matter how sophisticated an energy management system may be, energy controls are virtually worthless if they are operating an energy system that is poorly designed or inadequately maintained.

## Auxiliary Guest Services

Automation has simplified many auxiliary guest services, such as the placement of wake-up calls, voice messaging, and the delivery of messages to guests. These functions are often performed by devices marketed as stand-alone systems that can be interfaced to the rooms management module of a property management system.

Perhaps the main reason for interfacing auxiliary guest services to a property management system lies in the comprehensive coordination and tracking of guest-related functions. While automated wake-up call devices are often best operated as stand-alone units, it may be beneficial to interface a guest messaging system to the PMS. The ability to notify guests about messages waiting for them depends on access to the PMS mechanism that links with guestroom telephones and televisions.

An automated wake-up system permits front desk employees to input a guest's room number and requested wake-up time. At the specified time, the system automatically rings the room and calls back at predetermined intervals until the guest answers the phone. If there is no response on the third or fourth try, the system stops calling and makes note of the guest's failure to answer. If the guest answers the call, the system completes a prerecorded morning greeting and then disconnects. Some sophisticated wake-up devices require that the guest actually speak into the phone to confirm that he or she is awake. A notation of the answered call is often stored for the day within the system.

Electronic message-waiting systems and voice messaging systems are designed to let a guest know that a message is waiting and can be retrieved through the phone, television set, or other in-room device. Traditional message-waiting devices are capable of flashing a light on a telephone or television in the guest's room. Electronic systems are now available that actually display messages on the television screen in the guest's room. Other systems employ an automatic telephone calling pattern similar to that used in automated wake-up systems. The system's ability to keep calling until the guest answers is more economical and efficient than employing the time, patience, and persistence of a switchboard operator.

Hotels have also adopted voice mailboxes. These are devices that record telephone messages for guests. A caller who wishes to leave a message for a guest simply does so over the phone, and the message is recorded for the guest to access later. To retrieve a message, the guest typically dials a special telephone number, connects with the voice mailbox, and listens to the message delivered in the caller's own voice. By interfacing the voice mailbox service with the PMS, the recording of the message trips the message-waiting mechanism in the guestroom, leaving the switchboard staff free to perform other productive tasks.

# Guest-Operated Devices

Guest-operated devices can be located in a public area of the hotel or in private guestrooms. In-room guest-operated devices are designed to be user-friendly. An assortment of devices provides concierge-level service with in-room convenience. Guest-operated devices discussed in the following sections include:

- Self-check-in/self-check-out systems

- In-room entertainment systems

- In-room vending systems

- Information service systems

## Self-Check-In/Self-Check-Out Systems

**Self-check-in/self-check-out terminals** are typically located in the lobbies of fully automated hotels and can be accessed through guestroom televisions or telephones. These terminals vary in design. Some resemble automatic bank teller machines, while others are unique in design and may possess both video and audio capability.

In order to use one of these terminals, a guest typically must arrive at the hotel with an advance reservation and must possess a valid credit (or debit) card. The guest initiates the self-registration process by inserting the credit card into the terminal. The terminal then prompts the guest to use a keypad and enter necessary information. After collecting registration data, the terminal screen may display room types and rates. Since most terminals are interfaced to a property management system rooms management module, automatic room and rate assignment is possible. Once a room and rate have been determined, the terminal may automatically dispense an electronic keycard or tell the guest how to obtain a room key.

Lobby terminals are also capable of handling self-check-out procedures. Typically, the guest uses the credit or debit card used at check-in to access the appropriate folio and review its contents. After the guest completes the designated check-out procedures, the system automatically posts the account balance to the credit or debit card for billing and dispenses an itemized statement for the guest.

Self-check-in/self-check-out systems are also available for small properties. These systems allow the busy owner or manager of a small property to capitalize on technological advances that, in the past, have been available primarily to large properties. One system is capable of registering guests, assigning rooms, handling credit card or cash transactions, providing a room key or keycard, and printing a receipt for the guest.

One type of system has a secured face plate that mounts on an interior or exterior wall. For the convenience of guests, step-by-step instructions are printed on the face plate. The only way to access the machine's contents (such as cash) is from the rear of the machine, which generally opens into the manager's office or another secure area. As a security precaution, the system does not disburse cash. If a late-arriving guest uses the system and a credit is due from a cash overpayment, the guest is instructed to receive the change at the front desk in the morning. When a guest pays by credit or debit card, authorization is secured by telecommunications capability. If the guest's use of a credit or debit card is declined, special instructions can be displayed asking the guest to use another card or to pay by cash.

In addition, guests have the opportunity for both in-room folio review and **in-room check-out**. These systems may use in-room terminals, the property's television cable station, or guestroom telephones to access and display guest folio data on the guestroom television screen. When in-room terminals are interfaced with a property management system guest accounting module, they are able to access folio data and provide guests with a means to approve and settle their accounts. Some in-room folio review technology uses a guestroom telephone interface with the property management system to provide computer-synthesized voice responses. This system provides guests with folio totals (or details) and directs a self-check-out procedure. Folio copies are typically available for guests to pick up at the front desk or can be faxed or e-mailed to the departing guest.

Regardless of which kind of guest-operated device is used, self-check-in/ self-check-out terminals and in-room interfaces can significantly reduce the time it takes to process guest registrations, check-ins, and check-outs. In addition, some automated terminals have enhanced video capability enabling the property to introduce guests to the facilities and amenities available. Automated check-in and check-out devices can free front office employees to spend more time with those guests who require personal attention.

## In-Room Entertainment Systems

**In-room entertainment systems** can be interfaced with a hotel's property management system or can function as independent, stand-alone systems. When interfaced with the property management system, in-room movie systems provide guestroom entertainment either through synchronous programming (with specific start and end times) or asynchronous programming (on demand). The interface includes a timing device. After a special programming channel has been tuned in for a predetermined amount of time (usually several minutes), the device triggers an automatic charge posting to the appropriate guest folio.

Guest-disputed charges have plagued in-room entertainment systems since their inception. A guest may inadvertently turn on a special programming channel for background entertainment, only to discover at check-out that the set was tuned to a pay channel. Incorporating a free preview channel introducing the special programming offered can significantly reduce the number of disputed charges resulting from guests unknowingly selecting a pay-to-view channel. The preview channel permits a guest to view a small segment of each special program. In order to view an actual program, the guest must then physically switch the television from normal viewing to a pay-to-view mode.

In addition to movies, in-room entertainment systems may include:

- On-screen controls (offering DVD/CD functionality)
- CD library
- Digital music channels
- Music video library
- Video games

## In-Room Vending Systems

**In-room vending systems** are capable of monitoring sales transactions and determining inventory replenishment quantities. A popular in-room vending system is an in-room beverage system. There are two types of in-room beverage service systems: non-automated honor bars and microprocessor-based beverage devices.

**Non-automated honor bars** typically involve stocks of items that are held in both dry and cold storage areas within a guestroom. Changes in the bar's beginning inventory level are noted either by housekeeping room attendants during their normal rounds or by designated room service employees. In either case, the employee typically uses a hand-held portable computer terminal or the touch-tone telephone in the guestroom to connect with the remote dedicated bar computer. Once connection has been made, the employee enters the product code numbers of items that have been consumed. The bar system's CPU relays guest-room information and charges for consumed items to the property management system for proper folio posting and issues a stock replacement report.

Although non-automated honor bar systems are extremely convenient for guests, they may pose several problems for the hotel. For example, since the bar is always open, consumption is almost impossible to regulate. This service problem could result in underage access to alcohol or frequent late charges. Another potential problem is the high labor costs associated with taking the necessary physical inventory of each in-room bar.

**Microprocessor-based beverage devices** contain beverage items in see-through closed compartments. The compartment doors may be equipped with fiber optic sensors that record the removal of stored products. Once triggered, the sensors relay the transaction to a built-in microprocessor for recording. Individual room microprocessors are typically cabled to a remote CPU, which stores recorded transactions. This CPU converts transactions into accounting entries, and relays them to the property management system guest accounting module for folio posting. The bar system's CPU also maintains perpetual inventory replenishment data, which directs the restocking of vending units.

Microprocessor-based systems avoid some of the problems associated with honor bars. For example, hotel managers may use a remote central console to lock in-room vending units. Some systems enable guests to lock their in-room bar units with their guestroom keys. In addition, property management system interfacing minimizes late charges. Also, since microprocessor-based devices maintain a perpetual inventory record, labor costs associated with manual inventory tracking are reduced.

## Guest Information Services

Just as shopping malls have installed information terminals, so too have many hotels. Automated **guest information services** include devices in public hotel areas and in guestrooms that allow guests to inquire about in-house events and local activities. Transient guests, conference attendees, and casual observers alike can access information about the hotel, its outlets, and surrounding attractions.

Guest information systems, also called in-room electronic services, are an important guest amenity. These systems are television-based and may connect to cable broadcast systems, wire news services, transportation schedules, and restaurant and room service menus, and may also access the Internet. When in-room computers are able to connect to the Internet, guests may access:

- Airline schedules
- Local restaurant guides
- Entertainment guides and ticketing

- Stock market reports

- News and sports updates

- Shopping catalogs and transactions

- Video games and casino games

- Weather reports

In addition to the property management system interface, in-room guest information terminals may be connected to the hotel's cable television band. This connection enables the property to keep in-house guests and convention attendees informed about events and functions, to provide tourists with information about local attractions, and to inform business travelers about support services provided by the property.

# Key Terms

### Point-of-Sale Systems

**PC-based register system (PCR)**—A POS system design that networks terminals to form an integrated system that functions without a large, remote CPU.

**point-of-sale terminal**—Contains its own input/output component and may even possess a small storage (memory) capacity, but usually does not contain its own central processing unit.

### Call Accounting Systems

**active call accounting system**—Enables a hotel to take control over local and long-distance services and apply a markup to switchboard operations. Call accounting systems are capable of placing and pricing local and long-distance calls. Passive call accounting systems do not employ an automatic route selection switch with a least-cost routing device.

**automatic identification of outward dialing**—A feature of a call accounting system that immediately identifies the extension from which an outgoing call is placed.

**automatic route selection**—A feature of a call accounting system that provides the capability of connecting with a variety of common carriers.

**call record**—Electronic or hard copy documentation containing essential transactional support data for individually placed and rated telephone calls.

**common carrier**—Any recognized entity that transmits messages or other communication for general use at accepted rates.

**daily telephone revenue report**—Also called a daily profit report. It sorts traffic transaction data by type of call and records the cost, price, and gross profit earned for each call processed by a call accounting system.

**HOBIC**—Acronym for Hotel Billing Information Center, a service supplied by a telephone company that provides a means to record time and charges on each long-distance call that guests make.

**least-cost routing**—A feature of an active call accounting system that directs calls over the least-cost available line, regardless of carrier.

**passive call accounting system**—Under this system, no options are available to the call distribution network. Selection of a route is based on convenience rather than on minimizing expense.

**ringback mechanism**—A feature of a call accounting system that ensures that a guest is charged only for calls that are answered.

**station message detail record**—A feature of a call accounting system that charts and monitors telephone traffic.

**timeout feature**—A feature of a call accounting system that ensures that callers begin paying for calls only after a predetermined amount of time, thus allowing for wrong numbers.

**traffic transaction file**—Part of a call accounting system that maintains data necessary for generating reports for management.

*Electronic Locking Systems*

**hard-wired electronic locking system**—An electronic locking system that operates through a centralized master code console that is interfaced to every controlled guestroom door.

**micro-fitted electronic locking system**—An electronic locking system that operates as a stand-alone unit. Each door has its own microprocessor that contains a unique, predetermined sequence of codes. A master console at the front desk contains a record of all code sequences for each door.

*Energy Management Systems*

**demand control**—A feature of an energy management system that maintains usage levels below a given limit by shedding energy loads in an orderly fashion.

**duty cycling**—A feature of an energy management system that turns off equipment on a sequential basis for a given period of time each hour.

**room occupancy sensors**—Sensors that use either infrared light or ultrasonic waves to register the physical occupancy of a room.

*Guest-Operated Devices*

**guest information services**—These automated information devices in public hotel areas allow guests to inquire about in-house events and local activities.

**in-room check-out**—When in-room computers are interfaced with a computer-based property management system's guest accounting module, they are able to access folio data and provide guests with a way to approve and settle their accounts.

**in-room entertainment system**—When interfaced with a hotel property management system, an in-room movie system provides guestroom entertainment through a dedicated television pay channel.

**in-room vending system**—A system capable of monitoring sales transactions and determining inventory replenishment quantities. Two popular in-room beverage service systems are non-automated honor bars and microprocessor-based vending machines.

**microprocessor-based beverage device**—Vending machine that contains beverage items in see-through closed compartments. The compartment doors may be equipped with fiber optic sensors that record the removal of stored products. Once triggered, the sensors relay the transaction to a built-in microprocessor for recording. Individual room microprocessors are typically cabled to a large CPU, which stores recorded transactions.

**non-automated honor bar**—Typically involves stocks of items that are held in dry and cold storage areas within a guestroom. Changes in the bar's beginning inventory level are noted either by housekeeping room attendants during their normal rounds or by designated room service employees.

**self-check-in/self-check-out terminals**—Typically located in the lobbies of fully automated hotels, some resemble automatic bank teller machines, while others are unique in design and may possess both video and audio capability.

 **Review Questions**

1. What issues should hospitality managers consider before interfacing separate applications with a property management system?

2. What are typical POS data entry requirements for posting charges to appropriate guest folios?

3. What are some concerns that management should address in relation to interfacing a POS system to a PMS system?

4. What are the advantages of a call accounting system when compared with the HOBIC system?

5. What data are maintained by a CAS call record file? Explain how this data may be useful to management.

6. What are the major differences between hard-wired and micro-fitted electronic locking systems? Identify advantages and disadvantages of each system.

7. What are three energy control strategies that may be used by an energy management system?

8. How can lodging properties benefit from automated self-check-in/self-check-out systems?

9.  What are two in-room vending systems? Explain the advantages and disadvantages of each.

10. What external information services may guests be able to access from in-room computer terminals?

 **Internet Sites** ————————————————————————

For more information, visit the following Internet sites. Remember that Internet addresses can change without notice. If the site is no longer there, you can use a search engine to look for additional sites.

InfoGenesis
http://www.infogenesis.com

NCR Corporation
http://www.ncr.com

Remanco International Inc.
http://www.remanco.com

Squirrel Companies Inc.
http://www.squirrel-rms.com

System Concepts Inc.
http://www.foodtrak.com

Profit Watch, Metropolis Technologies
http://www.metropolis-tech.com

RBS Computer Corporation
http://www.rbscc.com

Hitachi Telecom (USA), Inc.
http://www.hitel.com/lodge.htm

Inn Room Video, Inc.
http://www.innroomvideo.com

INNCOM International Inc.
http://inncom.com

LodgeNet Entertainment
http://www.lodgenet.com

VingCard
http://www.vingcard.com

# Chapter 6 Outline

POS Order-Entry Units
    Keyboards and Monitors
    Touch-Screen Terminals
    OCR Terminals
    Wireless Hand-Held Terminals
POS Printers
    Guest Check Printers
    Receipt Printers
    Work Station Printers
    Journal Printers
Account Settlement
    Power Platforms
    Smart Cards
    Debit Cards
Managing Guest Accounts
POS Software
    Menu Item File
    Labor Master File
    Inventory File
    Consolidated Reports
Automated Beverage Control Systems
    Order-Entry Devices
    Delivery Networks
    Dispensing Units

# Competencies

1. Describe the features and functions of keyboards and monitors typically used by point-of-sale systems. (pp. 129–135)

2. Distinguish touch-screen point-of-sale terminals from OCR and wireless terminals. (pp. 135–140)

3. Describe the features and functions of various types of point-of-sale printers. (pp. 140–146)

4. Describe the features and functions of point-of-sale account settlement devices such as magnetic strip readers, power platforms, smart cards, and debit cards. (pp. 146–147)

5. Identify the major files typically maintained by point-of-sale software and describe how managers can use the various reports commonly generated by point-of-sale software. (pp. 147–153)

6. Describe the features and functions of an automated beverage control system. (pp. 153–159)

# 6

# Point-of-Sale Technology

WHILE AUTOMATED property management systems tend to consist of modules, restaurant management systems often involve speciality hardware components and a wide variety of application software packages. This chapter focuses on service-oriented applications that rely upon point-of-sale (POS) technology to monitor service area transactions through remote work station printers, displays, and printer controllers.

This chapter begins by identifying the necessary order-entry units of a restaurant-wide POS system. Input/output devices such as keyboards, monitors, touchscreen terminals, OCR terminals, and wireless terminals are discussed in detail. POS printers—guest check printers, receipt printers, work station printers, and journal printers—and POS account settlement devices—power platforms, smart cards, and debit cards—are also discussed. In addition, guest checks are examined in relation to enhancing management's control of operations.

Like other computer hardware components, POS terminals require software programs to instruct them in what to do, how to do it, and when to do it. POS software not only directs internal system operations, it also maintains files and produces reports for management's use. The chapter examines the types of data stored in major POS files and the kind of information contained in some of the more significant reports that can be generated.

The chapter closes with a section on automated beverage control systems. The discussion focuses on order-entry devices, delivery networks, and dispensing units.

## POS Order-Entry Units

In this chapter, the term **cashier terminal** refers to a POS device that is connected to a cash drawer. A terminal without a cash drawer is commonly called a **precheck terminal**. Precheck terminals are used to enter orders, not to settle accounts. For example, a server can use a precheck terminal located in a dining room service station to relay orders to the appropriate kitchen and/or bar production areas, but cannot use the terminal to settle guest checks. Only cashier terminals can be used for cash settlement.

Since POS devices are generally sold as modular units, everything but the basic terminal is considered optional equipment. The cash drawer is no exception. Management may connect several cash drawers to a single cashier terminal. Multiple cash drawers may enhance management's cash control system when several cashiers work at the same cashier terminal location during the same shift. Each cashier can be assigned a separate cash drawer so that, at the end of the shift, cash drawer receipts are individually reconciled.

A POS device with a cash drawer normally supports both prechecking and cashiering functions. For example, an employee at a cashier stand in a hotel restaurant may serve as the cashier for the food service outlet and as an order-entry person for room service. When answering room service calls, the employee uses the cashier terminal as a precheck terminal. The terminal relays the room service orders to the appropriate kitchen and/or bar production areas. Before delivering the room service order, a room service employee may need to stop at the cashier station and pick up the printed guest check from the cashier. After delivering the order, the room service employee presents the settled or signed guest check to the cashier, who then uses the cashier terminal to close the guest check or transfer the folio charge within the system.

POS order-entry units consist of keyboards and monitors. The following sections discuss these components. Keyboards are examined in relation to keyboard design, types of keys, and keyboard overlays. The section on monitors addresses important concerns, such as the size and function of operator displays and hand-held devices. Touch-screen POS devices, magnetic strip readers, and hand-held terminals are alternatives to traditional keyboard entry procedures. These devjces are described in detail later in the chapter.

## Keyboards and Monitors

The two primary types of keyboard surfaces are micro-motion and reed style. The micro-motion keyboard design has a flat, wet-proof surface. The reed keyboard design contains wet-proof keys raised above the surface of the keyboard. More important than the physical design of the device's surface is the number of hard and soft keys the keyboard or screen provides. **Hard keys** are dedicated to specific functions programmed by the manufacturer. **Soft keys** can be programmed by users to meet the specific needs of their restaurant operations.

Keyboard designs can usually support interchangeable menu boards. A **menu board** overlays the keyboard surface and identifies the function performed by each key during a specific meal period. Menu boards can be developed to meet the specific needs of individual properties. Exhibit 1 shows a sample menu board for a dinner period. Menu boards for both micro-motion and reed style keyboard designs can identify a number of different types of key functions. Key types may include:

- Preset keys (or screen icons).

- Price look-up (PLU) keys (or screen icons).

- Function keys.

- Settlement keys.

- Modifier keys.

- Numeric keypad.

**Exhibit 1    Sample Menu Board**

| CARAFE WHITE WINE | CARAFE RED WINE | BOURBON | VODKA | DECAF COFFEE | COFFEE | SALAD | BAKED POTATO | HASH BROWNS | FRENCH FRIES | SOUR CREAM | TIME IN |
|---|---|---|---|---|---|---|---|---|---|---|---|
| CARAFE ROSE WINE | SCOTCH | SODA | WATER | BLOODY MARY | TEA | WITH | WITH-OUT | BREAD | STEWED TOMATO | VEGETAB | TIME OUT |
| RARE | GIN | TONIC | COLA | SCREW-DRIVER | MILK | HOUSE DRESS | FRENCH DRESS | VINEGAR & OIL | EXTRA BUTTER | MUSHRM SAUCE | ACCOUNT # |
| MEDIUM | WELL | SAUTEED MUSHRMS | SHRIMP COCKTAIL | FRENCH ONION SOUP | CRAB MEAT COCKTAIL | OYSTERS ON 1/2 SHELL | ITALIAN DRESS | BLEU CHEESE DRESS | COUPON 1 | COUPON 2 | COUPON 3 |
| PRIME RIB | T-BONE | SHRIMP | LOBSTER | CIGARS | CASH BAR | CLEAR | ERROR CORRECT | CANCEL TRANS | CHECK TRANSFER | PAID OUT | TIPS PAID OUT |
| CHATEAU-BRIAND | FILET | CLAMS | TROUT | CANDY | SERVER # | TRAN CODE | SCREEN | NO SALE | CASHIER # | EMPL DISC | MGR DISC |
| TOP SIRLOIN 16 OZ | TOP SIRLOIN 12 OZ | SEA BASS | SCALLOPS | SNACKS | VOID ITEM | 7 | 8 | 9 | QUANTITY | ADD CHECK | CREDIT CARD 2 |
| PORTER-HOUSE | CHOPPED SIRLOIN | OYSTERS | ALASKAN KING CRAB | # PERSONS ADD ON | REVERSE RECEIPT | 4 | 5 | 6 | VOID TRANS | CHARGE TIPS | CREDIT CARD 1 |
| STEAK & CHICKEN | SURF & TURF | RED SNAPPER | SEA FOOD PLATTER | DINING ROOM SERVICE | PRICE LOOK UP | 1 | 2 | 3 | NEW CHECK | CASH BAR TOTAL | CHARGE |
| LEG OF LAMB | ROAST DUCK | PORK CHOPS | CHICKEN LIVERS | LOUNGE SERVICE | MODE SWITCH | 0 | | MENU 1 | PREVIOUS BALANCE | CHECK TOTAL | CASH TEND |

Source: Validec, Inc., San Carlos, California.

Servers enter orders by using preset keys and price look-up (PLU) keys. Modifier keys may be used in combination with preset and PLU keys to detail preparation instructions (such as rare, medium, well-done) for food production areas. Modifier keys may also be used to alter prices according to portion sizes (such as small, medium, and large). A numeric keypad facilitates various data-entry operations and enables cashiers to ring items by price when prices for items are not identified by preset keys or PLU numbers. Function keys and settlement keys are used to correct and complete transactions.

Generally, restaurant managers determine the positioning of most keys on a keyboard overlay. By positioning keys for similar items and functions together and arranging groups logically, managers can improve system performance and enhance operational controls. The following sections briefly discuss the types of keys commonly found on POS system keyboards.

**Preset Keys/Screen Icons.** These keys are programmed to maintain the price, descriptor, department, tax, and inventory status for a limited number of menu items. Automatic menu pricing speeds guest service, eliminates pricing errors, and permits greater menu flexibility. The term descriptor refers to the abbreviated description of a menu item, such as "SHRMPCKT" for shrimp cocktail or "PRIME" for

**Menu Board Overlay.** (Courtesy of National Cash Register Corporation)

prime rib. Although systems vary in the number of descriptor characters they can accommodate, most support descriptors 8 to 10 characters long.

Each **preset key** (or screen icon) is normally associated with a department code and a printer routing code. A department code refers to the menu category to which the preset item belongs—appetizer, entrée, dessert, and so on. A printer routing code, also used in conjunction with a remote work-station monitor, is used to direct preparation instructions to the proper production area. For example, the porterhouse steak on the keyboard in Exhibit 1 has a department code associated with entrée items. The porterhouse steak also has a printer routing code designating it as an item prepared at the hot food station of the kitchen. Other items on the same keyboard (salad, wine, etc.) may be assigned different department and printer routing codes.

Once a preset key is selected, a description of the item and its price are retrieved from memory and appear on the operator's monitor. This data may also be relayed (along with preparation instructions) to the appropriate production station and may be printed (or retained for later printing) on a guest check. In addition, the sales represented by this transaction are retained for revenue reporting and for tracking perpetual inventory levels. Sales data of individual items are important for guest check totaling as well as for production of management reports.

**Price Look-Up Keys.** Since terminals have a limited number of preset keys, **price look-up (PLU) keys** (or screen icons) are used to supplement transaction entries. PLU keys operate like preset keys, except that they require the user to identify a menu item by a unique reference code number (up to five digits) rather than by its name or descriptor. A server entering an order for prime rib on a preset keyboard would merely press the item's designated key. In the absence of a prime rib preset

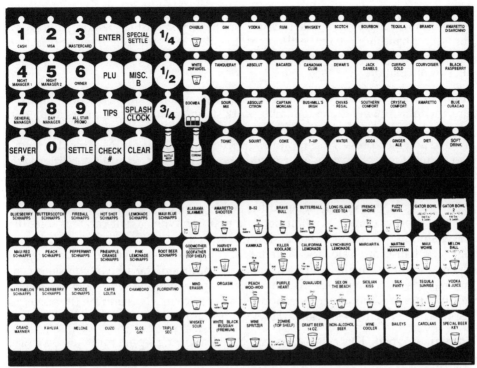

**Keyboard for an Automatic Dispensing System.** (Courtesy of American Business Computers)

key, the server would enter the item's code number (e.g., 7807) and then press the PLU key. PLU keys perform the same functions as preset keys. Preset keys and PLU keys enable the system to maintain a large file of menu items in terms of price, descriptor, tax, department, and inventory status.

**Function Keys.** While preset and PLU keys are used for order-entry purposes, function keys assist the user in processing transactions. Sample function keys include: clear, discount, void, and no-sale. Function keys are important for error correction (clear and void), legitimate price alteration (discount), and proper cash handling (no-sale). For example, a restaurant may attempt to increase weekly lunch sales by issuing coupons to nearby local businesses. When a coupon is used at the time of settlement, the cashier typically enters the value of the coupon and then presses the "discount" key. The value of the coupon is credited to the guest check and the remainder of the bill is settled through standard settlement procedures. The success of the promotion can be tracked if the system can retain itemized discounts and daily discount totals.

**Settlement Keys.** These keys are used to record the methods with which accounts are settled: by cash, credit card, house account, charge transfer, debit card, smart card, or other payment method. Settlement keys enhance revenue accounting controls because they classify transactions at the time of settlement. Although restaurants may use any one of a number of revenue accounting methods, most operations use either server banking or cashier banking. Server banking places the responsibility for guest check settlement on the server. Cashier banking involves a non-server handling account settlement. In either case, tracking the identification of the banker and the transaction settlement method facilitates a fast and accurate sales reconciliation.

**Modifier Keys.** These keys allow servers to relay preparation instructions (such as rare, medium, or well-done) to remote work station printers or monitors located in food and beverage production departments. Typically, a server enters the item ordered and then presses the appropriate preparation modifier. Modifier keys may also be used to legitimately alter menu item prices. For example, modifier keys may be useful to a restaurant that sells house wine by the carafe and half-carafe. Instead of tying up two preset keys (one for carafe, the other for half-carafe), a single preset key can be designated for house wine by the carafe and a modifier key can be programmed as a half-portion modifier. When a half-carafe is sold, the server simply presses both the carafe preset key and half-portion modifier key to register a half-carafe sale. The system will compute wine revenue by adding the dollar amount for the half-carafe sale only. In addition, the system adjusts inventory records accordingly. A forced modifier may be built into the system. A forced modifier requires the server to respond to a specific cue. By requiring the server to respond, the system is especially targeted for guest service.

**Numeric Keypad.** This set of keys can be used to ring up menu items by price, access PLU data by menu item code number, access open guest check accounts by serial number, record the number of items sold, and perform other data entry operations. For example, if the cashier terminal is used to record and store payroll data, employee identification numbers can be entered as employees begin and end their workshifts. In addition, menu item code numbers may be entered through the numeric keypad to access various files in order to make adjustments approved by management. The numeric keypad may also be used to enter report codes that initiate the production of management reports.

**Monitors.** A micro-motion or reed style POS terminal typically contains an **operator monitor** and may support a customer display unit as well. An operator monitor is generally a standard system component that enables the operator to view and edit transaction entries. The unit allows a user to monitor transactions in progress and also may serve as a prompt for various system procedures. The length and number of lines displayed are often an important consideration when selecting POS devices. Line lengths may range from 7 to 80 characters, and the number of lines available can vary from 1 to 24 (or more). An operator monitor is typically encased in the primary housing of the POS device. This is not always true for customer display units.

The designs of **customer display units** include those that rest atop, inside, or alongside the POS device. Although customer display units are more restricted in size and scope than operator monitors, they permit a guest to observe the operator's entries. In many table service restaurants, settlement activities often take place outside the view of guests; therefore, a customer display unit may not be

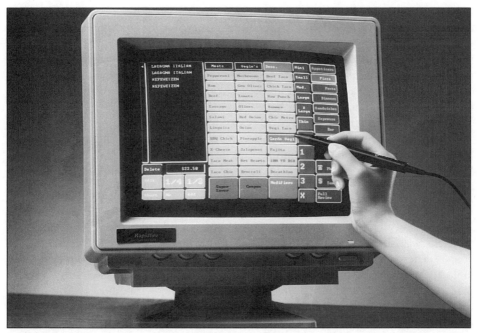

**Touch-Screen Terminal Activated by Touch or Light Pen.** (Courtesy of RapidFire Solutions, Hillsboro, Oregon)

warranted. In those restaurants where guests can view settlement transactions, serious consideration should be given to the use of a customer display monitor.

Customer display units also permit management to spot-check cashier activities. For example, an employee operating a cashier terminal without a customer display unit might ring up a $5 transaction as 50 cents. Later, to balance the cashier terminal's cash, the employee might take the $4.50 difference for personal use. This kind of theft is riskier when the terminal contains a customer display unit because a manager or the customer might observe the bogus 50-cent entry and take appropriate corrective action or request an explanation. Customer monitors are often more important for management control purposes than for the assurance they offer guests.

The importance of practical, easy-to-use, fast, and reliable input devices has prompted the development of touch-screen terminals, optical character recognition (OCR) terminals, and hand-held wireless server terminals. The following sections discuss each of these devices.

## Touch-Screen Terminals

There is perhaps no area of POS hardware that has received more research and development than touch-screen technology. Color touch-screen terminals are replacing monochrome touch-screen terminals, traditional keyboards, and other order-entry devices. Color touch-screen terminals have been developed for all types of food service operations, including those that allow customers to place their orders without interacting with counter employees.

A **touch-screen terminal** contains a unique adaptation of a cathode ray tube (CRT) screen and a special microprocessor to control it. The self-contained microprocessor displays data on areas of the screen that are sensitive to touch. Touching one of the sensitized areas produces an electronic charge that is translated into digital signals telling what area was touched for transmission to the microprocessor. This signal also instructs the microprocessor to display the next screen.

Terminal design varies from vendor to vendor. Flat, color touch-screen terminals are available that require significantly less counter space than the traditional POS terminals that they replace. Flat screens measure only a few inches thick and can be mounted from walls, ceilings, counters, or shelving units. Flat screens offer restaurants flexibility in determining where to locate the terminals.

**Touch-Screens and POS Systems.** Color touch-sensitive color screens simplify data entry and may be used in place of traditional CRT screens and POS keyboards. The previous discussion of POS system keyboards pointed out that price look-up keys (PLUs) must often be used to enter orders because many systems maintain a limited number of preset keys. Using PLUs generally requires additional order-entry procedures related to product code numbers assigned to menu items. In some cases, servers memorize these codes, or management tapes a list of the code numbers at keyboard terminals. Most touch-screen terminals eliminate the need for PLUs altogether, decreasing the time necessary to enter orders into the system.

Color touch-screen terminals are also interactive. That is, the system provides on-screen prompts guiding servers through order-entry or settlement procedures. For example, after a server enters an order for a menu item that needs preparation instructions (such as a New York strip steak), the screen shifts to display the appropriate modifiers (rare, medium rare, medium, medium well done, well done) or forced modifiers. Forced modifiers will not allow the user to proceed with order entry until a response is indicated. This eliminates the possibility of servers sending incomplete orders to production areas. The interactive nature of these systems decreases the time it takes to train new employees.

**Magnetic Strip Readers.** POS terminals may also be equipped with a magnetic strip reader that allows servers and managers to use company identification cards to sign in and out of the system. The magnetic strip reader can also be used to capture credit or debit card account information. One system ensures that immediately after employees sign into the system, a message screen is displayed. This message screen enables management to deliver messages to different categories of employees, or to individual employees. For example, employees with job codes corresponding to food servers might receive messages about daily specials and prices. Or an individual employee might receive a message from a supervisor about work schedule changes. Since employees must touch the message screen to complete sign-in procedures, management is assured that employees have received their messages.

**Customer Order-Entry Systems.** Some quick-service operations have installed countertop-recessed touch-screen terminals that customers can use to place their orders without interacting with counter employees. This self-service option helps to reduce labor costs and speed service. Some systems have color graphic components that entice customers to use the terminals. For example, icons (graphic images) can be used: caricature drawings representing chicken, fish, french fries, burgers, etc.; and company logos representing specific soft drink choices. Condiments can also be creatively displayed—with a lasso indicating ranch salad dressing, the Eiffel Tower indicating French salad dressing, and so on.

One system enables customers to place orders by following six simple steps. The customer activates the terminal by pressing a start feature on the screen. The screen then shifts to a display asking the customer to indicate whether the order will be take-out or whether the customer will dine on premises. Next, the screen shifts to display menu options. To order, the customer simply touches the desired item on the screen. As items are touched, a "video receipt" appears on the right side of the screen that keeps a running total during the ordering process. When the order is complete, the customer touches a "finished" box on the screen. At this point, a suggestive selling display appears, asking the customer if he or she would like soft drinks or desserts (if not ordered). The final screen displays the total amount due and settlement options.

## OCR Terminals

While **optical character recognition (OCR) terminals** have not been widely adopted, they may simplify data entry and can be used in place of traditional keyboards or touch-screen terminals. With this system, servers use hand-held, pen-like bar code readers to enter orders at service station terminals from a laminated bar-coded menu. Exhibit 2 presents a sample bar-coded menu.

Orders can be entered quickly at OCR terminals because no keystrokes are involved. Also, servers do not have to keep switching from one screen to another as with touch-screen terminals. In addition, server training time can be reduced because all orders are entered from a bar-coded menu.

## Wireless Hand-Held Terminals

Wireless order-entry terminals offer unique POS opportunities. When these terminals are small enough to hold in one's hand, they are called **hand-held terminals** (HHTs). These devices perform most of the functions of a precheck terminal. Wireless technology can be a major advantage for large establishments with drive-through facilities, long distances between service stations, outdoor dining areas, or very busy lounges where it is difficult to reach a precheck terminal. In any establishment, service may be enhanced because servers do not have to wait to use a precheck terminal during peak business periods and orders can be entered at tableside. Exhibit 3 outlines the features and benefits of wireless hand-held terminals.

Two-way communications not only allow a server to include special instructions, such as "no salt" or "medium rare" as part of an order, but also enable the

**Exhibit 2   Sample Bar-Coded Menu**

| COLD APPETIZERS | HOT APPETIZERS | PASTA | PASTA SIDES | MODIFIERS |
|---|---|---|---|---|
| ANTIPASTO MISTO | 1/2 HOT ANTIPASTO | ANGEL HAIR PRIMAVERA | ANGEL HAIR PRIMAVERA | *DISCOUNT AMOUNT |
| ANTIPASTO CASALINGO | ARTICHOKE CASINO | BAKED ZITI | BAKED ZITI | *WITH |
| CLAM COCKTAIL | CALAMARI FRITTI | CANNELLONI | CANNELLONI | *NO |
| CRAB MEAT COCKTAIL | CLAMS OREGANATE | FETT FILETTO DI POM | FETT FILETTO DI POM | *EAST ON |
| INSALATA MARINA | HOT ANTIPASTO | FETT ROMANISSIMO | FETT ROMANISSIMO | *EXTRA |
| M.C SHRIMP & LOBSTER | MOZZ IN CARROZZA | FETTUCINE ALFREDO | FETTUCINE ALFREDO | *ON SIDE |
| MOZZ, PROSC, & TOM | SNAILS BOURGUIGNONE | GNOCCHI | GNOCCHI | *INSTEAD OF |
| OYSTER COCKTAIL | SNAILS FRA DIAVOLO | LASAGNA | LASAGNA | *BAKED |
| PEPPERS & ANCHOVIES | SPIEDINI ALLA ROM | LINGUINE - GAR & OIL | LINGUINE - GAR & OIL | *STEAMED |
| PROSCIUTTO & MELON | STUFFED MUSHROOMS | LINGUINE - RED CLAM | LINGUINE - RED CLAM | *BOILED |
| SCUNGILLI SALAD | ZUPPA DI CLAMS | LINGUINE - WH CLAM | LINGUINE - WH CLAM | *HOT |
| SHRIMP & LOBSTER | ZUPPA DI MUSSELS | MANICOTTI | MANICOTTI | *COLD |
| SHRIMP COCKTAIL | *TODAY'S APPETIZER | RAVIOLI | RAVIOLI | *SPICY |
| SUN D.TOM.MOZZ.& B.P | **SALADS** | SPAGH.BOLOGNESE | SPAGH.BOLOGNESE | *NOT SPICY |
| *TODAY'S APPETIZER | *NO | SPAGH.MARINARA | SPAGH.MARINARA | *BLACK & BLUE |
| **CHICKEN** | *EXTRA | SPAGH.PESTO | SPAGH.PESTO | *PINK |
| CHICKEN CACCIATORE | *DRESSING | SPAGH.PUTANESCA | SPAGH.PUTANESCA | *VERY RARE |
| CHICKEN CHAMPAGNE | *ON SIDE | SPAGH.TOMATO SAUCE | SPAGH.TOMATO SAUCE | *RARE |
| CHICKEN FRANCESE | ROQUEFORT | ZITI ARRABIATI | ZITI ARRABIATI | *MED RARE |
| CHICKEN OREGANATA | ARUGULA & ORANGE | ALFREDO | ALFREDO | *MEDIUM |
| CHICKEN PARMIGIANA | BROCCOLI SALAD | ARRABIATI | ARRABIATI | *MED WELL |
| CHICKEN PARM W/SPAG | CAESAR SALAD | BOLOGNESE | BOLOGNESE | *WELL |
| CHICKEN PICCATA | ENDIVE SALAD | FILLETTO DI POMODORO | FILETTO DI POMODORO | *VERY WELL |
| CHICKEN PORTAFOGLIO | HEARTS OF PALM | GARLIC & OIL | GARLIC & OIL | *DRY |
| CHICKEN SCARPARIELLO | HOUSE SALAD | MARINARA | MARINARA | *SOFT |
| CHICKEN ZINGARA | SPINACH SALAD | PESTO | PESTO | *ANCHOVIES |
| ROASTED BABY CHICKEN | TOMATOES & ONION | PRIMAVERA | PRIMAVERA | *ARTICHOKES |
| **BEEF** | **VEAL** | PUTANESCA | PUTANESCA | *BALSAMIC VINEGAR |
| FILET MIGNON | VEAL CHAMPAGNE | RED CLAM SAUCE | RED CLAM SAUCE | *BASIL |
| MEDALIONS OF BEEF | VEAL CHOP MILANESE | ROMANISSIMO | ROMANISSIMO | *BEL PAESE |
| NEW YORK SIRLOIN | VEAL FRANCESE | TOMATO SAUCE | TOMATO SAUCE | *BREAD CRUMBS |
| STEAK ARRABBIATA | VEAL MARSALA | WHITE CLAM SAUCE | WHITE CLAM SAUCE | *BUTTER |
| STEAK PIZZAIOLA | VEAL PARMIGIANA | *TODAY'S PASTA | *TODAY'S PASTA | *CHEESE |
| **FISH** | VEAL PARM W/SPAG | *ANGEL HAIR | *ANGEL HAIR | |
| BROILED FILET SOLE | VEAL PICCATA | *FARFALLE | *FARFALLE | |
| CALAMARI MARINARA | VEAL PIZZAIOLA | *FETTUCINE | *FETTUCINE | |
| FILET OF SOLE | VEAL ROLLATINI | *GNOCCHI | *GNOCCHI | Copyright January 1989 |
| FILET SOLE MEUNIER | VEAL SALTIMBOCCA | *LINGUINE | *LINGUINE | Standard Commercial Systems |
| FRIED CALAMARI | VEAL VALDAOSTANA | *PENNE | *PENNE | Ridgewood, NJ 07450 |
| LOBSTER TAILS ROM | | *RIGATONI | *RIGATONI | 201-447-5350 • 212-505-9416 |

Source: Standard Commercial Systems, Ridgewood, New Jersey.

kitchen staff (or management) to immediately alert a server if an item is out of stock. Typically, when an order is ready for pick-up, the server receives a signal on the hand-held unit. In some cases, appetizers and drinks may be ready just seconds after a server has finished entering the order and left the table.

Since all items must be entered through a server's hand-held unit, the frequent problem of beverages or desserts inadvertently left off guest checks may be eliminated. Some wireless configurations enable managers to monitor service through their own hand-held units.

Exhibit 4 diagrams one type of hardware configuration for hand-held server terminals. The hand-held units have low-frequency FM radio transmitters and receivers. As orders are entered at the guest's table, signals are sent to **antenna units** located within the dining area. These antenna units relay the signals to a **radio base station** where they are sent to remote work station printers or kitchen monitors. A charged battery pack powers each hand-held server terminal. Fully charged, these battery packs may last for many hours. It is recommended that two fully charged battery packs be available for each hand-held unit.

Several antenna units may be connected to a radio base station. Before installation, a site survey should be conducted to determine the optimum locations for each antenna unit. The number and location of metal structures in a restaurant are important installation concerns.

**Exhibit 3   Sample Features and Benefits of Wireless Hand-Held Terminals**

## AMERANTH ®
### WIRELESS AT WORK

| Home | About Us | News | Products | Partners | Contact | Events | Careers |

**Features**

- **21st Century Restaurant**
  - Features
- **System Requirements**
- **Product Tour**
- **Download Brochure**

### *21ˢᵗ Century Restaurant®*

| Features | Benefits |
| --- | --- |
| Clock-In | The users can clock-in via the handheld device and select an appropriate job code. Only those employees with order entry privileges appear in job codes screen. |
| Deleting an Item | Items can be deleted from the order providing that the items have not already been sent to the kitchen. Held items can also be deleted. |
| Expand/Collapse Grids | The collapsed order grid (default) displays the item name. The user has the option of expanding the grid, which displays the status, price and exception modifiers associated with each item. |
| Failed Order Submissions | The handheld will inform the user if errors occur upon submitting the order. The order will be saved and the handheld will automatically be rebooted. Once the handheld has been rebooted, the order will be resubmitted. |
| Guest Count | Servers have the ability to enter the number of guests per table. |
| Hold/Release Items | Items can be placed on hold. Held items can then be released and sent to the kitchen. |
| Item Availability | Items can be marked as unavailable. The handheld will display message text to prevent the user from selling an item that is currently not available. |
| Login | Only those employees who have order entry privileges are allowed to login via the handheld. Servers, Managers and Bartenders have order entry privileges. Kitchen employees do not retain these privileges and therefore are not permitted to login using the handheld. Terminated employees are not permitted to login to the system. |
| Menu Selection | Menus are automatically displayed based on a user's job code. Events are supported but real-time events are not supported. To get a new menu, the user must logout and login again. |
| Mobile Printing | Receipts can be printed to a mobile printer. |
| | Each individual item can be modified. Users will be prompted when there are mandatory modifiers associated with an item. - Keypad |

*(continued)*

**Exhibit 3**   *(continued)*

| | | |
|---|---|---|
| | Modifiers | The Keypad allows the user to write unique instructions for a particular item. An image of a pencil will be placed to the left of the item that has been modified with the keypad.<br><br>**- Modifier Group Buttons**<br><br>A scrollable list of modifier group buttons is displayed for each item. However, the user can elect not to display the modifier group button on the handheld. |
| | Multiple Checks | More than one check can be associated with each table. The maximum number of checks per table is 20. |
| | Payment Processing | Cash, credit card, gift certificate and other payment options can be processed from the handheld. Credit card processing can be used in conjunction with a mobile credit card scanning device or the user can manually enter the credit card information. |
| | Pivot Seating | Associates an item with a seat number. Pivot seating must be highlighted and deleted in order to change the seat number once it has been assigned to an item. |
| | Tabs | Tabs allow the user to customize a check by name, most often used in a bar setting. Only the "Sees Tabs" setting is supported. |

Source: Ameranth Wireless, Inc., San Diego, Calif. For more information, browse the company's Web site at http://www.ameranth.com.

# POS Printers

Cashier terminal printers are sometimes described as either on-board or remote printing devices. On-board printing devices are normally located within six feet of the terminal that they serve. These devices include guest check printers and receipt printers. Remote printing devices include work station printers and journal printers that are located more than six feet from the terminal that they support. Each remote printing device requires separate cabling.

One of the most important peripheral devices in a POS system with remote work station devices is the **printer controller**, also called a network controller. A printer controller coordinates communications between cashier or precheck terminals and work station printers or remote monitors, while ensuring that servers need only enter orders once. Exhibit 5 diagrams the function of a printer controller.

When several precheck terminals send data to the same work station printer or remote monitor simultaneously, the printer controller processes data from one of the terminals immediately and temporarily stores (buffers) other communications until the remote device becomes available. As the remote printer or remote monitor outputs data sent from one terminal, the printer controller sends the next set of data, and so on, until all orders are printed or displayed. Since remote work station units are typically very fast, the time delay between order entry and printout is minimal—even for those orders temporarily held by the printer controller.

**Exhibit 4  Sample Hardware Configuration for Wireless Hand-Held Server Terminals**

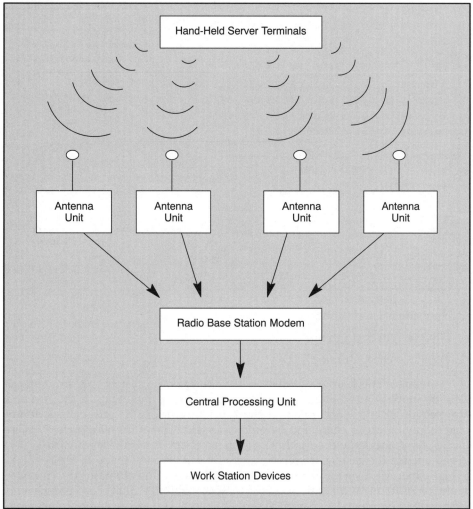

Without a printer controller, a remote work station unit would be able to receive and print only one set of data at a time. When the remote printer is receiving data from one terminal, servers entering orders at other precheck terminals would receive a "bottleneck" response, much like a telephone busy signal. Orders would have to be re-input, since the original orders would not have been received or stored anywhere in the POS system.

## Guest Check Printers

Sometimes called slip printers, **guest check printers** of most POS systems are capable of:

**Exhibit 5    The Function of a Printer Controller**

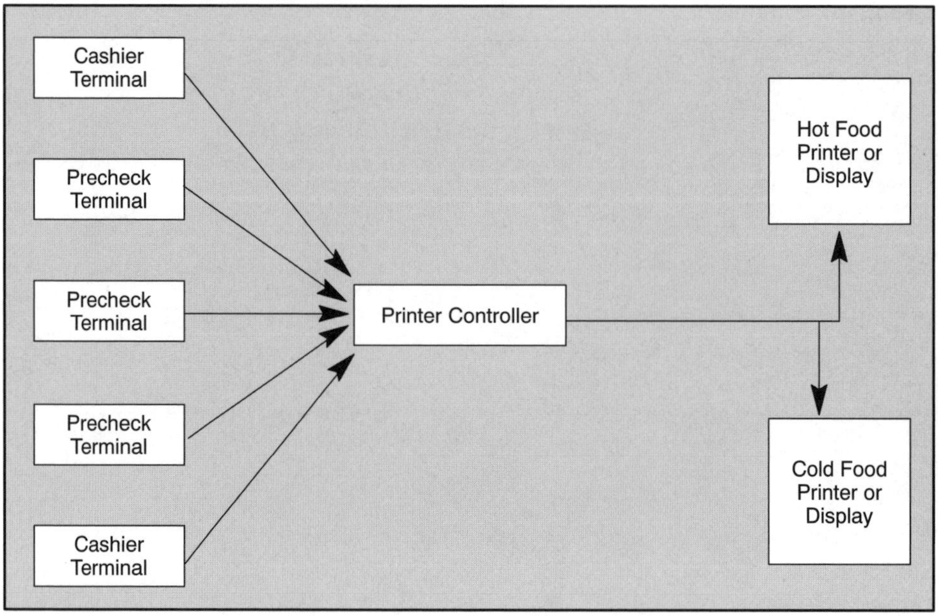

- Immediate check printing.
- Delayed check printing.
- Retained check printing.

Immediate check printing refers to the ability of the system to print items as they are input at a terminal; delayed check printing prints items at the end of a complete order entry; and retained check printing prints the guest check at any time following order entry and before settlement. There are two types of guest checks: **hard checks** and **soft checks**. A hard check is a stiff-paper card that is stored outside the cashier terminal system. A soft check is made of light-weight receipt paper. Hard check printers may be equipped with automatic form number reader (AFNR) and automatic slip feed (ASF) capabilities. Since hard checks tend to be serially numbered and printed sequentially as orders are entered, these features are quite important. Soft check printers, however, do not require such technology, since the complete guest check is printed just prior to settlement. Soft check devices are easy to use and popular because credit or debit card settlement can be recorded directly on the guest check.

An **automatic form number reader** facilitates order-entry procedures. Instead of a server manually inputting a guest check's serial number to access the account, a bar code imprinted on the guest check presents the check's serial number in a machine-readable format. A server simply slips the guest check into the terminal's AFNR unit, and the AFNR provides rapid access to the guest check account.

An **automatic slip feed** capability prevents overprinting items and amounts on guest checks. POS systems without ASF capability require that a server insert a guest check into the printer's slot and manually align the printer's ribbon with the next blank printing line on the guest check. This can be an awkward procedure for servers to follow during busy meal periods. If the alignment is not correct, the guest check appears disorganized and messy with items and amounts printed over one another or with large gaps between lines. A system with ASF capability retains a record of the line number of the last line printed for each open guest check. The server simply aligns the top edge of a guest check with the top edge of the printer's slot, and the terminal automatically moves the check to the next available printing line and prints the order-entry data. Since guest checks are placed within the printer's slot the same way every time, servers may spend less time manipulating machinery and more time meeting their guests' needs. In addition, guests receive neatly printed, easy-to-read checks for settlement.

Exhibit 6 presents an itemized hard check produced by a guest check printer with an automatic form number reader and automatic slip feed capability. The bar code is printed in the upper right-hand corner of the guest check. The printed order follows a sequence of departments rather than the sequence in which the server actually wrote the order or entered the order at a precheck terminal.

## Receipt Printers

These printing devices produce hard copy on narrow register tape. In addition to printing soft checks, a **receipt printer** may help control the production of menu items that are not prepared at departments receiving orders through remote display or printing devices. For example, when servers prepare desserts, and the pantry area is not equipped with a remote communication device, desserts could be served without ever being entered into the system. When this happens, it is also possible that desserts could be served without amounts ever being posted to guest checks and without the desserts being paid for. This situation can be avoided with a receipt printer. Servers preparing desserts may be required to deliver a receipt tape to the dessert pantry area as proof that the items are properly posted to guest checks for eventual settlement. This procedure ensures that every menu item served is printed somewhere in the system, enhancing management's internal control.

## Work Station Printers

Remote printers (or monitors) are usually placed at kitchen preparation areas and service bars. As orders are entered at precheck terminals, they are sent to a designated remote **work station printer** (or remote monitor) to initiate production. Exhibit 7 shows printouts produced by remote work station printers. The printouts correspond to items appearing on the sample guest check illustrated in Exhibit 6. This communications system enables servers to spend more time meeting their guests' needs while significantly reducing traffic between the dining room and the kitchen and also in bar areas.

If the need for hard copy output in production areas is not critical to an operation's internal control system, remote display units (also called **kitchen monitors**) may be viable alternatives to work station printers. Since these units display

**Exhibit 6   Sample Guest Check**

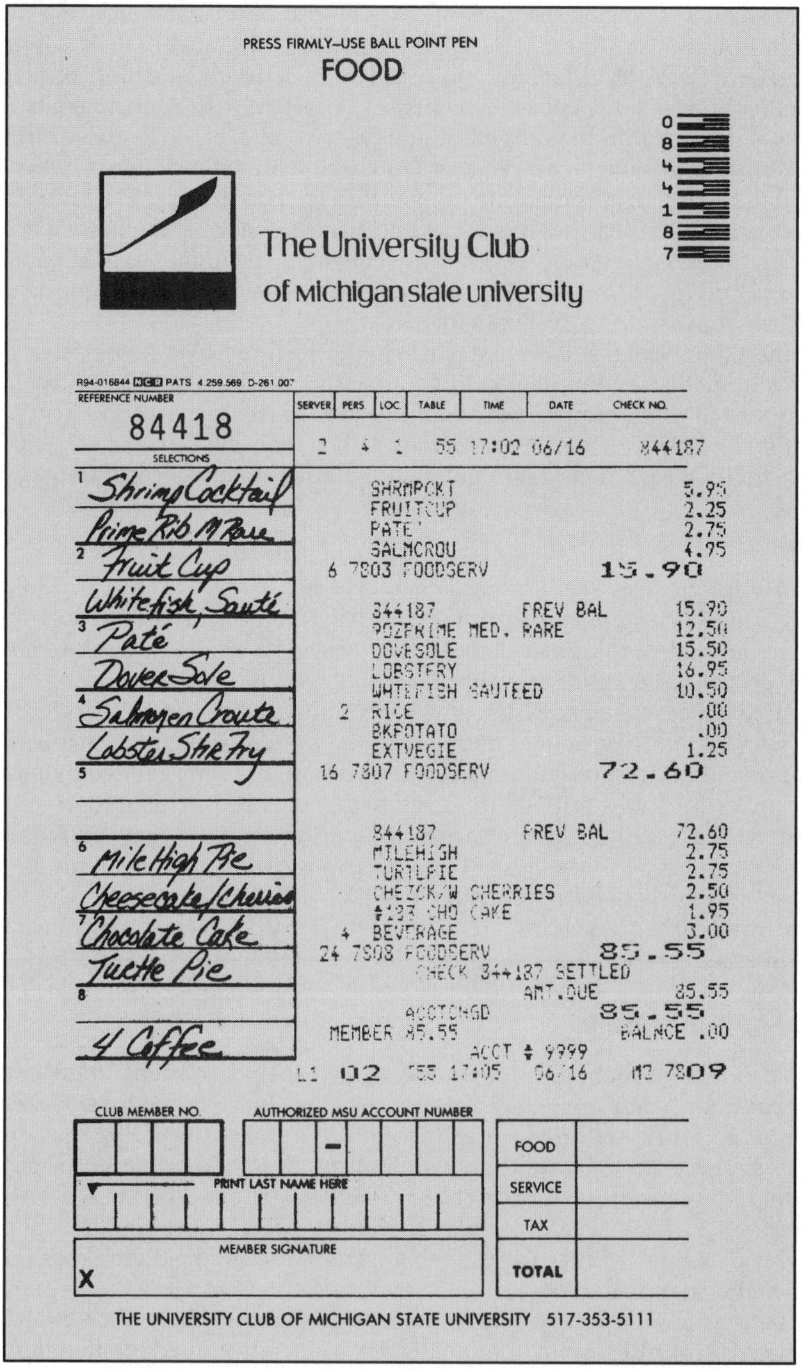

PRESS FIRMLY—USE BALL POINT PEN

## FOOD

The University Club
of michigan state university

| REFERENCE NUMBER | SERVER | PERS | LOC | TABLE | TIME | DATE | CHECK NO. |
|---|---|---|---|---|---|---|---|
| 84418 | 2 | 4 | 1 | 55 | 17:02 | 06/16 | 844187 |

SELECTIONS

1 *Shrimp Cocktail*
*Prime Rib N Rare*
2 *Fruit Cup*
*Whitefish, Sauté*
3 *Paté*
*Dover Sole*
4 *Salmon en Croute*
*Lobster Stir Fry*
5

6 *Mile High Pie*
*Cheesecake/Cherries*
7 *Chocolate Cake*
*Turtle Pie*
8

*4 Coffee*

```
                SHRMPCKT              5.95
                FRUITCUP              2.25
                PATE'                 2.75
                SALMCROU              4.95
         6 7803 FOODSERV             15.90

                844187      FREV BAL  15.90
                POZPRIME MED. RARE    12.50
                DOVESOLE              15.50
                LOBSTFRY              16.95
                WHTEFISH SAUTEED      10.50
             2  RICE                   .00
                BKPOTATO               .00
                EXTVEGIE              1.25
        16 7807 FOODSERV             72.60

                844187      FREV BAL  72.60
                MILEHIGH              2.75
                TURTLPIE              2.75
                CHEZCK/W CHERRIES     2.50
                #133 CHO CAKE         1.95
             4  BEVERAGE             3.00
        24 7808 FOODSERV             85.55
             CHECK 844187 SETTLED
                        AMT.DUE       85.55
                ACCTCHGD
        MEMBER 85.55          BALNCE  .00
                     ACCT # 9999
        L1 02   55 17:05   06/16   N2 7809
```

| CLUB MEMBER NO. | AUTHORIZED MSU ACCOUNT NUMBER | |
|---|---|---|
| | — | FOOD |
| PRINT LAST NAME HERE | | SERVICE |
| | | TAX |
| MEMBER SIGNATURE | | **TOTAL** |
| X | | |

THE UNIVERSITY CLUB OF MICHIGAN STATE UNIVERSITY   517-353-5111

Courtesy of The University Club, Michigan State University, East Lansing, Michigan

**Exhibit 7   Sample Work Station Printouts**

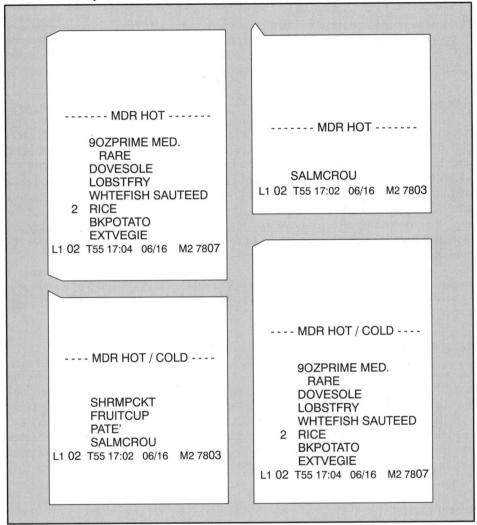

```
------- MDR HOT -------

  9OZPRIME MED.
   RARE
  DOVESOLE
  LOBSTFRY
  WHTEFISH SAUTEED
2  RICE
  BKPOTATO
  EXTVEGIE
L1 02  T55 17:04  06/16   M2 7807
```

```
------- MDR HOT -------



  SALMCROU
L1 02  T55 17:02  06/16   M2 7803
```

```
---- MDR HOT / COLD ----



  SHRMPCKT
  FRUITCUP
  PATE'
  SALMCROU
L1 02  T55 17:02  06/16   M2 7803
```

```
---- MDR HOT / COLD ----

  9OZPRIME MED.
   RARE
  DOVESOLE
  LOBSTFRY
  WHTEFISH SAUTEED
2  RICE
  BKPOTATO
  EXTVEGIE
L1 02  T55 17:04  06/16   M2 7807
```

Courtesy of The University Club, Michigan State University, East Lansing, Michigan

several orders on a single screen, kitchen employees do not have to handle numerous pieces of paper. An accompanying cursor control keypad enables kitchen employees to easily review previously submitted orders by scrolling full screens at a time.

## Journal Printers

A remote **journal printer** produces a continuous detailed record of all transactions entered anywhere in the POS system. Journal printers are usually located in secure areas away from service and production areas. Hard copy may be produced on narrow register tape (usually 20 columns wide) or printed on letter size (8 ¹/₂" by 11") paper, and it provides management with a thorough system audit. In addition to providing an audit trail, journal printers also print a variety of management reports. Management routinely reviews journal printouts to verify that the system is functioning properly.

# Account Settlement

A **magnetic strip reader** is an optional input device that connects to a cashier terminal. Magnetic strip readers do not replace keyboards, touch-screen devices, or optical character recognition terminals. Instead, they extend their capabilities. Magnetic strip readers are capable of collecting data stored on a magnetized film strip typically located on the back of a credit card, debit card, or house account card. As explained earlier, terminals equipped with magnetic strip readers can be used by employees with plastic, bar-coded identification cards to sign into the system. Also, managers can use specially encoded cards to access ongoing transactions and other operational data.

With magnetic strip readers, credit card, debit card, and house account transactions can be handled directly within a POS system. The connection of a magnetic strip reader to a cashier terminal allows rapid data entry and efficient settlement processing.

## Power Platforms

Processing credit and debit card transactions is simplified when a **power platform** is used to consolidate electronic communications between a hospitality establishment and a credit card authorization center. A POS power platform connects all POS terminals to a single processor for transaction settlement. This eliminates the need for individual telephone lines at each POS cashier terminal. Power platforms can capture credit card authorizations in a few seconds or less. This swift data retrieval helps reduce the time, cost, and risk associated with credit and debit card transactions.

## Smart Cards

**Smart cards** are made of plastic and are the same size as credit cards. Microchips embedded in smart cards store information that can be accessed by a specially designed card reader. Smart cards can store information in several files that are accessed for different functions. For example, a smart card could store a person's vital health statistics, dietary restrictions, credit card number, and bank account information. The security of information stored in smart cards is controlled through a personal identification number (PIN) that must be used to access files.

Since smart cards contain the necessary information for completing electronic purchases, a specially designed card reader processes the transaction and reduces the cash value stored on the card very quickly. No bank or credit company authorizations are required.

## Debit Cards

**Debit cards** differ from credit cards in that the cardholder must deposit money in a bank account in order to establish settlement value. The cardholder deposits money in advance of purchases through a debit card center, a bank, or an ATM. As purchases are made, the balance in the debit account is adjusted accordingly. For example, a cardholder who has deposited $300 to a debit card account has a value of $300 available for transaction settlement. As the cardholder makes purchases, the value of the debit account decreases accordingly. To settle the transaction, the money is electronically transferred from the customer's account to the business account. A debit card is similar to an ATM card in that the purchaser must have cash on account to complete a transaction successfully.

## Managing Guest Accounts

Managing guest accounts is important regardless of whether a hard check or soft check POS system is used. Before entering an order, the server "opens" the guest check within the system by inputting his or her identification number. Once the system has recognized the server and opened a new guest check, orders are entered and relayed to remote printers (or monitors) at production areas. The same items (with their selling prices) are printed on the server's guest check.

Once a guest check has been opened, it becomes part of the system's **open check file**. For each opened guest check, this file may contain the following data:

- Terminal number where the guest check was opened.
- Guest check serial number (if appropriate).
- Server identification number.
- Time guest check was created.
- Menu items ordered.
- Selling prices of items ordered.
- Applicable tax.
- Total amount due.

A server adds orders to the guest check by first inputting at the terminal the guest check's serial number (or other identifier) and then entering the additional items.

There are many variations of this automated system. As described earlier in this chapter, some systems use guest checks with bar codes corresponding to the pre-printed serial numbers. This eliminates the need for servers to input the guest check's serial number when opening a guest check or when adding items to guest checks already in use. When the guest check is placed in the guest check printer, the system reads the bar code and immediately accesses the appropriate file.

Soft check systems eliminate the traditional guest check altogether. These systems maintain only an electronic file for each open guest check. A receipt-like guest check can be printed at any time during service, but is usually not printed until after the meal when the server presents a final version of the check to the guest for settlement. Since no paper forms are used during service, the table number often is the tracking identifier for the order. With some systems, seat numbers are used for tracking multiple checks per table. When presenting soft checks to guests for settlement, the receipt-like guest checks can be inserted in high-quality paper, vinyl, or leather presentation jackets.

Most POS systems feature a soft guest check that also serves as a credit card or debit card voucher. This often reduces the time it takes servers to settle guest checks. Instead of presenting the guest check, collecting the guest's credit or debit card, printing a voucher, transferring information from the guest check to the voucher, and then presenting the voucher to the guest to sign, servers are able to present the guest check and the credit or debit card voucher simultaneously.

Point-of-sale technology simplifies guest check control functions and eliminates the need for time-consuming manual audit procedures. Automated pre-checking functions eliminate mistakes servers make in pricing items on guest checks or in calculating totals. When items must be voided, a supervisor (with a special identification number) accesses the system and deletes the items. Generally, automated systems produce a report that lists all guest checks with voided or returned items, the servers responsible, and the supervisors who voided the items. It is important for automated systems to distinguish voided from returned items because returned items should be included in inventory usage reports while voided items may not. If an item is voided after it has been prepared, the item typically is classified as "returned."

At any point, managers and supervisors can access the system and monitor the status of an open or closed guest check. This check-tracking capability can help identify potential walkouts, reduce server fraud, and tighten guest check and sales income control.

The status of a guest check changes from open to closed when payment is received from the guest and is recorded in the system. Most automated systems produce an **outstanding checks report** that lists all guest checks (by server) that have not been settled. These reports may list the guest check number, server identification number, time at which the guest check was opened, number of guests, table number, and guest check total. This makes it easier for managers to determine responsibility for unsettled guest checks. Exhibit 8 presents a sample server check-out report. Note that the report lists time in, time out, hours worked, number of guests served, tables attended, net sales, and tip information.

## POS Software

The hardware of any computer system does nothing by itself. There must be a set of software programs directing the system in what to do, how to do it, and when to do it. POS application software not only directs internal system operations, but also maintains files and produces reports for management. Files that may be stored and maintained by a POS systems include:

- Menu item file.
- Labor master file.
- Inventory file.

**Exhibit 8   Sample Server Check-Out Report**

# MRS
# DEMONSTRATION

Server: **ANNA**

Date: **11/20**

| In Time | Out Time | Total |
|---------|----------|-------|
| 12:36 | 15:23 | 02:47 |
| 15:25 | 15:26 | 00:01 |

Total Hours Worked: **02:48**

|         | Persons | Tables | Net | Tips |
|---------|---------|--------|--------|-------|
| Lunch:  | 19 | 6 | 290.55 | 39.71 |
| Dinner: | 0  | 0 | 0.00   | 0.00  |
| Total:  | 19 | 6 | 290.55 | 39.71 |

| | |
|---|---|
| Tips on Credit Cards: | 39.71 |
| Credit Card Surcharge: | 1.99 |
| Net Total Tips: | 37.72 |
| Balance Due: | **37.72** |

Source: Genlor Systems, Inc., Northport, New York.

Data maintained by these files (and others) can be accessed by POS terminals, and formatted reports can be generated. The following sections briefly examine these files and the types of data stored by each.

## Menu Item File

A **menu item file** usually contains data for all menu items tracked by a POS system. Records within this file may contain the following data:

- Identification number.
- Descriptor.
- Price.
- Tax.
- Applicable modifier keys.
- Amount totals for inventory reporting.
- Printer routing code.

This file is generally used to monitor menu keyboard operations. Management can control information about current menu items for various meal periods. Reports can be produced for each meal period identifying menu item descriptor, price, and applicable taxes. When menu items, prices, or taxes need to be changed, the menu item file is accessed and appropriate changes are entered according to procedures indicated in the user's manual provided by the system's vendor.

## Labor Master File

Some POS systems can be used as a time clock system, enabling employees to sign in and sign out. The software can then compute gross time worked based on a labor master file. The **labor master file** of a POS system contains one record for each employee and typically maintains the following data:

- Employee name.
- Employee number.
- Social security number.
- Authorized job codes.
- Hourly wage rates.

This file may also contain data required to produce labor reports for management. Each record in the labor master file may accumulate:

- Hours worked.
- Gross hourly wages.
- Declared wages.
- Tips (or tip credits).
- Credits for employee meals.
- Number of guests served (if appropriate).
- Gross sales generated.

Many POS systems are unable to compute net pay figures because of restricted processing ability and limited memory capacity. Data accumulated by the labor master file can be used to produce a number of reports, such as a labor master report and daily, weekly, and period labor reports. The labor master file can also be exported to a back office labor accounting software package to generate a comprehensive set of labor reports.

A POS **labor master report** contains general data maintained by the labor master file. This report is commonly used to verify an employee's hourly rate(s), job code(s), or social security number.

A POS **daily labor report** typically lists the names, employee numbers, hours worked, wages earned, and wages declared for each employee. A **weekly labor report** contains similar information and may be used to determine which employees are approaching overtime pay rates. A **period labor report** generally

**Exhibit 9    Sample Daily Labor Report**

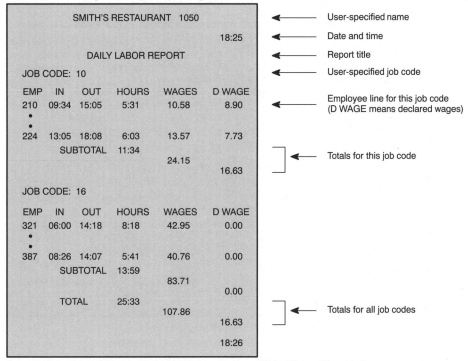

| SMITH'S RESTAURANT 1050 | | | | | | | User-specified name |
| | | | | | 18:25 | | Date and time |
| DAILY LABOR REPORT | | | | | | | Report title |
| JOB CODE: 10 | | | | | | | User-specified job code |
| EMP | IN | OUT | HOURS | WAGES | D WAGE | | Employee line for this job code (D WAGE means declared wages) |
| 210 | 09:34 | 15:05 | 5:31 | 10.58 | 8.90 | | |
| 224 | 13:05 | 18:08 | 6:03 | 13.57 | 7.73 | | |
| | SUBTOTAL | | 11:34 | | | | Totals for this job code |
| | | | | 24.15 | | | |
| | | | | | 16.63 | | |
| JOB CODE: 16 | | | | | | | |
| EMP | IN | OUT | HOURS | WAGES | D WAGE | | |
| 321 | 06:00 | 14:18 | 8:18 | 42.95 | 0.00 | | |
| 387 | 08:26 | 14:07 | 5:41 | 40.76 | 0.00 | | |
| | SUBTOTAL | | 13:59 | | | | |
| | | | | 83.71 | | | |
| | | | | | 0.00 | | |
| | TOTAL | | 25:33 | | | | Totals for all job codes |
| | | | | 107.86 | | | |
| | | | | | 16.63 | | |
| | | | | | 18:26 | | |

Source: International Business Machines Corporation, White Plains, New York.

lists hour and wage information for each employee who worked during the period specified by management. Exhibit 9 illustrates a sample POS daily labor report.

Data stored in the POS labor master file may also be used to produce daily, weekly, and period employee meal reports that show amounts for meals provided to employees. Also, a weekly and period employee tips report may be printed showing the total tips reported by each employee.

## Inventory File

The **inventory file** maintained by a POS system may not meet all the inventory control needs of some properties. Most POS systems are incapable of tracking the same item as it passes through the control points of receiving, storing, issuing, and production. Inventory data must be specific to each of these control points because purchase units (case, drum, etc.) commonly differ from storeroom inventory units (#10 can, gallon, etc.), which, in turn, differ from standard recipe units (ounce, cup, etc.). Many systems are not able to support the number of conversion tables necessary to track menu items through ingredient purchase, storage, and use (standard recipe).

Since operators do not purchase inventory ingredients on a pre-portioned basis, they very often encounter significant problems when trying to implement a

**Exhibit 10    Sample Sales and Payment Summary Report**

| SALES | | LUNCH | DINNER | BRUNCH | TOTAL |
|---|---|---|---|---|---|
| 1 NUMBER OF CUSTOMERS | | 110 | 89 | . | 199 |
| 2 TAXABLE FOOD TOTAL | | 2455.50 | 2093.00 | . | 4558.50 |
| 3 TAXABLE BEVERAGES TOTAL | | 1371.00 | 1382.75 | . | 2753.75 |
| TOTAL FOOD & BEVERAGE (before tax) | | 3826.50 | 3475.75 | . | 7302.25 |
| SALES TAX | | 315.69 | 286.75 | . | 602.44 |
| 4 NONTAXABLE FOOD TOTAL | | . | . | . | . |
| 5 NONTAXABLE BEVERAGE TOTAL | | . | . | . | . |
| TOTAL | | 4142.19 | 3762.50 | . | 7904.69 |
| % OF SALES | | 52.40 | 47.60 | . | |

| PAYMENTS | #CKS | TAXABLE | NONTAX. | TAX | TIPS | GROSS | CARD FEE | NET |
|---|---|---|---|---|---|---|---|---|
| 6 CASH | 3 | 482.50 | . | 39.81 | . | 522.31 | . | 482.50 |
| 7 CHECK | 3 | 318.25 | . | 26.26 | . | 344.51 | . | 318.25 |
| 8 HOUSE CH. | 3 | 1017.00 | . | 83.90 | 57.00 | 1157.90 | . | 1017.00 |
| 9 AMEX | 40 | 5484.50 | . | 452.47 | 298.50 | 6235.47 | 222.64 | 5261.86 |
| 10 DC | 0 | . | . | . | . | . | . | . |
| 11 VISA/MC | 0 | . | . | . | . | . | . | . |
| CARD SUBTOT | 40 | 5484.50 | . | 452.47 | 298.50 | 6235.47 | 222.64 | 5261.86 |
| TOTAL | 49 | 7302.25 | . | 602.44 | 355.50 | 8260.49 | 222.64 | 7079.61 |

Source: Integrated Restaurant Software, Fort Lee, New Jersey.

POS-based inventory control system. In addition, the initial creation of an ingredient file and the subsequent file updates (daily, weekly, monthly, etc.) can be an overwhelming task for some operations. For example, a restaurant typically carries an average of 400 menu items and an average inventory of 1,500 ingredients and monitors at least 12 to 18 high-cost inventory items on a perpetual basis. POS systems may not be able to support the files necessary for effective inventory control.

## Consolidated Reports

POS systems may access data contained in several files to produce consolidated reports for use by management. Such reports typically include daily revenue reports, sales analysis reports, summary **activity reports**, and productivity reports. Data captured by a POS system can be exported to a back office accounting software package for more extensive report generation.

A POS **sales and payment summary report** provides managers with a complete statement of daily or monthly sales (by shift and/or broken down by food and beverage categories). The report also summarizes settlement methods. Exhibit 10 illustrates a sample sales and payment summary report.

A POS **sales by time of day report** enables management to measure the sales performance of individual menu items by department or product category within certain time intervals (often called "day parts"). Time intervals may vary in relation to the type of food service operation. Quick service restaurants may desire **sales analysis reports** segmented by 15 minute intervals, table service restaurants

**Exhibit 11    Sample Sales by Time of Day Report**

```
        Date  8-30
        Time  5:31 A.M.        SALES BY TIME OF DAY
        --------- CURRENT --------    --------- TO DATE ---------
   Stn  Sales  Trans Cvrs  Avg    Avg    Sales    Trans Cvrs  Avg    Avg
                           $/Trns $/Cvr                       $/Trns $/Cvr

08:01- 09:00  01-  141.85   9   25  15.76  5.67    141.85    9   25  15.76  5.67
              02-  372.75  13   43  28.67  8.67    372.75   13   43  28.67  8.67
               -   514.60  22   68  23.39  7.57    514.60   22   68  23.39  7.57

09:01 - 10:00 01-   12.30   2    5   6.15  2.46     12.30    2    5   6.15  2.46
               -    12.30   2    5   6.15  2.46    242.40   18   36  13.47  6.73

10:01 - 11:00 01-  183.85  10   34  18.39  5.41    183.85   10   34  18.39  5.41
              02-  464.90  13   74  35.76  6.28  1,173.80   50  196  23.48  5.99
               -   648.75  23  108  28.21  6.01  1,357.65   60  230  22.63  5.90

11:01 - 12:00 01-   22.75   1    2  22.75 11.38     22.75    1    2  22.75 11.38
              02-   24.55   2    4  12.28  6.14    178.40   12   35  14.87  5.10
               -    47.30   3    6  15.77  7.88    201.15   13   37  15.47  5.44

12:01 - 13:00 01-   54.20   3    6  18.07  9.03     54.20    3    6  18.07  9.03
              02-   45.20   4    8  11.30  5.65     45.20    4    8  11.30  5.65
               -    99.40   7   14  14.20  7.10     99.40    7   14  14.20  7.10

13:01 - 14:00 01-   31.15   2    8  15.58  3.89     31.15    2    8  15.58  3.89
              02-   38.90   2    4  19.45  9.73     38.90    2    4  19.45  9.73
               -    70.05   4   12  17.51  5.84     70.05    4   12  17.51  5.84

   Total     - 1,392.40  61  213  22.83  6.54  2,485.25  124  397  20.04  6.26
```

Source: American Business Computers, Akron, Ohio.

by the hour, and institutional food service operations by meal period. A sales analysis report allows management to track individual item sales, analyze product acceptance, and monitor advertising and sales promotional efforts. A sample sales by time of day report is shown in Exhibit 11.

Exhibit 12 presents a sample POS **daily transactions report** that provides an in-depth analysis of sales transactions by individual server. POS **productivity reports** typically detail sales activity for all assigned server sales records. Daily productivity reports may be generated for each server and cashier in terms of guest count, total revenue, and average revenue. In addition, a weekly productivity report may be generated, showing average sales per guest for each server.

# Automated Beverage Control Systems

Automated beverage systems reduce many of the time-consuming management tasks associated with controlling beverage operations. While automated beverage

**Exhibit 12   Sample Daily Transactions Report**

|  |  | Date | 8-30 |  |  |  |  |  |  |  |  |  |  |
|---|---|---|---|---|---|---|---|---|---|---|---|---|---|
|  |  | Time | 5:31 A.M. |  | DAILY TRANSACTIONS |  |  |  |  |  |  |  |  |

| Guest Check | Tabl/ Covrs | Employee | ID | Time In | Time Out | Elapsed Time | Food | Bar | Wine | Guest Total | Tax | Tip | Settlement Method | Settlement Amount |
|---|---|---|---|---|---|---|---|---|---|---|---|---|---|---|
| 11378 | 2-2 | Jones | 4 | 8:23 | 9:00 | 0:37 | 13.75 | 0.00 | 3.50 | 17.25 | 0.87 | 2.00 | CASH | 20.12 |
| 11379 | 2-1 | Jones | 4 | 8:25 | 9:00 | 0:35 | 2.35 | 0.00 | 0.00 | 2.35 | 0.12 | 0.00 | COMP 1 0004 | 2.47 |
| 11380 | 3-3 | Jones | 4 | 8:32 | 9:01 | 0:29 | 13.15 | 0.00 | 5.50 | 18.65 | 0.93 | 0.00 | CASH COMP 2 0033 | 9.58 10.00 |
| 11381 | 4-4 | Jones | 4 | 8:34 | 9:16 | 0:42 | 9.05 | 0.00 | 0.00 | 9.05 | 0.47 | 0.00 | MC | 9.52 |
| 11382 | 3-2 | Jones | 4 | 8:40 | 9:18 | 0:38 | 6.20 | 0.00 | 5.50 | 11.70 | 0.60 | 0.00 | Cancelled | |
| 11383 | 3-2 | Jones | 4 | 8:41 | 9:19 | 0:38 | 4.35 | 0.00 | 0.00 | 4.35 | 0.22 | 0.00 | COMP 1 0004 | 4.57 |
| 11384 | 4-4 | Jones | 4 | 8:43 | 10:16 | 1:33 | 33.80 | 11.00 | 0.00 | 44.80 | 2.25 | 0.00 | AMEXPRESS | 47.05 |
| 11385 | 4-2 | Jones | 4 | 8:46 | 10:17 | 1:31 | 0.00 | 9.75 | 0.00 | 9.75 | 0.49 | 0.00 | VISA | 10.24 |
| 11386 | 4-5 | Jones | 4 | 8:51 | 10:17 | 1:26 | 0.00 | 18.50 | 0.00 | 18.50 | 0.91 | 0.00 | MC | 19.41 |
| 11387 | 8-2 | Jones | 4 | 8:54 | 10:18 | 1:24 | 14.65 | 2.50 | 0.00 | 17.15 | 0.85 | 0.00 | COMP 1 0004 | 18.00 |
| 11388 | 4-3 | Jones | 4 | 9:23 | 10:17 | 0:54 | 4.70 | 3.00 | 0.00 | 7.70 | 0.39 | 1.00 | CASH | 9.09 |
| 11389 | 2-2 | Jones | 4 | 9:34 | 10:16 | 0:42 | 4.60 | 0.00 | 0.00 | 4.60 | 0.24 | 0.00 | CASH | 4.84 |
| 11398 | 3-2 | Jones | 4 | 12:09 | 12:10 | 0:01 | 11.35 | 0.00 | 0.00 | 11.35 | 0.57 | 0.00 | CASH | 11.92 |
| 11399 | 3-2 | Jones | 4 | 12:20 | 12:21 | 0:01 | 10.25 | 2.00 | 0.00 | 12.25 | 0.61 | 0.00 | CASH | 12.86 |
| 21615 | 3-2 | Jones | 4 | 11:39 | 11:41 | 0:02 | 13.15 | 0.00 | 0.00 | 13.15 | 0.65 | 0.00 | CASH | 13.80 |
| 21616 | 1-2 | Jones | 4 | 11:40 | 11:41 | 0:01 | 7.90 | 0.00 | 3.50 | 11.40 | 0.58 | 0.00 | CASH | 11.98 |
| | Total cancelled | | 11.70 | | | | | | | | | | | |
| | **** Totals | | | | | | 143.05 | 46.75 | 12.50 | 202.30 | 10.15 | 3.00 | | 215.45 |

Source: American Business Computers, Akron, Ohio.

systems vary, most systems can dispense drinks according to the operation's standard drink recipes and monitor the number of drinks poured.

Automated beverage systems can be programmed to dispense both alcoholic and non-alcoholic products with different portion sizes. A beverage control system can also generate projected sales information based on different pricing periods as defined by management. With many systems the station at which drinks are prepared can be connected to a guest check printer that records every sale as drinks are dispensed. As a control technique, some systems require that a guest check be inserted into the printer before a drink can be dispensed. Most equipment can, and should, be connected to the bar POS system to automatically track all sales generated through automated equipment.

With one type of automated beverage system, liquor is stored at the bar. Price-coded pourers (special nozzles) are inserted into each bottle. These pourers cannot dispense liquor without a special activator ring. The bartender slips the neck of a liquor bottle (with the price-coded pourer already inserted) into the ring and prepares the drink with a conventional hand-pouring motion. A cord connects the activator ring to a master control panel that records the number of drinks poured at each price level. The master control panel is typically connected to a point-of-sale system that records the sale. Some master control panels are equipped with printers and can produce sales reports for each station. Reports indicate the number of drinks poured at different price levels and the total expected revenue from each station.

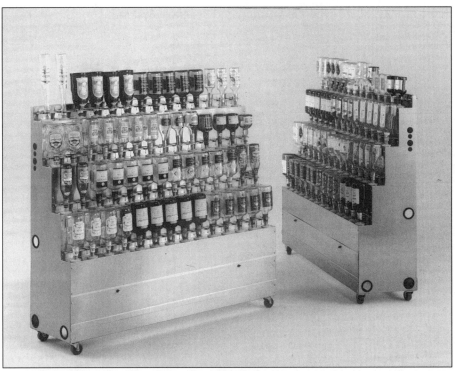

**An Automated Beverage Control and Storage System.** (Courtesy of American Business Computers, Akron, Ohio)

With another type of automated beverage system, liquor is stored in racks in a locked storage room located away from the service areas. The bartender prepares a drink by pushing the appropriate key on a keyboard. The liquor and necessary mixes travel to a dispensing device at the bar through separate, high quality, plastic tubing. The system pours the drink when the bartender holds the glass (with ice) under the dispensing device. The drink is then garnished and served to the guest. Exhibit 13 diagrams the layout of one type of keyboard-operated automated beverage control system.

Keyboard-operated automated beverage control systems may employ different types of sensing devices that increase operational controls and maintain data integrity within the system. Three common sensing devices are glass sensors, guest check sensors, and empty bottle sensors. A **glass sensor** is an electronic mechanism located in a bar dispensing unit that will not permit liquid to flow from the dispensing unit unless there is a glass in place to catch the liquid below the dispensing head. **Guest check sensors** prevent the system from fulfilling beverage orders unless they are first recorded on a guest check. When a server places a beverage order whose ingredients are close to becoming out-of-stock, an **empty bottle sensor** relays a signal to the order-entry device.

Automated beverage control systems can enhance production and service capabilities while improving accounting and operational controls. Systems can

**Exhibit 13   Keyboard-Operated Automated Beverage System**

OFFICE

⑤ *INVENTORY IS DEPLETED AT CPU/MRP*

③ *CPU INITIATES DISPENSING AT ECR*

① *DRINK SELECTION MADE AT ABC ECR*

BAR

⑤ *AS DRINK IS POURED PRICING IS INDICATED AT ECR*

**BOTTLE STORAGE**   ② *ECR REQUEST TRANSMITTED TO ABC CPU*

④ *COMPLETED DRINK REQUEST POURED. ALL INGREDIENTS FOR REQUEST POUR SIMULTANEOUSLY*

**ABC**   ABC BEVERAGE SYSTEM

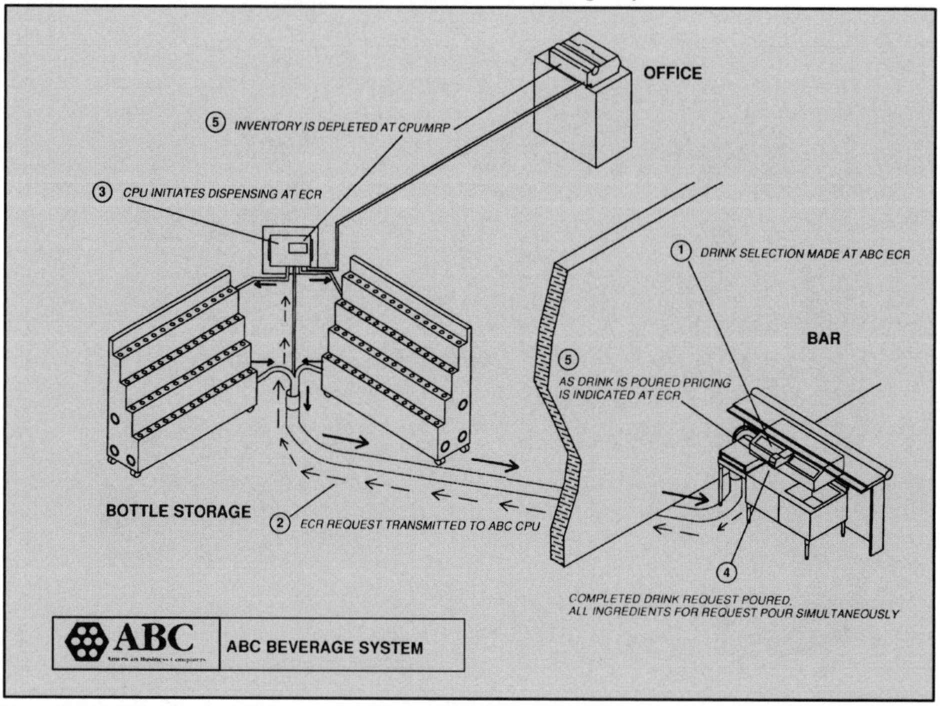

Source: American Business Computers, Akron, Ohio.

record data input through order-entry devices, transport beverage ingredients through a controlled delivery network, dispense ingredients for ordered items, and track important service and sales data that can be used to produce various reports for management. The following sections examine the basic components of an automated beverage control system: order-entry devices, delivery networks, and dispensing units.

## Order-Entry Devices

In an automated beverage control system, the primary function of an order-entry device is to initiate activities involved with recording, producing, and pricing beverage items requested by guests. There are two basic order-entry devices: a group of preset buttons located on a dispensing unit and keyboard units that function as precheck terminals.

A group of preset buttons on a dispensing unit is the most popular order-entry device. These devices may result in lower system costs because the dispensing unit serves as both an order entry and a delivery unit. However, since dispensing units may support a limited number of preset buttons, the number of beverage items under the control of the automated beverage system is limited.

Keyboard units function like precheck terminals; beverage dispensing is performed by a separate piece of hardware. Since keyboards support a full range of

**Exhibit 14    Delivery Network of an Automated Beverage Control System**

*Bottles are not pressurized*—so they can be changed while system is operating.

*Air filtration system*—provides clean, filtered air to the system.

*Automatic drain* prevents moisture from entering the liquor supply lines.

*Easily expandable*—reserves can be connected in series to allow added capacity on any brands.

*Patented Turbo Flo™ pump reserve system*—for high speed pumping of liquor, up to 6 stations.

*Air supply system*—oilless air compressor and air accumulator tank provide constant line pressure. Reserve capacity to pour 72 ounces of drinks even with air supply shut down.

*Components* made only with special "taste-free" materials.

*Liquor control unit*—can be located up to 500 ft. from liquor storage area.

*Master console*—segregated from liquid for added safety and dependability. Up to 3 sets of timers are built-in for control of different liquor viscosities.

*Flexible, stainless hose*—provides convenient 36" reach in the work storage area.

*Stylish, hand-held dispenser gun*—for no-splash portions, from $1/3$ to 6 ounces, with fingertip control.

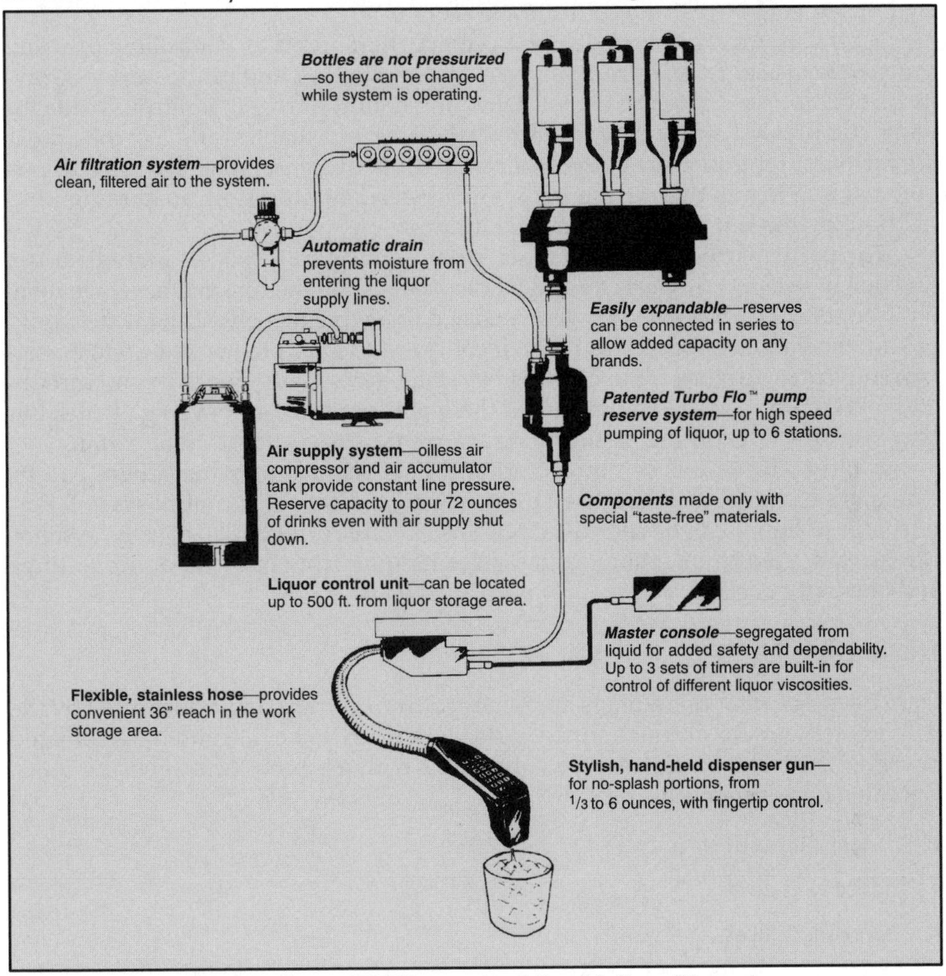

Source: Berg Company, A Division of DEC International, Inc., Madison, Wisconsin.

keys (including preset keys, price look-up keys, and modifier keys), keyboard units place a large number of beverage items under the control of the automated system. Keyboard units may be equipped with a guest check or receipt printer and may feature a colorful array of keys or icons.

## Delivery Networks

An automated beverage control system relies on a **delivery network** to transport beverage item ingredients from storage areas to dispensing units. Exhibit 14 diagrams one kind of delivery network. The delivery network must be a closed system capable of regulating temperature and pressure conditions at various locations and stages of delivery. To maintain proper temperature conditions, the delivery network typically employs a cooling sub-system that controls such mechanisms as cold plates, cold boxes, and cold storage rooms.

Most systems are able to deliver beverage ingredients by controlling pressure sources such as gravity, compressed air, carbon dioxide, and nitrous oxide. Gravity and compressed air are used for delivering liquor, nitrogen or nitrous oxide for wine, compressed air for beer, compressed air for perishables, and a carbon dioxide regulator for post-mixes. A post-mix soft drink dispenser places syrup and carbonated water together at the dispenser instead of storing, transporting, and distributing the soft drink as a finished product.

The particular pressure source selected to transport a specific ingredient is a function of its effect on the taste and wholesomeness of the finished beverage item. For example, if carbon dioxide were attached to a wine dispenser, the wine would be carbonated and spoiled. Similarly, if compressed air were hooked up to a post-mix soft drink dispenser, the finished beverage item would not have any carbonation. Pressure sources not only affect the quality of finished beverage items, but may also affect the timing, flow of mixture, portion size, and desired foaming.

Almost any brand of liquor and accompanying liquor ingredient can be stored, transported, and dispensed by an automated beverage control system. Portion sizes of liquor can be controlled with remarkable accuracy. Typically, systems can be calibrated to maintain portion sizes ranging from one-half ounce to three and one-half ounces.

## Dispensing Units

Once beverage item ingredients are removed from storage and transported by the delivery network to production areas, they are ready to be dispensed. Automated beverage control systems may be configured with a variety of dispensing units. Common dispensing units include:

- Touch-bar faucet.

- Hose and gun.

- Console faucet.

- Mini-tower pedestal.

- Bundled tower.

A touch-bar faucet can be located under the bar, behind the bar, on top of an ice machine, or on a pedestal stand. These devices may not have the versatility, flexibility, or expandability of other dispensing units. Typically, touch-bar faucets are dedicated to only a single beverage type and are preset for one portion size output per push on the bar lever. A double shot of bourbon, therefore, may require the bartender to push twice on the bar lever.

The hose and gun device is a popular dispensing unit. Control buttons on the handle of the gun can be connected to liquors, carbonated beverages, water, and wine tanks. These dispensers can be installed anywhere along the bar and are frequently included as standard equipment on portable bars and at service bar locations. Pressing a control button produces a pre-measured flow of the desired beverage. The number of beverage items under the control of a hose and gun dispensing unit is limited to the number of control buttons the device supports. Some newer units offer the bartender up to 16 buttons.

Console faucet dispensing units are similar to touch-bar faucet devices in that they can be located in almost any part of the bar area. In addition, these units may be located up to 300 feet from beverage storage areas. Unlike touch-bar faucet devices, console faucet units can dispense various beverages in a number of portion sizes. Using buttons located above the faucet unit, a bartender can trigger up to four different portion sizes from the same faucet head. An optional feature of this kind of dispensing device is a double hose faucet unit that provides the capability to transport large quantities of liquids in short amounts of time.

The mini-tower pedestal dispensing unit combines the button selection technique of hose and gun devices with the portion size capabilities of console faucet units. In addition, the mini-tower concept offers increased control of bar operations. In order for a beverage to be dispensed, the mini-tower unit requires that a button be pressed and a glass sensing device requires that a glass be placed directly under the dispensing head. This automated dispensing unit has been popular for dispensing beverage items that need no additional ingredients before service, such as wine, beer, and call brand liquors. A mini-tower unit can also be located on a wall, ice machine, or pedestal base in the bar area.

The most sophisticated and flexible dispensing unit is the bundled tower unit, also referred to as a tube tower unit. The bundled tower unit is designed to dispense a variety of beverage items. Beverage orders must be entered on a separate piece of hardware, not on the tower unit. Bundled tower units may support in excess of 110 beverage products and contain a glass-sensing element. Each liquor has its own line to the tower unit, and a variety of pressurized systems can be used to enhance delivery from storage areas. While other units sequentially dispense beverage item ingredients, the bundled tower unit simultaneously dispenses all ingredients required for a specific beverage item; bar servers merely garnish the finished product. This dispensing unit can be located up to 300 feet from beverage storage areas.

## 🔑 Key Terms

*POS System Hardware*

**automatic form number reader (AFNR)**—A feature of a guest check printer that facilitates order entry; instead of a server manually inputting a guest check's serial number to access the account, a bar code imprinted on the guest check presents the check's serial number in a machine-readable format.

**automatic slip feed (ASF)**—A feature of a guest check printer that prevents overprinting of items and amounts on guest checks.

**cashier terminal**—A POS device that is connected to a cash drawer.

**customer display unit**—A display screen that may rest atop, inside, or alongside the POS device.

**function keys**—When part of a POS system terminal, function keys help the user process transactions; they are important for error correction (clear and void), legitimate price alteration (discount), and proper cash handling (no-sale).

**guest check printer**—A POS on-board printing device that is sometimes called a slip printer. A sophisticated guest check printer may be equipped with an automatic form number reader and may possess automatic slip feed capabilities.

**hard checks**—Guest checks that are made of stiff-paper cards. Hard checks are stored outside the cashier terminal system.

**hard keys**—Keys on a POS system terminal dedicated to specific functions programmed by the manufacturer.

**journal printer**—A remote printing device of a POS system that produces a continuous detailed record of all transactions entered anywhere in the system. Hard copy is produced on narrow register tape (usually 20 columns wide) and provides management with a thorough system audit. In addition to providing an audit trail, journal printers are capable of printing a variety of management reports.

**kitchen monitor**—Video display units capable of displaying several orders on a single screen. An accompanying cursor control keypad enables kitchen employees to easily review previously submitted orders by scrolling full screens at a time.

**menu board**—A keyboard overlay for a POS system terminal that identifies the function performed by each key during a specific meal period.

**modifier keys**—Parts of a POS system keyboard used in combination with preset and price look-up keys to detail preparation instructions (such as rare, medium, and well-done) for food production areas; also used to alter prices according to designated portion sizes (such as small, medium, and large).

**operator monitor**—Part of a POS system terminal enabling the operator to review and edit transaction entries.

**precheck terminal**—A POS system terminal without a cash drawer; used to enter orders, not to settle accounts.

**preset key**—Part of a POS system keyboard programmed to maintain the price, descriptor, department, tax, and inventory status of a menu item.

**price look-up (PLU) key**—Part of a POS system keyboard that operates like a preset key, except that it requires the user to identify a menu item by its reference code number (up to five digits) rather than by its name or descriptor.

**printer controller**—Part of a POS system that coordinates communications between cashier or precheck terminals and work station printers or kitchen monitors, while ensuring that servers need enter their orders only once. Also called a network controller.

**receipt printer**—On-board printing devices that produce hard copy on narrow register tape.

**settlement keys**—Part of a POS system keyboard used to record the methods with which accounts are settled: cash, credit card, house account, charge transfer, or other payment.

**soft checks**—Guest checks made of flimsy receipt paper.

**soft keys**—Parts of a POS system keyboard that can be programmed by users to meet the specific needs of their restaurant operations.

**work station printer**—Remote printing devices usually placed at kitchen preparation areas and service bars.

*POS System Software*

**activity report**—A report generated by automated systems providing an in-depth analysis of sales transactions and actual labor hours during selected time periods.

**daily labor report**—A report generated by automated systems listing the names, employee numbers, hours worked, wages earned, and wages declared for each employee on a given workday.

**daily transactions report**—A report generated by automated food and beverage systems providing an in-depth analysis of sales transactions by individual server.

**inventory file**—A computer-based record of items in storage.

**labor master file**—A file maintained by sophisticated POS systems containing one record for each employee; it typically maintains the following data: employee name, employee number, social security number, authorized job codes, and corresponding hourly wage rates. This file may also contain data required to produce labor reports for management.

**labor master report**—A file maintained by sophisticated POS systems containing general data maintained by the labor master file; it is commonly used to verify an employee's hourly rate(s), job code(s), or social security number.

**menu item file**—A file maintained by sophisticated POS systems containing data for all meal periods and menu items sold. Important data maintained by this file may include: identification number, descriptor, recipe code number, selling price, ingredient quantities for inventory reporting, and sales totals.

**open check file**—A file maintained by sophisticated POS systems that maintains current data for all open guest checks; it is accessed to monitor items on a guest check, add items to a guest check after initial order entry, and close a guest check at the time of settlement.

**outstanding checks report**—A report produced by automated point-of-sale equipment that lists all guest checks (by server) that have not been settled; information may include: the guest check number, server identification number, time at which the guest check was opened, number of guests, table number, and guest check total.

**period labor report**—A report generated by automated systems listing hour and wage information for each employee who worked during a period specified by management.

**productivity reports**—In relation to automated food and beverage systems, reports that detail sales activity for all assigned server sales records; may be generated for each server and cashier in terms of guest count, total sales, and average sales.

**sales analysis report**—A report generated by automated food and beverage systems that enables management to measure the sales performance of individual menu items by department or product category over various time intervals.

**sales and payment summary report**—A report generated by automated food and beverage systems providing managers with a complete statement of daily or monthly sales (by shift or broken down by food and beverage categories) and a listing of settlement methods.

**sales by time of day report**—A report generated by automated food and beverage systems enabling managers to measure the sales performance of individual menu items by department or product category within certain time intervals.

**weekly labor report**—A report generated by automated food and beverage systems listing the names, employee numbers, hours worked, wages earned, and wages declared for each employee on a given workday; may be useful for determining which employees are approaching overtime pay rates.

*Other Peripherals*

**antenna units**—Part of a system that supports the use of wireless, hand-held server terminals. Antenna units relay signals from hand-held terminals to a radio base station.

**debit card**—These differ from credit cards in that the cardholder must deposit money in order to give the card value. The cardholder deposits money in advance of purchases through a debit card center or an electronic debit posting machine. As purchases are made, the balance on the debit card falls.

**hand-held terminal**—Wireless server terminal that performs most of the functions of a precheck terminal and enables servers to enter orders at tableside.

**magnetic strip reader**—Optional input device that connects to a POS system register or terminal capable of collecting data stored on a magnetized film strip typically located on the back of a credit card or house account card.

**optical character recognition (OCR) terminal**—A terminal activated by hand-held, pen-like bar code readers that servers use to enter orders at service station terminals from a laminated bar coded menu.

**power platform**—Consolidates electronic communications between a hospitality establishment and a credit card authorization center. Power platforms can capture credit card authorizations in three seconds or less. This swift data retrieval helps reduce the time, cost, and risk associated with credit card transactions. A POS power platform connects all POS terminals to a single processor for transaction settlement. This eliminates the need for individual telephone lines at each POS cashier terminal.

**radio base station**—Part of a wireless system supporting the use of hand-held server terminals that relays signals received from antenna units to a digital computer's processing unit.

**smart card**—Smart cards are made of plastic and are about the same size as credit cards. Microchips embedded in them store information that can be accessed by a specially designed card reader. Smart cards can store information in several files that are accessed for different functions, such as a person's vital health statistics, dietary restrictions, credit card number, and bank balance. The security of information stored in smart cards is controlled because a personal identification number (PIN) must be used to access files.

**touch-screen terminal**—A terminal that contains a unique adaptation of a cathode ray tube (CRT) screen and a special microprocessor to control it. The self-contained microprocessor displays data on areas of the screen that are sensitive to touch. Touching one of the sensitized areas produces an electronic charge that is translated into digital signals telling what area was touched for transmission to the microprocessor. This signal also instructs the microprocessor to display the next screen.

### Automated Beverage Control Systems

**delivery network**—Part of an automated beverage control unit that transports beverage item ingredients from storage areas to dispensing units.

**empty bottle sensor**—Can be part of an automated beverage control unit; relays a signal to the order-entry device.

**glass sensor**—Part of an automated beverage control unit, an electronic mechanism located in a bar dispensing unit that will not permit liquid to flow from the dispensing unit unless there is a glass positioned to catch the liquid below the dispensing head.

**guest check sensor**—Part of an automated beverage control unit preventing the system from fulfilling beverage orders unless they are first recorded on a guest check.

## Review Questions

1. What are the necessary hardware components of a POS system? Describe the varieties of each component.

2. How do preset keys differ from PLU keys?

3. What functions do modifier and numeric keys perform?

4. How can a customer display unit on a POS terminal enhance management's internal control system?

5. What are two important features available for traditional guest check printers?

6. How are guest checks opened and closed within a POS system?

7. What types of data are kept by the major files maintained by POS systems?

8. Why would managers prefer touch-screen, OCR, or wireless terminals to conventional keyboard order-entry devices?

9. What kinds of sensor devices do some types of automated beverage systems have?

10. What are the basic components of an automated beverage control system?

 **Internet Sites** ——————————————————————

For more information, visit the following Internet sites. Remember that Internet addresses can change without notice. If the site is no longer there, you can use a search engine to look for additional sites.

Ameranth Wireless
http://www.ameranth.com

Comtrex Systems Corporation
http://www.comtrex.com

Elo TouchSystems
http://www.elotouch.com

InfoGenesis
http://www.infogenesis.com

NCR Corporation
http://www.ncr.com

Palm Computing
http://www.palm.com

Remanco International Inc.
http://www.remanco.com

Restaurant Data Concepts
http://www.positouch.com

Squirrel Companies Inc.
http://www.squirrel-rms.com

System Concepts Inc.
http://www.foodtrak.com

Touch Menus, Inc.
http://www.touchmenus.com

# Chapter 7 Outline

Recipe Management
    Ingredient File
    Standard Recipe File
    Menu Item File
Sales Analysis
Menu Management
    Menu Item Analysis
    Menu Mix Analysis
    Menu Engineering Summary
    Four-Box Analysis
    Improving the Menu
Integrated Food Service Software
    Generic Software
    Precosting/Postcosting Applications
Automated Beverage System Reports

# Competencies

1.  Identify the files typically maintained by recipe management software applications for food and beverage operations. (p. 167)

2.  Describe how information from recipe management software applications helps managers control food and beverage operations. (pp. 167–172)

3.  Explain how food and beverage managers use various reports generated by sales analysis software applications. (pp. 172–174)

4.  Explain the features and functions of menu engineering software. (pp. 174–180)

5.  Describe the advantages of integrated food and beverage software in relation to precosting and postcosting functions. (pp. 180–181)

6.  Explain how managers use reports generated by automated beverage control systems. (pp. 182–189)

7

# Food and Beverage Management Applications

Restaurant managers are constantly challenged to find new ways to increase revenues while controlling and reducing costs. A major stumbling block for many managers is the lack of detailed, timely information about restaurant operations. Managers need timely information to measure current effectiveness and plan business strategies. The cost of collecting detailed information manually is often prohibitive. But an automated food service management system can provide needed information while improving operations and enhancing management's control.

Food and beverage management applications process data related to back-of-the-house food service activities. This chapter examines common food service management applications such as:

- Recipe management
- Sales analysis
- Menu management

This chapter also discusses the importance of integrated food service software for precosting and postcosting applications. In addition, reports generated by sophisticated automated beverage control systems are described.

## Recipe Management

The recipe management application maintains three of the most important files of an automated restaurant management system:

- Ingredient file
- Recipe file
- Menu item file

Most other food service applications have to access data contained within these files in order to effectively carry out their processing functions.

### Ingredient File

An **ingredient file** contains important data on each purchased ingredient. Data may include:

**167**

**Exhibit 1   Sample Ingredient Cost List**

```
01  - CHICKEN DELICIOUS, INC.                INGREDIENT COST LIST                        SA1222
001 - CHICKEN DELICIOUS #1                                                               10.35.19

        EXPENSE     INGRED.    INGREDIENT        PURCHASE    PURCHASE    RECIPE    RECIPE    RECIPE
        CATAGORY    NUMBER     DESCRIPTION       UNIT        COST        YIELD     UNIT      COST
          01          1        Chicken           Case         51.00       32.00    Head      1.5937
          02          41       Shortening        50 lb        19.12       50.00    lb         .3824
          03          42       Milk & Egg Dip    24 lb/cs     28.51       24.00    lb        1.1879
          03          43       Fine Salt         80 lb         7.98       80.00    lb         .0097
          03          44       Seasoning         24 lb/10     61.38       24.00    Pkts      2.5575
          03          45       Flour             25 lb         3.89        1.00    Bag       3.8900
          04          2        Roll              80/cs         6.76      180.00    Each       .0375
          05          3        Potato Mix        6 #10 Cans   31.88       34.80    lb         .9160
          06          49       Cabbage           50 lb        11.75       50.00    lb         .2350
          06          50       Onions            lb            1.70       50.00    lb         .0340
          06          52       Mayonnaise        4 Gal.       17.81       40.00    Gal.       .4452
          06          53       Salad Oil         4 Gal.       16.43       32.00    Pint       .5134
          06          54       Vinegar           4 Gal.       11.92       32.00    Pint       .3725
          06          55       Sugar             25 lb         8.98       25.00    lb         .3592
          06          56       Salt              80 lb         4.90       80.00    lb         .0612
          07          6        Gravy Mix         24 lb/cs     16.07       24.00    lb         .6695
          07          65       Pepper            1 lb          4.41        1.00    lb        4.4100
          07          66       Margarine Qtrs    30 lb        11.22       30.00    lb         .3740
          09          12       Bucket            100 cs       20.72      100.00    Each       .2072
          09          15       Dinner Box        250 cs       13.32      250.00    Each       .0532
          09          16       Snack Box         300 cs       12.54      300.00    Each       .0418
          09          17       Plastic Forks     6000 cs      37.47     6000.00    Each       .0062
          09          19       Napkins           6000 cs      31.68     6000.00    Each       .0052
          09          28       3.5 oz cup        2000 cs      29.10     2000.00    Each       .0145
          09          29       3.5 oz lid        2000 cs      14.20     2000.00    Each       .0071
          09          69       Labels            1000 cs       2.71     1000.00    Each       .0027
          10          75       Milk              1/2 Pint       .19        1.00    Each       .1900
          15          21       Chicken Livers    Case         72.00       72.00    1/2 lb    1.0000
          15          22       Breading          25 lb        25.00      650.00    1 Cup      .0384
```

Source: Tridata, Inc., Atlanta, Georgia.

- Ingredient code number
- Ingredient description
- Purchase unit
- Purchase unit cost
- Issue unit
- Issue unit cost
- Recipe unit
- Recipe unit cost

Exhibit 1 shows a sample ingredient cost list produced from some of the data maintained by an ingredient file. This report shows the current cost of each ingredient, the unit of measure by which each ingredient is purchased, the number of recipe portions by unit, and the recipe cost of each portion. The report is useful for verifying the accuracy of entered data, detailing unit expenditures at current costs, and monitoring relationships among various product units (such as purchase, issue, and recipe units of the same ingredient).

Some ingredient files may specify more than one recipe unit. For example, the recipe unit for bread used for french toast may be the slice; however, the recipe unit for bread used for stuffing may be the ounce. In addition, most restaurant operations enter non-food items into an ingredient file to ensure that the ingredient file contains a complete list of all purchased products. This list becomes especially important if purchase orders are eventually generated for complete ingredient inventory.

Additional data contained in the ingredient file may provide the basis for effective inventory control. **Conversion tables** can be maintained by which to track ingredients (by unit and by cost) as they pass through purchasing/receiving, storing/issuing, and production/service control points. In order to efficiently maintain a perpetual inventory record, a food service system must be able to automatically convert purchase units into issue units and recipe units (also called usable units).

Assume that an ingredient is purchased, issued, and used in different units. When a shipment of the ingredient arrives, it should be easy to update the inventory record by simply entering the purchase units received. The computer should then automatically convert this entry into issue units. Without this conversion capability, it would be necessary to manually calculate the number of units that will be stored, and increase the inventory record accordingly. Similarly, at the end of a meal period the system should update the inventory record by entering the standard recipe units that were used to prepare menu items. If the food and beverage system cannot convert issue units into recipe units, these calculations might also have to be performed manually and the inventory record decreased accordingly.

The system should also track the costs associated with these various ingredient units. Assume that bottle ketchup is purchased by the case (24 12-ounce bottles), issued from the storeroom to the kitchen by the bottle, and used in recipes by the ounce. Given information regarding the purchase unit's net weight and cost, the system should extend costs for issue and recipe unit(s). If the purchase unit's net weight is 18 pounds and its purchase price is $20.40, the system computes issue unit cost at $0.85 and recipe unit cost at slightly more than $0.07. To arrive at these costs through manual calculations an employee would first compute the price per ounce of the purchase unit. This is done by first converting 18 pounds to 288 ounces and then dividing $20.40 by 288 ounces to arrive at the recipe unit cost of $0.07 per ounce. Multiplying $0.07 by 12 ounces yields the issue unit cost of $0.85. Performing these calculations manually for every ingredient purchased can be a tedious, error-prone, time-consuming process. An ingredient file application package can perform these calculations in fractions of a second. Care must be taken to ensure that the ingredient file contains the necessary data, conversion definitions, and algorithms.

## Standard Recipe File

A standard recipe file must contain recipes for all menu items. Important data maintained by the standard recipe file may include:

- Recipe code number
- Recipe name
- Number of portions

**Exhibit 2    Sample Recipe File Printout**

| Item Name: New York Steak Dinner | | | | Code: 4 | | | Category: Dnnr = 2 |
|---|---|---|---|---|---|---|---|
| No. Ingredient | Code | Price/Oz. | Meas. | Lrg. Units | Sml. Units | Extension |
| 0   New York Strip | 2 | $0.2484 | 1 | 0.0 Pnds | 8.0 Ozs. | $1.9872 |
| 1   Russet Potatoes | 1 | $0.0125 | 1 | 0.0 Pnds | 9.0 Ozs. | $0.1125 |
| 2   Butter Chips | 10 | $0.1375 | 1 | 0.0 Pnds | 2.0 Ozs. | $0.2750 |
| 3   Salad Batch | 2R | $0.0247 | 1 | 0.0 Pnds | 6.0 Ozs. | $0.1482 |
| 4 | 0 | $0.0000 | 1 | 0.0 Pnds | 0.0 Ozs. | $0.0000 |
| 5 | 0 | $0.0000 | 1 | 0.0 Pnds | 0.0 Ozs. | $0.0000 |
| 6 | 0 | $0.0000 | 1 | 0.0 Pnds | 0.0 Ozs. | $0.0000 |
| 7 | 0 | $0.0000 | 1 | 0.0 Pnds | 0.0 Ozs. | $0.0000 |
| 8 | 0 | $0.0000 | 1 | 0.0 Pnds | 0.0 Ozs. | $0.0000 |
| 9 | 0 | $0.0000 | 1 | 0.0 Pnds | 0.0 Ozs. | $0.0000 |

Selling Price: $8.95           Yield: 100%        Total Food Extension:   $2.5228
Total Ozs. 25.0        Cost/Oz.:        $0.1189   +     Misc. Food Cost:   $0.0000
Base Recipe Code: 3 Dinner Set Up             +   Cost of Base Recipe:   $0.4500
Food Cst % = $2.9728 × 100/    $8.95    = 33.2%  =     Total Food Cost:   $2.9728
                    High Warning Flag Set At:   35%     Labor or Non-Food:   $0.0000
Profit = Selling Price − Total Cost =        $5.98   =        Total Cost:   $2.9728

* ENTER <1> TO MODIFY FILE, <2> TO EXIT *

Source: Advanced Analytical Computer Systems, Tarzana, California.

- Portion size
- Recipe unit
- Recipe unit cost
- Menu selling price
- Food cost percentage

Exhibit 2 presents a sample printout of some of the data contained in a recipe file. Up to ten ingredients can be listed for each recipe contained in this specific application. A feature of this recipe record is the "high warning flag," which signals when the current food cost exceeds a level designated by management. Recipe records are integral to purchase order systems, because stored recipes can indicate needed quantities before production and provide an index of perpetual inventory replenishment following production.

Some data in the standard recipe file overlap data within the ingredient file. This simplifies the creation and maintenance of recipe records, because data will not have to be re-entered. Recipe management applications can access specific elements of data contained in ingredient and recipe files and format different management reports.

Some recipe management applications provide space for preparation instructions (also called assembly instructions) that are typically found on standard recipe cards. Although this information is not accessed by other food service management applications, it allows management to print recipes for production personnel. This can be a useful feature when batch sizes (number of portions yielded by a particular standard recipe) need to be expanded or contracted to accommodate forecasted needs. For example, if a standard recipe is designed to yield 100 portions (batch size), but 530 portions are needed, it may be possible (depending on the item) to instruct the system to proportionately adjust the corresponding ingredient quantities. When batch size can be modified, unique recipes can be printed that include preparation information, providing a complete plan for recipe production.

Few restaurants purchase all menu item ingredients in ready-to-use or pre-portioned form. Some ingredients are made on the premises. This means that the ingredients within a standard recipe record may be either inventory items or references to other recipe files. Recipes included as ingredients within a standard recipe record are called **sub-recipes.** Including sub-recipes as ingredients for a particular standard recipe is called **recipe chaining.** Chaining recipes enables the system to maintain a record for a particular menu item that requires an unusually large number of ingredients. When ingredient costs change, automated recipe management applications must be capable of updating not only the costs of standard recipes, but also the cost of sub-recipes used as ingredients. If not, new cost data would have to be separately entered into each sub-recipe record. This can be a time-consuming and error-prone process. Exhibit 3 shows the recipe-building feature of a recipe management program. All items are selected from a list, including sub-recipes. The program also automatically reprices recipes as needed and can convert recipes to desired yields. Exhibit 4 presents a sample recipe printout that can be customized with preparation methods for food production staff.

## Menu Item File

A **menu item file** contains data for all meal periods and menu items sold. Important data maintained by this file may include:

- Identification number
- Descriptor
- Recipe code number
- Selling price
- Ingredient quantities for inventory reporting
- Sales totals

This file also stores historical information on the actual number of items sold. Generally, after a meal period, the actual number of menu items served is manually entered into the menu item file, or automatically transferred from a POS system through an interface to the food and beverage system. This data can be accessed by management or by sophisticated forecasting programs to project sales, determine the number of ingredient quantities to purchase, and schedule needed

**Exhibit 3    Sample Recipe Management Screen**

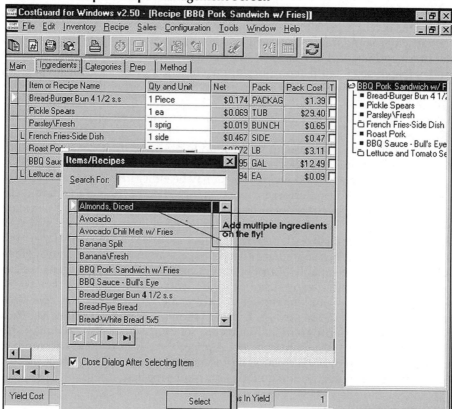

Source: CostGuard Food Service Software. For more information, browse the company's Web site at http://www.costguard.com

personnel. In addition, automated sales analysis applications access data in the menu item file to produce sales analysis reports for management. When menu items, prices, or tax tables need to be changed, the menu item file is accessed and appropriate changes are entered according to procedures indicated in the user's manual provided by the system's vendor.

## Sales Analysis

A POS system can store or maintain files that contain important data regarding daily food service operations. When a POS system is interfaced to a fully integrated management system, data maintained by POS system files can be accessed through an automated process. A POS interface enables a sales analysis application to merge data from the POS files with data from files maintained by a recipe management application. The sales analysis software can then process this combined data into numerous reports to help management monitor and control operations in such specific areas as:

**Exhibit 4    Sample Recipe Printout**

```
Date: 8/19/200X
Time: 1:31 PM
```

**BBQ Pork Sandwich w/ Fries**

```
Description:
        Yield: SERVING              Cost: $1.99              Type: Serving
        Portion: SERVING           Cost: $1.99          Portions In Yield: 1
```

|          | Cost   | Sells For | FC %   | Margin $ |
|----------|--------|-----------|--------|----------|
| Current: | $1.99  | $5.95     | 33.44% | $3.96    |
| Target:  |        | $6.22     | 32.00% | $4.23    |

| L | Quantity and Unit | Ingredient or Recipe | Net | Purchase | T | Prep Notes |
|---|-------------------|----------------------|-----|----------|---|------------|
|   | 1 Piece | Bread-Burger Bun 4 1/2 s.s | $0.17 | $1.39 | | |
|   | 1 ea | Pickle Spears | $0.07 | $29.40 | | |
|   | 1 sprig | Parsley\Fresh | $0.02 | $0.65 | | |
| * | 1 side | French Fries-Side Dish | $0.47 | $0.47 | | |
|   | 5 oz | Roast Pork | $0.97 | $3.11 | | |
|   | 2 foz | BBQ Sauce - Bull's Eye | $0.20 | $12.49 | | |
| * | 1 ea | Lettuce and Tomato Setup | $0.09 | $0.09 | | |

**Method:**

Source: CostGuard Food Service Software. For more information, browse the company's Web site at http://www.costguard.com

- Menu planning
- Sales forecasting
- Menu item pricing
- Ingredient purchasing
- Inventory control
- Labor scheduling
- Payroll accounting

Exhibit 5 presents a sample sales mix of a dinner menu. Sales figures can be entered manually or imported from a POS system. The program calculates food cost and depletes inventory amounts accordingly. Food service management systems typically produce a variety of sales reports. A **daily sales report** summarizes all sales revenue activity for a day. Revenue is itemized by the following categories:

- Net sales
- Tax
- Number of guest checks
- Number of covers
- Dollars per check
- Dollars per cover
- Sales category
- Day-part totals

**Exhibit 5    Sample Sales Mix of a Dinner Menu**

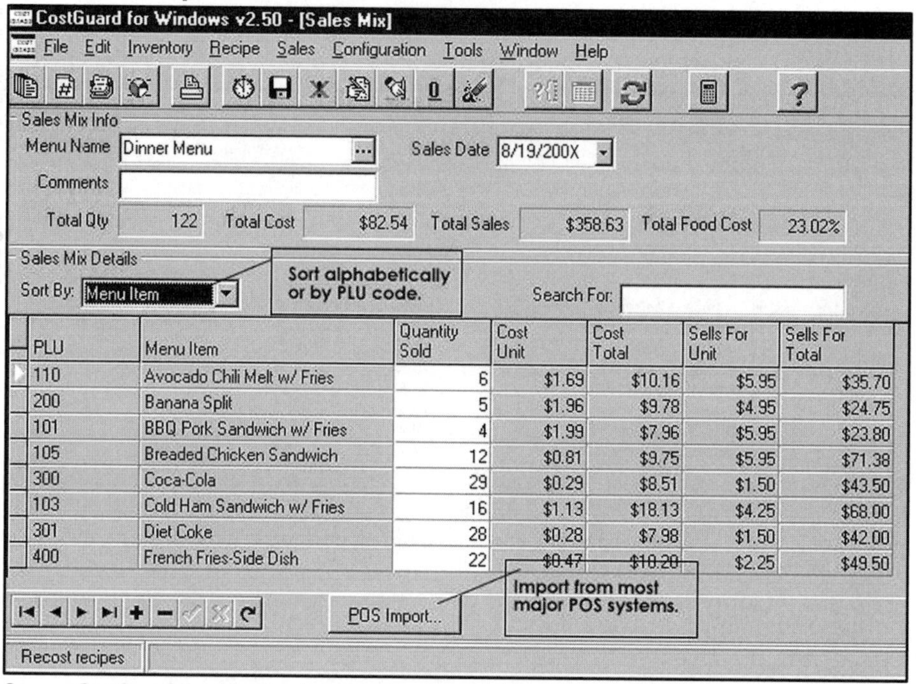

CostGuard for Windows v2.50 - [Sales Mix]

File  Edit  Inventory  Recipe  Sales  Configuration  Tools  Window  Help

**Sales Mix Info**

Menu Name: Dinner Menu          Sales Date: 8/19/200X

Comments:

| Total Qty | 122 | Total Cost | $82.54 | Total Sales | $358.63 | Total Food Cost | 23.02% |

**Sales Mix Details**

Sort By: Menu Item      *Sort alphabetically or by PLU code.*      Search For:

| PLU | Menu Item | Quantity Sold | Cost Unit | Cost Total | Sells For Unit | Sells For Total |
|-----|-----------|---------------|-----------|------------|----------------|-----------------|
| 110 | Avocado Chili Melt w/ Fries | 6 | $1.69 | $10.16 | $5.95 | $35.70 |
| 200 | Banana Split | 5 | $1.96 | $9.78 | $4.95 | $24.75 |
| 101 | BBQ Pork Sandwich w/ Fries | 4 | $1.99 | $7.96 | $5.95 | $23.80 |
| 105 | Breaded Chicken Sandwich | 12 | $0.81 | $9.75 | $5.95 | $71.38 |
| 300 | Coca-Cola | 29 | $0.29 | $8.51 | $1.50 | $43.50 |
| 103 | Cold Ham Sandwich w/ Fries | 16 | $1.13 | $18.13 | $4.25 | $68.00 |
| 301 | Diet Coke | 28 | $0.28 | $7.98 | $1.50 | $42.00 |
| 400 | French Fries-Side Dish | 22 | $0.47 | $10.20 | $2.25 | $49.50 |

POS Import...   *Import from most major POS systems.*

Recost recipes

Source: CostGuard Food Service Software. For more information, browse the company's Web site at http://www.costguard.com

In addition, affected general ledger accounts are listed, and associated food costs and sales percentage statistics are noted. A **weekly sales spreadsheet** provides a weekly summary of all information reported by daily sales reports.

A **sales category analysis report** shows relationships between amounts sold by sales category and day-parts as defined by management. This report enables management to see at a glance which menu items sell and the time of day they sell. A **marketing category report** compiles weekly totals summarizing the revenue earned by food and beverage departments (or categories).

## Menu Management

While most automated food service management applications sort and index data into timely, factual reports for management, menu management applications help management answer such questions as:

- What is the most profitable price to assign to a menu item?

- At what price level and sales mix does a food service operation maximize its profits?

- Which current menu items require repricing, retention, replacement, or repositioning on the menu?

- How should daily specials and new items be priced?

- How can the success of a menu change be evaluated?

**Menu engineering** is a menu management application used for evaluating decisions regarding current and future menu pricing, design, and contents. This application requires that management focus on the number of dollars a menu contributes to profit and not simply monitor cost percentages.

Menu engineering begins with an interactive analysis of menu mix (MM) and contribution margin (CM) data. Competing menu items are categorized as either high or low. A menu item is high when its MM is greater than or equal to 70 percent of its equal menu share, low when its MM is less than 70 percent of its equal menu share. The item's individual CM is similarly compared with the menu's average CM and categorized as either high or low. This analysis produces the following classifications:

- Menu items high in both MM and CM are stars (winners).

- Menu items high in MM but low in CM are plowhorses (marginal).

- Menu items low in MM but high in CM are puzzles (potential).

- Menu items low in MM and low in CM are dogs (losers).

The application goes a step further and identifies practical approaches by which to re-engineer the next menu. For example, simple strategies include:

- Retain stars

- Reprice plowhorses

- Reposition puzzles

- Remove dogs

Following data input and selection of the analysis option, the menu engineering application begins its work. As the analysis progresses, a menu item's contribution margin and unit sales activity will be categorized as relatively high or low. The menu engineering output is composed of several reports which include:

- Menu item analysis

- Menu mix analysis

- Menu engineering summary

- Four-box analysis

## Menu Item Analysis

Exhibit 6 illustrates the initial report in the menu engineering analysis. This is an item-by-item listing accompanied by selling price, portion cost, contribution margin, and item count (number sold). The primary purpose of this report is to provide the user with a means by which to verify the data that is to be analyzed. This can be helpful when data has been manually entered into the program.

**Exhibit 6   Menu Item Analysis**

| | | Item Analysis | | |
|---|---|---|---|---|
| Item Name | Item Price | Portion Cost | Contr. Margin | Item Count |
| Fried Shrimp | 7.95 | 4.85 | 3.10 | 210 |
| Fried Chicken | 4.95 | 2.21 | 2.74 | 420 |
| Chopped Sirloin | 4.50 | 1.95 | 2.55 | 90 |
| Prime Rib | 7.95 | 4.95 | 3.00 | 600 |
| King Prime Rib | 9.95 | 5.65 | 4.30 | 60 |
| NY Strip Steak | 8.50 | 4.50 | 4.00 | 360 |
| Top Sirloin | 7.95 | 4.30 | 3.65 | 510 |
| Red Snapper | 6.95 | 3.95 | 3.00 | 240 |
| Lobster Tail | 9.50 | 4.95 | 4.55 | 150 |
| Tenderloin Tips | 6.45 | 4.00 | 2.45 | 360 |

**Exhibit 7   Menu Mix Analysis**

| | | | Menu Mix Analysis | | | | |
|---|---|---|---|---|---|---|---|
| Item Name | MM Count | % MM Share | Group Rank | % CM Share | Contr. Margin | Group Rank | Menu Class |
| Fried Shrimp | 210 | 7.00 | HIGH | 6.73 | 3.10 | LOW | PLOWHORSE |
| Fried Chicken | 420 | 14.00 | HIGH | 11.89 | 2.74 | LOW | PLOWHORSE |
| Chopped Sirloin | 90 | 3.00 | LOW | 2.37 | 2.55 | LOW | << DOG >> |
| Prime Rib | 600 | 20.00 | HIGH | 18.60 | 3.00 | LOW | PLOWHORSE |
| King Prime Rib | 60 | 2.00 | LOW | 2.67 | 4.30 | HIGH | ?PUZZLE? |
| NY Strip Steak | 360 | 12.00 | HIGH | 14.88 | 4.00 | HIGH | **STAR** |
| Top Sirloin | 510 | 17.00 | HIGH | 19.24 | 3.65 | HIGH | **STAR** |
| Red Snapper | 240 | 8.00 | HIGH | 7.44 | 3.00 | LOW | PLOWHORSE |
| Lobster Tail | 150 | 5.00 | LOW | 7.05 | 4.55 | HIGH | ?PUZZLE? |
| Tenderloin Tips | 360 | 12.00 | HIGH | 9.12 | 2.45 | LOW | PLOWHORSE |

## Menu Mix Analysis

Exhibit 7 illustrates a menu mix analysis report. This report evaluates each item's participation in the overall menu's performance. The percentage of menu mix (*%MM Share*) is based upon each item's count divided by the total number of items sold. Each percentage is then ranked as high or low depending upon its comparison with the menu engineering rule for menu mix sufficiency. The percentage each item has contributed to the menu's total contribution margin is found in the

**Exhibit 8  Menu Engineering Summary**

| Menu Engineering Summary | | | | |
|---|---|---|---|---|
| | Total | Average | Low | High |
| Price ............... | 22050.00 | 7.35 | 4.50 | 9.95 |
| Food Cost .......... | 12374.70 | 4.12 | 1.95 | 5.65 |
| Contribution Margin ... | 9675.30 | 3.23 | 2.45 | 4.55 |
| Demand Factor ...... | 3000 | 300 | 60 | 600 |
| | | | | |
| Food Cost Percentage | 56.12% | | | |
| Number of Items ..... | 10 | | | |

column labeled *%CM Share*. Each item's contribution margin is then ranked according to how it compares with the menu's weighted average contribution margin. A menu classification for each item is determined by considering its MM group rank and CM group rank together.

## Menu Engineering Summary

Exhibit 8 illustrates a menu engineering summary report. Perhaps the most informative report produced by the menu engineering application, this analysis presents important information in capsule form to produce a concise statement of operations. The row labeled *Price* shows total menu revenue, average item selling price, lowest selling price, and highest selling price. The *Food Cost* row contains total menu costs, average item food cost, lowest cost item, and highest cost item. The *Contribution Margin* row shows total menu CM, average item CM, lowest item CM, and highest item CM. The *Demand Factor* row lists total number of covers (guests), average number of covers, lowest item count, and highest item count. Much of the information in the body of this report is used elsewhere in the overall menu engineering system. For example, the lowest and highest selling prices on the menu are termed price points and can be used to help identify target market success. This report also contains the menu's food cost percentage and number of items sold.

## Four-Box Analysis

Exhibit 9 illustrates a four-box analysis that indexes the menu classifications developed in the menu mix analysis report. Since menu engineering leads to a series of decision strategies specific to each menu classification, this report provides the user with insight about the number of items found in each category. For example, Exhibit 9 displays a menu composed of five plowhorses, two stars, two puzzles, and one dog. Are five plowhorses too many? This type of evaluation process begins with the four-box matrix and continues as management strives to improve the menu.

**Exhibit 9   Four-Box Analysis**

| | |
|---|---|
| PLOWHORSE<br>Fried Shrimp<br>Fried Chicken<br>Prime Rib<br>Red Snapper<br>Tenderloin Tips | STAR<br>NY Strip<br>Steak<br>Top Sirloin |
| DOG<br>Chopped Sirloin | PUZZLE<br>King Prime Rib<br>Lobster Tail |

## Improving the Menu

The benefits of menu engineering can accrue only if information gained from the menu engineering analysis is used to improve the menu. What can a food and beverage manager do with this knowledge about the various food item classifications?

**Managing Plowhorses.** First, let's consider plowhorses (those items low in contribution margin, but high in popularity). Guests like these items, but, unfortunately, plowhorses do not contribute their fair share of contribution margin. Possible strategies for managing a plowhorse menu item include:

- Increase prices carefully. Perhaps the item is popular because it represents a great value to guests. If prices could be increased, the item may still represent a good value, may remain popular, and may generate a higher contribution margin. This alternative may be most effective when the item is unique to the property and cannot be obtained elsewhere.

- Test for demand. If there is no strong resistance to price increases, it may be useful to complement an increased price with other strategies such as repackaging the item or repositioning it on the menu. These other strategies may be designed to maintain or increase the item's popularity while generating a higher contribution margin through the increase in selling price. If prices are to be increased, this should probably be done in several stages rather than all at once.

- Relocate the item to a lower profile on the menu. Depending upon the menu layout, certain areas of a menu represent a better location than others. A plowhorse can be relocated to a less desirable area of the menu. Since the item is popular, some guests will search it out. Others will be drawn to higher profile areas of the menu that list more profitable items the property wishes to sell.

- Shift demand to more desirable items. Menu engineering allows the manager to determine which items to sell—those high in popularity and high in contribution margin. Servers using suggestive selling techniques, for example, would *not* recommend plowhorses. Table tents and other point of sale tools would, likewise, suggest stars and puzzles (because of their high contribution margins); they would not suggest plowhorses.

- Combine with lower-cost products. The contribution margin of a plowhorse can be increased if lower-cost meal accompaniments are offered with the entree. Perhaps, for example, higher-priced vegetables and dessert accompaniments can be replaced with other, less expensive items without reducing the item's popularity. If this can be done, the contribution margin will increase.

- Assess the direct labor factor. The food and beverage manager should know if there is a significant amount of direct labor required to produce the plowhorse item. If an item with a low contribution margin does not have a significant amount of direct labor involved in production (a convenience food product, for example), the manager may be able to justify the lower contribution margin since fewer revenue dollars will be required to compensate for labor cost.

- Consider portion reduction. If the portion size is reduced, the product cost will be decreased and the contribution margin will increase. This alternative must be viewed with caution, of course, since the guest's perception of value may decrease when the portion size is reduced.

**Managing Puzzles.** Puzzles are items that are high in contribution margin but low in popularity—items the food and beverage manager desires to sell since their contribution margin is relatively high. The challenge is to find ways to increase the number of guests ordering these items. Alternatives include:

- Shift demand to these items. Techniques include repositioning the items to more visible areas of the menu, renaming them, using suggestive selling techniques, developing advertising campaigns, using table tents, using buttons and badges on server uniforms, highlighting items on menu boards at the entrance to the dining area, and other strategies to increase the item's popularity.

- Consider a price decrease. Perhaps an item is low in popularity because it does not represent a value to guests. If this is the case, the selling price might be decreased with the contribution margin still remaining higher than average. This could lead to increased popularity, since a reduced selling price would represent a greater value to the guest.

- Add value to the item. Offering a larger portion size, adding more expensive meal accompaniments or garnishes, and using higher-quality ingredients are among the ways that value can be increased. These techniques may lead to increased popularity and to a contribution margin that is lower, but still higher than the average generated by the menu.

**Managing Stars.** Stars are items that are high in contribution margin and high in popularity. The best advice for managing stars includes:

- Maintain rigid specifications. Do not attempt to alter the quality of the product being served.

- Place in a highly visible location on the menu. Stars are items that the food and beverage operator wants to sell. Therefore, make sure guests are aware of their availability.

- Test for selling price inelasticity. Perhaps the star is popular because it is a significant value to the guest. Or perhaps the star is not available in its existing form elsewhere in the marketplace. These might be two instances in which the price could be increased without a decrease in popularity.

- Use suggestive selling techniques. Some of the techniques for shifting demand to puzzles might also be useful for stars.

**Managing Dogs.** Dogs (items that are low in contribution margin and low in popularity) are obvious candidates for removal from the menu. After all, they do not contribute their fair share of contribution margin and they are not popular. Alternatively, the selling price could be increased, since this would at least generate a higher contribution margin. When a "dog" requires a significant amount of direct labor, does not permit sufficient use of leftovers, and has a relatively short storage life, the reasons for removing the item from the menu become more compelling.

# Integrated Food Service Software

Perhaps the most common mistake in choosing a food service system is deciding on hardware before considering software. Computer hardware is typically purchased on the basis of brand, advertising, price, accessories, and the like. Only after the purchase is made does the search for software begin.

Identifying software aimed at an operation's needs can be time-consuming and frustrating, but learning that the software selected is incompatible with already-purchased hardware can be devastating. The best way to avoid this disaster is to remember that finding hardware to support software packages is much easier than working with inadequate software.

## Generic Software

Standard word processing, electronic spreadsheet, and database management programs are powerful and versatile management tools, but they can also become an endless source of frustration. Consider the operator who selects a spreadsheet program to generate budgets, food costs, and daily reports. Each application requires that separate data be entered into specific cells located in distinct worksheet files. If the operator also wants to monitor inventory, the work it takes to support the automated applications may outweigh the savings in time and money. A food service operator who uses a word processing program for correspondence, an electronic spreadsheet program for financial analysis, and a database management program for inventory control may find that automation is more trouble than it is worth.

The limitations of free-standing, non-integrated, generic software become apparent when management tries to share or exchange data between programs.

Non-integrated application software seldom achieves the chief objectives of electronic data processing. These objectives are:

- To minimize the time it takes to process input into output (throughput).
- To minimize the handling and rehandling of data (efficiency).
- To minimize the amount of unnecessary output (streamlining).

Integrated food service software applications enable data to pass directly from one application to another. Data is entered only once. The following section illustrates the differences between integrated and non-integrated food service applications while describing precosting and postcosting applications.

## Precosting/Postcosting Applications

**Precosting** is a special type of forecasting that compares forecasted guest counts with standard menu item recipe costs to yield an index of expense before an actual meal period. Precosting software applications can project costs on a portion, batch, or meal period basis. This projected cost of sales figure enables management to review and adjust operations before an actual service period begins. If precosting finds projected costs to be outside an acceptable range, management may consider raising prices, decreasing portion sizes, altering accompaniments, or substituting menu items.

Precosting predictions are based on three types of data: an accurate cost of every item contained in the ingredient file; a set of standard recipes stored in the recipe file containing a precise list of ingredients, quantities, and production procedures; and a menu plan specifying each item on the menu and the projected number of portions to be consumed during a meal period. A commercial restaurant with a fixed menu and standard recipes would need to focus most of its attention on maintaining current cost data and developing sound sales mix forecasts.

Although nearly all restaurants have access to the data needed for precosting calculations, few actually perform the analysis manually because it can be time-consuming and error-prone. It can be almost as time-consuming for restaurants with non-integrated software packages. In a non-integrated food service software design, the necessary data—ingredient costs, recipe formulations, and menu plans—most likely would reside in separate software programs. Applying each ingredient data element against its recipe and menu plan would require intervention by the user, intermediate calculations, and re-entry of data, all of which is counter to the objectives of electronic data processing. To achieve accurate and timely precosting, the best approach is to use integrated software. Integrated file structures enable management to concentrate on designing menu plans without getting mired in repetitive clerical procedures. Exhibit 10 outlines the files accessed by a precosting management application.

**Postcosting** multiplies the number of menu items sold by standard recipe costs to determine a potential food cost amount. When actual recipe costs are known, these figures are multiplied by the number of menu items sold to produce an actual cost figure. Exhibit 11 outlines the files accessed by a postcosting management application. Exhibit 12 summarizes popular food-costing algorithms.

**Exhibit 10    Files Accessed by Precosting Applications**

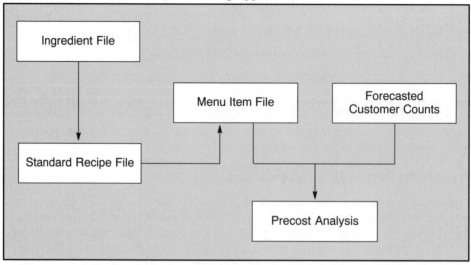

**Exhibit 11    Files Accessed by Postcosting Applications**

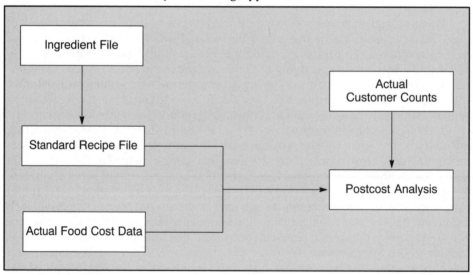

# Automated Beverage System Reports

Automated beverage control systems record and store data that can be accessed to produce valuable reports for management. Data may include:

- Beverage item
- Individual brands

**Exhibit 12 Popular Food-Costing Algorithms**

| Components: | Costing Scheme |
|---|---|
| (Standard Cost) (Forecasted Counts) | STANDARD COSTING |
| (Standard Cost) (Actual Counts) | POTENTIAL COSTING |
| (Actual Cost) (Actual Counts) | ACTUAL COSTING |

- Portion sizes
- Prices
- Sales
- Tax
- Tips
- Bar check numbers (if appropriate)
- Server identification codes
- Service location(s)

Beverage control systems are usually programmed to access specific types of data and can generate a variety of reports. Reports produced by an automated beverage system are similar to those produced by typical POS systems. These reports may include sales mix analysis, inventory usage reports, check tracking reports, server productivity reports, and others. Journal printers may be programmed to produce detailed accounting and financial reports.

For each shift and each station during a shift, automated beverage control systems can produce separate reports indicating:

- Sales by major beverage category, or grouping
- Sales by time of day
- Sales by server
- Sales by settlement methods
- Open, closed, and missing guest checks
- Sales mix by beverage product

Exhibits 13 through 19 show a series of reports generated by an automated beverage control system. The reports cover a single shift and integrate data from four separate stations.

Exhibit 13 reports the expected beverage **sales by major beverage category** for the four separate stations, as well as total sales figures combining the four

**Exhibit 13   Sales by Major Beverage Category Report**

| Ring Off #22 | — 2:52 a.m. | 1/06 | | | |
|---|---|---|---|---|---|
| Accumulators Cleared | — 8:00 a.m. | 1/05 | | | |

| Sales by Major Category | Station 1 Sales | Station 2 Sales | Station 3 Sales | Station 4 Sales | Total Sales |
|---|---|---|---|---|---|
| Liquor | 1,185.75 | 977.25 | 1,040.25 | 417.75 | 3,621.00 |
| Beer | 469.50 | 372.25 | 236.50 | 144.00 | 1,222.25 |
| Wine | 29.75 | 45.00 | 77.00 | 19.50 | 171.25 |
| Soft Drinks | 1.75 | 20.75 | 17.25 | 8.75 | 48.50 |
| Misc A | 34.50 | 61.15 | 88.70 | 117.90 | 302.25 |
| Btl Wine | .00 | .00 | .00 | .00 | .00 |
| Lookups | 57.85 | 94.55 | 23.80 | .00 | 176.20 |
| | | | | | |
| Price Mode 1 | 3.00 | 77.00 | 110.25 | .00 | 190.25 |
| Mode 2 | 1,776.10 | 1,492.20 | 1,363.25 | 707.90 | 5,339.45 |
| Mode 3 | .00 | 1.75 | 10.00 | .00 | 11.75 |
| | | | | | |
| Tax—Mode 1 | .00 | .00 | .00 | .00 | .00 |
| Mode 2 | .00 | .00 | .00 | .00 | .00 |
| Mode 3 | .00 | .00 | .00 | .00 | .00 |
| | | | | | |
| Tips | 1.50 | .00 | 11.10 | .00 | 12.60 |
| | | | | | |
| Gross Sales | 1,780.60 | 1,570.95 | 1,494.60 | 707.90 | 5,554.05 |
| | | | | | |
| Net Sales | 1,779.10 | 1,570.95 | 1,483.50 | 707.90 | 5,541.45 |
| | | | | | |
| Accumulated Sales | 919,058.24 | 43,281.83 | 50,696.30 | 30,780.18 | |
| | | | | | |
| Transactions | 16 | 190 | 24 | 93 | 323 |

Source: American Business Computers, Akron, Ohio.

stations. Exhibit 14 shows a **sales by beverage server report.** Note that the total sales figure at the bottom of this report ($5,524.05) is $30 less than the total standard beverage income listed in Exhibit 13 as $5,554.05 (total gross sales). An **outstanding guest checks report** (Exhibit 15) resolves this discrepancy. When bartenders close their stations, the system generates a **settlement methods report** (Exhibit 16), which indicates the amounts due in the form of credit card vouchers, house account charges, and cash. Note that the total of the settlement report (the amount of sales income that the bartenders will be held accountable for) does not include the $30 from the outstanding guest check.

Exhibit 17 shows a **net sales by time of day report.** This report is useful for forecasting sales and for scheduling servers and bartenders according to expected demand. Exhibit 18 shows the **sales mix by major product report** for the shift. Managers use these reports to monitor product sales trends and to adjust par inventory levels when necessary. The **product usage report** shown in Exhibit 19 enables managers to minimize inventory control problems.

**Exhibit 14   Sales by Beverage Server Report**

| Server | Reported Tips | Total Sales | Cash | Visa | Dine | Amex | Prom | Comp | Disc | Dire |
|---|---|---|---|---|---|---|---|---|---|---|
| 1 | 6.10 | 1252.05 | 1160.45 | .00 | .00 | 91.60 | .00 | .00 | .00 | .00 |
| 4 | .00 | 197.45 | 197.45 | .00 | .00 | .00 | .00 | .00 | .00 | .00 |
| 5 | .00 | 223.40 | 223.40 | .00 | .00 | .00 | .00 | .00 | .00 | .00 |
| 6 | .00 | 493.50 | 493.50 | .00 | .00 | .00 | .00 | .00 | .00 | .00 |
| 12 | 1.50 | 785.65 | 553.70 | .00 | 179.70 | 52.25 | .00 | .00 | .00 | .00 |
| 15 | .00 | 644.75 | 644.75 | .00 | .00 | .00 | .00 | .00 | .00 | .00 |
| 16 | .00 | 5.00 | 5.00 | .00 | .00 | .00 | .00 | .00 | .00 | .00 |
| 17 | .00 | 288.90 | 288.90 | .00 | .00 | .00 | .00 | .00 | .00 | .00 |
| 27 | .00 | 111.75 | 111.75 | .00 | .00 | .00 | .00 | .00 | .00 | .00 |
| 35 | .00 | 21.00 | 21.00 | .00 | .00 | .00 | .00 | .00 | .00 | .00 |
| 37 | .00 | 28.25 | 28.25 | .00 | .00 | .00 | .00 | .00 | .00 | .00 |
| 39 | .00 | 36.50 | 36.50 | .00 | .00 | .00 | .00 | .00 | .00 | .00 |
| 40 | .00 | 276.20 | 276.20 | .00 | .00 | .00 | .00 | .00 | .00 | .00 |
| 41 | .00 | 18.00 | 18.00 | .00 | .00 | .00 | .00 | .00 | .00 | .00 |
| 43 | .00 | 244.25 | 233.50 | 10.75 | .00 | .00 | .00 | .00 | .00 | .00 |
| 44 | .00 | 5.95 | 5.95 | .00 | .00 | .00 | .00 | .00 | .00 | .00 |
| 45 | .00 | 85.95 | 85.95 | .00 | .00 | .00 | .00 | .00 | .00 | .00 |
| 47 | 5.00 | 30.50 | 25.50 | .00 | .00 | 5.00 | .00 | .00 | .00 | .00 |
| 56 | .00 | 166.25 | 166.25 | .00 | .00 | .00 | .00 | .00 | .00 | .00 |
| 58 | .00 | 84.25 | 84.25 | .00 | .00 | .00 | .00 | .00 | .00 | .00 |
| 60 | .00 | 7.75 | 7.75 | .00 | .00 | .00 | .00 | .00 | .00 | .00 |
| 65 | .00 | 13.00 | 13.00 | .00 | .00 | .00 | .00 | .00 | .00 | .00 |
| 66 | .00 | 235.50 | 235.50 | .00 | .00 | .00 | .00 | .00 | .00 | .00 |
| 67 | .00 | 2.50 | 2.50 | .00 | .00 | .00 | .00 | .00 | .00 | .00 |
| 68 | .00 | 21.00 | 21.00 | .00 | .00 | .00 | .00 | .00 | .00 | .00 |
| 71 | .00 | 24.25 | .00 | .00 | .00 | 24.25 | .00 | .00 | .00 | .00 |
| 78 | .00 | 208.25 | 208.25 | .00 | .00 | .00 | .00 | .00 | .00 | .00 |
| 80 | .00 | 10.50 | 10.50 | .00 | .00 | .00 | .00 | .00 | .00 | .00 |
| 93 | .00 | 1.75 | 1.75 | .00 | .00 | .00 | .00 | .00 | .00 | .00 |
| Totals | 12.60 | 5524.05 | 5160.50 | 10.75 | 179.70 | 173.10 | .00 | .00 | .00 | .00 |

Note: (All Sales Include Tax and Tips)

Ring Off #22 —2:52 a.m. 1/06
Accumulators Cleared —8:00 a.m. 1/05

Source: American Business Computers, Akron, Ohio.

**Exhibit 15   Outstanding Guest Checks Report**

Ring Off #22 — 2:52 a.m. 1/06
Accumulators Cleared — 8:00 a.m. 1/05

| Outstanding Guest Checks | Server | Check Total |
|---|---|---|
| #4567 | 05 | 30.00 |
| Total | | 30.00 |

Source: American Business Computers, Akron, Ohio.

## Exhibit 16    Settlement Methods Report

**Ring Off #22          —2:52 a.m.   1/06**
**Accumulators Cleared—8:00 a.m.   1/05**

| Settlement Methods | STATION 1 SALES | STATION 2 SALES | STATION 3 SALES | STATION 4 SALES | TOTAL SALES |
|---|---|---|---|---|---|
| Cash | 1548.65 | 1560.20 | 1368.00 | 683.65 | 5160.50 |
| Visa/MC | .00 | 10.75 | .00 | .00 | 10.75 |
| Diners | 179.70 | .00 | .00 | .00 | 179.70 |
| Amex | 52.25 | .00 | 96.60 | 24.25 | 173.10 |
| Promo | .00 | .00 | .00 | .00 | .00 |
| Company | .00 | .00 | .00 | .00 | .00 |
| Discovery | .00 | .00 | .00 | .00 | .00 |
| Direct Bill | .00 | .00 | .00 | .00 | .00 |
| Total Settlements | 1780.60 | 1570.95 | 1464.60 | 707.90 | 5524.05 |

Source: American Business Computers, Akron, Ohio.

## Exhibit 17    Net Sales by Time of Day Report

**Ring Off #22          — 2:52 a.m.      1/06**
**Accumulators Cleared      — 8:00 a.m.      1/05**

| Net Sales by Time of Day | Station 1 Sales | Station 2 Sales | Station 3 Sales | Station 4 Sales | Total Sales |
|---|---|---|---|---|---|
| 6 - 7 A.M. | .00 | .00 | .00 | .00 | .00 |
| 7 - 8 | .00 | .00 | .00 | .00 | .00 |
| 8 - 9 | .00 | .00 | .00 | .00 | .00 |
| 9 - 10 | .00 | .00 | .00 | .00 | .00 |
| 10 - 11 | .00 | .00 | .00 | .00 | .00 |
| 11 - 12 | .00 | .00 | .00 | .00 | .00 |
| 12 - 1 P.M. | .00 | .00 | .00 | .00 | .00 |
| 1 - 2 | .00 | .00 | .00 | .00 | .00 |
| 2 - 3 | .00 | .00 | .00 | .00 | .00 |
| 3 - 4 | .00 | .00 | .00 | .00 | .00 |
| 4 - 5 | .00 | 3.25 | 16.50 | .00 | 19.75 |
| 5 - 6 | .00 | 14.00 | 32.25 | .00 | 46.25 |
| 6 - 7 | .00 | 43.00 | 68.25 | .00 | 111.25 |
| 7 - 8 | 40.70 | 58.00 | 112.50 | 6.25 | 217.45 |
| 8 - 9 | 123.75 | 77.40 | 170.85 | 55.40 | 427.40 |
| 9 - 10 | 297.75 | 272.50 | 217.00 | 180.15 | 957.40 |
| 10 - 11 | 343.50 | 361.65 | 282.90 | 221.50 | 1,209.55 |
| 11 - 12 | 346.00 | 250.40 | 218.75 | 194.85 | 1,010.00 |
| 12 - 1 A.M. | 276.90 | 276.05 | 208.50 | 49.75 | 811.20 |
| 1 - 2 | 233.00 | 183.45 | 126.00 | .00 | 542.45 |
| 2 - 3 | 117.50 | 31.25 | 30.00 | .00 | 178.75 |
| 3 - 4 | .00 | .00 | .00 | .00 | .00 |
| 4 - 5 | .00 | .00 | .00 | .00 | .00 |
| 5 - 6 A.M. | .00 | .00 | .00 | .00 | .00 |
| Total Net Sales | 1,779.10 | 1,570.95 | 1,483.50 | 707.90 | 5,541.45 |

Source: American Business Computers, Akron, Ohio.

# Exhibit 18  Sales Mix by Major Product Report

| Ring Off #22 | –2:52 a.m. | 1/06 |
| --- | --- | --- |
| Accumulators Cleared | –8:00 a.m. | 1/05 |

| Sales Mix By Major Product | STATION 1 SALES | STATION 2 SALES | STATION 3 SALES | STATION 4 SALES | TOTAL SALES |
| --- | --- | --- | --- | --- | --- |
| Scotch | 30.00/ 12 | 46.00/ 22 | 45.00/ 18 | 15.00/ 6 | 136.00/ 58 |
| Chivas | .00 | .00 | 12.50/ 6 | .00 | 12.50/ 6 |
| Cutty | .00 | 4.50/ 2 | .00 | .00 | 4.50/ 2 |
| Dewar's | 46.75/ 17 | 30.00/ 12 | 36.50/ 14 | 46.75/ 17 | 160.00/ 60 |
| J&B | 11.00/ 4 | 8.25/ 3 | 32.00/ 12 | .00 | 51.25/ 19 |
| JW Black | 8.25/ 3 | 13.75/ 5 | 2.75/ 1 | 2.75/ 1 | 27.50/ 10 |
| Bourbon | 47.50/ 19 | 15.50/ 7 | 21.50/ 9 | 5.00/ 2 | 89.50/ 37 |
| Granddad | .00 | 5.25/ 3 | .00 | .00 | 5.25/ 3 |
| WildTurk | 5.50/ 2 | 8.25/ 3 | .00 | .00 | 13.75/ 5 |
| JDaniels | 74.25/ 27 | 90.75/ 33 | 65.25/ 27 | 35.75/ 13 | 266.00/ 100 |
| Seag 7 | 52.50/ 21 | 15.00/ 6 | 13.00/ 6 | 30.00/ 12 | 110.50/ 45 |
| MakrMark | 5.50/ 2 | 18.25/ 7 | 2.75/ 1 | 11.00/ 4 | 37.50/ 14 |
| Seag VO | 22.00/ 8 | 40.00/ 16 | 45.75/ 17 | 27.50/ 10 | 135.25/ 51 |
| Cr Royal | 13.75/ 5 | 19.25/ 7 | 2.75/ 1 | .00 | 35.75/ 13 |
| C Club | 8.25/ 3 | 82.00/ 32 | 35.75/ 13 | 8.25/ 3 | 134.25/ 51 |
| Tanquray | 60.50/ 22 | 46.75/ 17 | 51.00/ 20 | 22.00/ 8 | 180.25/ 67 |
| Beefeatr | 2.75/ 1 | 2.75/ 1 | 8.25/ 3 | .00 | 13.75/ 5 |
| Gin | 25.00/ 10 | 10.00/ 4 | 7.50/ 3 | 2.50/ 1 | 45.00/ 18 |
| Bombay | 11.00/ 4 | .00 | .00 | .00 | 11.00/ 4 |
| Absolut | 16.50/ 6 | 38.50/ 14 | 16.50/ 6 | 2.75/ 1 | 74.25/ 27 |
| Vodka | 145.00/ 58 | 130.00/ 52 | 205.50/ 85 | 45.00/ 18 | 525.50/ 213 |
| Stoli | 46.75/ 17 | 40.25/ 15 | 76.00/ 28 | 19.25/ 7 | 182.25/ 67 |
| Smirnoff | 24.75/ 9 | 13.75/ 5 | .00 | .00 | 38.50/ 14 |
| Rum | 30.00/ 12 | 5.00/ 2 | 28.00/ 12 | 5.00/ 2 | 68.00/ 28 |
| Bacardi | .00 | .00 | .00 | 11.00/ 4 | 11.00/ 4 |
| Trip Sec | .00 | 2.50/ 1 | .00 | .00 | 2.50/ 1 |
| Peach | 75.00/ 30 | 27.50/ 11 | 5.00/ 2 | 17.50/ 7 | 125.00/ 50 |
| Sloe Gin | .00 | 2.50/ 1 | .00 | .00 | 2.50/ 1 |
| Dom Beer | 428.25/ 191 | 321.00/ 145 | 218.25/ 99 | 119.25/ 53 | 1086.75/ 488 |
| Imp Beer | 41.25/ 15 | 51.25/ 19 | 18.25/ 7 | 24.75/ 9 | 135.50/ 50 |
| Tequila | 5.00/ 2 | .00 | 12.50/ 5 | 2.50/ 1 | 20.00/ 8 |
| Cuervo G | 2.75/ 1 | 24.75/ 9 | 5.50/ 2 | .00 | 33.00/ 12 |
| Gr Marn | .00 | 6.50/ 2 | 19.50/ 6 | 6.50/ 2 | 32.50/ 10 |
| Brandy | 12.50/ 5 | .00 | .00 | .00 | 12.50/ 5 |
| Menthe L | 17.50/ 7 | .00 | 7.50/ 3 | .00 | 25.00/ 10 |
| Menthe G | .00 | .00 | 2.50/ 1 | .00 | 2.50/ 1 |
| Cacao Dk | 2.50/ 1 | .00 | .00 | .00 | 2.50/ 1 |
| Drambuie | 19.50/ 6 | 6.50/ 2 | .00 | .00 | 26.00/ 8 |
| Di Saron | 6.50/ 2 | 3.25/ 1 | .00 | .00 | 9.75/ 3 |
| Amorita | 19.50/ 6 | 7.50/ 3 | .00 | .00 | 27.25/ 9 |
| Frngelco | .00 | .00 | 3.25/ 1 | .00 | 3.25/ 1 |
| Chrdonay | .00 | 3.00/ 1 | .00 | 3.00/ 1 | 6.00/ 2 |
| Kamora | 32.50/ 10 | .00 | 4.50/ 2 | .00 | 37.00/ 12 |

| Sales Mix By Major Product | STATION 1 SALES | STATION 2 SALES | STATION 3 SALES | STATION 4 SALES | TOTAL SALES |
| --- | --- | --- | --- | --- | --- |
| Midori | 3.25/ 1 | .00 | .00 | .00 | 3.25/ 1 |
| Chablis | 5.25/ 3 | 15.75/ 9 | 21.75/ 13 | 8.75/ 5 | 51.50/ 30 |
| Sambuca | .00 | 26.00/ 8 | 45.50/ 14 | .00 | 71.50/ 22 |
| TiaMaria | .00 | .00 | 7.75/ 3 | .00 | 7.75/ 3 |
| Zinfndel | 21.00/ 7 | 21.00/ 7 | 36.00/ 12 | 6.00/ 2 | 84.00/ 28 |
| Soda | .00 | .00/ 1 | 1.75/ 5 | .00/ 3 | 1.75/ 9 |
| LemLime | 1.75/ 2 | .00 | 1.75/ 1 | .00/ 1 | 3.50/ 4 |
| SeagCool | .00 | 12.25/ 7 | 1.75/ 1 | .00 | 14.00/ 8 |
| Cola | .00 | 1.75/ 3 | 10.25/ 6 | 1.75/ 6 | 13.75/ 15 |
| Tonic | .00 | .00/ 1 | 1.75/ 1 | .00 | 1.75/ 2 |
| Diet | .00 | 5.00/ 3 | 1.75/ 1 | 7.00/ 6 | 13.75/ 10 |
| Martini | 10.25/ 3 | 13.75/ 4 | 21.25/ 7 | 78.75/ 23 | 124.00/ 37 |
| Manhattn | 3.25/ 1 | 3.25/ 1 | 40.25/ 13 | .00 | 46.75/ 15 |
| Mai-Tai | 11.00/ 3 | .00 | .00 | .00 | 11.00/ 3 |
| Wh Sour | 5.75/ 2 | 28.75/ 10 | 15.50/ 5 | .00 | 50.00/ 17 |
| TCollins | 5.00/ 2 | 7.50/ 3 | 10.00/ 4 | .00 | 22.50/ 9 |
| Daiquiri | .00 | .00 | 1.50/ 1 | 3.00/ 1 | 4.50/ 2 |
| Bl Russn | 13.00/ 4 | 2.25/ 1 | 2.25/ 1 | .00 | 17.50/ 6 |
| Rusty Nl | .00 | .00 | 6.50/ 2 | .00 | 6.50/ 2 |
| Stinger | 19.50/ 6 | .00 | .00 | .00 | 19.50/ 6 |
| Kamikaze | 85.00/ 34 | 85.00/ 34 | 27.50/ 11 | .00 | 197.50/ 79 |
| Spritzer | 1.75/ 1 | 3.50/ 2 | 17.50/ 10 | 1.75/ 1 | 24.50/ 14 |
| Ice Tea | 26.00/ 8 | 32.50/ 10 | 26.00/ 8 | 9.75/ 3 | 91.25/ 29 |
| Lemonade | .00 | 6.50/ 2 | .00 | 3.25/ 1 | 9.75/ 3 |
| W Cooler | 1.75/ 1 | 1.75/ 1 | 1.75/ 1 | .00 | 5.25/ 3 |
| Margrita | 10.00/ 4 | 2.50/ 1 | 2.50/ 1 | .00 | 15.00/ 6 |
| PeachDaq | .00 | 3.50/ 1 | .00 | .00 | 3.50/ 1 |
| B-52 | 52.00/ 16 | 6.50/ 2 | 3.25/ 1 | .00 | 61.75/ 19 |
| V Hammer | .00 | .00 | .00 | 7.00/ 2 | 7.00/ 2 |
| LaBoomer | .00 | .00 | 3.50/ 1 | .00 | 3.50/ 1 |
| Spec Ctl | 58.50/ 18 | 9.75/ 3 | 35.75/ 11 | .00 | 104.00/ 32 |
| Totals | 1686.75 | 1415.25 | 1371.00 | 590.00 | 5063.00 |

| Sales Mix By Produce Lookup | STATION 1 SALES | STATION 2 SALES | STATION 3 SALES | STATION 4 SALES | TOTAL SALES |
| --- | --- | --- | --- | --- | --- |
| Moet Chandon | 38.00/ 1 | 38.00/ 1 | .00 | .00 | 76.00/ 2 |
| Cajun | .00 | .00 | 6.95/ 1 | .00 | 6.95/ 1 |
| Barb Chick | 6.95/ 1 | 13.90/ 2 | .00 | .00 | 20.85/ 3 |
| Wild Mush | .00 | 6.95/ 1 | .00 | .00 | 6.95/ 1 |
| Brie | .00 | .00 | 4.95/ 1 | .00 | 4.95/ 1 |
| Thai Chick | 6.95/ 1 | .00 | .00 | .00 | 6.95/ 1 |
| Reuben | .00 | 5.95/ 1 | .00 | .00 | 5.95/ 1 |
| Mush Pep Sau | 5.95/ 1 | 29.75/ 5 | 11.90/ 2 | .00 | 47.60/ 8 |
| Totals | 57.85 | 94.55 | 23.80 | .00 | 176.20 |

continued

Source: American Business Computers, Akron, Ohio.

## Exhibit 19    Product Usage Report

| Ring Off #22 | —2:52 a.m. | 1/06 |
| Accumulators Cleared | —8:01 a.m. | 1/05 |

| Product Usage | Bottle Size | Ounces Poured | Bottles Emptied | Product | Size | Poured | Emptied |
|---|---|---|---|---|---|---|---|
| Scotch | 1.75 L | 77 | 1 | Almond | Liter | 4 | |
| Chivas Regal | 1.75 L | 7 | | Cacao Dark | Liter | 3 | |
| Cutty Sark | 1.75 L | 2 | | Cacao Light | Liter | 1 | |
| Dewar's | 1.75 L | 82 | 1 | Menthe Green | Liter | 1 | |
| J&B | 1.75 L | 24 | | Menthe Light | Liter | 15 | |
| JWalker Black | 1.75 L | 17 | | | | | |
| | | | | Midori | Liter | 2 | |
| Bourbon | 1.75 L | 54 | 1 | Peach Schnaps | 1.75 L | 68 | 1 |
| Jack Daniels | 1.75 L | 130 | 2 | Sloe Gin | Liter | 1 | |
| Jim Beam | 1.75 L | | | Triple Sec | 1.75 L | 42 | 1 |
| Makers Mark | 1.75 L | 17 | | | | | |
| Old Granddad | 1.75 L | 3 | | Di Saronna | 1.75 L | 3 | |
| Wild Turkey | 1.75 L | 6 | | Amorita | Liter | 27 | |
| | | | | Drambuie | 1.75 L | 12 | 1 |
| Canadian Club | 1.75 L | 64 | 1 | Frangelico | 750ml | 1 | |
| Crown Royal | 1.75 L | 17 | | Grand Marnier | 1.75 L | 19 | 1 |
| Irish Whiskey | 1.75 L | 1 | | | | | |
| Seagram's 7 | 1.75 L | 60 | 1 | Kahlua | 1.75 L | 4 | |
| Seagram's VO | 1.75 L | 73 | 2 | Kamora | Liter | 29 | 1 |
| | | | | Sambuca | 750ml | 28 | 1 |
| Gin | 1.75 L | 43 | 1 | Tia Maria | Liter | 15 | 1 |
| Beefeater | 1.75 L | 6 | | | | | |
| Bombay | 1.75 L | 5 | | Chablis | 1 Gal | 234 | 1 |
| Tanqueray | 1.75 L | 92 | 1 | Chardonnay | 1 Gal | 10 | |
| | | | | Wht Zinfandel | 1 Gal | 159 | 1 |
| Vodka | 1.75 L | 414 | 7 | | | | |
| Absolut | 1.75 L | 34 | 1 | Margarita Mix | 5 Gal | 2 | 1 |
| Smirnoff | 1.75 L | 18 | | Sour Mix | 5 Gal | 138 | |
| Stolichnaya | Liter | 111 | 3 | | | | |
| | | | | LemLime Syrup | 1 Gal | 32 | |
| Rum | 1.75 L | 66 | 1 | Seagrams Coolr | 1 Gal | 7 | |
| Bacardi | 1.75 L | 5 | | Cola Syrup | 1 Gal | 36 | 1 |
| Myers's | 1.75 L | | | Tonic syrup | 1 Gal | 40 | 1 |
| | | | | Diet Syrup | 1 Gal | 9 | |
| Tequilla | 1.75 L | 15 | | | | | |
| Cuervo Gold | 1.75 L | 15 | | Soda | 1 Gal | 799 | 6 |
| | | | | Water | 1 Gal | 42 | |
| Brandy | 1.75 L | 15 | 1 | | | | |
| Apricot | Liter | | | | | | |

**continued**

Source: American Business Computers, Akron, Ohio.

Automated beverage systems can greatly enhance management's control of beverage operations. At the least, the system provides accurate information about the number of drinks and/or ounces sold. At best, such a system will not allow a drink to be served without its being entered as a sale within the system.

However, automated equipment cannot solve the problem of assessing standard income from beverage sales completely because:

- Some beverage products will not be on the system. For example, bottled beer and some mixed cocktails such as frozen daiquiris are not generally metered by automated equipment.

- Dishonest personnel can almost always find a way to work outside or around the system.

- Should the equipment break down, manual income control systems are still necessary.

Perhaps the best approach for controlling sales income with an automated beverage system is to make sure that it complements the income collection system used in the food and beverage operation.

## 🔑 Key Terms

**conversion tables**—Track ingredients (by unit and by cost) as they pass through purchasing/receiving, storing/issuing, and production/service control points.

**daily sales report**—Summarizes all sales revenue activity for a day. Revenue is itemized by the following categories: net sales, tax, number of guest checks, number of covers, dollars per check, dollars per cover, sales category, day-part totals. Affected general ledger accounts are listed, and associated food costs and sales percentage statistics are noted.

**ingredient file**—Contains important data on each purchased ingredient, such as ingredient code number, ingredient description, purchase unit, purchase unit cost, issue unit, issue unit cost, recipe unit, and recipe unit cost.

**marketing category report**—Compiles weekly totals summarizing the revenue earned by food and beverage departments (or categories).

**menu engineering**—A menu management application for evaluating decisions regarding current and future menu pricing, design, and contents. This application requires that management focus on the number of dollars a menu contributes to profit and not simply monitor cost percentages.

**menu item file**—Contains data for all meal periods and menu items sold.

**net sales by time of day report**—A report produced by sophisticated automated beverage systems indicating hourly sales; the report is useful for forecasting sales and scheduling servers and bartenders according to expected demand.

**outstanding guest checks report**—A report produced by sophisticated automated beverage systems to resolve any discrepancy existing between the sales by major beverage category report and the sales by beverage server report.

**postcosting**—Multiplies the number of menu items sold by standard recipe costs to determine a potential food cost amount. When actual recipe costs are known, these figures are multiplied by the number of menu items sold to produce an actual cost figure.

**precosting**—A special type of forecasting that compares forecasted guest counts with standard menu item recipe costs to yield an index of expense before an actual meal period.

**product usage report**—A report produced by sophisticated automated beverage systems indicating amounts of beverage products sold during a shift; the report enables managers to minimize inventory control problems.

**recipe chaining**—Including sub-recipes as ingredients for a particular standard recipe. This enables the computer-based restaurant management system to maintain a record for a particular menu item that requires an unusually large number of ingredients.

**sales by beverage server report**—A report produced by sophisticated automated beverage systems indicating the total sales of each beverage server during a shift.

**sales by major beverage category report**—A report produced by sophisticated automated beverage systems indicating the expected beverage income by major beverage category (liquor, beer, wine, etc.).

**sales category analysis report**—Shows relationships between amounts sold by sales category and day-parts defined by management; enables management to view at a glance which menu items sell and when they sell.

**sales mix by major product report**—A report produced by sophisticated automated beverage systems indicating how much of each beverage product was sold during a shift; the report is useful for monitoring product sales trends and adjusting par inventory levels when necessary.

**settlement methods report**—A report produced by sophisticated automated beverage systems indicating the amounts due in the form of cash, credit card vouchers, and house account charges for sales made during a shift.

**sub-recipe**—Recipes that are included as ingredients within a standard recipe record.

**weekly sales spreadsheet**—Provides a weekly summary of all information reported by relevant daily sales reports.

# Review Questions

1. What three files does a recipe management application maintain?

2. How can other management applications use the data in recipe management files?

3. What does the term "sub-recipes" mean? Explain how sub-recipes are used in an ingredient file of a recipe management application.

4. Why is it useful for a sales analysis application to be able to access POS system files?

5. What problems could managers encounter when the restaurant operation uses generic software applications to manage information?

6. How can managers benefit from integrated software applications?

7. What do the terms "precosting" and "postcosting" mean?

8. How are menu management applications, such as menu engineering, different from most other management applications?

9. How can managers use the results of menu engineering to improve the profitability of their operations?

10. What are some of the reports produced by automated beverage systems that enhance management's control of operations?

## Internet Sites

For more information, visit the following Internet sites. Remember that Internet addresses can change without notice. If the site is no longer there, you can use a search engine to look for additional sites.

CLS Software
http://www.hospitalitynet.nl/cls

Comtrex Systems Corporation
http://www.comtrex.com

Comus Restaurant Systems
http://www.comus.com

CostGuard Food Service Software
http://www.costguard.com

Eatec Corporation
http://www.eatec.com

Geac Computer Corporation Limited
http://www.geac.com

Instill Corporation
http://www.instill.com

Integrated Restaurant Software
http://www.rmstouch.com

Micros Systems, Inc.
http://www.micros.com

System Concepts, Inc.
http://www.foodtrak.com

# Chapter 8 Outline

Hotel Sales Office Automation
    Group Guestroom Sales
    Function and Banquet Room Sales
    Sales Filing Systems
    Sales Forecasts and Performance
       Reports
Revenue Management
    Elements of Revenue Management
    Using Revenue Management
    Revenue Management Software
Catering Software
    Off-Premises Catering
    Home Delivery Catering

# Competencies

1. Identify characteristics of guestroom and function room sales that affect the design and operation of hotel sales software. (pp. 193–198)

2. Identify the types of data, files, and reports used in the operation of a hotel sales office. (pp. 198–203)

3. Identify characteristics of revenue management in hotel operations that affect the design and operation of hotel sales software. (pp. 203–209)

4. Describe the features and functions of software designed for off-premises catering operations. (pp. 209–213)

# 8

# Sales and Catering Applications

A TYPICAL HOTEL sales or food service catering operation generates an incredible amount of paperwork, and a great part of each day is spent managing the information collected through prospecting, selling, booking, and reporting. Today, at many properties, these time-consuming and costly efforts are handled with automated systems. During the past decade, sales and catering applications have enabled operations to:

- Accomplish tedious tasks quickly and efficiently.

- Access sales information rapidly.

- Facilitate personalized mailings through database marketing.

- Reduce data-handling errors.

- Decrease training costs by implementing automated procedures.

- Access customer profile information for sales promotions to client groups or individuals.

- Enhance communication among affiliated properties, greatly facilitating the sales effort in large hotel chains.

The following sections explore software applications in relation to hotel sales office functions and revenue management strategies, as well as off-premises and home-delivery food service operations.

## Hotel Sales Office Automation

Sales records are a vital part of a sales office's communication system. They are important in establishing new accounts, servicing existing accounts, and generating repeat business. In a non-automated sales office, it is essential that salespeople familiarize themselves with sales forms, learn to complete them properly, and file them in accordance with sales office procedures. Many of these mechanical and often detailed office procedures are streamlined or eliminated in automated sales offices. Exhibit 1 summarizes a few of the differences between non-automated and automated systems. The following sections compare non-automated and automated sales office functions in relation to group guestroom sales, function and banquet room sales, and sales office filing systems.[1] In addition, the sections describe sales forecasts and performance reports generated by automated sales systems.

**Exhibit 1   Non-Automated vs. Automated Sales Systems**

| Non-Automated | Automated |
|---|---|
| 1. Account and booking information is entered on a scratch sheet. | All information is entered directly into the computer. If the account is an established one, entering the first few letters brings the name, address, contact person, and all other relevant information onto the screen. If the new booking is similar to a previous booking, the old entry can be duplicated and modified if necessary. |
| 2. The same account and booking information is entered into the group room control log—the log is summarized manually. | The log is updated automatically; summary and forecast are calculated automatically. |
| 3. The secretary types up group room block and function information. | The recap is automatically printed and includes all details on the group room block and the function events. |
| 4. The same account and booking information is retyped in a confirmation letter. | Confirmation is produced automatically. |
| 5. The same information is retyped in a contract. | Contract is produced automatically. |
| 6. The banquet event order is typed and retyped with corrections using the same information as well as detailed menus, resource items, and comments. | Banquet event order is automatically generated by selecting menus and resources from the screen. Costs, consumption, and use at the time of the event are displayed. |
| 7. Related follow-up correspondence is typed, referring to the same account and booking information. | Follow-up correspondence is traced and generated automatically. |
| 8. In order to execute market research and/or telemarketing activity, a database is built by re-entering the same booking and account information. | Integrated account booking information is available for database search for marketing, telemarketing, service history, and lost business tracking. |
| 9. Reports are created by a review of the forecast books, diaries, and booking recaps. Summary of data is entered. | Diary is automatically updated each time a booking is entered; summary and forecast are automatically calculated. |
| 10. Salesperson booking pace and productivity reports are created through manual tabulation. | Reports are generated automatically using data in the system. |
| 11. Tracing is done by manual entry on 3- by 5-inch cards. Traced files are delivered by secretaries to sales manager where they pile up on desks. | All activities are traced to the salesperson in accordance with a pre-developed plan. Daily trace reports remind the sales staff of such critical account and booking details as contracts due, credit checks to be done, block pick-ups, menus, and follow-up sales calls. Tentative and definite bookings are displayed and traced for follow-up. Numerous user-defined account traces and booking traces are generated for action steps. |

Source: Adapted from *HSMAI Marketing Review.*

## Group Guestroom Sales

In most non-automated sales offices, a guestroom control book is used to monitor the number of guestrooms committed to groups. Because front desk, reservations, and sales office employees all book guestroom business, it is important that all of these personnel be aware of group allotments and avoid overbooking.

Many properties implement revenue management strategies that are designed to maximize rooms revenue by establishing a desired mix of group, tour and travel, and individual guest business for specific time periods. A later section in this chapter discusses revenue management in greater detail. For the purposes of our discussion here, it is important to note that the **guestroom control book** guides guestroom booking activity by providing the sales office with the maximum number of guestrooms it can sell to groups on a given day. This quota is usually set by the general manager and the head of the marketing and sales department. The remaining guestrooms (and any unsold guestrooms allotted to groups) are available for individual guests. These guestrooms can generally be sold by front desk and reservations staff at higher rates than they could be sold to groups.

A major challenge of non-automated sales offices is maintaining an up-to-date and accurate guestroom control book. Difficulties arise during busy periods when bookings or cancellations are not recorded as soon as they occur. Therefore, before booking guestroom business, it is not unusual for a salesperson to double-check the reliability of guestroom control data by asking other sales staff members about recent activity regarding the days in question.

Automated sales offices overcome many of these problems simply because every salesperson with a terminal has immediate access to guestroom control information. Bookings and cancellations can be quickly processed as they occur—even as the salesperson is on the telephone with the client. This helps ensure that every salesperson has access to exactly the same information, and that "definite" and "tentative" bookings are clearly identified to prevent errors.

Exhibit 2 shows the screen of a guestroom control log from a Windows-based hotel sales program. For each day of the week, the screen shows the total number of rooms still available for sale, as well as the number of rooms allocated to definite and tentative group bookings and the number of rooms protected for front office sales to transient business. Room sales are coordinated in real time as salespeople, the rooms manager, and the general manager have instant access to the most current information. The booking evaluator, also shown in Exhibit 2, enables everyone to assess the impact of individual group bookings on budgeted targets for rooms sales, average rate, and revenue per available room.

## Function and Banquet Room Sales

In non-automated properties, the key to successful function and banquet space control is the function book. This record shows the occupancies and vacancies of specific function and banquet rooms and facilitates the effective planning of functions.

Function books normally are divided into pages for each day of the year, with sections set aside for each meeting or function room. Information recorded in the

**Exhibit 2   Guest Rooms Control Log**

| 8 Bookings | | | | Sun 10/12 | Mon 10/13 | Tue 10/14 | Wed 10/15 | Thu 10/16 | Fri 10/17 | Sat 10/18 | Sun 10/19 |
|---|---|---|---|---|---|---|---|---|---|---|---|
| 19XX | | | | | | | | | | | |
| Total Available | | | | 210 | 25 | -35 | 75 | 52 | 300 | 300 | 340 |
| Grp Definite | | | | 130 | 190 | 150 | 40 | 45 | 15 | 15 | 0 |
| Grp Tentative | | | | 0 | 0 | 0 | 0 | 68 | 75 | 75 | 0 |
| Trans Protected | | | | 75 | 200 | 300 | 300 | 250 | 25 | 25 | 75 |
| MAR | | | | 100 | 110 | 110 | 105 | 90 | 85 | 90 | 100 |
| Court Report | D | IS | 89 | 50 | 75 | 55 | | | | | |
| Bose Corp. | D | CA | 45 | 50 | 75 | 55 | | | | | |
| UNH Alumni | D | CA | 133 | 30 | 40 | 30 | 30 | 30 | | | |
| U.S. Airforce | D | CA | 92 | | | 10 | 10 | 15 | 15 | 15 | |
| Int'l Dental | T | EMF | 34 | | | | | 23 | 30 | 30 | |
| IDS Board | T | DH | 83 | | | | | 45 | 45 | 45 | |
| Reader's Digest | P | CA | 99 | | | | | | 50 | 122 | |
| Delphi User Grp | P | CA | 113 | | | | | | | 50 | 50 |

**Booking Evaluator**

October, 20XX     Post As: Bose Speakers Audio Show

| | Rooms | Avg. Rate | Revenue | Revenue PAR |
|---|---|---|---|---|
| Budget: | 14280 | 102.00 | 1,456,560.00 | 78.31 |
| Without Booking: | 14107 | 101.75 | 1,435,387.25 | 77.17 |
| With Booking: | 14290 | 103.25 | 1,475,442.50 | 79.32 |

Dates: October, 20XX

Source: Delphi 7/Newmarket Software Systems, Inc., Durham, New Hampshire. For more information, browse the company's Web site at http://wwwnewmarketinc.com

function book includes the organization or group scheduling the space; the name, address, and telephone number of the group's contact person; the type of function; the time required for the function; the total time required for preparation, breakdown, and cleanup; the number of people expected; the type of setup(s) required; the rates quoted; the nature of the contract; and any pertinent remarks to help property personnel stage a successful function. Function book entries are always made in pencil because changes can occur even when a commitment seems firm. As with the guestroom control book, only one function book should be maintained to prevent mismatching of entries or double bookings.

Information from the function book and other files is eventually transcribed on a **banquet event order (BEO).** Since a BEO generally serves as a final contract for the client and as a work order for the catering department, problems arise when the function book contains inaccurate or incomplete information.

**Exhibit 3 Sample Banquet Event Order**

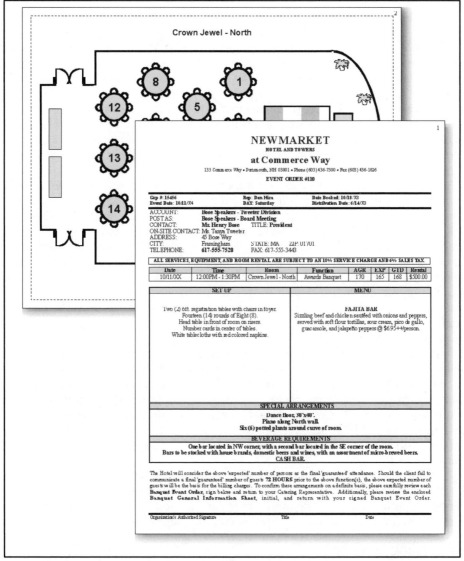

Source: Delphi 7/Newmarket Software Systems, Inc., Durham, New Hampshire. For more information, browse the company's Web site at http://www.newmarketinc.com

Automated sales systems build a BEO as information is gathered and input by the salesperson in the client's account file. Exhibit 3 shows a sample BEO. Sophisticated sales and catering software packages are generally able to supplement information provided by BEOs. For example, for a specific date or range of dates, an automated sales system can produce kitchen reports (listing all menu items needed by preparation area), setup reports (listing all resource items

requested on BEOs for those events), and revenue forecast reports (based on anticipated revenue from BEOs).

Problems non-automated properties encounter in maintaining the function
book are similar to those they encounter in maintaining the guestroom control
book. For example, consider the following scenario. A meeting planner calls and
requests the best rate the hotel can offer for 50 rooms for 3 nights in April with a
general session meeting room (set up classroom style with a head table for 5) and 3
break-out rooms (set up conference style). To respond to this request, the salesperson must first match April availability dates in the guestroom control book
with open dates for four meeting rooms in the function book. Next, the salesperson
may want to double-check the accuracy of each book's information with several
members of the sales staff. Finally, the salesperson would likely have to check with
the department manager before quoting a rate.

In an automated sales office, a salesperson could respond much more quickly.
Availability of both group guestrooms and function room space could be checked
simultaneously on a single screen of information displayed by the terminal. The
salesperson could use a special search function of the system to match the meeting
planner's needs with the hotel's offerings by providing a list of best available dates
to accommodate the group (based on projected occupancy). This allows a hotel
salesperson to quickly check the status of the meeting planner's preferred dates,
and to suggest alternative days if the requested days are booked. If the property's
revenue management strategies are programmed into the system, the terminal
could also provide a range of rates that the salesperson could negotiate without
authorization from the department manager.

Exhibit 4 shows the screen of a function diary from a Windows-based hotel
sales program. Each function room is listed down the left side of the screen with
each hour of a particular day listed across the top. Functions are blocked by room
and time of day, with easy access to individual account information and room
setup requirements. The program enables sales, banquets, and convention services
managers to maximize function space and minimize room turns by scheduling
groups with the same setup requirements in the same room at different times of
the same day.

With sophisticated sales office software packages, once a booking is entered
into the system, it is automatically integrated, tracked, and traced for management
reports, contracts, proposals, and the tediously detailed banquet event order.
Incomplete information is traced for completion. Illegible information never exists.

## Sales Filing Systems

For maximum efficiency in the sales office, an effective filing system is required.
Up-to-date information is essential for a successful sales effort, and information
must be available quickly. Most non-automated hotels use three separate files to
record client information: the trace (or tickler) file, the account file, and the master
card file. The contents of these files vary from property to property.

**Trace Files.** In non-automated sales offices a trace file (also known as a tickler file,
bring-up file, or follow-up file) is used as an aid for following up accounts. A
reminder note or card is filed in the tickler file by month and date; as seen in

**Exhibit 4  Sample Function Space Profile**

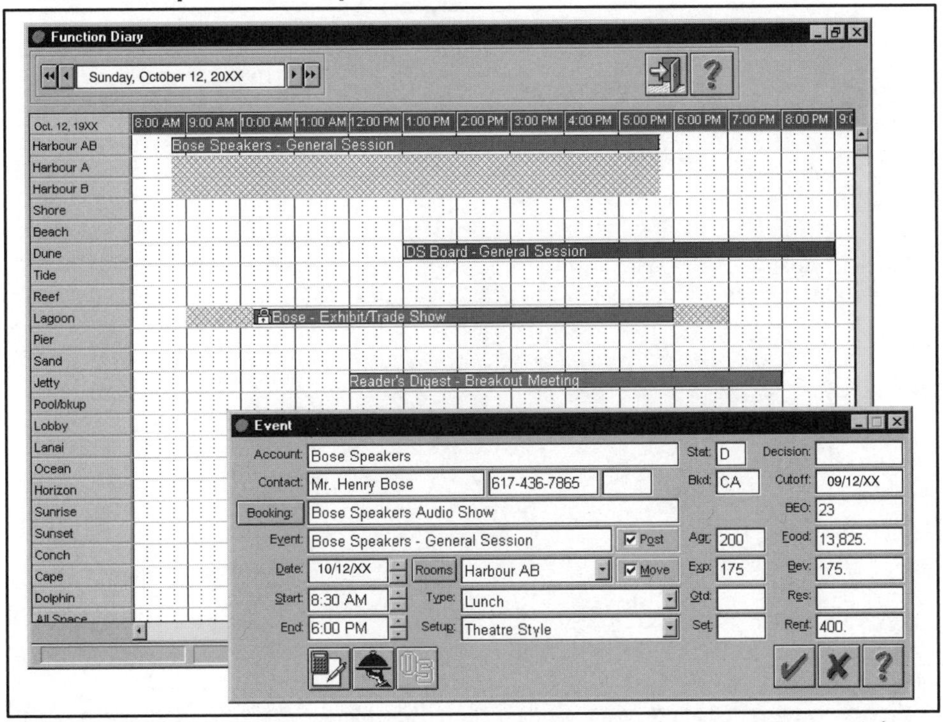

Source: Delphi 7/Newmarket Software Systems, Inc., Durham, New Hampshire. For more information, browse the company's Web site at http://www.newmarketinc.com

Exhibit 5, daily dividers are arranged chronologically for the current month. The system is designed to remind the user of correspondence, telephone calls, or contacts that he or she must handle on a particular date.

For example, suppose a client has reserved space for a training meeting at the property in April. The salesperson will want to contact the client no later than February 15 to finalize meeting plans, so the salesperson would slip a note or a 3 × 5 inch index card (often called a "trace card") dated February 15 into the February tickler divider. On February 1, the notes and trace cards for February would be arranged according to date, and the reminder to contact the meeting planner would be placed into the 15th slot.

This system, as long as it is updated and checked daily, works well and takes very little time to implement. However, the system also depends entirely on the accuracy, efficiency, and completeness with which individual salespersons maintain their trace files.

In automated sales offices, all traces input within the system are activated on the appropriate dates and printed for each salesperson every morning. As the salesperson reads through each trace message, he or she decides whether to act on the trace or to trace it to another date. Throughout the day, the salesperson records notes on the report regarding each trace. At the end of the day, the report is handed

**Exhibit 5   Sample Tickler File**

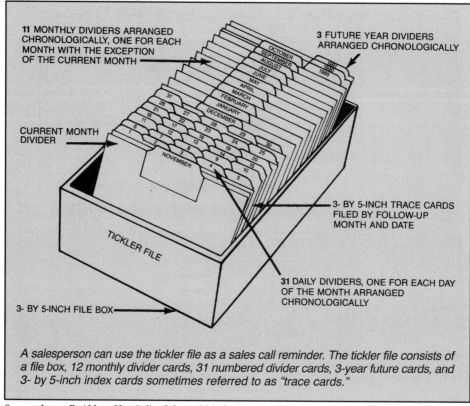

11 MONTHLY DIVIDERS ARRANGED CHRONOLOGICALLY, ONE FOR EACH MONTH WITH THE EXCEPTION OF THE CURRENT MONTH

3 FUTURE YEAR DIVIDERS ARRANGED CHRONOLOGICALLY

CURRENT MONTH DIVIDER

3- BY 5-INCH TRACE CARDS FILED BY FOLLOW-UP MONTH AND DATE

TICKLER FILE

31 DAILY DIVIDERS, ONE FOR EACH DAY OF THE MONTH ARRANGED CHRONOLOGICALLY

3- BY 5-INCH FILE BOX

*A salesperson can use the tickler file as a sales call reminder. The tickler file consists of a file box, 12 monthly divider cards, 31 numbered divider cards, 3-year future cards, and 3- by 5-inch index cards sometimes referred to as "trace cards."*

Source: James R. Abbey, *Hospitality Sales and Marketing,* 4th ed. (Lansing, Mich.: Educational Institute of the American Hotel & Lodging Association, 2003).

to a staff associate who keys in the notes and updates the report for the next morning. Those traces that have been completed will no longer appear on the report, while those traces awaiting action will continue to appear on future reports until action is taken.

**Account Files.** In non-automated sales offices, account files are standard-size file folders holding information needed for serving the basic business needs of clients. An account file is started at the time of initial contact with a prospective client and may include programs from previous conventions or meetings the organization has held, convention bureau bulletins, and information relating to the organization that has appeared in newspapers or trade journals. Sales reports and all correspondence relating to previous efforts to secure business should also be in the file. All information in the account file should be in reverse chronological order—that is, the newest paperwork first. Account files are usually filed alphabetically and are often color-coded by geographic location or, more commonly, by market segment.

When an account file is removed, a guide card detailing the name of the group, its file number, the date of removal, and the initials of the person removing the file should be left in the file drawer in place of the file. This ensures that the sales staff will have easy access to the whereabouts of the file.

In automated sales offices, current account information is available to all sales staff networked to account manager files of the automated sales program. Typically, the salesperson accessing the program determines the extent of the information displayed. Exhibit 6 shows the screen of an account manager system from a Windows-based hotel sales program. From this main menu, salespeople can simply point and click to access detailed, current information about customer contacts (decision-makers, telephone numbers, etc.), account activity, past and future bookings, traces, and call reports.

**Master Card Files and Automated Search Routines.** In non-automated sales offices, a master card (usually a 5 × 8 inch index card) contains a summary of everything needed for an effective sales effort: the organization's name, the names and titles of key executives, addresses, phone numbers, month or months in which the group meets, the size of the group, where the group has met in the past, the group's decision-maker, and other pertinent data that can help to obtain and keep that account's business. Master card files are also used to create mailing lists and quickly obtain addresses or phone numbers for additional sales efforts or follow-ups.

Master cards are often color-coded to draw attention to specific areas of consideration: geographic location, months of meetings, follow-ups required, and size of group. Some properties also arrange master cards alphabetically by market segment. For example, IBM and Xerox would be sorted alphabetically under "Corporate Business." Other properties may not separate master cards by market segment, but may use a color code system to easily identify specific market segments within the file. For example, an association account may be flagged in blue, a government account in yellow, and so on.

Some properties keep a geographic file of master cards. These cards are organized according to the geographic location of the decision-maker. This type of file enables sales personnel to quickly identify accounts in cities to which they are traveling. Salespeople can simply pull the names of the decision-makers located in the area they are visiting and call on them during the sales trip.

Master card files can easily become overloaded with data as salespeople place more and more demands on the type of information they need to prospect, book, and service clients. In automated sales offices, the functions of a master card filing system are quickly and easily performed by search routines with selection criteria defined by the salesperson's or manager's immediate needs. For example, a salesperson can call up specific information needed for an account, whether it be the names of contacts, notes on follow-up calls, or remarks that can help other members of the sales team answer questions regarding the account in the absence of the salesperson who made the call(s). In addition, a salesperson can search the database of accounts for clients likely to fit the future booking needs of the hotel. For example, a salesperson could search for only those accounts in the northeast states that book in July for Sunday night arrival. If, on the first run, the generated list is too long or too short, the salesperson could run the search again with different criteria such as rate or space requirements.

**Exhibit 6    Sample Account Manager Program**

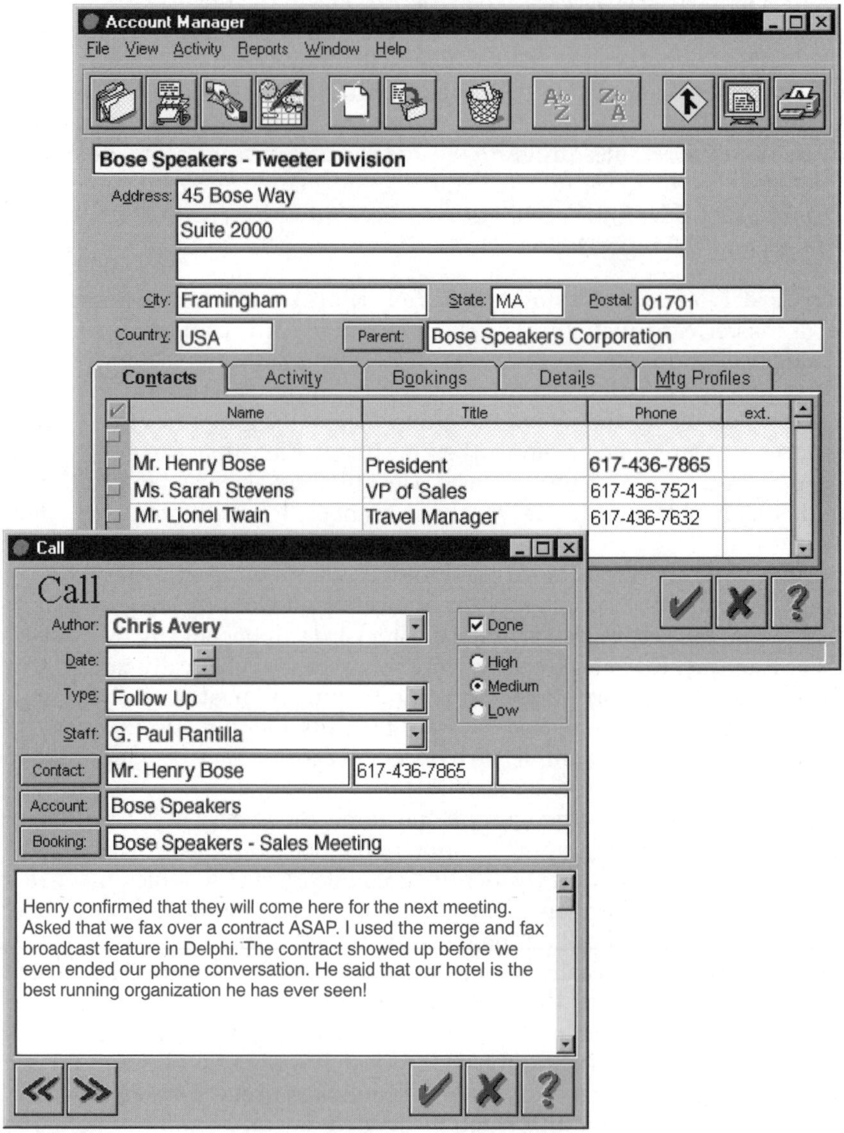

Source: Delphi 7/Newmarket Software Systems, Inc., Durham, New Hampshire. For more information, browse the company's Web site at http://www.newmarketinc.com

## Sales Forecasts and Performance Reports

An automated sales office system can produce reports that provide information on
accounts, bookings, market segments, sales staff productivity, average room rates,
occupancy, revenue, service history, lost business, and important marketing data.

Many of these reports would take several hours to produce manually. The following sections describe some of these reports.

**Cover Count and Revenue Summary Report.** To produce a monthly catering sales forecast at a non-automated property, someone must carefully review each page for a particular month in the function book and calculate (or estimate) each day's cover count and revenue forecast. This could take several hours. A sample cover count and revenue summary can be produced in seconds by a sales software package with integrated files. The daily revenue summary figures can be calculated on the basis of estimates (such as multiplying cover counts by check averages for meal periods), they can represent actual revenue figures drawn from completed banquet event orders, or they can be a combination of both methods.

**Sales Performance by Market Segment Report.** Sales software packages can also produce sales performance by market segment report that analyzes a salesperson's booking activity by market segment during a specified time period. This report can be used to evaluate the performance of salespersons.

# Revenue Management

**Revenue management,** sometimes called yield management, is a set of demand-forecasting techniques used to determine whether prices should be raised or lowered and whether a reservation request should be accepted or rejected in order to maximize revenue. Revenue management is based on supply and demand. Prices tend to rise when demand exceeds supply; prices tend to fall when supply exceeds demand. Pricing is the key to profitability. By increasing bookings on low-demand days and by selling rooms at higher prices on high-demand days, a hotel improves its profitability. In general, room rates should be higher when demand exceeds supply. They should be lower (in order to increase occupancy) when supply exceeds demand.

One of the principal computations involved in revenue management is **yield,** which is the ratio of actual revenue to potential revenue. Actual revenue is the revenue generated by the number of rooms sold. Potential revenue is the amount of money that the property would receive if all of its rooms were sold at full rack rates. There are many formulas used to implement revenue management strategies.[2]

## Elements of Revenue Management

Revenue management takes into account as many of the factors influencing business trends as possible. There are various approaches to revenue management. Often, each approach is modeled to meet the needs of the individual property or company.

Revenue management can be used to determine whether all room rates should be raised or lowered—for example, when the hotel moves out of or into its off-season—and whether selective room rate changes are called for. Revenue management becomes more complex when room rate changes are implemented on a selective rather than a general basis, and when it involves selling rooms for which there may be competing buyers. Hotels frequently offer discounts to guests falling into certain categories (for example, senior citizens or government employees). Hotels must also decide whether to accept or refuse group business at a discounted rate.

The following elements must be included in the development of a successful yield strategy:

- Group room sales

- Transient (or FIT) room sales

- Food and beverage activity

- Local and area-wide conventions

- Special events

This section focuses on group room sales.[3]

For many hotels, groups form the foundation of future business. It is common to have reservations for group sales three months to two years in advance. Some international hotels and resorts commonly book groups more than two years in advance. Therefore, understanding group booking trends and requirements can be critical to the success of revenue management.

To clearly understand how group sales affect overall room revenue, the hotel should collect as much of the following types of data as possible:

- Business already on the books (reservations)

- Group booking pace (the rate at which group business is being booked)

- Business not yet on the books but likely to return

- Room booking lead time

- Displacement of transient business

**Business Already on the Books.** Management should determine whether the group blocks already in the reservation file should be reduced because of anticipated cancellations or overestimation of the group's size. If the group has booked at the hotel before, management can often determine this information by looking at the group's booking history. Groups often block 5 percent to 10 percent more rooms than they need to ensure that they will have sufficient space for their members. The deletion of unnecessary group rooms from the group block is called the **wash factor.**

**Group Booking Pace.** The rate at which group business is being booked is called the **group booking pace.** ("Booking" in this context refers to the initial agreement between the group and the hotel, not to the booking of individual rooms in the block by group members.) For example, suppose that in April of a given year, a hotel has 300 rooms in group blocks due to arrive in October of that year. If the hotel had only 250 group rooms booked for October at the same time the year before, the booking pace would be 20 percent ahead of the previous year's pace. Once a hotel has accumulated several years of operational data, it can often determine a historical trend that reveals the normal booking pace for each month of the year. While simple on the surface, this method of forecasting can become very complicated due to yearly fluctuations. Management should try to keep the method for tracking the group booking pace forecast as simple as possible.

**Unbooked Business Likely to Return.** Most national, regional, and state associations, as well as some corporations, have policies governing the locations of annual meetings. For example, a group may rotate among three cities, returning to each every three years. Although a contract may not yet be signed, hotel management may be quite confident that the group will return according to the cycle. In addition, tentative bookings that await final contract negotiations are normally included in the yield analysis.

**Booking Lead Time.** **Booking lead time** measures how far in advance bookings are made. Some hotels have average lead times of two months. For many hotels, group bookings are usually made within one year of actual arrival. Management should determine its hotel's lead time for group bookings so that a booking trend can be charted. This trend can be combined with booking pace information on a graph to illustrate the rate at which the hotel is booking business compared with historical trends (see Exhibit 7). This information can be very important when determining whether to accept an additional group and at what room rate to book the group. If the current booking pace is lower than expected or lags behind the historical trend, it may be necessary to offer a lower room rate to stimulate business through increased occupancy. On the other hand, if demand is strong and the group booking pace is ahead of anticipated or historical trends, it may not be appropriate to discount room rates to increase room revenue.

**Displacement of Transient Business.** Management should consult its demand forecast when determining whether to accept group business. **Displacement** occurs when a hotel accepts group business at the expense of turning away transient guests. Transient rooms are guestrooms sold to guests who are not affiliated with a group staying at the hotel. These guests, usually called transient guests or FITs (free independent travelers), are often businesspeople or vacationers. Since transient guests often pay higher room rates than group business, any situation involving displacement should be looked at very carefully.

Assume that a 400-room hotel has a **potential average rate** of $100, an actual transient rate of $80, an actual group rate of $60, and a marginal cost (i.e., the variable cost) of $15 per room. Consider the impact of a group requesting a block of 60 rooms during the following four days:

|  | Tuesday | Wednesday | Thursday | Friday |
|---|---|---|---|---|
| Room Nights Available | 400 | 400 | 400 | 400 |
| Definite Group Demand | 140 | 140 | 150 | 150 |
| Expected Transient Demand | 200 | 180 | 220 | 210 |
| Available Rooms | 60 | 80 | 30 | 40 |
| Suggested Group | 60 | 60 | 60 | 60 |
| Transient Displacement | 0 | 0 | 30 | 20 |

If this group is accepted, no displacement occurs on Tuesday and Wednesday; the hotel clearly benefits on these days because it sells rooms it did not expect to sell

**Exhibit 7   Lead Time/Booking Pace for Sample Hotel**

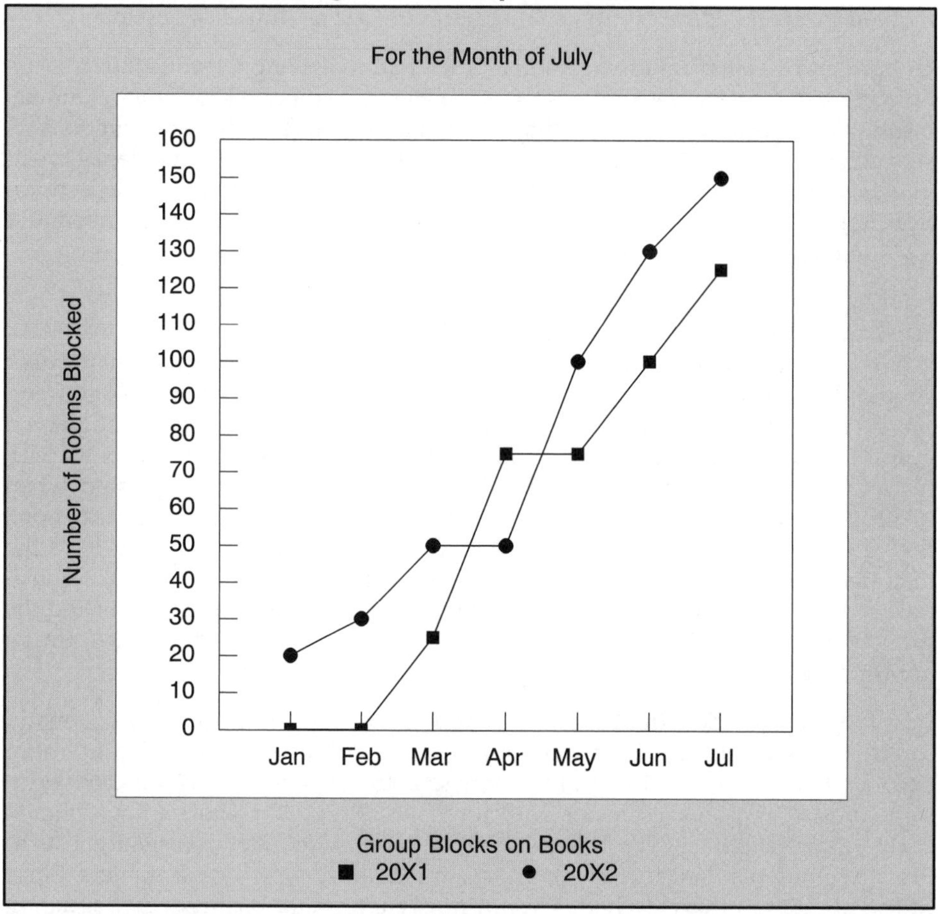

For the Month of July

Group Blocks on Books
■ 20X1      ● 20X2

Source: Michael L. Kasavana and Richard M. Brooks, *Managing Front Office Operations*, 6th ed. (Lansing, Mich.: Educational Institute of the American Hotel & Lodging Association, 2001), p. 450.

(earning an additional $3,600 gross and $2,700 net room revenue each day). On Thursday and Friday, however, 30 and 20 transient guests, respectively, will be displaced. Still, as shown in Exhibit 8, Thursday's room revenue will rise by $1,200 gross and $750 net if the group is accepted. Friday's room revenue will rise by $2,000 gross and $1,400 net if the group is accepted. In other words, accepting the group business will increase the hotel's yield for all four days. Since it also raises the hotel's occupancy, the group business will probably increase non-room revenue as well.

Several factors help determine whether a group reservation should be accepted. As just illustrated, the hotel should first look at revenue factors. A group should probably be accepted if the expected revenue gain (including that from non-room revenue centers) offsets the transient guest revenue loss. In addition, management must consider what happens to the transient guests who cannot be

**Exhibit 8    Revenue and Yield Calculations**

|  | Tuesday | | Wednesday | | Thursday | | Friday | |
|---|---|---|---|---|---|---|---|---|
|  | Without Group | With Group | Without Group | With Group | Without Group | With Group | Without Group | With Group |
| Gross revenue | $24,400 | $28,000 | $22,800 | $26,400 | $26,600 | $27,800 | $25,800 | $27,800 |
| Contribution* | 19,300 | 22,000 | 18,000 | 20,700 | 21,050 | 21,800 | 20,400 | 21,800 |
| Yield** | 61.0% | 70.0% | 57.0% | 66.0% | 66.5% | 69.5% | 64.5% | 69.5% |

*Based on a marginal cost of $15.
**Potential revenue = $100 potential average rate × 400 rooms = $40,000.

Source: Michael L. Kasavana and Richard M. Brooks, *Managing Front Office Operations,* 6th ed. (Lansing, Mich.: Educational Institute of the American Hotel & Lodging Association, 2001), p. 452.

accommodated. Whether they are frequent or first-time guests, they may decide not to return after the way they are treated. The transient revenue lost may not be confined simply to the nights in question if frequent guests choose not to return. Of course, turning away the group business may also reduce the chance that the group will return. Deciding whether to accept a group that forces transient displacement is more than an issue of easily identifiable numbers. Management must also consider the longer-term impact on future business.

## Using Revenue Management

All elements of revenue management (group room sales, transient room sales, food and beverage activity, local and area-wide conventions, and special events) should be viewed together in order to make the appropriate decisions. While it is potentially complex, a failure to include relevant factors may make revenue management efforts less successful than they could be.

Yield should be tracked daily. Tracking yield for past days can help reveal trends. However, to use revenue management properly, management must track yield for *future* days. Calculations must be done every day for a future period, depending on how far in advance the hotel books business. If a hotel is currently at 50 percent yield for a day three weeks away, there may be plenty of time to put strategies in place to raise that number. Discounts may be opened to raise occupancy, or some discounts may be closed to raise average rate. It is the balance of occupancy and rate that achieves the highest yield. If achieving the potential room revenue is not possible (and it usually is not), the manager must decide on the best combination of rate and occupancy in order to get the highest yield.

Each piece of group business should be looked at individually. It should be compared to historical trends as well as to the budget. A hotel usually has a group sales target or budgeted figure for each month. Each group should be examined to see if it will contribute to meeting the budget. If demand is strong and the group will create low revenue, the hotel may decide not to book it. If demand is weak, the hotel may decide to accept the group simply to create revenue from rooms that would not otherwise be occupied. Using the group booking pace analysis will help management determine whether the hotel is on track for its target.

Another factor is the actual group booking pattern already on the books. For example, due to booked groups, a hotel may have two days between groups that are not busy. Management may take a lower-revenue-producing group just to fill the gap. The opposite may also occur. A group may want to come in over a period when the hotel is near filling its goal of group rooms. The group may take the hotel over its goal. While this appears to be good, it may displace higher-rated transient business. If the hotel wants the group, it may quote such a rate to the group that will help make up the lost revenue caused by the displacement of transient guests.

The same type of analysis is needed for transient business. For example, due to the discounts the hotel offers, corporate and government business may be assigned the standard category of rooms. As these standard rooms fill, the hotel may only have deluxe rooms left to sell. If demand is not strong, management may decide to sell the deluxe rooms at the standard rack rate to remain competitive. It is best to look at a combined picture (group and transient business) before making these occupancy and rate decisions.

It is important to remember that historical trends do not always apply. More recent trends must also be taken into consideration. For example, if historical trends have been strong, but recent business has been weak, it is better to plan for weak business and attempt to attract as much as possible through low rates. Likewise, if recent occupancy has been very strong, it is appropriate to follow that trend instead of a history showing lower demand.

Since the objective of revenue management is to maximize revenue, tracking business by revenue source will also help management determine when to allow discounted business and when not to allow it. Some hotels may decide to allow specific types of discounted business, such as corporate business, since they are responsible for many repeat guests. As the various sources of business are determined, each should be analyzed to understand its impact on total revenue. Quite often, managers will take discounted business if it generates frequent customers, since the long-term impact is very positive.

## Revenue Management Software

Although the individual tasks of revenue management can be performed manually, doing so is very difficult and time-consuming. The most efficient means of handling data and generating yield statistics is through application software. Revenue management software can integrate room demand and room price statistics, and project the highest revenue-generating product mix. These packages often consider what the competition is charging.

Revenue management software does not make decisions for managers. It merely provides them with information and support for their decisions. The advantage of using revenue management software is that it can store, quickly retrieve, and manipulate great amounts of data on a broad range of factors influencing room revenue. Over time, revenue management software can help management create models showing the probable results of decisions; these models are based on history, forecasts, and booked business.

Those industries that have applied automated revenue management solutions have achieved the following results:

- Continual monitoring: an automated revenue management system can track and analyze business conditions 24 hours a day, 7 days a week.

- Consistency: software can respond to changes in the marketplace, according to corporate or local management rules built into the software.

- Information availability: revenue management software can provide improved management information that, in turn, may help managers make more intelligent decisions more quickly.

- Performance tracking: an automated system is capable of analyzing sales and revenue transactions occurring within a business period to determine how well revenue management goals were achieved.

Revenue management software is also able to generate a number of special reports. The following reports are representative of revenue management software output.

**Market Segment Report.** This report provides information regarding customer mix. This information is important to effective forecasting by market segment.

**Calendar/Booking Graph.** This graph presents room-night demands and volume of reservations on a daily basis.

**Booking Overrides Report.** A booking overrides report lists all bookings that fail to meet contribution margins or availability constraints as determined by management. The report provides management with information necessary to evaluate questionable bookings before contracts are sent to clients.

**Future Arrival Dates Status Report.** This report furnishes demand data for each day of the week. The report contains a variety of forecasting information that allows for the discovery of occupancy trends by comparative analysis of weekdays. It can be designed to cover several future periods.

**Single Arrival Date History Report.** This report indicates the hotel's booking patterns (trends in reservations). The report relates to the booking graph by documenting how a specific day was constructed on the graph.

**Weekly Recap Report.** This report contains the sell rates for rooms and the number of rooms authorized and sold in marketing programs with special or discounted rates.

**Room Statistics Tracking Sheet.** This report tracks no-shows, guaranteed no-shows, walk-ins, and turn-aways. This information can be instrumental in accurate forecasting.

# Catering Software

While catering is similar in many ways to traditional restaurant operations, there are unique characteristics that are addressed by specific software applicatons. There are two different types of catering for which software applications have been developed: off-premises catering and **finished product** (or home delivery) **catering**. These are discussed in the following sections.

## Off-Premises Catering

There are many details involved in the proposal, planning, and execution stages of an off-premises catering activity. Initially, the caterer suggests a standard menu or set of menus to a client for consideration. The client either selects from available offerings or requests a special meal plan. In either case, the caterer develops a proposal for the function.

Caterers are responsible for food and beverage service and may also be contracted to provide furnishings, entertainment, decorations, and the like. Before an event, the caterer typically plans for necessary purchases, personnel, production, transportation, service, and rental equipment. Generally, the caterer arrives at a catered event with all these requirements, because supplemental equipment, product replenishment, and additional staff are usually not available at the catered site. After the activity, the caterer must be sure that the client settles the account.

Catering software monitors and controls the activities associated with each stage of **off-premises catering service**. Many of the files created through the use of catering software packages perform functions similar to automated restaurant management applications. Typical files contained in a catering software package include:

- Ingredient file
- Recipe file
- Menu item file
- Proposal/contract file
- Inventory file
- General accounting files

In addition to containing data on all purchased food and beverage products, the ingredient file includes data on such non-food items as labor, serving utensils, production equipment, rental equipment, disposable items, and entertainment options. The more complete this file, the easier it becomes for the caterer to assemble an entire catering service package.

While standard recipes for food service operations list ingredients and a set of assembly instructions, an off-premises catering recipe generally contains "ingredients" for non-food items as well. For example, a table and chairs recipe may be recorded in a recipe file to assist in determining the number of tables and chairs required for a particular catered event. A caterer who seats eight persons per table would input this as a recipe. If the caterer were planning an off-premises catering activity for 240 persons, the table and chairs recipe would state 30 tables and 240 chairs as required ingredients. In addition, the recipe file generally accesses cost data contained in the ingredient file and can generate the cost of supplying any number of tables and chairs. The table and chairs recipe would be used as a sub-recipe within a larger recipe. Any number of sub-recipes can be chained to

produce a single recipe that contains a large number and wide range of ingredients. Cost figures for all food, beverage, and non-food ingredients can be generated for almost any recipe.

The menu item file contains meal plans for specific catered activities. Catering
menu item files contain recipes for consumable as well as non-consumable items.
Some catering software packages remind users to create recipes for determining
required gratuities, insurance, and taxes. All of these recipes are collected within a
menu item file for specific catered events.

A proposal/contract file accesses data contained in the menu item file, develops prices for menu items, and maintains a record of commitments. The inventory
file and general accounting files perform the same functions as inventory and back
office accounting applications.

Off-premises catering applications provide event calendars that list customer
names, addresses, and notes that apply to specific events. A calendar may list
events by a specific date, or it may cover a longer time period and list events
assigned to a particular manager. Some applications convert information from the
event calendars into production requirements for different preparation areas such
as hot foods, cold foods, rentals, and cutlery and linen. This feature is particularly
helpful because customers are likely to change the number of people expected in
their party up to 24 hours before the event.

Exhibit 9 depicts a sample event worksheet. The worksheet can be used to
plan an event with a customer. Also, the manager of the event uses the worksheet
as a checklist to ensure that all requested items are properly prepared and readied
for the event. The worksheet lists the number of people in the party, the manager
in charge of the event, the employees scheduled to work the event, the customer's
name and address, and all of the food, furniture, props, and other items requested.

Once entered within the system, an event worksheet can be converted into a
cost analysis report. Exhibit 10 shows information a catering manager uses when
pricing a particular event. If a customer requests changes, a new cost analysis is
prepared for the new event worksheet. Exhibit 11 illustrates an invoice prepared
from data contained in the sample event worksheet and the accompanying cost
analysis.

## Home Delivery Catering

Some multi-unit food service operators have home delivery networks that are similar in design to hotel central reservation systems. The focal point of the network is
an order-taking center connected to remote production and delivery stations. As
orders are transmitted to remote work stations, so too is the responsibility for their
fulfillment and eventual home delivery.

In the case of single independent units, the order process originates with the
order-taker entering the caller's telephone number and address into the home
delivery system. Entering this data normally triggers an internal database search
through the system's customer master file, generating a customer history report.

If the customer has not placed an order before, a customer record is created as
a consequence of the order-taking routine. With some systems this routine begins
with the order-taker using the system's area or street index to determine whether

**Exhibit 9    Sample Event Worksheet**

```
Event:01234  Date:06/21        Start:19:30  End:21:30              Page:  1

Party:00085  Mgr:SAM

Account:GREENJ    (Cash)

Jane Green
301 Saddle River Road
Saddle River, NJ 07450
201-447-5350


Tent must be installed on Wed at 3:00pm.
         1  Buffet
        85  Crudite with Dips
        85  Assorted Cheeses
        85  Eggplant Caviar
        85  Assorted Canapes
        85  Sesame Chicken Brst
        85  Pasta Bar
        45  Assorted Pastries
         2  Chocolate Cake
         1  Ice Carving
         2  8-ft Banquet Table
        45  White Chair

Start at14:30  for  05:00    OC:D    Bert Brent     201-444-8732
        15:30  for  04:00    OC:A    Andrea Andersen    201-889-8989
        15:00  for  03:50    OC:B    Charles Cook   201-447-3212
```

Source: Standard Commercial Systems, Ridgewood, New Jersey.

the customer is within the establishment's delivery area. If so, the order-taker enters a street code and the customer's house number and telephone number. The system then creates a customer record and automatically completes mailing information (city, state, and ZIP code) for future direct mail promotions. Some systems also add map coordinates and route information to the customer record. This information automatically appears on the receipt for the customer's order, thus helping the driver to deliver the order in a timely manner.

If the customer has placed an order at the establishment before, an electronic customer record is retrieved from the database. Exhibit 12 shows one type of order-entry screen format. Note that the screen displays the customer's total sales to date. This helps the order-taker know when he or she is talking to one of the establishment's loyal customers.

Many automated home delivery systems also provide establishments with files for scheduling employees, recording time worked by employees, analyzing sales, and recording accounts payable data. Exhibit 13 shows a special check-out screen used by delivery drivers at the end of their shifts. The system prompts the employee to enter ending mileage, coupons accepted (up to six different coupons),

**Exhibit 10   Sample Cost Analysis Report**

| | | | ----Cost---- | | ----Retail---- | | |
|---|---|---|---|---|---|---|---|

The Modern Caterer                    Cost Analysis                                      Page 1
Jane Green                                                        Invoice No:01234A
301 Saddle River Road                                    Deliver on:06/21
Saddle River, NJ 07450                                   Persons:  85

201-447-5350

| Code | | Qty | Price | Amount | Price | Amount | Margin |
|---|---|---|---|---|---|---|---|
| S3 | Buffet @ 1.25 | 85 | | | 150.00 | 256.25 | |
| G1 | Crudite with Dips | 85 | .45 | 38.25 | 1.50 | 127.50 | 89.25 |
| G2 | Assorted Cheeses | 85 | .45 | 38.25 | 1.75 | 148.75 | 110.50 |
| G3 | Eggplant Caviar | 85 | .75 | 63.75 | 2.50 | 212.50 | 148.75 |
| G4 | Assorted Canapes | 85 | .55 | 46.75 | 1.00 | 85.00 | 38.25 |
| G5 | Sesame Chicken Brst | 85 | .35 | 29.75 | .95 | 80.75 | 51.00 |
| G6 | Pasta Bar | 85 | .35 | 29.75 | 1.25 | 106.25 | 76.50 |
| D2 | Assorted Pastries | 45 | .50 | 22.50 | 2.00 | 90.00 | 67.50 |
| D1 | Chocolate Cake | 2 | 3.00 | 6.00 | 15.00 | 30.00 | 24.00 |
| D5 | Ice Carving | 1 | 100.00 | 100.00 | 300.00 | 300.00 | 200.00 |
| F5 | 8-ft Banquet Table | 2 | 1.00 | 2.00 | 12.00 | 24.00 | 22.00 |
| F6 | White Chair | 45 | .25 | 11.25 | 3.00 | 135.00 | 123.75 |
| | | | 107.65 | 388.25 | 490.95 | 1,596.00 | 1,207.75 |

Cost Per Person = 4.56          Retail Cost Per Person = 18.77

Source: Standard Commercial Systems, Ridgewood, New Jersey.

and any gasoline expense. The amount due from the driver is calculated. With this particular system, it is also possible to reimburse drivers who use their own cars. The compensation can be made on the basis of a percentage of the total deliveries.

# Endnotes

1. For more information on non-automated and automated marketing and sales offices, see James R. Abbey, *Hospitality Sales and Marketing,* 4th ed. (Lansing, Mich.: Educational Institute of the American Hotel & Lodging Association, 2003), Chapter 3.

2. For a complete discussion of these formulas, see Michael L. Kasavana and Richard M. Brooks, *Managing Front Office Operations,* 6th ed. (Lansing, Mich.: Educational Institute of the American Hotel & Lodging Association, 2001), Chapter 13.

3. For a detailed discussion of the other major elements of revenue management, see Kasavana and Brooks.

# Key Terms

**banquet event order (BEO)**—Information from the function book and other files is eventually transcribed on a banquet event order (BEO). A BEO generally serves as a final contract for the client and as a work order for the catering department.

**Exhibit 11  Sample Invoice**

```
                    The Modern Caterer
                     1988 Main Street
                  Anywhere, US 12345-6789
                      201-447-5350

Invoice No:01234A  Event Date:06/21  7:30pm      85 Persons

Jane Green
301 Saddle River Road
Saddle River, NJ 12345
201-447-5350

     1   Buffet                          256.25
    85   Crudite with Dips               127.50
    85   Assorted Cheeses                148.75
    85   Eggplant Caviar                 212.50
    85   Assorted Canapes                 85.00
    85   Sesame Chicken Brst              80.75
    85   Pasta Bar                       106.25
    45   Assorted Pastries                90.00
     2   Chocolate Cake                   30.00
     1   Ice Carving                     300.00
     2   8-ft Banquet Table               24.00
    45   White Chair                     135.00

                          Total   >>   1,596.00
                            Tax   >>     131.67
                   Less Deposit   >>     500.00
                Pay this amount   >>   1,227.67

    Use these two lines for advertisements,
    special announcements, etc. . . . . . . . . . . .
```

Source: Standard Commercial Systems, Ridgewood, New Jersey.

**booking lead time**—A measurement of how far in advance bookings are made.

**displacement**—The turning away of transient guests for lack of rooms due to the acceptance of group business.

**finished product catering**—Home delivery catering services.

**group booking pace**—The rate at which group business is being booked.

**guestroom control book**—Guides guestroom booking activity by providing the sales office with the maximum number of guestrooms it can sell to groups on a given day. The remaining guestrooms (and any unsold guestrooms allotted to groups) are available for individual guests.

**off-premises catering service**—A catering service that typically requires the caterer to be responsible for food and beverage production and service and possibly for providing furnishings, entertainment, decorations, and the like.

**Exhibit 12  Sample Home-Delivery Order-Entry Screen**

```
           F O O D M A N  -  Order-Taker  -  02/15        19:36

     1. Action:0  Telephone:447-5350      Order No:2023      Date:0125
```

|  |  |  |  |  |
|--|--|--|--|--|
| 2. Name: | Paula Paterson | House#:345 | Street:ZW | |
| | Addr: 345 Shelton Avenue | | Del/PU:D | |
| | Addr: Apt 3b | | Del by: 9:00PM | |
| | City: Midland Park | State:NJ | Zip:07432 | Sales |
| | SI: Use rear of driveway | | Brthdy:0215 | $263.12 |

| 01 | 01 | LA  LL  LM  LR | Personal Pizza/Extra Cheese/Pepperoni/Mushrooms |
|----|----|----------------|--------------------------------------------------|
| 02 | 01 | EL | Pepsi-Cola |
| 03 |    | (these are menu | |
| 04 |    | codes for the | (Line items are displayed in this section |
| 05 |    | items ordered) | for operator verification and read-back) |

```
Actions:  O = New Order  T = Take-out    C = Change Order    Price:   6.50
          S = Search     N = Next Order  I = Print Invoice   Tax:      .39
          D = Delete     P = Punch-in/out Q = Quit           Total:   6.89
```

Source: Standard Commercial Systems, Ridgewood, New Jersey.

**Exhibit 13  Sample Home-Delivery Employee Check-Out Screen**

```
           F O O D M A N  -  Operations Manager  -  02/15   12:00

     1.Action:0              Employee:ARD
```

Press F1 to start over if you make an error
Enter ending mileage:004534    Total Mileage:  54
Enter gasoline expense:  5.00       Deliveries:  12  Amount: 185.76
                              Total Coupons:  17.00
                              Car Allowance:
                                 Total Due:163.76


Enter Coupons Below:

Code:V1  Qty:6    Code:V2  Qty:11    Code:    Qty:
Code:    Qty:     Code:    Qty:      Code:    Qty:


Punch-In at:16:45              Occupation:D
Punch-Out at:19:50 on 2/15    Total time was:03:05

Source: Standard Commercial Systems, Ridgewood, New Jersey.

**potential average rate**—A collective statistic that effectively combines the potential average single and double rates, multiple occupancy percentage, and rate spread to produce the average rate that would apply if all rooms were sold at their full rack rates.

**revenue management**—A set of demand-forecasting techniques used to determine whether prices should be raised or lowered and whether a reservation request should be accepted or rejected in order to maximize revenue.

**wash factor**—The deletion of unnecessary group rooms from a group block.

**yield**—The ratio of actual revenue to potential revenue.

 # Review Questions

1. What are the advantages an automated sales office has over a non-automated sales office?

2. What are the advantages of using an automated sales system to create a function book and a banquet event order?

3. How does automation facilitate trace file, account file, and master card file systems?

4. What is the goal of revenue management?

5. What role does booking pace play in revenue management?

6. Why is transient displacement analysis so important in determining whether to accept a group reservation?

7. What does the term "off-premises catering" mean?

8. What does "finished product catering" mean?

9. What files are typically included in catering software packages?

10. What competitive advantages do automated home delivery systems offer?

 # Internet Sites

For more information, visit the following Internet sites. Remember that Internet addresses can change without notice. If the site is no longer there, you can use a search engine to look for additional sites.

Hospitality Sales & Marketing
Association International
http://www.hsmai.org

CaterWare Inc.
http://www.caterware.com

CaterMate Event Management
Software
http://www.catermate.com

National Restaurant Register's
Online Menus
http://www.onlinemenus.com

Newmarket Software Systems, Inc.
http://www.newmarketinc.com

World Wide Waiter
http://www.waiter.com

# Chapter 9 Outline

Accounts Receivable Module
    Customer Master File
    Management Reports
Accounts Payable Module
    Vendor Master File
    Invoice Register File
    Check Register File
Payroll Module
    Employee Master File
    Payroll Register File
    Other Functions
Inventory Module
    Inventory Status
    Inventory Valuation
    Special Food and Beverage Concerns
Purchasing Module
    Purchase Order File
    Telecommunication of Purchase Orders
    Other Functions
    EProcurement
Financial Reporting Module
    Chart of Accounts
    Trial Balance File
    Financial Statements
    Ratio Analysis
    Enterprise Reporting

# Competencies

1. Identify features and functions of an accounts receivable module for an automated accounting system and explain how managers use accounts receivable reports generated by the accounting system. (pp. 219–222)

2. Identify features and functions of an accounts payable module for an automated accounting system and explain how managers use accounts payable reports generated by the accounting system. (pp. 222–226)

3. Identify characteristics of hospitality operations that affect the design of a back office payroll module for an automated accounting system. (pp. 226–228)

4. Identify characteristics of hospitality operations that affect the design of inventory and purchasing modules for an automated accounting system. (pp. 229–240)

5. Identify features and functions of a financial reporting module for an automated accounting system. (pp. 240–246)

# 9

# Accounting Applications

**H**OSPITALITY INDUSTRY back office packages vary in the number of accounting applications they provide. This chapter focuses on software modules that are typically included in back office packages:

- Accounts receivable
- Accounts payable
- Payroll accounting
- Inventory accounting
- Purchasing
- Financial reporting

The specific needs and requirements of individual properties determine whether these modules are purchased and operated separately or as an integrated back office application package. Since the greatest value (in terms of capitalizing on technology) is derived from a fully integrated system, this chapter treats each back office module as if it were part of an overall hospitality management system.

## Accounts Receivable Module

The term **accounts receivable** refers to obligations owed to a lodging or food service operation from sales made on credit. An accounts receivable application typically performs the following functions:

- Maintains account balances
- Processes billings
- Monitors collection activities
- Generates aging of accounts receivable reports
- Produces an audit report indicating all accounts receivable transactions

Management can also set various credit limits and the module can print reports that list all accounts with balances above their established credit limit. For each account, the module can maintain a variety of credit history data. These data typically indicate the number of days elapsed between payments and the oldest invoice to which the last payment applied.

With an integrated system, accounts receivable balances may be automatically transferred from a front office accounting module to a back office accounts receivable module during the system update routine. The **city ledger** is a subsidiary ledger listing accounts receivable balances of guests who have checked out, and other receivables as well. Data from the front office accounting module (such as balances from guest folios, non-guest accounts, bill-to accounts, credit card billings, and others) form part of the **city ledger file** of the back office accounts receivable module.

Some front office systems simplify account billing procedures by creating semi-permanent and permanent folios. Semi-permanent folios are assigned to guest or non-guest accounts designated for direct billing. Permanent folios are assigned to credit card companies and other long-term contracted credit relationships.

As payments are received or additional charges incurred, they are posted to the appropriate city ledger account. Payments or charges posted to the accounts receivable module immediately update the city ledger file, helping to ensure that all account balances are current.

## Customer Master File

A **customer master file** provides a basis for collecting and storing billing information. Customer data maintained in this file may include:

- Account code
- Name of guest or account
- Address
- Telephone number
- E-mail address
- Web site address
- Contact person
- Type of account
- Credit limit
- Last payment date
- Last payment amount
- Credit history

Generally, management identifies the names of the various types of accounts. These accounts are not mutually exclusive and can be classified as transient, permanent, credit card company, direct billing, and so on. Accounts receivable modules automatically generate individual account invoices.

## Management Reports

An accounts receivable module generally allows management to access data on any account stored in an accounts receivable file. Many modules maintain an **accounts aging file**, containing data that can be formatted into a variety of aging reports. An **aging of accounts receivable schedule** breaks down each account in

**Exhibit 1    Sample Aging of Accounts Receivable Report**

| | | | | | | | | |
|---|---|---|---|---|---|---|---|---|
| DATE: | | | ACCOUNTS RECEIVABLE<br>AGED ACCOUNTS RECEIVABLE REPORT<br>01 - ABC RESTAURANT INC.<br>Aging Date: | | | | | PAGE: 1 |

| --------CUSTOMER-------- | | -------INVOICE----- | | | | | |
|---|---|---|---|---|---|---|---|
| NUMBER | NAME | NUMBER | DATE DUE | CURRENT | OVER 30 | OVER 60 | OVER 90 |
| 1 | AMERICAN EXPRESS | 10577 | | 0.00 | 2,442.53 | 0.00 | 0.00 |
| 1 | AMERICAN EXPRESS | 10776 | | 567.71 | 0.00 | 0.00 | 0.00 |
| | | | | 567.71 | 2,442.53 | 0.00 | 0.00 |
| 2 | MASTERCARD | 10578 | | 0.00 | 1,676.77 | 0.00 | 0.00 |
| 2 | MASTERCARD | 10777 | | 97.98 | 0.00 | 0.00 | 0.00 |
| | | | | 97.98 | 1,676.7 | 0.00 | 0.00 |
| 10 | JAMES JOHNSON | 10774 | | 122.56 | 0.00 | 0.00 | 0.00 |
| 10 | JAMES JOHNSON | 10775 | | 165.36 | 0.00 | 0.00 | 0.00 |
| | | | | 287.92 | 0.00 | 0.00 | 0.00 |

AGED ACCOUNTS RECEIVABLE TOTALS
Aging Date:

| ---CURRENT--- | | ---OVER 30--- | | ---OVER 60--- | | ---OVER 90--- | |
|---|---|---|---|---|---|---|---|
| NO. | AMOUNT | NO. | AMOUNT | NO. | AMOUNT | NO. | AMOUNT |
| 3 | 953.61 | 2 | 4119.30 | 0 | 0.00 | 1 | 0.00 |

Source: Datachecker Systems Inc., a subsidiary of National Semiconductor Corporation, Santa Clara, California.

the accounts aging file according to the date of the initial charge. Exhibit 1 illustrates a sample aging of accounts receivable report produced by a restaurant back office accounting system.

Although aging schedules can be printed on demand, they are routinely generated during month-end file updates. In addition, an accounts receivable module can automatically print (on letter-head stationery) a series of standard dunning letters for all accounts in 30-day and delinquent payment categories. A dunning letter is a request for payment of an outstanding balance.

An accounts receivable module can streamline reports for specific users. Much of the detailed information in an aging schedule may not be necessary for some accounting functions. In these cases, data maintained in the accounts aging file can be selected according to the user's specific needs for customized aging reports. In addition, a summary aging of accounts receivable report may be produced for management.

For security, some accounts receivable modules issue an audit report showing accounts receivable transactions. An audit report usually charts each account by account code, account name, invoice number(s) and amount(s), and the types of transactions processed over a specified time period.

# Accounts Payable Module

The term **accounts payable** refers to liabilities incurred for merchandise, equipment, or other goods and services purchased by the hospitality operation on account. The accounts payable module can be a stand-alone system or it can work with other modules of an automated accounting system. When this module is part of an accounting system, it maintains current payables records through online automatic posting of transactions to the financial reporting (or general ledger) module. This helps prevent duplicate entries of invoices and gives management up-to-date information on invoices and vendors.

An accounts payable application maintains a vendor master file, an invoice register file, and a check register file, and typically performs the following functions:

- Posts purveyor invoices
- Monitors vendor payment discount periods
- Determines amounts due
- Produces checks for payment
- Facilitates the reconciliation of cleared checks
- Generates numerous management reports

With a fully integrated hotel property management system, an accounts payable module can also access travel agent commission data from the front office reservations module to print travel agent commission checks. Along with each check, the module can print a voucher that lists guest name, arrival date, and other reservations data. Alternatively, accounts payable modules without access to reservations data require staff to hand-process commission checks, treating them as typical accounts payable invoices.

Additional reports that can be produced from data in accounts payable module files are payables aging reports, vendor status reports, vendor activity reports, and monthly check registers. A **check register** is a printout of the checks written during a specified time period. The checks can be sorted by vendor or by the invoice due date. An **accounts payable aging report** can contain several aging columns and list invoices by vendor number, vendor name, invoice number, and invoice date. Generally, this report can be printed on demand and streamlined to meet the needs of users. A **monthly check register** provides a hard copy audit trail of payments made to vendors. This report also identifies checks that have not been accounted for. Exhibit 2 shows a sample vendor status report.

## Vendor Master File

The **vendor master file** maintains records of all current vendors. Data contained in this file may include:

## Exhibit 2    Sample Vendor Status Report

| | VENDOR STATUS REPORT BY VENDOR NUMBER ECI HOTEL PROPERTIES, INC. | | | | | |
|---|---|---|---|---|---|---|
| Vendor | Vendor Name | Balance Accruals | MTD Payments | MTD Accruals | YTD Payments | YTD |
| 051462 | Spunky's Produce | 150.00 | 150.00 | 143.36 | 603.36 | 453.36 |
| 051562 | Upton's Fish Market | 0.00 | -159.63 | -159.63 | 0.00 | 0.00 |
| 051662 | Cory Cow's Dairy Farm | 0.00 | 0.00 | 101.92 | 101.92 | 101.92 |
| 051762 | Capital Dry Goods | 0.00 | 0.00 | 65.00 | 65.00 | 65.00 |
| 051862 | Dolly Madison Bakery | | | 0.00 | 0.00 | |
| 051962 | Miltons Meat Market | 0.00 | 0.00 | 269.00 | 269.00 | 269.00 |
| 052062 | Amy's Amenities | 0.00 | 0.00 | 500.00 | 500.00 | 500.00 |
| 052162 | Denmark Data Forms | 0.00 | 0.00 | 2500.00 | 2500.00 | 2500.00 |
| 052262 | Suttons Pool Supplies | | | 0.00 | 0.00 | |
| 121213 | Carmen's Cleaning Service | 92.00 | 92.00 | 0.00 | 92.00 | |
| 121214 | S&S Quality Produce | 1500.00 | 0.00 | 500.00 | 2000.00 | 500.00 |
| 121215 | G&G Produce | | | 0.00 | 0.00 | |
| 121217 | Sounds of Music | 0.00 | 0.00 | 890.00 | 890.00 | 890.00 |
| 121231 | Coors Dist. | 0.00 | 0.00 | 1300.30 | 1300.30 | 1300.30 |
| 121235 | Nordic Princess Cheesecak | | | 0.00 | 0.00 | |
| 121313 | Southwest Laund | 125.00 | 248.00 | 123.00 | 248.00 | 123.00 |
| 171717 | Southern California | | | 0.00 | 0.00 | |
| 1000000 | ABC Lumber | | | | | |
| 1212121 | Pacific Bell | 500.00 | 500.00 | 1000.00 | 1500.00 | 1000.00 |
| 1212129 | Artistic Florist | 0.00 | 0.00 | 175.00 | 175.00 | 175.00 |
| 1234698 | Keenan's Uniform Supplies | 0.00 | 0.00 | 15069.69 | 33659.02 | 33659.02 |
| 1256153 | Martins Flower Shop | 0.00 | 0.00 | 0.00 | 300.00 | 300.00 |
| 3249874 | Eat Um Up Food Service | 0.00 | 0.00 | 10002.38 | 10002.38 | 10002.38 |
| 4151265 | Pacific Gas Company | | | 0.00 | 0.00 | |
| 5261235 | Bostonian Federal | | | 0.00 | 0.00 | |
| 5468923 | Halp Company | | | 0.00 | 0.00 | |
| 6587463 | Liquid Refreshment Inc. | 0.00 | 0.00 | 2253.68 | 2253.68 | 2253.68 |
| 7878787 | First Intermedian Bank | 526.34 | 526.34 | 526.34 | 1052.68 | 526.34 |
| 8585858 | Tony's Seafood | | | 0.00 | 0.00 | |
| 9999999 | Onetime Vendor | 0.00 | 250.00 | 350.00 | 350.00 | 350.00 |
| | | 2893.34 | 1606.71 | 35610.04 | 57862.34 | 54969.00 |

[405] 30 Items Listed.

Source: ECI Computer Inc., Santa Ana, California.

- Vendor number
- Vendor name
- Contact name
- Address

- Telephone number
- E-mail address
- Web site address
- Vendor payment priority
- Discount terms
- Discount account number
- Invoice description
- Payment date
- Year-to-date purchases

A **vendor status report**, such as that shown in Exhibit 2, presents summary accounts payable information. A **vendor activity report** can list gross amount invoiced, discounts taken, number of invoices, and other vendor data.

## Invoice Register File

An **invoice register file** keeps a list of all invoices currently outstanding and payable. The accounts payable module can select invoices for payment by due date or by payment discount date. The **payment discount date** is the last day on which it is possible for the operation to take advantage of a cash payment discount offered by a vendor. Many vendors offer a discount on the invoice amount if payment is made within a specified time frame. For example, the terms of an invoice could be stated as: $2/10$ net 30 days, meaning that the buyer applies a 2 percent discount to the invoice amount if payment is made within 10 days of the date on which the invoice was issued; if the discount period elapses, full payment is expected within 30 days of the original invoice date. Tracking discount payment dates is often a tedious and time-consuming task in non-automated hotel or restaurant properties. The accounts payable module lets employees perform more productive tasks and lets management take advantage of significant savings monitored by this module.

Although accounts payable modules can automatically select invoices for payment, they typically allow management to override selected invoices. **Override options** give management complete control over cash disbursements before engaging the check-writing feature of the accounts payable module. Options that management may wish to exercise include:

- Selecting invoices for payment that are not yet due
- Making partial payments of certain invoices
- Suspending payments of certain invoices
- Adding reference data to invoices (to be printed on check stubs)

After management has exercised its options, a **cash requirements report** can be printed. This report lists all invoices selected for payment and the corresponding cash requirements. These reports can be prepared by vendor number,

## Exhibit 3   Sample Cash Requirements Report

**CASH REQUIREMENTS REPORT BY VENDOR NUMBER**
**ECI HOTEL PROPERTIES, INC.**

| Vendor | Vendor Name | Invoice | D/Due | Gross | 07/15 | 07/22 | 07/29 | 08/05 | 08/12 | 08/19 | Future |
|---|---|---|---|---|---|---|---|---|---|---|---|
| 051462 | Spunky's Produce | 12312 | 06/15 | 150.00 | 150.00 | | | | | | |
| | | | | 150.00 | 150.00 | 0.00 | 0.00 | 0.00 | 0.00 | 0.00 | 0.00 |
| 121213 | Carmen's Cleaning Serv | 98798 | | 25.00 | 25.00 | | | | | | |
| | | 1-6766 | 07/10 | 52.00 | 52.00 | | | | | | |
| | | 111 | 07/20 | 40.00 | 40.00 | | | | | | |
| | | | | 117.00 | 117.00 | 0.00 | 0.00 | 0.00 | 0.00 | 0.00 | 0.00 |
| 121214 | S&S Quality Produce | 121214 | 03/15 | 1500.00 | 1500.00 | | | | | | |
| | | | | 1500.00 | 1500.00 | 0.00 | 0.00 | 0.00 | 0.00 | 0.00 | 0.00 |
| 121313 | Southwest Laundry | 99998 | 08/10 | 125.00 | | | | 125.00 | | | |
| | | | | 125.00 | 0.00 | 0.00 | 0.00 | 125.00 | 0.00 | 0.00 | 0.00 |
| 1212121 | Pacific Bell | 12 | 07/20 | 500.00 | 500.00 | | | | | | |
| | | | | 500.00 | 500.00 | 0.00 | 0.00 | 0.00 | 0.00 | 0.00 | 0.00 |
| 7878787 | First Intermedian Bank | 1-6766 | 07/10 | 526.34 | 526.34 | | | | | | |
| | | | | 526.34 | 526.34 | 0.00 | 0.00 | 0.00 | 0.00 | 0.00 | 0.00 |
| Total for 6 Vendors | | | | 2918.34 | 2793.34 | 0.00 | 0.00 | 125.00 | 0.00 | 0.00 | 0.00 |

Source: ECI Computer Inc., Santa Ana, California.

vendor name, due date, item, or group code. They typically include vendor number, vendor name, invoice number, due date, balance due, and amount to be paid. Exhibit 3 shows a sample cash requirements report prepared by vendor number. Most accounts payable modules can print a cash requirements report at any time, basing it on a list of all open invoices.

## Check Register File

The **check register file** monitors the calculation and printing of bank checks for payments of selected invoices. After printing checks, the accounts payable module deletes paid invoices from the invoice register file, preventing the possibility of double payments. With a fully integrated property management system, the check-writing routine updates account balances maintained by the general ledger module. After the checks have been written, the accounts payable module prints a check register by check number, which also may be sorted by vendor or by invoice due date.

Accounts payable modules can process hand-written checks and voided checks as well. Once hand-written checks are posted, the entire system is updated. Generally, the checks that are input as hand-written are highlighted on the check register printout. When a voided check is entered in the accounts payable module, the accounting system is also updated. The invoice is added back to the invoice register file, and the voided check is highlighted on the check register printout. Highlighting hand-written and voided checks on the printout enhances management's internal control.

After all entries have been made for hand-written and voided checks, the accounts payable module may print an **outstanding checks list**. This list details all checks that have been issued but remain outstanding. The outstanding checks list can be used to reconcile checks issued against canceled checks appearing on bank statements. While actual procedures for **check reconciliation** vary from one system to another, the procedure could prompt the user to enter check numbers and amounts from a bank statement. As each check is entered, the accounts payable module verifies the entry and removes (clears) the check from the outstanding checks list. When all checks have been reconciled, the system can print a **reconciliation audit report**. This report balances the total of checks removed from the outstanding checks list with the total of cleared checks appearing on the bank statement. After a check reconciliation routine, the accounts payable module typically prints an updated list of all checks still outstanding.

# Payroll Module

Calculating each employee's pay, developing the accounting records, and preparing the necessary reports required by federal, state, and local governments are recurrent tasks carried out by a hotel's accounting department. Payroll accounting can be time-consuming in non-automated properties. Not only do pay rates vary with job classifications, but, in the hospitality industry, a single employee could also work at different tasks over a number of workshifts, each of which could call for a different pay rate. Unlike many other accounting functions, payroll system requirements are defined by sources other than property management officials. Government agencies, unions, pension trust funds, credit unions, banks, and employees themselves often have input into how payroll information is stored and reported.

A back office payroll module must be flexible enough to meet all the demands placed on it with a minimum of programming changes. Often a module utility program allows a property to define its own pay period (daily, weekly, biweekly, or monthly). Payroll modules generally perform the following functions:

- Maintain an employee master file
- Calculate gross and net pay for salaried and hourly employees
- Print paychecks
- Produce payroll tax registers and reports
- Prepare labor cost reports for use by management

## Employee Master File

An employee master file maintains payroll and personnel data on each employee. Data contained in this file may include:

- Company employee number
- Name of employee
- Address of employee
- E-mail address of employee
- Social security number
- Job classification code(s)
- Wage rate code(s)
- Withholdings
- Deductions

This file can be extensive. Appropriate deductions and withholding amounts are subtracted from each employee's gross pay to arrive at net pay. **Withholdings** are for income and social security taxes. Since federal tax regulations frequently change and since state withholdings vary across the country, many payroll modules are designed so that the user can make the necessary programming adjustments. **Deductions** are usually voluntary and depend on the types of benefits available from the employer. Exhibit 4 lists some of the subtractions made from the gross pay of hospitality industry employees.

## Payroll Register File

In order to calculate gross and net pay for hourly employees, the payroll module relies on a **payroll register file** to access the number of hours each employee worked during the pay period and other data that can require special tax calculations, such as:

- Sick leave pay
- Bonus pay
- Tips
- Expense reimbursements

In some properties, a **computerized time-clock system** records time in and time out for employees. Exhibit 5 depicts a time card produced by a computerized time-clock system. When a time-clock system is interfaced to a host system, data may be transferred each day to the back office payroll module and the previous day's pay calculated for each employee.

As noted earlier, the payroll module must be flexible enough to handle several pay categories per employee and several non-tax deductions (which may be required on either a fixed or a variable basis). Payroll modules typically provide override options with which management can adjust pay.

Exhibit 4    Sample Payroll Withholdings and Deductions

**TAXES**

- Federal, state, and city withholding amounts for income taxes
- Federal Insurance Contribution Act tax (Social Security tax)
- State unemployment compensation (selected states)

**OTHER**

- Savings bonds
- Medical insurance
- Life insurance
- Retirement contribution
- Charitable contribution
- Capital stock purchase plan
- Savings plan, credit union
- Charge for meals
- Payroll advance
- Garnishment of wages
- Union dues

## Other Functions

A payroll module can also print paychecks, paycheck registers, payroll detail registers, and deduction registers. This module generally maintains a government reporting file for quarter-to-date and year-to-date federal and state tax histories. Deduction reports can be produced with year-to-date computations. Exhibit 6 shows a sample payroll check register produced by a food and beverage back office accounting system. The check register summarizes payroll information for each employee.

Like the accounts payable module, a back office payroll module can accommodate hand-written payroll checks and voided payroll checks. The module reconciles outstanding paychecks (checks that have been issued) with paychecks that have cleared the bank and appear on bank statements. Generally, at the end of a check reconciliation routine, the payroll module prints an updated list of outstanding checks.

In addition to printing paychecks, payroll modules can calculate sick leave and vacation hours accrued (earned) by employees in one of several ways: accrual each pay period, accrual periodically (for example, on the first pay period of the month), or accrual yearly on the basis of the employee's anniversary date.

With each employee's hourly rate (which is previously stored in the system) and calculations of pay for salaried employees, payroll modules can determine departmental labor costs. A **payroll cost report**, by department or job classification, may also be prepared for management.

## Exhibit 5  Sample Time Card

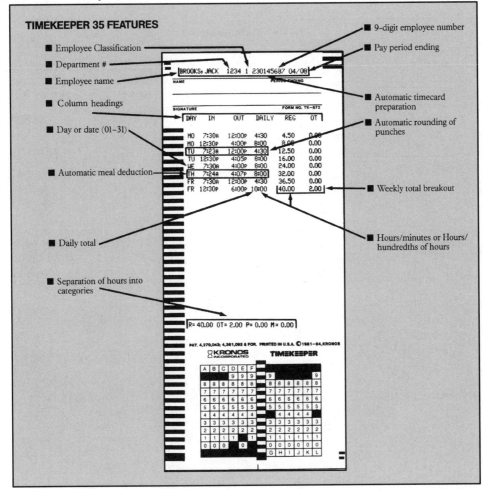

Source: Kronos Inc., Waltham, Massachusetts.

## Inventory Module

An accounting system may use an inventory module for internal control. Internal control is essential to efficient hospitality industry operations. Basic inventory data is stored in an **inventory master file**, which typically holds the following information:

- Item name
- Item description (brief)
- Inventory code number
- Storeroom location code

**Exhibit 6   Sample Payroll Check Register**

DATE 09-08            PAYROLL CHECK REGISTER                          PAGE 1
                        01 - ABC RESTAURANT INC

| Employee | EARNINGS Category | Hours | Amount | DEDUCTIONS Category | Amount |
|---|---|---|---|---|---|
| 10 | Salary | 50.00 | 500.00 | Federal | 59.99 |
| Jones, Henry | | | | FICA | 35.75 |
| | | | | State | 13.12 |
| | | | | Meals | 17.50 |
| | | | | Add'n Fed'l | 12.00 |
| | | | | Insurance | 5.00 |

Check Number    125
Hours Worked     50.00
** Gross Pay    500.00
**** Net Pay    356.64

| Employee | EARNINGS Category | Hours | Amount | DEDUCTIONS Category | Amount |
|---|---|---|---|---|---|
| 20 | Tipped Wages | 40.00 | 80.40 | Federal | 36.61 |
| Williamson, Johnny | Overtime | 10.00 | 50.30 | FICA | 26.04 |
| | Rptd Tips | | 233.50 | State | 6.50 |
| | Gross Rcpts | | 2918.75 | Uniforms | 4.00 |
| | Tip Credit | | 53.60 | Meals | 17.50 |
| | | | | Add'n Fed'l | 7.32 |

Check Number    126
Hours Worked     50.00
** Gross Pay    130.70
**** Net Pay     32.73

***** END OF COMPANY SUMMARY *****

| Employee | EARNINGS Category | Hours | Amount | DEDUCTIONS Category | Amount |
|---|---|---|---|---|---|
| 01 | Salary | 50.00 | 500.00 | Federal | 96.60 |
| ABC RESTAURANT INC | Tipped Wages | 40.00 | 80.40 | FICA | 61.79 |
| | Overtime | 10.00 | 50.30 | State | 19.62 |
| | Rptd Tips | | 233.50 | Uniforms | 4.00 |
| | Gross Repts | | 2918.75 | Meals | 35.00 |
| | Tip Credit | | 53.60 | Add'n Fed'l | 19.32 |
| | | | | Insurance | 5.00 |

No of Checks      2
Hours Worked    100.00
** Gross Pay    630.70
**** Net Pay    389.37

***** EMPLOYER TAXES *****

| | | | | | |
|---|---|---|---|---|---|
| Matching FICA | (630.7 | + | 53.60) | * | 7.15% = | 48.93 |
| FUI Requirements | | | 0.00 | * | 2.00% = | 0.00 |
| SUI Requirements | | | 130.70 | * | 2.00% = | 2.61 |

                                                              2.61

***** STATE TAX TABLE TOTALS *****
                    GA

                  19.62

Source: Datachecker Systems Inc., a subsidiary of National Semiconductor Corporation, Santa Clara, California.

- Item purchase unit

- Purchase unit price

- Item issue unit

- Product group code

- Vendor identification number

- Order lead time

- Minimum-maximum stock levels

- Date of last purchase

With this data, a back office inventory module can address three of the most common inventory concerns: inventory status, inventory variance, and inventory valuation.

## Inventory Status

**Inventory status** is an account of how much of each item is in storage. Inventory status may be determined by a physical inventory or a perpetual inventory, or both. With a **physical inventory system,** property staff periodically observe and count items in storage. With a **perpetual inventory system,** a back office inventory module maintains an **inventory status file** that keeps a running balance of the quantity of issued/stored items. In general, this module carries over the ending inventory of the prior period as the beginning inventory of the current period and adds all newly purchased items as they enter storage areas and subtracts all quantities issued from storage to production areas. Exhibit 7 shows a sample inventory directory report presenting a snapshot of stored items detailed in relation to purchase units, storage ("pack") units, and recipe units. Sorting options of the inventory module make it easy for managers to retrieve the precise information they need. When management uses a perpetual inventory system, a physical inventory is still taken at the end of each accounting period to verify the accuracy of inventory balances tracked by the inventory module.

Inventory modules may accommodate hand-held, wireless, mobile devices that significantly speed up the process of taking physical inventory. These devices can also be use to receive orders, create requisitions and transfers, and build shopping lists. In addition, some inventory modules can track by separate inventory locations and enable managers to print inventory count sheets that match the layout of each location. This feature can also speed up the process of taking physical inventory.

The term **inventory variance** refers to differences between a physical count of an item and the balance maintained by the perpetual inventory system. Significant variances may indicate control problems requiring investigation and correction. Inventory modules may generate a variety of variance reports. The report shown in Exhibit 8 alerts managers to the difference between amounts of inventory that should have been used and what was actually used over a given period of time. This enables managers to quickly identify potential problems and take appropriate corrective actions.

## Exhibit 7   Sample Inventory Directory Report

| | PURCHASE | | PACK | | | RECIPE UNITS | | |
|---|---|---|---|---|---|---|---|---|
| Item Name | Cost Desc | Last Priced | Cost Desc | Size | Packs/ Purch. | Cost Unit | # Per Pack | Shrink (%) |
| Almonds, Diced | $92.58 CASE | 1/18/2002 | $15.43 #10CAN | #10CAN | 6.00 | $0.24 OZ | 64.00 | 0.00 |
| Avocado | $68.00 CASE | 1/18/2001 | $2.43 EA | 1 EA | 28.00 | $0.27 slice | 9.00 | 25.00 |
| Banana\Fresh | $0.61 LB | 1/18/2002 | $0.61 LB | LB | 1.00 | $0.24 EA | 2.50 | 0.00 |
| | | | | | | $0.28 CUP | 2.18 | 0.00 |
| BBQ Sauce - Bull's Eye | $49.97 CASE | | $12.49 GAL | GAL | 4.00 | $0.00 | 0.00 | 0.00 |
| Bread-Burger Bun 4 1/2 s.s | $1.39 PACKAG | 1/18/2001 | $1.39 PACKAGE | PACKA | 1.00 | $0.17 PIECE | 8.00 | 0.00 |
| Bread-Rye Bread | $2.30 LOAF | 1/18/2001 | $2.30 LOAF | LOAF | 1.00 | $0.09 SLICE | 27.00 | 0.00 |
| Bread-White Bread 5x5 | $1.91 LOAF | 1/18/2002 | $1.91 LOAF | LOAF | 1.00 | $0.09 SLICE | 22.00 | 0.00 |
| Breaded Chicken | $32.50 CASE | 1/18/2002 | $3.25 LB | LB | 10.00 | $0.81 PIECE | 4.00 | 0.00 |
| Cheese\Swiss | $2.96 LB | | $2.96 LB | LB | 1.00 | $0.12 SLICE | 25.00 | 0.00 |
| Chocolate Syrup | $42.09 CASE | | $7.02 CAN | CAN | 6.00 | $0.06 OZ | 108.00 | 0.00 |
| | | | | | | $0.52 CUP | 13.50 | 0.00 |
| Coca-Cola | $7.04 CASE | 1/18/2002 | $0.29 BOTTLE | 20 FLOZ | 24.00 | $0.00 | 0.00 | 0.00 |
| Diet Coke | $6.84 CASE | 1/18/2002 | $0.28 BOTTLE | 20 OZ | 24.00 | $0.00 | 0.00 | 0.00 |
| French Fries | $18.67 CASE | 1/18/2001 | $3.11 BAG | 4.5LB | 6.00 | $0.00 | 0.00 | 0.00 |
| Ham | $1.66 LB | 1/18/2002 | $1.66 LB | LB | 1.00 | $0.00 | 0.00 | 0.00 |

Date: 8/19/200X  Time: 10:14 AM  Sorted by: Alpha — Inventory Directory, Wawa, Unit: SAMP

Source: CostGuard Food Service Software. For more information, browse the company's Web site at http://www.costguard.com

## Exhibit 8   Sample Inventory Variance Report

| Item Name | Item Unit | $ | Actual Usage Unit | $ | FC% | Ideal Usage Units | $ | FC% | Variance Units | Last $ | Counted | % of Sales |
|---|---|---|---|---|---|---|---|---|---|---|---|---|
| Whipped Topping | S GAL | 38.95 | 6.0 | 233.70 | 9.9 | 0.3 | 9.99 | 0.4 | 5.7 | 223.72 | 01/21/02 | 9.4 |
| Avocado | CASE | 68.00 | 2.0 | 136.00 | 5.1 | 0.5 | 30.78 | 1.2 | 1.5 | 105.24 | 01/21/02 | 4.0 |
| Oleo Blend Margarine | LB | 1.08 | 70.0 | 75.60 | 2.9 | 2.4 | 2.57 | 0.1 | 67.6 | 73.03 | 01/21/02 | 2.8 |
| Breaded Chicken | CASE | 32.50 | 4.8 | 156.00 | 5.9 | 2.7 | 86.94 | 3.3 | 2.1 | 69.06 | 01/21/02 | 2.8 |
| Lettuce\Iceberg | CASE | 24.00 | 2.3 | 54.00 | 2.0 | 0.2 | 5.23 | 0.2 | 2.0 | 48.77 | 01/21/02 | 1.8 |
| Ice Cream\Sherbet | TUB | 12.78 | 5.0 | 87.41 | 2.5 | 1.7 | 21.36 | 0.8 | 3.3 | 48.05 | 01/21/02 | 1.7 |
| French Fries | CASE | 18.67 | 7.0 | 128.89 | 4.8 | 4.7 | 87.90 | 3.3 | 2.3 | 38.99 | 01/21/02 | 1.5 |
| Strawberry Topping | CASE | 42.95 | 1.0 | 40.89 | 1.5 | 0.2 | 6.87 | 0.3 | 0.8 | 34.20 | 01/21/02 | 1.3 |
| Almonds. Diced | CASE | 92.58 | 0.3 | 23.15 | 0.9 | 0.0 | 2.47 | 0.1 | 0.2 | 20.87 | 01/21/02 | 0.8 |
| *** Grand Total | | | 98.3 | 913.62 | 34.5 | 12.5 | 253.88 | 9.8 | 85.8 | 659.74 | | 24.9 |

Date: 8/21/200X  Time: 4:32 PM  Inventory Variance Alert Report, Your Company Name Here, Unit: SAMP  Page: 1. From 1/1/200X to 12/31/200X (# of days: 365)  Details: Yes  Range: Top 10 Items  Total Sales: $2651.65

Source: CostGuard Food Service Software. For more information, browse the company's Web site at http://www.costguard.com

## Inventory Valuation

The term **inventory valuation** refers to the value of items in inventory. An **inventory valuation file** is used to determine the cost of goods sold and/or the replacement cost of items listed in the inventory master file. Exhibit 9 presents a screen

**Exhibit 9    Sample Inventory Module Screen**

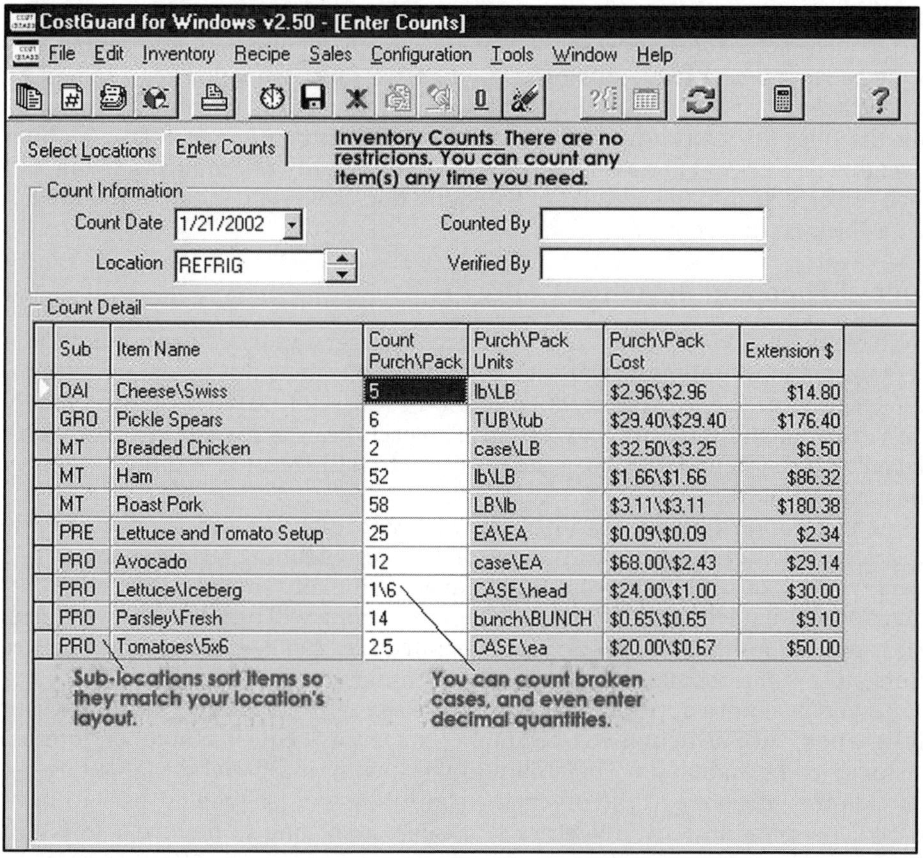

CostGuard for Windows v2.50 - [Enter Counts]

File   Edit   Inventory   Recipe   Sales   Configuration   Tools   Window   Help

| Select Locations | Enter Counts | **Inventory Counts** There are no restrictions. You can count any item(s) any time you need. |

Count Information

Count Date 1/21/2002        Counted By

Location REFRIG             Verified By

Count Detail

| | Sub | Item Name | Count Purch\Pack | Purch\Pack Units | Purch\Pack Cost | Extension $ |
|---|---|---|---|---|---|---|
| | DAI | Cheese\Swiss | 5 | lb\LB | $2.96\$2.96 | $14.80 |
| | GRO | Pickle Spears | 6 | TUB\tub | $29.40\$29.40 | $176.40 |
| | MT | Breaded Chicken | 2 | case\LB | $32.50\$3.25 | $6.50 |
| | MT | Ham | 52 | lb\LB | $1.66\$1.66 | $86.32 |
| | MT | Roast Pork | 58 | LB\lb | $3.11\$3.11 | $180.38 |
| | PRE | Lettuce and Tomato Setup | 25 | EA\EA | $0.09\$0.09 | $2.34 |
| | PRO | Avocado | 12 | case\EA | $68.00\$2.43 | $29.14 |
| | PRO | Lettuce\Iceberg | 1\6 | CASE\head | $24.00\$1.00 | $30.00 |
| | PRO | Parsley\Fresh | 14 | bunch\BUNCH | $0.65\$0.65 | $9.10 |
| | PRO | Tomatoes\5x6 | 2.5 | CASE\ea | $20.00\$0.67 | $50.00 |

Sub-locations sort items so they match your location's layout.

You can count broken cases, and even enter decimal quantities.

Source: CostGuard Food Service Software. For more information, browse the company's Web site at http://www.costguard.com

shot from an inventory module that shows amounts of items in inventory in terms of purchase units and extends the inventory value of each item.

Since methods of inventory valuation vary, management must be careful to clarify which methods a particular food service inventory package should support.

An inventory valuation file tracks the value of items in inventory by any of the four generally accepted methods of inventory valuation:

- First in, first out (FIFO)
- Last in, first out (LIFO)
- Actual cost
- Weighted average

When a **first in, first out (FIFO)** method of inventory valuation is used, the products in storage areas are valued at the level of the most recently purchased items in storage. With a **last in, first out (LIFO)** method, the inventory value is assumed to be represented by the cost of items which were placed in storage the earliest. The **actual cost** approach values inventory only in relation to actual costs of items stored. The value of stored products is, then, the value represented by individual unit costs. The **weighted average** method values inventory by considering the quantity of products purchased at different unit costs. This method "weights" the prices to be averaged based on the quantity of products in storage at each price. Note that the method of valuation does not relate to the actual flow of items through storerooms.

## Special Food and Beverage Concerns

From the point of view of food and beverage managers, an inventory application is perhaps the most important part of a back office package. But inventory applications tend to be the least uniform of all food service software. They vary widely with respect to file capacity and design. The usefulness of inventory reports produced by the system depends on the details within file records and the aptness of the formulas used.

The creation of a food and beverage ingredient file and subsequent file updates (daily, weekly, monthly, etc.) can be overwhelming tasks for some food service operations. Also, if errors are made when initially entering data, all subsequent processing will be unreliable and system reports will be relatively worthless. And applications that do not support integrated files can be cumbersome because users must re-input data from several files in order to run a program.

Some inventory applications provide file space for more than one ingredient designation, such as item file code number, inventory sequence number, internal customer code, and so on. The ability to work with additional designations can increase the efficiency of the inventory control system, enabling a user to print ingredients on a physical inventory worksheet according to the order in which they are shelved, for example.

Inventory is critical to a food service operation, because many POS systems cannot track an item as it passes through the control points of receiving, storing/issuing, and production. The data maintained by the inventory files of a back office package must be specific to each of these control points, because most ingredients are purchased, stored, and used in different quantities. Food and beverage inventory applications should enable users to specify tables for converting purchase units, issue units, and recipe units for individual inventory items. When conversion tables are not part of the application's design, data processing may have to be supplemented by cumbersome and time-consuming manual procedures.

Another concern is how usage is charted by the inventory application—by unit, by cost, or by both unit and cost. A system that charts items by unit might be able to report changes in stock levels, but might not provide financial data necessary for food costing. On the other hand, a system that charts items primarily by product cost may not facilitate spot-checks of items in storage. The most effective inventory applications are those that track both unit and cost.

Management should also make clear how basic food service concepts are defined within the inventory application design. For example, is an inventory item considered "used" (for costing purposes) at the time it is received, when it is issued to the kitchen, or at the time of service? The time that is best for an operation may not be the time frame built into the application's design.

# Purchasing Module

Effective purchasing methods are extremely important because cost savings directly affect bottom-line profitability—each dollar saved is an additional dollar of profit. Since a large percentage of sales income is spent on purchasing, it is critical that all procedures include effective controls. A back office purchasing module especially enhances management's control over purchase ordering and receiving practices.

## Purchase Order File

Back office purchasing modules maintain a purchase order file that is typically organized by vendor and purchase order number. Although purchase orders can always be generated by hand and later entered into the purchase order file, the value of a purchasing module lies in its ability to generate purchase orders and internally update its purchase order file.

Purchase orders can be generated by a purchasing module that accesses and analyzes minimum/maximum inventory data. **Minimum/maximum inventory levels** help managers determine when products need to be purchased and how much of each product to order. For each purchase item, management sets a minimum quantity below which inventory levels should not fall and a maximum quantity above which inventory levels should not rise. The minimum level is the safety level—the number of purchase units that must always remain in inventory. The maximum level is the greatest number of purchase units permitted in storage. Using minimum/maximum inventory level data transferred from the inventory module, the purchasing module generates purchase orders based on an order point established through usage rate and lead-time factors.

The usage rate is the number of purchase units used per order period. This is an important factor for determining when more purchase units need to be ordered. In addition to usage rates, managers must also determine a lead-time quantity for each purchase item. **Lead-time quantity** refers to the anticipated number of purchase units taken from inventory between the time an order is placed and the time it is delivered. Purchase units are counted in terms of normally sized shipping containers.

The order point is the number of purchase units in stock when an order is placed. The order point is reached when the number of purchase units in inventory equals the lead-time quantity plus the safety (minimum) level. If products are ordered at the order point, the quantity in inventory will be reduced to the safety (minimum) level by the time products are received. When the order arrives, the inventory levels for the product will be brought back to the maximum level. The screen shot shown in Exhibit 10 indicates the variables that managers can use when generating purchase orders. The system automatically detects lower prices and calculates potential savings.

**Exhibit 10  Generating Purchase Orders**

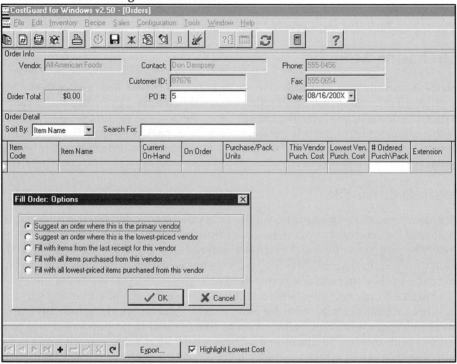

Source: CostGuard Food Service Software. For more information, browse the company's Web site at http://www.costguard.com

Purchase orders can also be generated by a purchasing module that analyzes sales forecast data. This method assumes a zero-based inventory system for developing purchase orders. Rather than reference existing inventory levels, the purchasing module forecasts anticipated revenue, projects needed inventory items, and automatically generates the necessary purchase orders.

Regardless of the method by which purchase orders are produced, purchasing modules typically provide override options allowing management to alter items and quantities before the final preparation and distribution of purchase orders. In addition to override capabilities, systems can add routine purchases (furnishings, amenities, supplies, food, and the like) to purveyor orders by predetermined date. For example, the systematic ordering of one case of bathroom cleaner each month can be added to a purchase order, eliminating the possibility of omission in ordering.

## Telecommunication of Purchase Orders

A growing trend among system vendors and food service purveyors is to install order entry telephone lines for telecommunication of purchase orders directly from customer properties. The property must first develop its own purchase order

**Exhibit 11    Sample Vendor Order Guide**

| Item Name | Item Code | Case Cost | Pu De |
|-----------|-----------|-----------|-------|
| ICE CREAM VAN CLASSIC | 1921089 | $15.53 | CS |
| ICE CREAM CHOC | 6412852 | $13.63 | CS |
| ICE CREAM STRAWBERRY | 1921105 | $16.46 | CS |
| CHEESE MOZZARELLA LOAF PRT | 2170215 | $16.24 | CS |
| OMELET EGG CHEESE | 2232965 | $30.54 | CS |
| CREAM SOUR CUP NO FAT | 2343333 | $8.98 | CS |
| ICE CREAM CUP VAN NFAT/NSA | 2403582 | $13.68 | CS |
| ICE CREAM CUP CHOC NFAT/NSA | 2403590 | $13.68 | CS |
| ICE CREAM CUP STRAW | 2403608 | $13.68 | CS |
| CREAMER HALF & HALF CUP UHT | 2444669 | $8.19 | CS |

*Vendor Edit - [Sysco]*
Search For: Sysco
Main | Vendor Items
Clear... | Import... | Import Format: Sysco
Close

Source: CostGuard Food Service Software. For more information, browse the company's Web site at http://www.costguard.com

file and then use communications software to communicate purchase orders to the purveyor's system. The screen shot shown in Exhibit 11 presents a sample vendor's order guide that managers use to import bids and export orders.

Some purveyors allow clients to use autodial modems. An autodial modem functions without user intervention, enabling late night transmission of purchase orders for next day processing. Some purchase order telecommunication links provide for two-way communication (duplex) between purveyor and property. This allows the operation to make online inquiries about current prices and stock availability at the purveyor's location, and permits the purveyor to send information about featured items, price specials, and close-out sales to the property.

## Other Functions

Properties dealing with more than one purveyor may collect competitive bids and store them in a **bid specification file,** which typically contains the specific characteristics of purchased items. Purveyors are asked to quote prices for products that meet or exceed stated specifications. Normally, a **bid specification form** can be printed at any time, upon demand. Once bids are obtained, they can be entered into the system, and the purchasing module may be able to sort items to be purchased by vendor and lowest bid.

Back office purchasing modules may simplify receiving practices. Receiving practices in non-automated properties can be tedious and time-consuming. Typically, a receiving clerk manually verifies shipments received by cross-checking each item against the original purchase order. The list of items received is used to make price extensions. That is, the quoted price of each purchased item is multiplied by the quantities received to yield an approximate cost of goods purchased. These price extensions are later used to scrutinize billings from purveyors. Following price extension, the quantities received are entered on an inventory worksheet alongside the name of the proper inventory item.

Purchasing modules can streamline receiving practices and simplify inventory updating. A receiving clerk may verify shipments by cross-checking items received against a list of product names and ordered quantities. Or a property may institute a blind receiving practice by supplying the receiving clerk with a list of product names (only) and requiring the clerk to record quantities received.

Once receiving is completed, amounts can be entered into the purchasing module by accessing and updating the stored purchase order. When the purchase order quantities reflect received quantities, inventory files can be instantly updated with a release to inventory function. All items and quantities on the receiving list (the updated purchase order) are added to the former perpetual inventory quantities.

The purchase price variance report, designed to notify purchasers, accounting personnel, and others when the recent price of an item exceeds the level of variance previously established by top management officials, is another popular purchasing report. This report enables management to react to price changes on a timely basis. With a fully integrated system, data from the purchasing module can also be transferred to the accounts payable module so that updated cash requirements reports can be produced.

## E-Procurement

All businesses perform some sort of purchasing function, and the great challenge facing purchasing managers and organizations is how to make the procurement process more efficient and realize additional bottom-line savings.[1] In some industries a minimal savings in procurement costs can result in a disproportionately large increase in operating profit.

**E-procurement** refers to the purchasing of goods and services over the Internet. Using a computer and a standard Web browser, buyers can look through product catalogs, review services, compare products, place orders, and pay for purchases. There are three common approaches to online purchasing:

- Sell-side model
- Buy-side model
- E-marketplace model

The **sell-side model** involves placing an order directly with a supplier over the Internet.

In this many-to-one environment (many buyers, one seller), the buyer generally accesses the supplier's own Web site to do research and make purchases. The sell-side model applies to companies who use Web technologies to sell their goods and services to other companies.

The **buy-side model** is a "one buyer, many sellers" approach. Buyers purchase Web-based services or use self-supported systems to buy from approved vendors electronically. In the case of third-party intermediary involvement, the service is frequently tailored to a particular buyer's needs, providing access to customized catalogs of goods and services offered by multiple suppliers. Once an order is placed, the intermediary in turn transmits the order to the supplier. The buyer and supplier then complete the financial transaction while the intermediary provides tracking and communication support. Several major hotel chains and related purchasing consortia use this model.

Companies can choose to operate their own electronic purchasing environment, but would need to assume the significant responsibility of managing their own content and technology. The buy-side model offers key opportunities to reduce costs, including procurement, production, and operations by streamlining the purchasing process. It focuses on quick and thorough searches to compare desired product offerings, minimize paperwork, and produce clear, consistent product and vendor information, thereby reducing ordering errors.

The **e-marketplace model** represents a virtual shopping mall where many buyers and many sellers transact business. Such communities connect customers directly with suppliers to serve a broad array of business segments. They typically draw on a larger universe of buyers, often formed into purchasing groups (PGs) that consolidate the volume from otherwise unrelated businesses, interested in purchasing similar products and services. Costs are reduced because purchasing transactions can be completed online leveraging the efficiency of the Internet as a distribution channel, and because the efficiency this model allows buyers to collaborate with their peers to procure products for general business or industry-specific requirements.

The key benefit to buyers under each of the three approaches is the ability to view online catalogs containing detailed product descriptions, receive timely pricing information, place orders online 24 hours a day, seven days a week, and reduce costs by eliminating ordering errors and unnecessary paperwork. The buy-side model and the e-marketplace model offer the added advantage of pooling many customers' orders to create buying economies and achieve better volume discounts. An even bigger benefit of these two models is the added cost savings of fully automating the purchasing process from order placement through payment. These options also offer the ability to track and analyze purchases through all stages of the purchasing cycle, allowing sellers to better control costs and manage inventory.

E-procurement solutions have broad appeal because they span all market sectors and many industries. E-procurement can deliver significant cost reductions through a variety of ways, including automation of manual processes, improved

**contract compliance**, and empowerment of purchasing employees. In general, e-procurement customers report a relatively quick return on investment and high satisfaction levels.

# Financial Reporting Module

The financial reporting module, also called a general ledger module, maintains account balances and is used to prepare trial balances, financial statements, and a variety of reports for management's use. In order to assist accounting personnel in the preparation of these documents (statements and reports), the financial reporting module must have access to account balances maintained by other system modules. When the financial reporting module has limited access to data maintained by other modules or when the module serves as a stand-alone general ledger system, data may be entered directly into the module's files. Most modules can generate reports relating to individual operating departments, support centers, divisions, or entire properties (for multi-unit corporations).

Many financial reporting modules can be adapted to the needs and requirements of individual hospitality properties. Flexible codes, screen designs, and report formats allow properties to customize applications. Management may design the format of the property's financial statements by controlling headings, spacing, indentation, sub-titles, underlining, and other formatting features.

## Chart of Accounts

An industry-accepted uniform system of accounts provides a logical approach to back office design because it guides accounting personnel in the preparation and presentation of financial statements by standardizing formats and account classifications. This standardization permits users of financial statements to compare the financial position and operational performance of a particular hospitality property to similar types of properties in the industry. For new businesses entering the hospitality industry, a uniform system of accounts serves as a turnkey accounting system that can be quickly adapted to meet the needs of the business.

A **chart of accounts** lists general ledger accounts by type of account, including account number and account title. The account names found in the **chart of accounts file** are listed in a sequence that parallels the order of their appearance on the financial statements and general ledger. The **general ledger** is the principal accounting ledger containing all of the balance sheet and statement of income accounts.

A chart of accounts shows no account balances. The main purpose of a chart of accounts is to serve as a "table of contents" to guide bookkeepers as they enter the results of business transactions in accounting records. Bookkeepers are generally not allowed to use an account unless it specifically appears on the company's chart of accounts.

For most businesses, the chart of accounts arranges accounts according to their major classification. Accounts are classified as either asset, liability, equity, revenue, or expense accounts. Asset, liability, and equity accounts form the basis for preparation of a balance sheet. Revenue or expense accounts form the basis for preparation of the statement of income. The sequence of major account classifications appearing on a chart of accounts typically is as follows:

- Asset accounts
- Liability accounts
- Equity accounts
- Revenue accounts
- Expense accounts

The use of a computer in the input (recording) phase requires that each account be assigned an account number. The account number is usually designed so that a significant digit represents one of the major account classifications (asset, liability, equity, revenue, or expense accounts). The digits that follow normally define the individual account's sequential relationship within that classification.

For example, assume that management has designed a three-digit account numbering system. Since the first major account classification is assets, the number 1 might be assigned as the first digit for all asset account numbers. The number series of 1xx will therefore include all asset accounts. Since cash is typically the first account to appear within the sequence of accounts classified as asset accounts, the three-digit account number assigned to the cash account will be 101. Since liabilities are the second major account classification, the number 2 can be assigned as the first digit for all liability accounts. Thus, the number series 2xx includes all liability accounts.

A business can use any account numbering system that meets its particular requirements. Some general ledger systems accommodate up to 12-character account numbers and maintain an array of accounts for multiple corporate properties. The variety of accounts and the design of numbering systems can vary from business to business, depending on the company's size and the detail of management information desired. Some businesses that use a manual accounting system may also use a variation of an account numbering system.

## Trial Balance File

A **trial balance file** maintains a list of accounts with debit and credit balances. With a fully integrated hotel property management system, the daily system update is responsible for transferring data from front office and back office modules to the general ledger, ensuring that the balances held in the financial reporting module are current. A **trial balance** is prepared to test the equality of these balances (debits and credits). In a non-automated back office system, the trial balance is prepared as follows:

1. Determine the balance of each account in the ledger.
2. List the accounts and show debit balances in one column and credit balances in a separate column.
3. Add the debit balances.

4. Add the credit balances.

5. Compare the totals of the debit and credit balances.

When the total of debit balance accounts equals the total of credit balance accounts, the trial balance is said to be in balance. If debits and credits do not balance, the bookkeeper has made errors in recording the transactions, in determining the balances of each account, or in preparing the trial balance. It is important to note that a balanced trial balance is not proof that all transactions have been properly recorded. The trial balance, if correct, only indicates that debits equal credits.

Preparing a trial balance in a non-automated system can be an error-prone and time-consuming task. In an automated system, the general ledger function of the financial reporting module can generate an accurate trial balance upon demand.

The general ledger function of the financial reporting module also simplifies the closing process at the end of an accounting period. The module audits accounting files for any out-of-balance conditions. It also searches for invoices or journals that are not fully posted to the general ledger and produces a report disclosing all errors.

Some modules allow the current period to remain open while postings are made to future periods. When the current period closes, the module computes opening balances for the next accounting period. Once a period is closed, errors are generally corrected with journal entries made to the current period. Some modules can reopen previously closed periods for correcting entries.

## Financial Statements

A back office financial reporting module can access relevant data from front office and back office modules and generate balance sheets and statements of income. Most modules can also produce statements of cash flows.

The **balance sheet** provides important information on the financial position of a hospitality business by showing its assets, liabilities, and equity on a particular date. Simply stated, assets represent anything a business owns that has commercial or exchange value, liabilities represent the claims of outsiders (such as creditors) to assets, and owners' equity represents the claims of owners to assets. On every balance sheet, the total assets must always agree (that is, balance) with the combined totals of the liabilities and equity sections. In essence, the format of the balance sheet reflects the fundamental accounting equation:

$$\text{Assets} = \text{Liabilities} + \text{Equity}$$

Financial reporting modules should be able to produce balance sheets (and other financial statements) that compare current figures with those of prior periods. In addition, modules should be able to generate comparative and common-size balance sheets for managerial review.

Comparative balance sheets present two sets of figures for each balance sheet line item. One set of figures is from the current balance sheet; the other set, from the balance sheet of a previous period. Changes in amounts of line items from one period to the next are reported in both absolute and relative terms. Absolute changes show the change in dollars between two periods, while relative changes (also referred to as percentage changes) are calculated by dividing the absolute change by the amount known for the previous period. Significant changes should be brought to management's attention.

**Common-size balance sheets** also present two sets of figures for each balance sheet line item. One set of figures is from the current balance sheet; the other set, from the balance sheet of a previous period. All amounts are reduced to percentages of their account classification. That is, the total assets on each balance sheet are set at 100 percent, and each asset category is reported as a percentage of the total (100 percent). This same procedure is followed for the total liabilities and owners' equity sections. The percentages found on the two balance sheets are then compared and significant changes are brought to management's attention.

The **statement of income** (also called the profit and loss statement) provides important financial information about the results of operations for a given period of time. The time period may be as short as one month and does not usually exceed one business year. The business year is called the **fiscal year**. Since this statement reveals the bottom line (net income for a given period of time), it should be one of the most important financial statements managers use to evaluate the success of operations. It may also be an important measure of managerial effectiveness and efficiency. Most financial reporting modules are able to generate both comparative and common-size income statements. Exhibit 12 shows a comparative income statement produced by a restaurant back office accounting system.

Financial reporting modules also produce condensed income statements comparing results of the current month with previous months, same month of previous years, and budgeted amounts. These reports may also compare year-to-date results with results of previous years.

Some financial reporting modules have extensive graphics capabilities. The phrase "a picture is worth a thousand words" certainly applies here. Although graphs do not usually provide detail, managers can track recent performance trends more easily by reviewing results through line drawings. Departmental expenses can be shown using pie charts, departmental revenue using bar charts, and so on. Charts tend to be easy to understand, and they can be used to demonstrate operational results more successfully than the traditional financial statements, which may at times appear as a confusing list of numbers.

## Ratio Analysis

Hospitality industry financial statements contain a considerable amount of information. A thorough analysis of this information may require more than simply reading the reported facts and figures. Users of financial statements need to be able to interpret the contents of these documents so that critical aspects of the property's financial situation do not go unnoticed. Interpretation is often accomplished through **ratio analysis**. A **ratio** gives mathematical expression to a significant relationship between two figures. It is calculated by dividing one figure by the other.

Ratio results are meaningful only when compared against useful criteria. Useful criteria against which to compare the results of ratio analysis normally include:

## Exhibit 12 Sample Comparative Income Statement

Comparative Income and Expense
Microbilt Restaurant #10

| Description | Curr Month This Year | % Of Total | Curr Month Last Year | % Of Total | Y-T-D This Year | % Of Total | Y-T-D Last Year | % Of Total |
|---|---|---|---|---|---|---|---|---|
| REVENUE | | | | | | | | |
| Food | 186,682.00 | 68.0 | 174,645.00 | 68.9 | 2,683,148.19 | 69.9 | 2,267,895.00 | 70.1 |
| Beverage | 86,500.00 | 31.5 | 77,880.00 | 30.7 | 1,145,800.00 | 29.8 | 959,245.00 | 29.7 |
| Miscellaneous Income | 1,200.00 | .4 | 800.00 | .3 | 7,500.00 | .2 | 7,500.00 | .2 |
| TOTAL REVENUE | 274,382.00 | 100.0 | 253,325.00 | 100.0 | 3,839,348.19 | 100.00 | 3,234,640.00 | 100.0 |
| COST OF SALES | | | | | | | | |
| Food | 76,410.00 | 27.9 | 74,100.00 | 29.3 | 1,087,651.63 | 28.3 | 947,650.00 | 29.3 |
| Beverage | 750.00 | .3 | 1,156.00 | .5 | 11,486.00 | .3 | 9,432.00 | .3 |
| Cost of Well Brands | 7,273.00 | 2.7 | 7,191.00 | 2.8 | 95,549.00 | 2.5 | 87,750.00 | 2.7 |
| Cost of Call Level 1 | 5,326.00 | 1.9 | 4,980.00 | 2.0 | 69,238.00 | 1.8 | 58,145.00 | 1.8 |
| Cost of Call Level 2 | 4,547.00 | 1.7 | 4,750.00 | 1.9 | 64,111.00 | 1.7 | 58,250.00 | 1.8 |
| Cost of House Wines | 1,234.00 | .5 | 679.00 | .3 | 12,510.00 | .3 | 10,555.00 | .3 |
| Cost of Fine Wines | 554.00 | .2 | 1,915.00 | .8 | 12,756.00 | .3 | 10,775.00 | .3 |
| Cost of Brandy & Liqueurs | 925.00 | .3 | 1,470.00 | .6 | 17,523.00 | .5 | 14,225.00 | .4 |
| Cost of Bar Garnishes | 231.00 | .1 | 182.00 | .1 | 2,772.00 | .1 | 2,327.00 | .1 |
| Cost of Bar Mixes | 205.00 | .1 | 224.00 | .1 | 2,460.00 | .1 | 2,239.00 | .1 |
| TOTAL COST OF SALES | 97,455.00 | 35.5 | 96,647.00 | 38.2 | 1,376,056.63 | 35.8 | 1,201,348.00 | 37.1 |
| GROSS PROFIT | 176,927.00 | 64.5 | 156,678.00 | 61.9 | 2,463,291.56 | 64.2 | 2,033,292.00 | 62.9 |
| OTHER INCOME | | | | | | | | |
| Vending Machines | 2,406.00 | .9 | 2,145.00 | .9 | 24,812.00 | .7 | 22,600.00 | .7 |
| TOTAL OTHER INCOME | 2,406.00 | .9 | 2,145.00 | .9 | 24,812.00 | .7 | 22,600.00 | .7 |
| TOTAL INCOME | 179,333.00 | 65.4 | 158,823.00 | 62.7 | 2,488,103.00 | 64.8 | 2,055,892.00 | 63.6 |
| CONTROLLABLE EXPENSES | | | | | | | | |
| Salaries and Wages | 75,320.00 | 27.5 | 65,900.00 | 26.0 | 960,640.00 | 25.0 | 810,650.00 | 25.1 |
| Employee Benefits | 14,125.00 | 5.2 | 12,800.00 | 5.1 | 197,050.00 | 5.1 | 166,550.00 | 5.2 |
| Direct Operating ExpeNses | 17,560.00 | 6.4 | 16,995.00 | 6.7 | 258,720.00 | 6.7 | 237,220.00 | 7.3 |
| Music and Entertainment | 2,410.00 | .9 | 2,240.00 | .9 | 34,020.00 | .9 | 28,400.00 | .9 |
| Marketing | 5,130.00 | 1.9 | 4,750.00 | 1.9 | 73,960.00 | 1.9 | 62,000.00 | 1.9 |
| Energy and Utility Serv's | 5,600.00 | 2.0 | 5,050.00 | 2.0 | 80,200.00 | 2.1 | 67,800.00 | 2.1 |
| Administrative/General | 18,000.00 | 6.6 | 18,400.00 | 7.3 | 222,800.00 | 5.8 | 188,900.00 | 5.8 |
| Repairs and Maintenance | 4,200.00 | 1.5 | 4,710.00 | 1.9 | 58,800.00 | 1.5 | 50,100.00 | 1.6 |
| TOTAL CONTROLLABLE EXPENSES | 142,345.00 | 51.9 | 130,845.00 | 51.7 | 1,886,190.00 | 49.1 | 1,611,620.00 | 49.8 |
| INCOME BEFORE RENT & OTHER OCCUP. COSTS | 36,988.00 | 13.5 | 27,978.00 | 11.0 | 601,913.56 | 15.7 | 444,272.00 | 13.7 |
| RENT & OTHER OCCUP. COSTS | | | | | | | | |
| Rent And Other Occ. Costs | 11,330.00 | 4.1 | 10,000.00 | 4.0 | 132,260.00 | 3.4 | 115,900.00 | 3.6 |
| INCOME BEFORE Interest | 25,658.00 | 9.4 | 17,978.00 | 7.1 | 469,653.56 | 12.2 | 328,372.00 | 10.2 |
| INTEREST | 1,850.00 | .7 | 2,000.00 | .8 | 25,900.00 | .7 | 22,000.00 | .7 |
| Depreciation | 4,733.00 | 1.7 | 5,000.00 | 2.0 | 66,266.00 | 1.7 | 56,950.00 | 1.8 |
| TOTAL RENT & OTHER OCCUP. COSTS | 17,913.00 | 6.5 | 17,000.00 | 6.7 | 224,426.00 | 5.9 | 194,850.00 | 6.0 |
| INCOME BEFORE PROVISION FOR INC. TAXES | 19,075.00 | 7.0 | 10,978.00 | 4.3 | 377,487.56 | 9.8 | 249,422.00 | 7.7 |
| PROVISION FOR INC. TAXES | | | | | | | | |
| Income Taxes | 6,625.00 | 2.4 | 5,625.00 | 2.2 | 92,750.00 | 2.4 | 78,575.00 | 2.4 |
| TOTAL PROVISION FOR INC. TAXES | 6,625.00 | 2.4 | 5,625.00 | 2.2 | 92,750.00 | 2.4 | 78,575.00 | 2.4 |
| NET INCOME | 12,450.00 | 4.5 | 5,353.00 | 2.1 | 284,737.56 | 7.4 | 170,847.00 | 5.3 |

Source: MicroBilt Corporation, Atlanta, Georgia.

- Corresponding ratios calculated for a prior period
- Corresponding ratios of other properties
- Industry averages
- Planned ratio goals

Ratio analysis can be extremely useful to owners, creditors, and managers in evaluating the financial condition and operation of a hotel. Users of ratio analysis must be careful when comparing two different properties because the accounting procedures of one may differ from those of another. Moreover, ratios are only indicators; they do not resolve problems or reveal what problems may exist. At best, ratios that vary significantly from past periods, budgeted standards, or industry averages indicate a reason for investigation. When problems appear to exist, considerably more analysis and investigation are necessary to determine appropriate corrective action.

Assuming that necessary financial data are stored, ratio statistics can be generated almost at will. Many ratios need not be calculated on a daily basis. In fact, if their analysis is based on too short a period of time, they may fail to provide meaningful information. It is important that management officials determine which ratios are to be calculated and how often. If all ratios were calculated daily, there could be a risk of information overload. In other words, so many statistics would be generated that the manager would not have the time—or the inclination—to search for critical information.

Operating ratios, on the other hand, may be an exception to this rule. They can be very useful when prepared on a frequent basis. For example, when a hotel's night audit is automated, many operating ratio computations (such as average daily rate, occupancy percentage, double occupancy percentage, and others) are a by-product of the system update routine. These statistics can then be compared against budgeted goals to present management with a timely (and convenient) measure of operational success.

## Enterprise Reporting

Enterprise information systems are designed for hospitality corporations and management companies that need to consolidate multi-unit data into useful reports for corporate staff as well as for managers at the unit level. Some of these systems resemble data warehouses. They can have extremely large databases and are designed to support decision-making within organizations. The database is structured to conduct a variety of analyses, including elaborate queries on large amounts of data that can require extensive searching.

Enterprise information systems enable corporate managers to monitor transactions and affect unit-level operations such as:

- Sorting data from units grouped by regions, price points, or other variables.
- Implementing pricing changes for a single unit, the entire company, or for a select group of business units.

- Implementing accounting changes (such as a new tax table) for a single unit, the entire company, or for a select group of business units.

With data warehouses, data are typically historical and static and may also contain numerous summaries. With enterprise reporting via Internet connection, however, "real-time" reporting enables managers to monitor sales, promotions, labor costs, etc., from a web browser anytime, anywhere. User names and passwords control the degree of access granted to various management levels.

# Endnotes

1. The section on e-procurement was adapted from *e-Commerce: Frequently Asked Questions*, written by Victor L. Vesnaver, Principal, V2 Consultants, with an editorial review by David Sjolander, Carlson Hospitality Corporation, and produced by the Technology Committee of the American Hotel & Lodging Association with a grant from the American Hotel & Lodging Foundation.

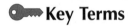

# Key Terms

### Accounts Receivable Module

**accounts aging file**—Contains accounts receivable data that can be formatted into a variety of aging reports that segment accounts in the file according to the date the charge originated.

**accounts receivable**—Obligations owed an organization from sales made on credit.

**aging of accounts receivable schedule**—Segments each account in the accounts aging file according to the date the charge originated.

**city ledger**—A subsidiary ledger listing accounts receivable balances of guests who have checked out, and other receivables as well.

**city ledger file**—Contains data from the front office guest accounting module, such as balances from guest folios, non-guest accounts, bill-to accounts, credit card billings, and others.

**customer master file**—Sets up billing information. Customer data maintained in this file includes: account code, name of guest or account, address, telephone number, contact person, type of account, credit limit, last payment date, last payment amount, and credit history.

### Accounts Payable Module

**accounts payable**—Liabilities incurred for merchandise, equipment, or other goods and services that have been purchased on account.

**accounts payable aging report**—Contains several columns listing invoices by vendor number, vendor name, invoice number, and invoice date.

**cash requirements report**—Lists all invoices selected for payment and the corresponding cash requirement totals; prepared by vendor number, vendor name, due date, item, or group code and typically including vendor number, vendor name, invoice number, due date, balance due, and amount to be paid.

**check reconciliation**—Balancing the total of checks removed from the outstanding checks list with the total of cleared checks appearing on the bank statement.

**check register**—After the check writing routine, the accounts payable module prints a check register by check number. The check register also may be sorted by vendor or by invoice due date.

**check register file**—Monitors the calculation and printing of bank checks for payments of selected invoices.

**invoice register file**—Maintains a complete list of all invoices currently outstanding and payable.

**monthly check register**—Provides a hard copy audit trail of payments made to vendors. This report also identifies checks that have not yet been accounted for.

**outstanding checks list**—Details all checks that have been issued but remain outstanding; can be used to reconcile checks issued against canceled checks appearing on bank statements.

**override options**—Provide management with complete control over cash disbursements before engaging the automatic check writing feature of the accounts payable module.

**payment discount date**—The last day on which it is possible for a lodging operation to take advantage of a cash payment discount that may be offered by a specific vendor.

**reconciliation audit report**—Balances the total of checks removed from the outstanding checks list with the total of cleared checks appearing on the bank statement.

**vendor activity report**—Lists gross amount invoiced, discounts taken, number of invoices, and other vendor data.

**vendor master file**—Maintains records of all current vendors. Data contained in this file includes: vendor number, vendor name, contact name, address, telephone number, vendor payment priority, discount terms, discount account number, invoice description, payment date, and year-to-date purchases.

**vendor status report**—Presents summary accounts payable information.

*Payroll Module*

**computerized time-clock system**—Records time in and time out for employees.

**deductions**—Subtractions from gross pay that are usually voluntary and depend on the types of benefits available from the employer.

**payroll cost report**—Shows labor costs by department or job classifications.

**payroll register file**—Maintains the number of hours each employee works during a pay period and other data that may require special tax calculations, such as sick leave pay, bonus pay, tips, and expense reimbursements.

**withholdings**—Subtractions from gross pay for income and social security taxes.

### Inventory Module

**actual cost**—A method of inventory valuation. Values inventory only in relation to actual costs of items stored. The value of stored products is, then, the value represented by the sum of individual unit costs.

**first in, first out (FIFO)**—A method of valuing inventory; the products in storage areas are valued at the level of the most recently purchased items to be placed in inventory.

**inventory master file**—Maintains basic inventory data, such as item name, item description (brief), inventory code number, storeroom location code, item purchase unit, purchase unit price, item issue unit, product group code, vendor identification number, order lead time, minimum-maximum stock levels, and date of last purchase.

**inventory status**—An account of how much of each item is in storage. Inventory status may be determined by a physical inventory or a perpetual inventory.

**inventory status file**—In a perpetual inventory system, keeps a running balance of the quantity of issued/stored items.

**inventory valuation**—The value of items in inventory.

**inventory valuation file**—Contains data for determining the cost of goods sold and the replacement cost of items listed in the inventory master file.

**inventory variance**—Differences between a physical count of an item and the balance maintained by the perpetual inventory system.

**last in, first out (LIFO)**—An inventory valuation method that assumes that the products that are most recently purchased are used first. The inventory value is assumed to be represented by the cost of items placed in storage the earliest.

**perpetual inventory system**—An inventory system that keeps records up-to-date by tracking all additions to and subtractions from stock.

**physical inventory system**—An inventory system in which property employees periodically observe and count items in storage.

**weighted average**—An inventory valuation method that considers the quantity of products purchased at different unit costs. This method "weights" the prices to be averaged based on the quantity of products in storage at each price.

### Purchasing Module

**bid specification file**—Contains the specific characteristics of purchased items. Purveyors are asked to quote prices for products that meet or exceed stated specifications.

**bid specification form**—Submitted to vendors to obtain item quotations.

**buy-side e-procurement model**—a "one buyer, many sellers" approach. Buyers purchase Web-based services or use self-supported systems to buy from approved vendors electronically.

**contract compliance**—utilizing volume purchasing contracts that have been negotiated by a company's corporate purchasing group or by a hotel chain, franchise organization, association, purchasing consortia, or representation firm.

**e-marketplace e-procurement model**—represents a virtual shopping mall where many buyers and many sellers transact business. Such communities connect customers directly with suppliers to serve a broad array of business segments.

**e-procurement**—purchasing goods and services over the Internet.

**daily receiving report**—Lists details of all items received on a given day.

**lead-time quantity**—The anticipated number of purchase units withdrawn from inventory between the time an order is placed and the time it is delivered.

**minimum/maximum inventory levels**—Help managers determine when products need to be purchased and how much of each product to order. For each purchase item, management sets a minimum quantity below which inventory levels should not fall and a maximum quantity above which inventory levels should not rise.

**sell-side e-procurement model**—involves placing an order directly with a supplier over the Internet. In this many-to-one environment (many buyers, one seller), the buyer generally accesses the supplier's own Web site to do research and make purchases.

*Financial Reporting Module*

**balance sheet**—Provides important information on the financial position of a hospitality business by showing its assets, liabilities, and equity on a particular date.

**chart of accounts**—Lists general ledger accounts by type of account including account number and account title.

**chart of accounts file**—Lists the names of accounts in a sequence that parallels the order of their appearance on the financial statements and general ledger.

**common-size balance sheets**—Present two sets of figures for each balance sheet line item. One set of figures is from the current balance sheet; the other set is from the balance sheet of a previous period. All amounts are reduced to percentages of their account classification.

**fiscal year**—Twelve consecutive months that define a business year.

**general ledger**—The principal accounting ledger containing all of the balance sheet and statement of income accounts.

**ratio**—Gives mathematical expression to a significant relationship between two figures. It is calculated by dividing one figure by the other.

**ratio analysis**—Analysis of financial statements and operating results through the use of ratios.

**statement of income**—Also called the profit and loss statement, provides important financial information about the results of operations for a given period of time.

**trial balance**—Tests the equality of debit and credit account balances.

**trial balance file**—Maintains a list of accounts with debit and credit balances.

 **Review Questions** ─────────────────────────────────

1. What functions are performed by an accounts receivable module?

2. How can management use an aging of accounts receivable schedule?

3. What functions does an accounts payable module perform?

4. What override options provided by accounts payable modules may be useful to management?

5. What are some uses of the cash requirements report produced by an accounts payable module?

6. What functions are performed by a payroll module?

7. What are some of the characteristics of hospitality operations that complicate the design of a back office payroll module?

8. How can differences among purchase units, issue units, and standard recipe units complicate the design of a back office inventory module?

9. What are two basic ways by which a purchasing module may automatically generate purchase orders?

10. What does a financial reporting module perform?

 **Internet Sites** ─────────────────────────────────

For more information, visit the following Internet sites. Remember that Internet addresses can change without notice. If the site is no longer there, you can use a search engine to look for additional sites.

*Hospitality Accounting Organizations*

Hospitality Industry Technology
Exposition and Conference
http://www.hitecshow.org

Hospitality Finance and Technology
Professionals (HFTP)
http://www.hftp.org

*Hotel Property Management Systems with Accounting Applications*

CLS Software
http://www.hospitalitynet.nl/cls

CMS Hospitality
http://www.cmshosp.com.au

Execu/Tech Systems, Incorporated
http://execu-tech.com

Fidelio
http://www.micros.com

HOST Group
http://www.hostgroup.com

Lodging Touch International
http://www.lodgingtouch.com

Resort Systems Incorporated
http://www.resortsystems.ca

Western Hospitality Systems—InnSure
http://www.lodgingsystems.com

## Food and Beverage Systems with Accounting Applications

CLS Software
http://www.hospitalitynet.nl/cls

CMS Hospitality
http://www.cmshosp.com.au

Comtrex Systems Corporation
http://www.comtrex.com

Comus Restaurant Systems
http://www.comus.com

CostGuard Food Service Software
http://www.costguard.com

Eatec Corporation
http://www.eatec.com

Geac Computer Corporation Limited
http://www.geac.com

Instill Corporation
http://www.instill.com

Integrated Restaurant Software
http://www.rmstouch.com

Micros Systems, Inc.
http://www.micros.com

Sulcus Computer Corporation
http://www.sulcus.com

System Concepts, Inc.
http://www.foodtrak.com

# Chapter 10 Outline

Management Information System
    MIS Personnel
Electronic Data Processing
    Advantages of Electronic Data
        Processing
    Types of Data
    Binary Coding
Database Management
    Files, Records, and Fields
    Database Structures
    Input/Output Specifications
    Database Management  Commands
Multidimensional Databases
    Guest Relationship Management
    Frequent Diner Applications

# Competencies

1. Define the purpose of management information systems and describe functions performed by information technology. (pp. 253–254)

2. Describe the typical responsibilities of managers and staff working in the information systems area of a hospitality operation. (pp. 254–257)

3. Describe the data processing cycle and cite the advantages of electronic data processing. (pp. 258–260)

4. Identify the types of data and distinguish bits from bytes. (pp. 260–261)

5. Identify major features of database management software and describe how they can be used by hospitality operations. (pp. 261–263)

6. Distinguish hierarchical database structures from relational database structures. (pp. 263–268)

7. Distinguish multidimensional database structures from traditional database structures. (pp. 268–270)

8. Describe the features and functions of frequent diner applications. (pp. 270–271)

# 10

# Information Management

THE INFORMATION SYSTEMS of automated hotels and restaurants can produce liter-
ally hundreds of reports for managers. However, simply distributing reports does
not in itself ensure an effective information system. To achieve the full potential of
an automated information system, system functions must be integrated with management's information needs.

Information systems also streamline the process of collecting and recording
data and expand the ways in which information is organized and reported. These
systems enable management to speed up the process by which useful information
is made available to those who make decisions.

This chapter examines the design and functions of an MIS and describes the
major responsibilities of information system managers. The fundamentals of data
processing and database management are also addressed. The chapter closes with
an overview of how databases are used to provide management with information
to better manage relationships with guests.

## Management Information System

A **management information system (MIS)** is designed to provide managers with
the necessary information needed to plan, organize, staff, direct, and control
operations. The design of an effective MIS is built around the information needs of
managers. As managers define and prioritize their specific information needs, an
information system can be designed to organize system applications so that they
support decision-making activities at all levels within the organization. An effective MIS extends its power beyond routine report generation and provides managers with the information they need to:

- Monitor progress toward achieving organizational goals

- Measure performance

- Identify trends and patterns

- Evaluate alternatives

- Support decision-making

- Assist in corrective action

The levels of decision-making supported by an MIS are: strategic planning,
tactical decision-making, and operational decision-making. Strategic planning
refers to decision-making activities through which future-oriented goals and

objectives of an organization are established. Tactical decisions relate to activities required to implement strategic planning decisions. Operational decisions address specific tasks that normally follow previously established rules and patterns.

Once the information needs of managers have been identified, an MIS is designed to perform the following functions:

- Enable managers to better monitor and administer business transactions and activities.

- Provide a high level of operational and internal control over business resources.

- Produce timely and comprehensive reports formatted to the specific needs of managers.

- Reduce managerial paperwork and operational expenses by eliminating unnecessary source documents and streamlining data transfer and recording procedures.

To perform these functions effectively, an MIS uses a variety of information technology and decision support systems. **Information technology (IT)** establishes a communication process in which data are transferred from related systems, such as a hotel's reservations system, front office modules, point-of-sale system, accounting applications, or sales applications. The transferred data are processed according to pre-established decision-making rules, financial models, or other analytical methods. The processed data are then stored in information formats tailored to the needs of individual managers and become available on demand or at set intervals.

Information technology also includes simulation capability and the incorporation of expert systems. Decision support systems with simulation capability enable managers to explore "what if" possibilities. These systems are interactive information systems that use decision models and a comprehensive database to provide information customized to support specific decisions that managers face. Expert systems differ from decision support systems in that they apply specialized problem-solving expertise and are used to indicate the most probable solution. Therefore, an expert system helps or replaces an expert to solve problems.

## MIS Personnel

In large, fully automated hospitality properties, the MIS management staff may consist of a property systems manager and department systems supervisors. Generally, the **property systems manager** participates in the evaluation, selection, and installation of system hardware and is trained in the operation of software applications used throughout the property. The property systems manager, also known simply as the systems manager, provides on-premises systems support and, when necessary, functions as a network administrator and/or an applications software troubleshooter. **Department systems supervisors** are typically individuals already employed within a specific department who receive extensive training in the operation of hardware, software applications, and network components used in their departments. Department systems supervisors train others within their departments and provide technical support services as appropriate.

The property systems manager has a wide range of responsibilities. More often a generalist than a technician, the systems manager must understand advanced technology (including hardware, software, and network components), information processing techniques, and interrelations of functional areas within the property. Without this understanding, it would be difficult to direct the MIS to meet the specific information needs of managers throughout the property. The systems manager must also be skilled in system vendor relations and provide a reliable and efficient information distribution system for management and staff. Other duties of a property systems manager include:

- Planning and controlling MIS activities, which includes identifying the processing priorities within the system

- Selecting department systems managers and establishing training programs

- Managing multi-processor environments, which includes developing system configuration and design alternatives in relation to the placement and processing capabilities of system components

- Designing and implementing information back-up and security controls

In addition to the above responsibilities, the systems manager also periodically reviews the MIS and presents requests for system modification to management. If the modifications are approved, the systems manager discusses desired changes with appropriate system vendors. Subsequent system changes are documented by the systems manager.

Professional certification in the area of hospitality technology is offered by Hospitality Financial and Technology Professionals (HFTP). Exhibit 1 presents basic information concerning the designation of Certified Hospitality Technology Professional (CHTP). For more information about HFTP and professional certification, visit the association's Web site at http://www.hftp.org.

The systems manager is also responsible for planning and maintaining the hardware configuration. The most common hardware configuration for property-based systems is the client-server model. This model uses a powerful file server PC in the computer room to hold the software application and all the data, and to communicate with the PC workstations at each user's location over a local area network (LAN). It sometimes seems as if every systems vendor requires a separate server for its products, which can lead to a large number of PCs filling the computer room.

There is some justification for this setup, in that keeping the software applications separate reduces the chance of one application interfering with another and makes troubleshooting easier. However, sometimes a property may end up spending more money on hardware than is really necessary. Going too far in the other direction and putting as many applications as possible on one server may save hardware costs, but it increases the property's vulnerability to server failure, as all systems would be lost at once.

**Exhibit 1   Certified Hospitality Technology Professional (CHTP)**

# CERTIFIED HOSPITALITY TECHNOLOGY PROFESSIONAL (CHTP)

The Certified Hospitality Technology Professional (CHTP) program is recognized as THE symbol of achievement and competence in hospitality information technology knowledge. Developed jointly by Hospitality Financial and Technology Professionals (HFTP) and the Educational Institute of the American Hotel and Lodging Association (AH&LA), the designation elevates the professionalism of both the recipient and the industry by helping to set standards for the field. Those who earn the CHTP designation demonstrate a higher level of dedication to their profession.

## The CHTP Professional Certification

- Identifies you as possessing a basic level of technical competency;
- Recognizes your commitment to professionalism;
- Raises colleague respect, offering you greater recognition on the job;
- Provides the opportunity for continual self-improvement;
- Indicates a mastery of key knowledge and skills;
- Serves as a valuable career tool; and
- Raises the professionalism of your company and identifies it as being committed to hiring quality professionals.

## CHTP Qualification Requirements

To earn the CHTP designation, applicants must pass a four-hour examination covering a wide range of technology principles. To qualify to take the exam, an applicant must have earned a minimum of 100 points which are awarded for evidence of an applicants's education, industry experience and/or HFTP or AH&LA membership. Here's a breakdown of the points and categories:

**Education:** The types of education eligible for points are an associate's degree, a bachelor's degree, graduate degree, college credit for hours above and beyond conferred degrees; HFTP/Educational Institute workshops and seminars that are technology-related; and non-HFTP workshops and seminars which are technology-related. The successful applicant must earn a minimum of 40 points in this category.

**Experience:** Points are earned annually based upon your specific work experience. Key areas of knowledge include: telecommunications systems; specialized systems specific to a particular segment of the hospitality industry (i.e. clubs, hotels, casinos, etc.); systems administration and operation; management practices; and property-based applications such as property management, accounting, and food and beverage. The successful applicant must receive a minimum of 40 points in this category.

**HFTP/AH&LA Membership:** Although membership is not required to take the exam, 10 points will be awarded for each year of membership in HFTP or AH&LA.

**Exhibit 1**  *(continued)*

**Examination**

The exam is comprised of a set of 250 questions and divided into sections. A passing grade of 75% must be accomplished for each section in order to pass the exam in its entirety. The contents of the exam will test the candidate's knowledge in technology concepts; specific hotel systems (i.e. PMS); systems rooted in other industries but also used in the hospitality sector (i.e. the Internet); and general hotel management practices. The candidate should also possess a basic knowledge of hotel accounting, be familiar with procedures relating to risk management, know the basics of sales management procedures as it relates to sales management systems, and understand the workings of telephone revenue accounting and facility management systems.

A breakdown of the exam sections is noted below:

| Technology Concepts | Hotel Technology |
|---|---|
| Network Administration | Accounting/Payroll/HR |
| Emerging Technologies | Food and Beverage |
| Telecommunications | Lodging Applications |
| System Architecture | Sales and Catering |
| **Targeted Technology** | **Managing Technology** |
| Facilities | Human Resources |
| Club Applications | General Management |
| Resort/Spa Applications | System Strategies |
| Marketing/Web Applications | System Analysis |
| | System Selection |

Source: Hospitality Financial and Technology Professionals. For more information, browse the association's Internet site at http://www.hftp.org

The other systems configuration is the application service provider (ASP) model, more properly called a remote-server model. In this scenario, the application software is physically located somewhere other than at the property, such as at the vendor's or hotel or restaurant chain's headquarters or even at a third party's site. The users' workstations at the property are connected to the server over a wide area network (WAN), and the system is paid for on a monthly rental or a per-transaction fee basis.

Much of the recent publicity ASPs have received comes from the emergence of the public Internet as an inexpensive way to implement this configuration, but ASPs can also be used (and with greater guarantees of security and performance) over dedicated private networks. The benefit to the property is the removal of worries about server reliability, data back-ups, and software upgrades, since the ASP vendor takes care of them. The tradeoffs are the long-range cost of using the system, and the vulnerability of the operation to the loss of the network connection. It's an analysis all potential ASP users have to work out for themselves.

**Exhibit 2    The Data Processing Cycle**

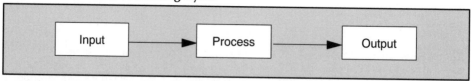

## Electronic Data Processing

Data are facts and/or figures to be processed into useful information. Data processing involves transforming raw facts and isolated figures into timely, accurate, and useful information. Every day, hospitality managers are bombarded with facts and figures about the results of operations. However, these individual pieces of data are relatively meaningless until they undergo a process that organizes or manipulates them into useful information.

Information, the result of data processing, is clearly one of the most valuable resources of a hospitality business. Information can increase a manager's knowledge regarding guests, service, labor, finance, and other areas of concern. Also, information may reduce the uncertainty that managers may experience in decision-making situations. And, after decisions have been made, information can provide managers with important feedback on the effectiveness of their decisions and may even indicate new areas of concern that call for corrective action.

Data processing is not unique to the world of business; it is an important function that occurs in everyday life as well. Everyone processes data. For example, consider what may happen on a typical payday.

After receiving a paycheck, a person may consider all of the items he or she would like to purchase, the cost of those items, and the difference between the amount of the paycheck and the total amount of the planned purchases. If the amount of the paycheck is greater than the amount of planned purchases, the person may decide to place the surplus amount in a savings account. If, on the other hand, the total amount of planned purchases is greater than the amount of the paycheck, the person may reconsider the purchase options, or, perhaps, consider taking out a loan.

In this example of data processing, a collection of data (the amount of the paycheck and the purchase options) is processed (totaled and compared) and, thus, transformed into information (surplus or deficit) useful in making decisions (what to buy, how much to save, or how much to borrow).

The conversion of data into information is accomplished through a cycle of events identified as input, process, and output. Using the terms of our previous example of data processing in everyday life, the paycheck and the purchase options are inputs; totaling the planned purchases and comparing that total with the amount of the paycheck is the processing; and the resulting surplus or deficit is the output. The sequence of input, process, and output is the basic data processing cycle as illustrated in Exhibit 2.

During input, data are collected and organized to simplify subsequent processing functions. During processing, input data are mathematically manipulated

**Exhibit 3   The Electronic Data Processing Cycle**

```
   ┌──────────┐            ┌──────────┐            ┌──────────┐
   │  Input   │ ─────────► │ Process  │ ─────────► │  Output  │
   └──────────┘            └──────────┘            └──────────┘
        │                       ▲
        │                       │
        │       ┌──────────┐    │
        └─────► │  Memory  │────┘
                └──────────┘
```

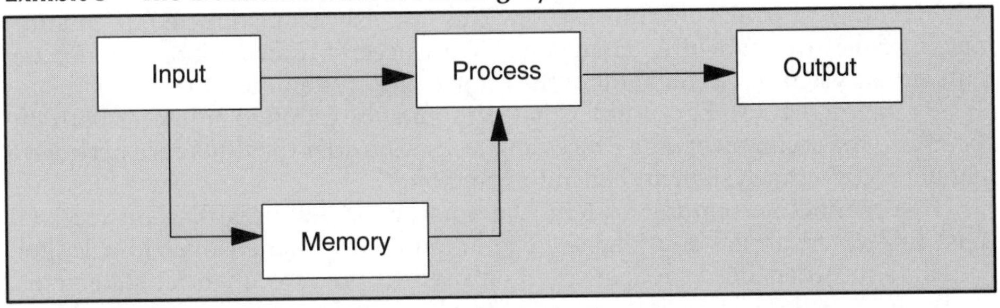

or logically arranged to generate meaningful output. The output can be reported for immediate use or saved for future reference.

The data processing cycle is not new, nor is it limited to automated applications. For example, standard recipes can be viewed as data processing techniques that food service operations have used for a long time to convert raw ingredients into finished menu items. Viewed from the perspective of the data processing cycle, ingredients and their corresponding quantities are the inputs to recipe production; following the recipe's instructions is the process by which the desired recipe output (the number of standard portions) is produced.

The speed, accuracy, and efficiency required for an effective information system are often best achieved through electronic data processing. The difference between data processing and electronic data processing lies in the automation of the process and the addition of a memory unit. Exhibit 3 illustrates the electronic data processing cycle.

Electronic data processing employs an automated system. The automation of input, process, and output events within the basic data processing cycle results in faster and more efficient operation. Also, the addition of a memory unit allows for the storage of data or instructions for more reliable and thorough processing.

## Advantages of Electronic Data Processing

Electronic data processing transforms data into timely, accurate, and useful information by reducing throughput, streamlining output, and minimizing the handling of data.

**Throughput** (formerly termed "turnaround time") refers to the time that elapses between data input and information output. Automated systems are able to minimize throughput for almost all data processing tasks. Inquiry and search procedures are usually performed within an acceptable response time. For example, if a hotel front desk employee needs to find out in which room a guest is registered, the information should be generated quickly. Also, a busy food and beverage manager would appreciate the speed and accuracy of an effective automated system when spot-checking the inventory levels of expensive ingredients immediately following a meal period. Simply stated, throughput is a measure of data processing efficiency.

**Streamlining** the output of an automated system means generating only those reports that are requested by those who will actually use the information. A frequent criticism of electronic data processing is that automated systems produce large volumes of irrelevant information. This criticism is misdirected. If an automated system overwhelms management with useless information, it is not the fault of the system—it is the fault of the information system design.

Reducing the number of times that data must be handled enhances both the speed and the accuracy of data processing tasks. Consider the difference between a manual accounting system and an automated one.

In a manual accounting system, the amounts of invoices that are received must first be recorded in a journal. The amounts are carried over to a ledger. Amounts recorded in the ledger are then used to prepare financial statements. During each of these steps it is possible for a bookkeeper to make any number of mistakes such as recording the wrong number, writing a number's digits in the wrong order (transposing them), calculating a total incorrectly, and so on. The greater the number of times data must be handled, the greater the possibility for error.

In an automated data processing system, the invoice amount is entered only once. The amount can then be accessed by the programs which prepare the journal, ledger, and financial statements. Therefore, when the amount of the invoice is entered correctly, all of the subsequent financial statements will be mathematically correct. If the amount is entered incorrectly, but the mistake identified and corrected, the correction automatically flows from the journal through to the financial statements. With electronic data processing, there are fewer opportunities for error, because it is not necessary to rehandle the same data at each step in the accounting process.

## Types of Data

There are three distinct types of data. One type is called "alpha data" because it consists only of letters of the alphabet. For example, the names of menu items, servers, and hotel guests are all types of alpha data. A second kind of data is called "numeric data" because it consists only of numbers. Menu prices, room numbers, guest check serial numbers, and occupancy percentages are all forms of numeric data. The third type of data is termed "alphanumeric data" because it is made up of both letters and numbers. A hotel's street address, a menu item's description, and personnel records are all examples of alphanumeric data used in the hospitality industry.

Classifying data by type can be very helpful when users are operating in an automated environment. When a data processing system is programmed, each data element must be "introduced" to the system so that the type of data and the maximum number of characters (i.e., letters, numbers, or symbols) it may have. Once the system is programmed with this information, it will not allow users to input data that does not meet specifications. For example, if a reservation system expects the telephone number of a guest to have ten numeric characters, and a user mistakenly enters nine numbers and a single letter, the system will refuse the data entry and inform the user that he or she has made a mistake. This feature reduces the potential number of data entry errors and enhances the reliability of the data entered into the electronic data processing system.

## Binary Coding

Regardless of whether alpha, numeric, or alphanumeric data are to be entered into an electronic data processing system, in order for the system to process it, the data must be translated into a binary code. The **binary code** is a counting system based on two digits, zero and one. This is the easiest way for an automated system to handle data because electronic circuits have two natural states: "on," usually represented by binary digit one; and "off," represented by binary digit zero.

A **bit** is the smallest unit of electronic data. The term bit is short for a *BI*nary digi*T* (which is either zero or one). All characters (letters, numbers, and symbols) are represented by a special sequence of binary digits. For example, the characters "A," "B," and "C" may be converted into binary code as follows:

$$A + 01000001$$

$$B + 01000010$$

$$C + 01000011$$

A special sequence of bits representing a single character is called a **byte**. A byte is a group of adjacent bits that work, or are operated on, as a unit. Theoretically, a byte may be any length, but the most common length for a byte is eight bits.

Bytes take up memory space.. A **kilobyte** represents approximately one thousand bytes (1,024 bytes). Kilobyte is often abbreviated as "K" or "Kb" and is used to describe memory capacity. A **megabyte**, abbreviated as "Mb," represents approximately one million bytes (1,048,576 bytes). A **gigabyte**, abbreviated as "Gb," represents approximately one billion bytes (1,073,741,834 bytes). A **terabyte**, abbreviated as "Tb," represents approximately one trillion bytes.

## Database Management

Database management is a term for applications that allow users to catalog and store information about their businesses for future use. A **database** is a collection of related facts and figures designed to serve a specific purpose.

People have been routinely using dozens of types of databases for centuries. For example, a personal checkbook is a database; it collects facts and figures that are designed to monitor personal finances. Other common databases include address books, telephone books, and dictionaries.

The design and organization of these everyday databases are essential to users. The data within an address book, telephone book, and dictionary are sorted alphabetically so that users can quickly access the particular data they need. The checks in a personal checkbook are numbered sequentially. If an individual keeps to this numbered sequence when issuing checks, the returned canceled checks can be stored in the same numbered sequence, enabling the person to easily retrieve any particular check.

Think of a database management system as a filing cabinet. The way information is organized within a filing cabinet will depend on the kind of information that is stored and the particular needs of the user. File cabinets have separate file

**Exhibit 4   Database Files, Records, and Fields**

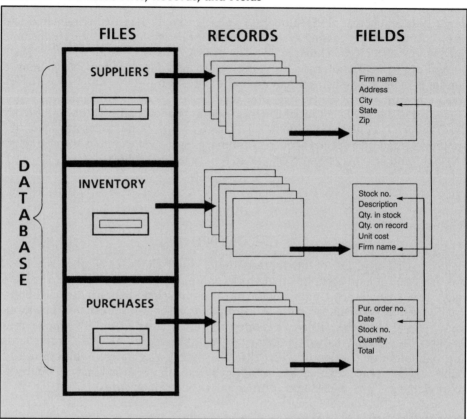

drawers. Each file drawer contains separate file folders. The folders within each drawer contain similar records of related information. Each record within a folder contains specific facts and/or figures.

Exhibit 4 diagrams the similarity between a typical office file cabinet and a database management system. In the language of database management, the file cabinet is called the database, the drawers of the cabinet are called **database files**, the folders within the drawers are called **database records**, and the detailed facts and/or figures in the records are called **database fields**.

For example, an inventory database might be set up for inventory control. Assume that this database is made up of a single file. The file would contain one record for each inventory item, and each record would contain a number of fields, such as the item's name, number, cost, quantity on hand, reorder point, and so on. Users of the computer system can access this database to perform any number of desired functions, such as:

- Generate inventory checklists to assist managers and supervisors in taking physical inventory.

- Perform variance analyses on the differences between actual quantities of items on hand versus the quantities projected (perpetual inventory) by the system.

- Calculate the total value of items in inventory.

There are hundreds of uses for database management applications in the hospitality industry. These applications are used in relation to personnel file management, payroll processing, marketing research, general ledger accounting, tax reporting, direct mail advertising, sales reporting, and countless other areas.

Database management applications control the structure and organization of databases as well as the means by which data is handled within a system. These applications limit the number of times that data must be handled and ensure that all users accessing the database are working with the same information. In addition, these programs enable users to create, access, and merge data files; to add, select, and delete data; and to index, sort, and search data files for information that is eventually printed as reports for use by management.

## Files, Records, and Fields

In a database management system, fields are labeled by categories that identify the kind of information they contain. Records are identified in terms of a primary key field, also called a primary key, which contains unique information. The name of the key field becomes the basis for searching through a data file for a particular record.

Consider the organization of a master payroll file. The file would contain a record for each employee. Each record would be made up of fields identified by labels such as employee number, employee name, address, pay rate, withholdings, deductions, and so on. One of these fields would serve as the primary key field, which could be used to search the data file for a particular record. Since the primary key field must contain unique information, the employee number field would function best as the key field of the master payroll file. Two employees may, by chance, have the same name, but when a company assigns employee numbers on a sequential basis, it guarantees that a particular number in the sequence identifies one particular employee named John Smith, who lives at a particular address, and so on.

The database of a hospitality business may be organized into many data files (such as personnel files, financial data files, guest history files, etc.). These files may contain dozens of records and scores of fields containing thousands of pieces of data. Database management applications structure the relationships among files, records, and fields in a way that ensures rapid access to information. However, not all database management software applications structure a database in the same manner.

## Database Structures

Database management applications structure a database by organizing data files, records, and fields in ways that facilitate searching for data, updating data, and generating accurate, timely, and useful reports for management. Database

**Exhibit 5** **Hierarchical Database Structure**

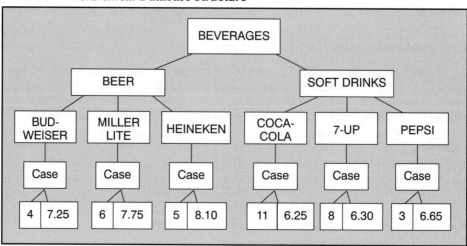

applications manage databases through either hierarchical structures or relational structures.

A **hierarchical database structure** arranges data files, records, and fields into formations that resemble the structure of the roots of a tree. As the trunk of a tree leads into major roots, which in turn branch off into entire networks of roots, so a hierarchically structured database begins with a data file (the trunk), which opens onto a number of master records (the major roots), which in turn lead to intricate networks of other subordinate records. Exhibit 5 illustrates the structure of a hierarchical database. In order to access data contained in subordinate records, the database management system must first access the data file, then the parent root, then a key field of the subordinate record network.

Database management applications that arrange data in hierarchical structures are able to carry out precise data searches and generate comprehensive statistical analyses. However, they are dependent upon rigid parameters that define the nature of fields and records. It may be difficult and time consuming to incorporate new data definitions into a hierarchically structured database.

**Relational database structures** have become popular because of the simplicity of data arrangement, the ease of data manipulation, and the flexibility of data handling. The data files of a relational database management program are formatted as rectangular tables of rows and columns and are similar in appearance to electronic spreadsheets.

Column headings identify fields (some relational database management packages refer to fields as attributes) such as an employee's number, name, address, work history, pay rate, skill code, and so on. When a column is read down through the rows, it reveals the same type of data about many employees. Each row is a record. When a row is read completely across the columns it reveals all the different types of data that have been input regarding a single employee. A key field (such as, in our previous example, employee number) is used to identify the

**Exhibit 6    Relational Database Structure**

| Beverages | Brand | Unit | Qty. | Cost |
|-----------|-------|------|------|------|
| BEER | BUDWEISER | Case | 4 | 7.25 |
| BEER | MILLER LITE | Case | 6 | 7.75 |
| BEER | HEINEKEN | Case | 5 | 8.10 |
| SOFT DRINK | COCA-COLA | Case | 11 | 6.25 |
| SOFT DRINK | 7-UP | Case | 8 | 6.30 |
| SOFT DRINK | PEPSI | Case | 3 | 6.65 |

**Exhibit 7    Personnel Data**

**Hierarchical Database Structure**

Name: Dagan, Toby
Emp. Number: 48824

Emp. No. 48824
Personal Data
29 Market Street
(413) 247-0962

Emp. No. 48824
Work History
Start: 4/29/XX
End:

Emp. No. 48824
Salary History
Start: $10.50
Current: $13.75

**Rational Database Structure**

**Fields**

| R E C O R D S | Name | Address | City, State | Emp. No. |
|-----|------|---------|-------------|----------|
| | Dagan, Toby | 29 Market St. | E. Natick, MA | 48824 |
| | Michael, Greg | 11 Arnold Pl. | N. Hampton, MA | 48895 |
| | Steven, Liz | 87 E. 204th St. | S. Queens, MA | 48864 |
| | Vaugh, Betty | 42 Summer St. | Carrick, MA | 48827 |

record. Exhibit 6 illustrates how the same data presented in Exhibit 5 would appear in a relational database structure. Exhibit 7 uses personnel data to illustrate the difference between hierarchical and relational database structures.

## Input/Output Specifications

Database applications require users to define an input area for data entry, a criteria area for directing queries, and an output area for directing results. Although database applications usually provide predetermined specifications (also referred to as default settings), users are encouraged to define specifications for these areas that best meet their particular needs.

Input area specifications define data entry procedures. Screen templates can be designed to guide users with data input responsibilities. For example, the display monitor at the front desk of a hotel may guide front desk employees in entering specific data regarding guests during check-in. The use of a screen or window template would ensure that important data are collected and properly entered into the system.

Criteria area specifications define query procedures. A query is usually a request for a few pieces of data that does not necessitate the completion of a lengthy report, such as information regarding a guest's credit limit. Most database management programs support a query language that enables users to make requests through the keyboard. Criteria area specifications define the necessary sequence of keystrokes. For example, inputting a query may necessitate the following keystrokes or menu bar selections:

- Entering a command or selecting a menu bar option

- Defining the scope of the command

- Specifying command conditions

Database management commands are usually entered by identifying a simple word (such as DISPLAY, SUM, COUNT, LOCATE, LIST, and so on). Defining the scope of the command identifies which areas of the database will be affected by the command. Specifying command conditions stipulates the circumstances under which the command will operate. For example, given a particular database management program, entering the following sequence of keystrokes: DISPLAY NAME, ADDRESS, CITY, STATE FOR SOCSEC + '384-42-1999' would lead the system to carry out the command (DISPLAY) for the field names listed (NAME, ADDRESS, CITY, STATE) when a specified condition is met (the existence of a Social Security number of 384-42-1999). The system will respond by displaying the person's name, address, city, and state only if there actually is an employee in the database with the specified Social Security number.

Output area specifications control the generation and formatting of reports and additional database files. Since data stored in a database are independent of its application, database applications are able to separate related information and generate a variety of reports.

## Database Management Commands

Once a database has been designed and the data input, records within database files can be accessed by a number of users, and various types of information can be obtained through database management commands or menu options. Database management applications provide a number of commands that enable users to organize records within database files and to search for information that may be contained in several files. A few of the more common commands are briefly described in the following sections.

**Organizing Records in Database Files.** Two of the most frequently used commands that organize records in database files are the "index" and "sort" commands. The index command does not rearrange the records of a database file. Instead, it provides a limited working file that identifies records containing certain data, somewhat as the index of a textbook identifies page numbers containing a certain type of information. When a database file is retrieved and the sort command issued, a new database file is created that is equal in size and content of the original (source) file. However, the sort command changes the order of the records in the source file according to a field category designated by the user.

Assume that a large hospitality corporation is considering increasing the life insurance benefits of employees who have been continuously employed by the company for ten years. A user retrieves the personnel database file and the records containing employee numbers, employee names, addresses, length of employment, and so on, and discovers that the records are arranged by employee number. Through the database management application, the user issues a command to sort the file and reorder the records by length of employment. The sorted file can then be printed as a report revealing the employees affected by the new insurance benefit, or the sorted file can become the basis for further processing.

It is important to note that an indexed file generally maintains a direct connection with the source file from which it was created. Therefore, the indexed file will immediately reflect any changes that are made to the source file, and vice versa. This is not the case with sorted files. A sorted file is generally independent of the source file from which it was created. Therefore, any changes made to the source file, such as updating the records, will have to be transferred to the previously sorted file. If extensive updating of database records occurs regularly, new sorted files must be created.

**Searching Records.** The "find" command or the "locate" command is used to search for specific records in database files. The find command normally functions more quickly than the locate command. However, it generally works only with files that have been indexed in terms of the specific field category for which the user is searching. The locate command functions by matching file entries with the character string for which the user is searching. Searches issued by the locate command tend to be less efficient and more time consuming than searches issued by the find command, especially when large database files are involved.

**Multiple Searches.** The real strength of a database management application lies in its ability to perform multiple searches across a broad spectrum of field categories. For example, consider the advantages of a "multiple-search" routine for processing room requests from walk-ins. Assume that a guest arrives at the front desk of a large hotel and requests an upper-floor suite with two double beds. The front desk employee conducts a multiple search through the rooms availability database file. The first search indexes the database file in terms of a primary key field, which is the broadest field category involved in the search. In our example, the primary key would be the type of room—a suite. Subsequent searches focus on secondary keys, which order and limit the primary key field. In our example, the number of beds in a room and floor location would be the secondary keys that order the primary key field of suites. Using the multiple-search feature of a database management application, the front desk employee would have the necessary information for the guest within seconds.

Multiple-search routines can be extremely useful when users work with large and complex databases. Consider how a multiple-search routine can be used by a large food and beverage operation to find a substitute server who is available on Tuesday evenings between 4 and 7 P.M. Initially, a personnel database file would be searched for all persons qualified as food servers. Subsequent search passes through the file would result in a selective deletion of names whose work availability schedules fail to coincide with the day and time criteria. Remaining records would be those that satisfy the multiple-search criteria.

**Calculations.** Most database management applications have built-in calculators that are capable of carrying out basic arithmetical and statistical operations. Standard mathematical conventions are adhered to, with multiplication and division taking precedence over addition and subtraction. The calculator feature can be extremely useful because it can be accessed at any point in a database application.

Since the results of calculations can be stored and later referenced, the calculator dimension extends the usefulness of the application. For example, a specific command files the results of calculations under a named memory variable. A hotel's average room rate, which is calculated by dividing rooms revenue by the number of rooms sold, can be computed and filed under a unique name, such as "ADR." Later, when the data are needed, they can be easily retrieved.

Database management applications allow the user to store both numeric and alpha data as memory variables. This feature enhances the recall capabilities of the application without necessitating the creation of separate database files that would have to be indexed, sorted, or searched.

# Multidimensional Databases

For decades, hospitality businesses have electronically captured and stored transactional data. However, the manner in which they did so made it difficult to access and analyze data for decision-making purposes. Modern technology enables individual properties as well as chain organizations to more easily identify relationships, patterns, and trends within large, centralized databases also known as data warehouses. A **data warehouse** is a database designed to support decision-making in an organization. The data in a data warehouse is structured to support a variety of analyses, including elaborate queries on large amounts of data that can require extensive searching. When the database is organized for one department or function, it is often called a **data mart** rather than a data warehouse.

**Online analytical processing (OLAP)** is decision support software that allows the user to quickly access data and analyze information that has been summarized into multidimensional views and hierarchies. OLAP works with databases that are structured as multidimensional cubes rather than as the two-dimensional rows and columns typical of relational databases. Data are stored as dimensions or subject domains and the cube structure allows different views of the data to be displayed quickly. The ability to quickly switch between one slice of

**Exhibit 8 Multidimensional Data Cube**

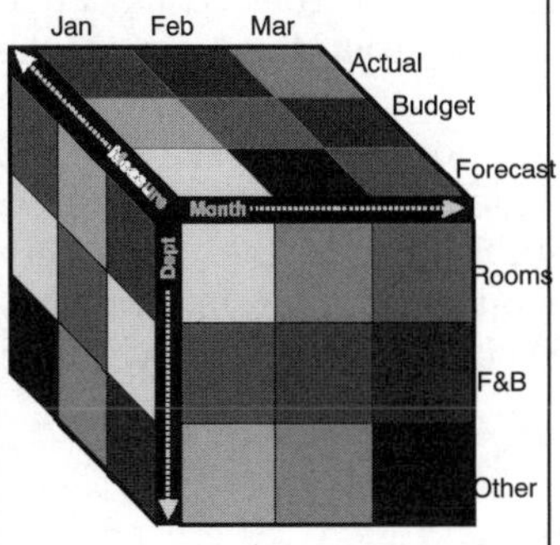


Querying the cube for data is as simple as specifying specific elements. For example, if you specified

**Jan, Forecast, Rooms**, you would end up with one number:

| | | | |
|---|---|---|---|
| Jan | Forecast | Rooms | 100 |

**Feb, Forecast** would produce three numbers:

| | | | |
|---|---|---|---|
| Feb | Forecast | Rooms | 200 |
| | | F&B | 300 |
| | | Other | 400 |

If you specified just **Mar**, you'd get 9 numbers:

| | | | |
|---|---|---|---|
| Mar | Actual | Rooms | 500 |
| | | F&B | 600 |
| | | Other | 700 |
| | Budget | Rooms | 800 |
| | | F&B | 900 |
| | | Other | 100 |
| | Forecast | Rooms | 200 |
| | | F&B | 300 |
| | | Other | 400 |

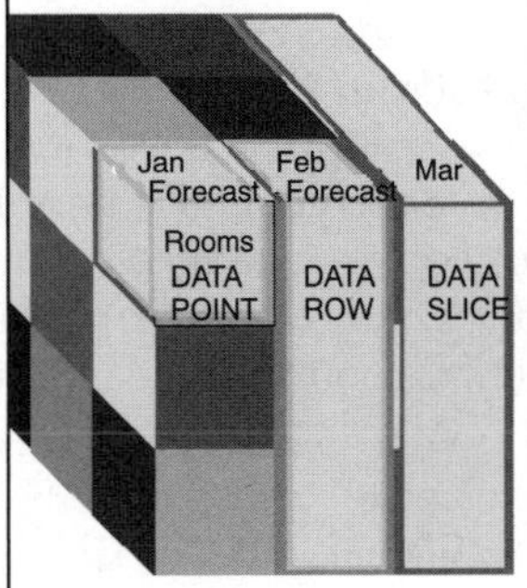


Source: Datavision Technologies, Inc. For more information, browse the company's Internet site at http://www.datavisiontech.com

data and another allows users to analyze their information in small palatable chunks instead of through a giant report that can be confusing. The data cube presented in Exhibit 8 shows three dimensions. If data were filled in the cube, "Months" could be listed across the top, "Actual," "Budget," and "Forecast" could be listed down the top, and "Payroll Departments" could be listed down the side.

The dimensions, or subject domains, are defined in terms of decision support requirements. Traditional hospitality database systems are organized around operational transactions such as reservations, registration, rooms management, guest accounting, etc. Multidimensional databases, on the other hand, can be organized around subject areas such as guests, spending pattern, bundled purchases, length of stay, etc. These dimensions are created to support managerial decision-making, not simply to reflect business processes. OLAP tools enable managers to drill down into masses of data to isolate only that data needed for specific decision-making purposes. For example, when managers are seeking data about guests from New York State, with only three clicks of the mouse they can "drill down" from "World" to "North America" to "U.S.A." to "New York." **Data mining** is the process of exploring (digging through tons of data) to uncover patterns and relationships relevant to the decision or issue at hand. Data mining can be done manually by slicing and dicing the data until a pattern becomes obvious, or it can be done with programs that analyze the data automatically.

## Guest Relationship Management

Hospitality marketing identifies large markets (such as business travelers, leisure travelers, corporate business, etc.) and targets marketing and sales efforts to specific groupings, or segments, of guests and potential guests within those markets (such as working women between the ages of 25 and 40). Advances in information technology and database management tools have made it possible to create a market of one. Given the appropriate technology and transaction history, marketing and sales staff can access the significant information (room types, spending pattern, preferred entrées, etc.) needed to understand an individual guest, contact that guest, and sell additional hospitality products and services that directly meet the guest's needs.

A popular form of one-to-one marketing is the use of personalized e-mails. These are generally permission-based programs in which guests opt-in, or agree, to receive messages from the hospitality company. Southwest Airlines has a very successful e-mail program (Click 'n Save) that has more than 3.5 million subscribers. Similarly, Wyndham has more than 350,000 customers in its Wyndham By Request program.

## Frequent Diner Applications

A direct descendant of the airline industry's frequent flyer clubs, frequent diner applications enable a restaurant to gain valuable marketing information while rewarding brand loyalty and building future sales. The benefits are balanced: while the restaurant builds a guest history database, the guest reaps the rewards offered through the frequent diner program.

Customers are generally able to enroll in a frequent diner program in a number of different ways: in person, over the telephone, or by fax, e-mail, or online. During the enrollment process, restaurants obtain data such as: customer name, street and e-mail addresses (home and work), demographic information (such as family status and birthday dates), special interests, and preferred frequent dining plan (if options exist). An enrollment fee is usually credited back to the member's account or is offset by discount incentives or redeemable points.

Upon completion of enrollment, an electronic file is created and the member may be issued a frequent diner card—a magnetic stripe plastic card or a smart card (with an embedded microchip). Automated frequent diner programs post transactions at the point of sale. The member presents a card at the point of purchase and the transaction is posted to the database. As part of the transaction, the member accrues awards (points, discounts, merchandise, etc.) based on the number of visits and the value of the transaction.

Member account balances can be maintained in a database (locally, regionally, or nationally) or they can be stored on a member's smart card. A current account balance is the accumulation of points attained less the points used to redeem appropriate rewards. An important consideration in account tracking is that the member should be able to view the account balance, either at each point of sale or through an online access.

Depending on the format of the databases, restaurants may be able to pose complex queries and search multiple databases containing transactional data, accrued points, issued vouchers, and redemption activity. Most frequent diner applications can identify and generate information in categories such as:

- Best customers

- Customer frequency (number of visits)

- Popularity of menu items

- Purchase patterns

- Bundled purchases

- Promotion items

- Redemption points

- Marketing/advertising campaign success

- Special promotion effectiveness

Frequent diner applications vary in terms of the method used to capture transactions. Some POS systems have built-in frequent diner applications. These applications poll detailed customer transaction information captured at the time of sale and automatically post amounts to member accounts. Electronic data capture (EDC) is another method. An EDC-based application relies on the data processing features of an external credit, debit, or smart card banking service to recognize, sort, and apply qualified transactional data to member accounts. The external company (or its intermediary) uses software capable of separating transactions by enrolled member and award criteria. A third option exists with stand-alone frequent diner applications that operate similarly to POS-based applications.

# Key Terms

**department systems supervisor**—An individual already employed within a specific department who receives extensive training in the operation of hardware, software applications, and network components, and afterward conducts training sessions for others and provides some technical support services.

**information technology (IT)**—Technology that establishes a communication process in which data are transferred from related systems; processed according to pre-established decision-making rules, financial models, or other analytical methods; and stored in information formats tailored to the needs of individual managers. Includes decision support systems and the incorporation of expert systems.

**management information system (MIS)**—A system designed to provide managers with the necessary information needed to plan, organize, staff, direct, and control operations.

**property systems manager**—Participates in the evaluation, selection, and installation of system hardware and is trained in the operation of software applications used throughout the property. The property systems manager, also known simply as the systems manager, provides on-premises systems support and, when necessary, functions as a network administrator and/or an applications software troubleshooter.

## Data Processing

**binary code**—A code based on only two digits, zero and one. This is the form of data a computer can handle with greatest ease because electronic circuits have two natural states: "on," usually represented by the binary digit one; and "off," represented by the binary digit zero.

**bit**—The smallest unit of electronic data. The term is short for *BInary digiT* (which is either zero or one). All characters (letters, numbers, and symbols) are represented by a special sequence of binary digits.

**byte**—A special sequence of bits (electronic data) representing a single character. A byte is a group of adjacent bits that work, or are operated on, as a unit. Theoretically, a byte may be any length, but the most common length for a byte is eight bits, with some computers using seven.

**data**—Facts or figures to be processed into useful information. Three types of data are alpha data, numeric data, and alphanumeric data.

**data processing**—A cycle of events identified as input, process, and output that transforms raw facts and isolated figures into timely, accurate, and useful information.

**gigabyte**—Often abbreviated as "Gb," equal to 1,073,741,834 bytes, and commonly used to describe computer memory capacity.

**kilobyte**—Often abbreviated as "K" or "Kb," equal to 1,024 bytes, and commonly used to describe computer memory capacity.

**megabyte**—Often abbreviated as "Mb," equal to 1,048,576 bytes, and commonly used to describe computer memory capacity.

**streamlining**—An electronic data processing practice of generating only those reports that are requested by staff members who will actually use the information.

**terabyte**—Often abbreviated as "Tb," equal to one trillion bytes, and commonly used to describe computer memory capacity.

**throughput**—An electronic data processing term referring to the time that elapses between data input and information output.

*Database Management*

**data mart**—A multidimensional database organized for one department or function.

**data mining**—Process of exploring a database (digging through tons of data) to uncover patterns and relationships relevant to the decision or issue at hand.

**data warehouse**—A database designed to support decision-making in an organization; structured to support a variety of analyses, including elaborate queries on large amounts of data that can require extensive searching.

**database**—A collection of related facts and figures designed to serve a specific purpose.

**database fields**—The detailed facts or figures contained in database records.

**database files**—A collection of database records and fields.

**database records**—A collection of database fields.

**hierarchical database structure**—In database management software, arranges data files, records, and fields into formations that resemble the structure of the roots of a tree.

**online analytical processing (OLAP)**—Decision support software that allows the user to quickly analyze information that has been summarized into multidimensional views and hierarchies.

**relational database structure**—A database structure in which the data files are formatted as rectangular tables of rows and columns and are similar in appearance to electronic spreadsheets.

 **Review Questions**

1. What is the purpose of a management information system?

2. What are the typical duties and responsibilities of a property systems manager? Of a department systems supervisor?

3. What are the three phases of the data processing cycle? Describe the functions performed in each phase.

4. What does the term "binary code" mean?

5. What is the difference between a bit and a byte? A kilobyte and a megabyte? A megabyte and a gigabyte? A gigabyte and a terabyte?

6. What does the term "database" mean? Explain how database management programs can be useful to managers of hospitality operations.

7. What are "files," "records," and "fields"? Explain how they are organized within hierarchical and relational database structures.

8. How do primary and secondary keys function in relation to multiple searches across a broad spectrum of field categories within a large database?

9. What is the difference between data warehouses and data marts?

10. What are the different methods by which frequent diner applications can capture transactions?

 **Internet Sites**

For more information, visit the following Internet sites. Remember that Internet addresses can change without notice. If the site is no longer there, you can use a search engine to look for additional sites.

Eatec Corporation
http://www.eatec.com

CMS Hospitality
http://www.cmshosp.com.au

Fidelio
http://www.micros.com

Datavision Technologies
http://www.datavisiontech.com

Comtrex Systems Corporation
http://www.comtrex.com

Comus Restaurant Systems
http://www.comus.com

InfoGenesis
http://www.infogenesis.com

NCR Corporation
http://www.ncr.com

Resort Systems Incorporated
http://www.resortsystems.ca

System Concepts, Inc.
http://www.foodtrak.com

# Chapter 11 Outline

Analyzing Current Information Needs
Collecting Sales Information
Establishing System Requirements
Requesting Proposals from Vendors
    Site Surveys
    Evaluating Vendor Proposals
    Vendor Product Demonstrations
Contract Negotiations
    Contract Provisions
    Contractual Arrangements
Installation Factors
    Training
    Site Preparation
    Design of Printed Materials
    Initial Entry of Database Elements
    Acceptance Testing
    System Conversion
    Documentation
    Contingency Planning

# Competencies

1. Describe ways in which hospitality managers can analyze current information needs. (pp. 277–282)

2. Explain how managers can establish basic technology system requirements. (pp. 283–284)

3. Explain the purpose of a Request for Proposal (RFP). (pp. 284–287)

4. Describe how managers can evaluate proposals submitted by technology system vendors. (pp. 287–289)

5. Describe how managers can get the most value out of technology product demonstrations. (p. 290)

6. Identify provisions and arrangements that hospitality managers generally negotiate with vendors of hospitality technology systems. (pp. 291–293)

7. Identify factors involved in the installation of technology systems in hospitality operations. (pp. 293–298)

# 11

# System Selection

THE IDENTIFICATION, EVALUATION, and selection of hospitality technology systems can be complex and time consuming. Many properties appoint a project team. The project leader generally has overall responsibility for purchasing the technology system. This person determines a schedule for the purchasing process and monitors the team's progress. The process begins as the team analyzes the current information needs of the business, collects relevant technology sales literature, and establishes system requirements. The results of this preliminary research are used to solicit proposals from vendors. The process continues with the evaluation of proposals and product demonstrations, contract negotiations, and the implementation of the new system. Throughout the process, it is helpful to keep the "Nevers" of technology purchasing in mind:

- Never purchase hardware before software. After selecting software first, identify the hardware it requires.

- Never make a purchase decision based solely on cost. Too often, economic factors are given a disproportionate weight in the decision process.

- Never lose control of the purchasing process. Develop request for proposal documents, script on-site vendor demonstrations, and apply uniform criteria when evaluating vendor proposals.

- Never rely on enhancement promises. A system feature that is advertised, but not yet available for sale, may not actually become available for months.

- Never be the first system user. New systems have no operational history and, therefore, are difficult to evaluate.

- Never allow technology to dictate operations. Changing operations to fit the demands of the technology is a case of the tail wagging the dog.

- Never be the largest system user. Pushing the envelope of a system's processing speed, file parameters, memory capabilities, and other functions may lead to a series of problems that the vendor may not be able to solve in a timely fashion.

- Never be the last system user. System maintenance, on-going technical support, enhancements, and the like may be difficult or impossible to obtain.

- Never allow a vendor to rewrite the business's technology requirements. A system that meets vendor specifications may not meet your business needs; stand firm on system requirements.

## Analyzing Current Information Needs

The first step in analyzing the current information needs of a business is to identify the types of information that various levels of management use in the course of everyday operations. This can be accomplished by compiling samples of all reports presently prepared for management's use. These reports include the daily operations report, basic financial statements, and other reports similar to those listed in Exhibit 1. Once collected, the reports can be analyzed in relation to such variables as purpose, content, users, and frequency of preparation.

This kind of analysis identifies the types of information management currently uses, but it does not necessarily reveal all the current information needs of the business. A survey should be conducted asking managers to evaluate the effectiveness of the format and content of reports they receive. The survey results should provide the basis for immediate improvements in the current information system and should also enable management to conduct a more in-depth analysis with flowcharts and a property profile.

**Flowcharts** use specially designed symbols for diagramming the flow of data and documents through an information system. Flowchart symbols have been standardized by the United States of America Standards Institute. Some of the more commonly used symbols are illustrated in Exhibit 2. Standardization is achieved by using common symbols and also by drawing flowcharts according to established procedures.

Since flowcharts reveal the origin, processing, and final disposition of each document, they are valuable techniques for evaluating the current information system of a hospitality business. Weaknesses, overlapping functions, and other redundancies can be identified, enabling management to revise and streamline current information needs that must eventually be met by the future system.

An alternative to detailed flowchart depictions of an information system is a series of written narrative descriptions. Written narratives are less efficient than flowcharts because they are time-consuming to write and to read. It may require a written narrative of six to eight pages to communicate the same information a detailed flowchart presents in a single page.

A **property profile** compiles statistics about the current information system. Exhibits 3 and 4 illustrate sample property profile formats for lodging operations and food service operations, respectively. The types of categories and number of individual entries will vary from property to property. A property profile proves useful when communicating information needs of the business to technology system vendors. The property profile allows vendors to compare the property's information system to those of similar properties that have already installed systems. In addition, a property profile enables management to conduct a more informed and efficient review of technology sales literature.

## Collecting Sales Information

After creating a property profile, management should collect sales literature on a variety of technology systems that meet the general information needs of the business by:

## Exhibit 1 Typical Management Reports

| Report | Frequency | Content | Comparisons | Who Gets It | Purpose |
|---|---|---|---|---|---|
| Daily Report of Operations | Daily, on a cumulative basis for the month, the year to date. | Occupancy, average rate, revenue by outlet, and pertinent statistics. | To operating plan for current period and to prior year results. | Top management and supervisors responsible for day to day operation. | Basis for evaluating the current health of the enterprise. |
| Weekly Forecasts | Weekly. | Volume in covers, occupancy. | Previous periods. | Top management and supervisory personnel. | Staffing and scheduling; promotion. |
| Summary Report—Flash | Monthly at end of month (prior to monthly financial statement). | Known elements of revenue and direct costs; estimated departmental indirect costs. | To operating plan; to prior year results. | Top management and supervisory personnel responsible for function reported. | Provides immediate information on financial results for rooms, food and beverages, and other. |
| Cash Flow Analysis | Monthly (and on a revolving 12-month basis). | Receipts and disbursements by time periods. | With cash flow plan for month and for year to date. | Top management. | Predicts availability of cash for operating needs. Provides information on interim financing requirements. |
| Labor Productivity Analysis | Daily. Weekly. Monthly. | Dollar cost; manpower hours expended; hours as related to sales and services (covers, rooms occupied, etc.). | To committed hours in the operating plan (standards for amount of work to prior year statistics). | Top management and supervisory personnel. | Labor cost control through informed staffing and scheduling. Helps refine forecasting. |
| Departmental Analysis | Monthly (early in following month). | Details on main categories of income; same on expense. | To operating plan (month and year to date) and to prior year. | Top management and supervisors by function (e.g., rooms, each food and beverage outlet, laundry, telephone, other profit centers). | Knowing where business stands, and immediate corrective actions. |
| Room Rate Analysis | Daily, monthly, year to date. | Actual rates compared to rack rates by rate category or type of room. | To operating plan and to prior year results. | Top management and supervisors of sales and front office operations. | If goal is not being achieved, analysis of strengths and weaknesses is prompted. |
| Return on Investment | Actual computation, at least twice a year. Computation based on forecast, immediately prior to plan for year ahead. | Earnings as a percentage rate of return on average investment or equity committed. | To plan for operation and to prior periods. | Top management. | If goal is not being achieved, prompt assessment of strengths and weaknesses. |
| Long-Range Planning | Annually. | 5-year projections of revenue and expenses. Operating plan expressed in financial terms. | Prior years. | Top management. | Involves staff in success or failure of enterprise. Injects more realism into plans for property and service modifications. |
| Exception Reporting | Concurrent with monthly reports and financial statements. | Summary listing of line item variances from predetermined norm. | With operating budgets. | Top management and supervisors responsible for function reported. | Immediate focusing on problem before more detailed statement analysis can be made. |
| Guest History Analysis | At least semi-annually; quarterly or monthly is recommended. | Historical records of corporate business, travel agencies, group bookings. | With previous reports. | Top management and sales. | Give direction to marketing efforts. |
| Future Bookings Report | Monthly. | Analysis of reservations and bookings. | With several prior years. | Top management, sales and marketing, department management. | Provides information on changing guest profile. Exposes strong and weak points of facility. Guides (1) sales planning and (2) expansion plans. |

**Exhibit 2 Common Flowchart Symbols**

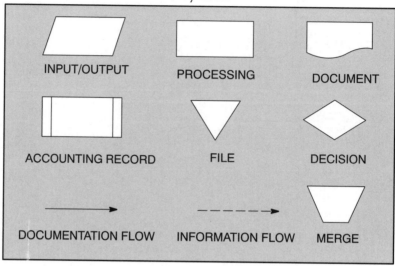

- Sending inquiries to state and national trade associations
- Attending industry trade shows
- Visiting area technology system vendors
- Making broadcast mailings to hospitality technology system vendors

State, national, and international hospitality trade associations, such as the American Hotel & Lodging Association (AH&LA), Hospitality Financial and Technology Professionals (HFTP), the National Restaurant Association (NRA), Club Managers Association of America (CMAA), the Information Technology Association (HITA), and the International Association of Conference Centers (IACC), provide information services for their members. While these organizations will not recommend specific products, they can assist members seeking information about current technology designs for hospitality operations. The Internet sites of these associations provide informative links to hospitality technology vendors.

In addition, these trade associations and other organizations regularly sponsor state, regional, and national trade shows. Attendance at trade shows typically places management in direct contact with hospitality technology vendors.

Management can also secure product information by visiting local system vendors. But this can be time-consuming, and it might not result in a representative view of the range of products on the market.

Perhaps the most effective approach to fact-finding is to use the information obtained through inquiries to trade associations, attendance at trade shows, and visits to local vendors to formulate a general interest letter to be mailed or e-mailed to all known vendors of hospitality technology systems. This broadcast mailing approach can be an efficient means of securing necessary information on various

## Exhibit 3   Sample Lodging Property Profile

**General**
___ Type of property (resort, hotel, motel, convention, condo, roadside, etc.)
___ Total number of rooms
___ Annual occupancy
___ Average room rate
___ Number of types of rooms
___ Number of suites
___ Percentage of annual occupancy from groups (tours, airlines, travel agencies, etc.)
___ Seasonal period(s); seasonal rates
___ Average length of stay
___ Number of permanent guests
___ Number of meeting rooms
___ Arrival/departure patterns
___ Number of revenue centers and locations

**Reservations**
___ Volume of reservation transactions (phone, telex, letter, etc.)
___ Volume of each type of reservation transaction
___ Percentage of reservations that require special handling (deposits, confirmations, etc.)
___ Hours of coverage
___ Average wage per employee
___ Annual overtime costs
___ If unionized department—will employees get raises because of automation?
___ Outside reservation services
___ Travel agent handling
___ Forecasting
___ Number of employees

**Switchboard**
___ Number of positions at switchboard
___ Type of equipment
___ Number of employees per shift (average/maximum)

**Housekeeping**
___ Number of floors
___ Number of rooms per floor (average)
___ Number of rooms or units cleaned per room attendant
___ Number of room attendants
___ Number of inspectors
___ Number of room attendants per inspector

**Food and Beverage**
___ Number of outlets
___ Location of outlets
___ Volume of sales
___ Number of sales
___ Number of menu items
___ Type of service

___ Number of covers
___ Average check
___ Present food and beverage registers
___ Present form of check used
___ Prechecking techniques (if applicable)
___ Inventory control methods
___ Inventory volumes
___ Percentage of sales charged to guestrooms
___ Number of employees
___ Number of function rooms

**Accounting**
___ Number of A/R accounts
___ Number of A/P accounts
___ Total A/R revenue handled per month (average/maximum)
___ Total A/P revenue handled per month (average/maximum)
___ Number of employees for A/R
___ Number of employees for A/P
___ Number of employees for general ledger
___ Number of employees for payroll
___ Number of employees for other accounting functions
___ Total number of employees on payroll (average/maximum)
___ Number of service bureaus presently employed
___ Cost of service bureaus
___ Number of travel agent accounts
___ Number of corporate accounts
___ Number of airline accounts
___ Number of special accounts
___ Present back office equipment
___ Cost/value/maintenance of present equipment
___ Supply cost of present equipment

**Front Desk**
___ Number of registration windows
___ Number of cashiering windows
___ Can registration and cashiering be done by same clerk?
___ Present equipment in use
___ Cost/value of present equipment
___ Maintenance of present equipment
___ Cost of supplies for present equipment (tapes, forms, etc.)
___ Number of employees per shift (average/maximum)
___ Average wage and benefit cost per employee
___ Number of registrants per day (average/maximum)
___ Number of check-outs per day (average/maximum)
___ Number of postings per day (average/maximum)

**Exhibit 4    Sample Food Service Property Profile**

---

**FILE AND TRANSACTION VOLUMES**

**Sales and Cash Receipts**

___ Number of seats
___ Number of covers per day
___ Number of daily menu items
___ Total number of menu items

**Food Inventory**

___ Number of inventory items (ingredients)
___ Daily inventory receipts (vendors)
___ Number of inventory items (classifications) per receipt
___ Daily inventory requisitions (from storeroom)
___ Number of recipes
___ Number of ingredients per recipe

**Liquor Inventory**

___ Number of inventory items
___ Daily storeroom requisitions (item classifications)
___ Number of recipes

**Accounts Payable**

___ Number of vendors
___ Invoices per day
___ Expense distributions per invoice
___ Checks (disbursements) per day

**Accounts Receivable**

___ Number of house accounts
___ Number of daily charges on account
___ Number of external charge media (American Express, etc.)
___ Number of daily receipts on account

**Payroll and Labor Analysis**

___ Number of employees
___ New hires per year
___ Number of W-2s prepared

**General Ledger**

___ Number of accounting periods
___ Number of accounts
___ Standard (recurring) monthly (journal entries)
___ Monthly general ledger postings (journal entries)

---

products and product lines. Management may also choose to use broadcast mailings to secure more specific information, such as:

• Hardware documentation

• Software documentation

• Lists of current product users

• Sample report formats

• Sample training materials

• Annual financial statements of the vendor's business

• Purchase/lease options

• User support and maintenance programs

Gathering this information early may prove valuable later when standardizing the form that selected vendors will use when submitting system proposals to top management officials. Before formulating the issues and categories of response that will appear on the proposal form, management must analyze the information needs of the business in light of the sales information collected.

# Establishing System Requirements

After management has analyzed the information needs of the business and collected sales literature describing relevant technology systems, the next step is to establish system requirements. This does not mean that hospitality managers must become experts in technology system design. Managers do not need to know the mechanics and details of electronic circuitry, but they must be able to make general decisions, such as:

- Determining what data to process
- Establishing how that data is to be processed
- Identifying formats in which processed data will be output as information

Determining what data to process involves identifying the information tasks that can best be performed by the technology system. Management must carefully weigh what is to be gained through automation. Will automation improve guest services? Will it increase the efficiency of operations? Will it enhance management's effectiveness in decision-making situations? Other factors to consider when determining which data to process include the ease of identifying, collecting, entering, and coding data. These factors are essential to the timely processing and output of information.

Determining how data is to be processed is a matter of making sure that the algorithmic design of the software programs corresponds to the actual formulas management wishes to use. The term "algorithm" refers to a prescribed set of well-defined, unambiguous rules or procedures leading to the solution of a problem. Too often, management assumes that hospitality industry jargon, such as "occupancy percentage" and "food cost percentage," means the same thing to all system designers. The truth is that hospitality properties themselves differ in terms of the variables going into basic calculations.

Throughout the lodging industry, occupancy percentage is calculated by dividing rooms sold by rooms available for sale. But properties may vary in their definitions of the terms "rooms sold" and "rooms available for sale." Actual occupancy percentage calculations produced by the basic formula depend on how properties take account of complimentary rooms, out-of-order rooms, no-show rooms, and other variables. Similarly, in relation to food service operations, the formulas used to calculate food cost information may vary widely. Some properties may cost food when received, others when it is issued to the kitchen, others when the food is sold, and so on.

In order to ensure that the eventual system will process data according to the property's standards, management must survey individual departments and compile a master list of important formulas, along with detailed explanations of how the terms within each formula are defined. This master list of formulas and the accompanying explanations identify major system requirements that vendors will be asked to meet as they submit proposals to top management officials.

Determining the formats in which processed data will be output as information involves decisions that may change the structure and style of current business forms, guest folios, guest checks, management reports, and other printed materials. The information needs of the business and the format preferences of managers should dictate the choice of printing capabilities of the system. The sample report formats collected from various vendors during the early fact-finding stage should serve as a good starting point for management's determination of preferred formats for the property's printed materials. If the vendors solicited have installed systems in other hospitality operations, management should be able to secure sample designs for many kinds of printed materials, including:

- Reservation confirmation notices

- Registration cards

- Guest folios

- Billing statements

- Payroll checks

It is important that management give early attention to this area of system design. If management waits too long, it could lose control of the situation. When this happens, the capabilities of the system control management's preferences, rather than management's preferences controlling the capabilities of the system.

## Requesting Proposals from Vendors

After translating information needs into system requirements, management is ready to request proposals from vendors. A **request for proposal (RFP)** is typically made up of three major sections. One section tells the vendor about management's business operations; a second section establishes bidding requirements for vendor proposals; and a third section deals specifically with user application requirements.

This first section of the RFP should contain an overview of the hospitality business, list objectives and broad operational requirements for the system, and briefly explain the vendor's future responsibilities. This overview of the hospitality business should include a brief description of the operation and the detailed property profile management created earlier when analyzing the information needs of the business. Listing objectives and broad operational requirements for the system offers management the opportunity to identify particular system features as either mandatory or optional, thus assisting vendors in the preparation of their proposals. The outline of the vendor's future responsibilities should designate when the vendor's proposal must be submitted for management's consideration, and it should request vendors to submit as much information as possible concerning such areas as:

- Hardware configurations

- Software descriptions

- Maintenance and support services

- Installation and training programs

- Guarantees and warranties

**Exhibit 5    Sample Cost Summary Table**

| REQUIREMENTS | PRICE | MAINTENANCE | COMMENTS |
|---|---|---|---|
| Hardware<br>Software<br>Other (specify)<br>Discount<br>Sub-Total | | | |
| **NON-RECURRING COSTS** | **PRICE** | **MAINTENANCE** | **COMMENTS** |
| Site Prep<br>Delivery<br>Installation<br>Training<br>Other (specify)<br>Discount<br>Sub-Total | | | |
| Total | | | |

- Payment options
- Future expandability of the proposed system

The second section of the RFP establishes bidding requirements for vendor proposals. Allowing vendors to formulate their bids within their own chosen formats may force management to adopt a tedious and unstructured evaluation process. All proposals should be submitted on a standardized response form created by management to facilitate price and performance comparisons. Exhibit 5 shows a sample cost summary table. Note how the structured formatting enables management to make intelligent comparisons between all proposals along a common set of dimensions. Vendors should also be asked to include a statement of their company's financial stability.

The final section of the RFP states specific system application requirements. Exhibit 6 shows a sample RFP form that structures vendors' responses to application requirements. Once again, note that since all vendors are asked to follow the same response format, top management officials will not waste time sifting through proposals that differ radically in both form and content.

Once created, the RFP form is distributed to the vendor community for response. After receiving an RFP, most vendors will contact management and schedule a site survey.

## Site Surveys

After receiving an RFP, conscientious vendors typically schedule a visit to the property in order to conduct a **site survey**. The purpose of a site survey is to

**Exhibit 6   Sample Format for Listing Application Requirements**

Instructions: Vendors are to indicate the applications they offer which are identical to those desired by the user (YES—Same), similar in function to those desired by the user (YES—Similar), function not now available but will develop (NO—Soon), or function not available (NO).

*   check appropriate column   *

| FUNCTION: | YES Same | YES Similar | NO Soon | NO |
|---|---|---|---|---|
| Ingredient file of food items | | | | |
| Recipe file of ingredients | | | | |
| Menu file of recipe and subrecipes | | | | |
| Inventory file of food items | | | | |
| Payroll master file of employees | | | | |
| Purchase order file by purveyor | | | | |
| Check register of issued checks | | | | |
| Daily transaction register | | | | |
| Payroll register | | | | |
| Accounts receivable ledger module | | | | |
| Accounts payable ledger module | | | | |
| General ledger module | | | | |
| Income statement | | | | |
| Balance sheet | | | | |

identify important factors regarding specific business operations within a property that may affect system design. The physical parameters of a property often determine appropriate types of hardware configurations.

During a site survey, a vendor may analyze many other characteristics specific to business operations that are important to overall system planning. Many details regarding the business's internal organization, policies and procedures, and daily operations directly affect the vendor's system proposal in relation to such areas as:

- Training programs

- Exceptional cost considerations

- System security features

- Installation schedules

- Backup system design

- Communication links

In order to secure all the information necessary to complete their proposals, vendors may require a great deal of information from different departments. This may involve the cooperation of personnel from several managerial levels within the property. To facilitate the vendor's access to necessary information and key personnel, top management officials may designate a management representative to coordinate the flow of information and help minimize disruptions to daily operations. When several vendors are scheduled to conduct site surveys at various times, it is wise to schedule the same management representative to serve as coordinator. This person may be able to provide management decision-makers with valuable information on the efficiency with which vendors conduct their surveys. Such information may become an important factor in evaluating the different proposals submitted by vendors.

## Evaluating Vendor Proposals

After conducting site surveys, vendors complete their system proposals and submit them for management's consideration. While there are many ways to evaluate a set of proposals, a multiple rating system can be an efficient and effective method.

A multiple rating system uses the same criteria to judge the worth of each vendor's proposal. Generally, the criteria consist of several issues that management considers critical to the business. Management rates each vendor's response to each issue on a scale from 1 to 100. The higher the rating, the better the proposal is judged to handle the issue. Because some issues will always be considered more important than others, simply totaling the ratings on key issues may not necessarily identify the best system proposal. In order to identify the best proposal, management must rank the issues in the order of their importance, and assign a percentage value to each, denoting its relative importance within the overall evaluation scheme. The ratings for each issue are multiplied by their appropriate percentage values and *then* totaled to yield an overall score for each proposal. The proposals receiving the highest overall score identify the vendors with whom management should seriously consider scheduling product demonstrations. The following example illustrates how a multiple rating system can be used to evaluate proposals from three different vendors.

Assume that a business receives three different proposals, one from vendor A, one from vendor B, and one from vendor C. Assume further that top management officials have decided to evaluate each proposal on three key issues—product performance, vendor's business reputation, and cost.

The first issue focuses on product performance—how well the proposed system fits the information needs of the business. Each vendor's proposal is studied and given a rating from 1 to 100. For the sake of this example, assume that vendor A receives a rating of 80, vendor B a rating of 70, and vendor C a rating of 50. Furthermore, assume that management officials decide that product performance is the most important of the three issues and, accordingly, they assign this issue a relative value of 45 percent. Each vendor's rating on the first issue is then multiplied by 45 percent to arrive at a score that is relative to the entire evaluation scheme. Vendor A scores 36 points ($80 \times .45 = 36$); vendor B scores 32 points ($70 \times .45 = 32$); and vendor C scores 23 points ($50 \times .45 = 23$).

The second issue focuses on the vendor's business reputation and includes such factors as the vendor's track record in the marketplace, the degree of system support that the vendor can provide, and the financial stability of the vendor's business. In relation to this issue, management is interested in answers to such questions as:

- How long has the vendor been in the hospitality technology business?
- Are hospitality systems the vendor's principal business?
- How many installations does the vendor currently support?
- How satisfied are current users?
- Is the vendor's business financially stable?
- Is the vendor expected to remain in business?

Each vendor's proposal is studied and given a rating from 1 to 100. Vendor A receives a rating of 60, vendor B a rating of 95, and vendor C a rating of 80. Although management officials consider product performance to be their primary concern, they also consider the vendor's business reputation to be important, and, therefore, they assign this issue a relative value of 30 percent. Each vendor's rating on the second issue is then multiplied by 30 percent to arrive at a score that is relative to the entire evaluation scheme. Vendor A scores 18 points ($60 \times .30 = 18$); vendor B scores 29 points ($95 \times .30 = 29$); and vendor C scores 24 points ($80 \times .30 = 24$).

The third issue identified by management centers on economic factors such as direct, indirect, and hidden costs of purchasing the technology. Assume that management officials were well-prepared and designed a portion of the RFP asking vendors to list the **direct costs** of individual system components. Avoiding a lump summary of direct expenditures enables management to:

- Consider the benefits of installing the system in phases rather than all at once.
- Eliminate unnecessary hardware devices or software programs.
- Conduct comparative price shopping for individual system components.

Assume further that management officials researched **indirect costs** that businesses typically incur in relation to the installation, operation, and maintenance of systems. A portion of the RFP asked vendors to estimate such indirect costs as taxes, insurance, shipping, and other costs that may result from:

**Exhibit 7    Multiple Rating Results**

| CRITERIA | VENDORS | | |
|---|---|---|---|
| | A | B | C |
| Product Performance | 80  × .45  = 36 | 70  × .45  = 32 | 50  × .45  = 23 |
| Vendor Reputation | 60  × .30  = 18 | 95  × .30  = 29 | 80  × .30  = 24 |
| System Cost | 90  × .25  = 23 | 70  × .25  = 18 | 80  × .25  = 20 |
| Overall Score | 77 | 79 | 67 |

- Modifying the property's air conditioning, electrical, and telephone wiring systems
- Establishing contingency programs
- Installing uninterruptible power sources
- Maintaining an inventory of spare parts

Another portion of the RFP asked vendors to estimate additional expenses, sometimes referred to as **hidden costs**, which include costs associated with supplies, customized forms, training, overtime pay, and data conversion.

Each vendor's proposal is studied in relation to these cost factors and given a rating from 1 to 100. Vendor A receives a rating of 90, vendor B a rating of 70, and vendor C a rating of 80. Because management officials believe product performance and vendor reliability are important steps toward fiscal responsibility, the cost issue is assigned a somewhat lower relative value—25 percent. Each vendor's rating on the third issue is then multiplied by 25 percent to arrive at a score that is relative to the entire evaluation scheme. Vendor A scores 23 points $(90 \times .25 = 23)$; vendor B scores 18 points $(70 \times .25 = 18)$; and vendor C scores 20 points $(80 \times .25 = 20)$.

Exhibit 7 shows the results of the multiple rating system used in this example. Vendor C's proposal will probably not receive any further consideration because it did not score well on any of the three key issues. Also, note that although vendor A offered the best system in terms of product performance, vendor B received the highest overall score due to its excellent reputation. However, since the overall scores of vendors A and B are so close, both vendors would likely be asked to schedule product demonstrations.

The previous example is meant only to illustrate a multiple rating system. Properties should take particular care to identify and rank key issues that relate specifically to the needs and requirements of their individual business operations. And, just as issues and their order of importance will vary from property to property, so will the relative percentage values assigned to each key issue.

## Vendor Product Demonstrations

Scripted product demonstrations (scripted demos) prevent vendor presentations from becoming a confusing show of "neat system tricks." With scripted demos, management provides each vendor with a script indicating what to demonstrate, thereby ensuring that the demo covers features relevant to the business—and that every demonstration covers the same information.

When preparing scripts for vendor presentations, determine the most important system capabilities to be demonstrated. Meet with appropriate managers and staff to determine potentially problematic areas that should be addressed during the demonstration.

In addition to adhering to management's script, the vendor should be required to use the actual hardware components and application software included within the proposal. It is essential that all components that are needed to carry out the scripted scenarios are included in the demonstration. For example, if a review of the output from a remote work station printer is part of one of the scripted scenarios, the vendor should include a remote work station printer in the demonstration. If magnetic stripe readers, bar code devices, or other units are included in the vendor's proposal, the vendor should be required to demonstrate these capabilities during the scripted demonstration session.

If applicable, develop guest scenarios to be scripted. Have members of the staff propose typical guest behaviors and preferences, and describe unusual patterns of business to be monitored by the system. For example, have visiting vendors program their systems with the actual menu items offered by the restaurant so as to closely simulate actual orders, modifications, and settlement procedures.

Arrange scenarios in a logical order but stagger the processing of transactions to simulate actual business conditions. This will test the system's ability to perform a variety of transactions in a random fashion. During the demonstration, vendors should demonstrate the scripted guest scenarios one at a time and in the sequence established by management. Scenarios should not be modified or rearranged or reorganized in any manner.

Identify future events that may be relevant to the system, such as physical plant expansion, changes in staff size, the use of online credit card authorization, satellite system interfacing, the use of electronic mail and online communication to purveyors, and so on.

Limit the vendor's demonstration time. This directs the vendor to address features and functions that management and staff are most interested in seeing rather than what the vendor is most interested in showing. A 90-minute presentation period should be sufficient.

Vendors should be informed that those who successfully pass the scripted demo stage will be invited back for a second visit. At that time, vendors may demonstrate any additional system features that the scenarios failed to illustrate. A second visit ensures the vendor a more serious and interested audience while providing an opportunity to establish product differentiation among competitors. After the second visits, management should be able to select the most appropriate product and begin contract negotiations with the vendor.

# Contract Negotiations

Before entering into contract negotiations with a vendor, management should secure copies of several standard contracts used by vendors of hospitality technology applications. These standard contracts are typically written in favor of the vendors and may not provide the kind of protection that the business may require. Management should examine these contracts carefully and obtain legal advice from a qualified attorney. If the attorney has no working knowledge of technology applications, management may also need assistance from an experienced technology applications consultant. In any case, the standard contract offered by a vendor serves only as the starting point for contract negotiations. Since the actual sale has not yet been made, the potential buyer may maintain a great deal of leverage in negotiating changes to the vendor's standard contract.

## Contract Provisions

The general contents of technology applications contracts can be divided into several areas. While some areas may be executed as separate contracts or subcontracts, properties may find that one master contract best meets the needs of their businesses. Three basic areas of a typical technology system contract are:

- General provisions
- Hardware provisions (including maintenance)
- Software provisions (including maintenance)

General contract provisions address standard contractual terms, such as the following, which are typically addressed in most purchasing agreements:

- Terms of delivery
- Terms of payment
- Survival past delivery
- Saleable product warranty
- Catastrophe remedies
- Provisions for breach of contract

Survival past delivery refers to the responsibilities of both parties once the product arrives on the buyer's premises. Saleable product warranty provides buyer assurance that the seller has a legal, marketable right to warrant the purchased product. Catastrophe remedies refer to penalties and relief in the event of a major failure of the product.

Hardware contract provisions relate to the purchase and operation of the technology equipment, including the operating system software that typically accompanies the hardware. Key areas addressed in the hardware section of a contract include:

- Specifications and performance criteria
- Delivery, installation, and testing requirements

- Costs and terms of payment

- Reliability tolerances

- Maintenance program options

Software contract provisions tend to be more difficult to negotiate because of the complex nature of software ownership. Since application programs are a compilation of ideas and processes proprietary to the seller, title is not automatically transferred to the buyer. Instead, the software often remains the property of the vendor and the buyer is granted a non-exclusive license to use the software programs. Key areas of a software contract are similar to those listed for hardware; however, the contract should demand that a copy of the source code in which the software was originally written be placed in escrow (in care of an independent third party) and released to the buyer should the vendor fail to carry out provisions stated within the contract.

## Contractual Arrangements

In relation to hospitality technology, there are several basic types of contractual arrangements. Three common types of agreements are:

- Single-vendor contracts

- Multi-vendor contracts

- Other equipment manufacturer (OEM) contracts

A **single-vendor contract** refers to an agreement to purchase hardware and software from the same vendor. In most of these cases, the vendor makes the necessary hardware and software modifications prior to system implementation. A single-vendor contract clearly identifies the vendor's responsibilities in relation to hardware and software performance and avoids the kind of confusion that may arise in other contractual arrangements when the lines of responsibility are not so clearly defined.

A **multi-vendor contract** refers to an agreement to purchase hardware and software from separate sources. The hardware components may be purchased directly from the manufacturer or purchased through the software vendor, who serves as a value-added dealer or value-added re-marketer. In either case, the hardware components or the accompanying operating system may require modifications by the software company in order to perform effectively.

When a business purchases (or repurchases) hardware components from one source that must be modified to perform according to specifications set by another source, confusion can arise with respect to guarantees and warranties. For example, when a software vendor modifies hardware components in order for the system to support special application programs, guarantees and warranties offered by the hardware manufacturer could become invalid. Hardware manufacturers generally assume responsibility for product performance only in relation to designated performance specifications. Whenever hardware components must be modified to perform according to specifications that differ from those originally designated by the hardware manufacturer, management should insist that whoever modifies the equipment backs the performance of that equipment with guarantees and warranty conditions similar to those originally provided by the hardware manufacturer.

Another area of concern in multi-vendor contracts relates to trouble-shooting and maintenance. For example, when a problem arises in the operation of a hotel's reservation system, the reservations staff may scramble to implement a manual backup operation while management contacts the hardware vendor. The hardware vendor listens to management's description of the problem and, after asking a few questions, concludes that the company can't help because the hotel's problem is really a software problem. Management then contacts the software vendor. The software vendor listens to management's description of the problem and, after asking a few questions, concludes that the hotel's problem is really a hardware problem and advises management to call the hardware vendor and carefully explain the situation once again. Meanwhile, managers waste time, tempers shorten, and room sales may be lost.

Clearly, managers engaged in the daily operation of a hospitality business cannot be burdened with diagnosing a technology application problem and determining whether the hardware or software vendor is responsible for resolving the situation. When negotiating a multi-vendor contract agreement, management should seek legal advice from a qualified attorney and technical assistance from an experienced technology applications consultant.

An **other equipment manufacturer (OEM) contract** refers to a situation in which a business agrees to purchase hardware components and software packages from a single source, and this single source takes full responsibility for the performance of the technology application. OEM contracts generally involve purchasing turnkey packages. In relation to hospitality technology applications, a turnkey package is a complete system that arrives at the property ready for installation. Once installed, the business "turns the key" and the system is ready to perform. This kind of contractual arrangement provides a business with the equivalent of a single-vendor contract, because all hardware and software customizing is performed by the OEM.

## Installation Factors

After completing contract negotiations, management must make final decisions on such installation factors as:

- Training
- Site preparation
- Design of printed materials
- Initial entry of database elements
- Acceptance testing
- System conversion
- Documentation
- Contingency planning

The following sections discuss each of these installation factors in some detail.

## Training

Training should begin before installation of the technology application and continue throughout the implementation process. The primary users of the system will be those individuals responsible for data entry, report generation, and system maintenance. These persons should begin active (hands-on) training with hardware components and software applications before installation. Training sessions may be conducted by the vendor or through seminars, textbooks, video, and other tutorial media.

Training conducted by the vendor can take place at the user's site or at the vendor's site. Regardless of location, management should insist that these training sessions involve hands-on experience with hardware and software identical to that being installed at the property. Although the costs of training are negotiable, the hospitality business generally assumes responsibility for any out-of-pocket expenses incurred by the vendor at the user's site. In addition, the hospitality business might have to bear the costs of securing any additional training equipment needed to accommodate large groups at the property.

Technology application experts often conduct seminars on specific topics, ranging from the essentials of technology applications to the details of particular software programs. There has been a rapid growth in these types of seminars. Although the training received by individuals attending these seminars may include hands-on experience, the hardware components and software applications used during the seminar may not be identical to those that are to be installed at the property. First-time users who receive training on one kind of technology application may become very confused and frustrated when they find out that they are to work on an entirely different technology application.

Technology training through textbooks can be laborious and confusing for first-time technology users. Written materials are better suited for supplementing the knowledge of those who are already familiar with basic technology operations. Textbooks can also be helpful for introducing experienced users to new software applications.

Video and tutorial media have proven to be highly effective training methods. Videotapes, designed to teach specific applications, generally allow a learner to progress through the materials at his or her own speed. The same is true for tutorial media (such as CD-ROM or Web-based training materials), which typically permit a learner to skip over previously mastered areas and concentrate on sessions involving applications that he or she finds more difficult.

The amount of training needed by managers will vary from property to property. Generally, managers are not directly involved in the daily input and processing functions of the technology application. However, since they depend on its output, it is vital that managers fully understand the system's capabilities. Since the success or failure of automating information needs often is a function of the degree of management involvement and commitment, managers must provide continual support and encouragement for personnel being trained as primary users and operators of the system.

## Site Preparation

Site preparation refers to architectural or engineering changes that must be made before the technology system can be installed. The extent of these changes depends on the size of the property and the kind of technology application that is to be installed. Depending on the circumstances, site preparation may include:

- Modifications to the property's air conditioning system, electrical wiring system, and telephone system
- Construction of individual work stations to accommodate hardware components and necessary cabling
- Installation of uninterruptible power sources
- Construction of a technology room

These facets of site preparation must be carefully planned and executed in order to prevent disruptions to operations during installation and later when the system is fully operational.

## Design of Printed Materials

Many general questions about printed materials must already have been answered in order for a business to purchase the appropriate printing devices for the technology application. Details regarding the nature of printed materials must also be addressed before full implementation of the technology application.

Lodging properties may choose to design new formats for reservation confirmation notices, registration cards, guest folios, room key envelopes, billing statements, payroll checks, and many management reports that are prepared on a daily basis. Printed materials that may be redesigned by food service businesses include guest checks, menus, promotional materials, and various management reports.

Other questions about printed materials that must be answered include the following:

- Which forms will be printed in multiple copies?
- Will different qualities of paper stock be used for different print jobs?
- Which forms and reports will use paper pre-printed with the business's logo and other artwork?

Answering these questions during site preparation will ensure smoother installation of the technology equipment and enable management to refine aspects of printed materials during acceptance testing of the technology application. In addition, appropriate personnel will be able to receive the more specific kind of training that may be necessary in order to prepare and print intricate forms and reports.

## Initial Entry of Database Elements

Long before system installation, management officials and vendor representatives should develop a plan for data entry that will populate the application database.

This is a critical area of technology planning. Once the system is installed and implemented, the content of the database will govern the scope of potential applications.

While database design specifications are usually the mutual responsibility of the vendor and management officials, the actual entering of data elements according to design specifications is the responsibility of trained property employees. Initial data entry can be a time-consuming process. For most lodging properties, initial data entry entails inputting room types, room numbers, room rates, revenue center codes, employee identification numbers, posting codes, settlement plans, sales history data, guest history files, and so on. For most food service operations, initial data entry entails inputting ingredient lists, recipe and sub-recipe codes, meal plans, menu prices, identification of house accounts, historical menu mix (sales) data, and much more. It is extremely important that initial data entry be completed within a time frame that permits extensive acceptance testing before the business converts to full automation.

## Acceptance Testing

Before adopting or upgrading a new technology application, management should conduct extensive acceptance testing of the candidate application. Acceptance testing involves more than simply checking whether the application works. Tests should be developed to determine whether automated operations function according to standards defined by management. Fundamental areas of acceptance testing include:

- Hardware efficiency
- Software reliability
- Data integrity

Hardware efficiency refers to the ease of use of system equipment and the suspense time involved in searching for necessary data. These areas must be tested and found acceptable. Users must be able to retrieve necessary data in the timely fashion required by management.

Software reliability refers to the accuracy with which the programs process data. The reliability of application software programs should be challenged with a set of test data. This can be done by processing a known set of data through the technology application and comparing the system's output with calculated results generated by the previous information system. Lodging operations can input data from a previous month and process a series of statistical reports and financial statements through the technology application. These reports and statements can then be compared with the actual reports and statements prepared by the previous information system. Similarly, food service operations can input data from a prior period and test the accuracy of the application software in calculating food cost percentages, menu counts, and payroll expenses. In any case, the use of previously processed data can be extremely helpful in verifying the new technology application's algorithmic design.

Data, or system, integrity refers to the degree of software integration. Sharing files to produce comprehensive reports is typically a major issue in the selection of one technology application over another. System testing should prove that such integration does in fact exist and that it functions according to standards defined by management.

## System Conversion

**System conversion** is the process of switching from an installed system to a new system. System conversion within a hospitality operation can be a difficult, if not trying, experience. Two commonly used conversion strategies are parallel conversion and direct cutover conversion.

With **parallel conversion**, the property continues to operate the old system while incrementally installing parts of the new system. The two information systems operate simultaneously. Both systems are maintained for one accounting period. When comfortable with the new system's operation, management directs a complete conversion to the new system. While there is relatively little risk involved with parallel conversion, it has the main disadvantage of the high costs of operating two information systems simultaneously.

With **direct cutover conversion**, management chooses a date on which the property is to switch from the current system to the new system. Direct cutover is also called "cold turkey" because it involves a complete withdrawal from the previous information system. This approach may be especially effective when the previous system is perceived as cumbersome and inadequate, or when the new technology is perceived as a great enhancement over the former system. The major advantage of a direct cutover conversion is that the hospitality business is not required to operate two different information systems simultaneously. The major disadvantage is the potential risk of adopting a new system without the ability to revert to old processes and procedures.

There are a number of conversion strategies that combine aspects of both parallel conversion and direct cutover strategies. For example, lodging properties may choose to immediately convert areas such as reservations, rooms management, and guest accounting, but maintain parallel conversion procedures for a full accounting period for payroll and general ledger applications. Whatever the selected strategy, operational costs should be balanced against risks. Risks can often be minimized by careful attention to acceptance testing, training, and contingency planning.

## Documentation

Securing adequate documentation of each technology application component is critical to the success of system operations beyond the installation period. Documentation is essential for the ongoing training of staff and for identifying underutilized system capabilities and possible weaknesses within the technology application. The three most important forms of documentation in relation to technology applications are operator's guides, technical manuals, and system flowcharts.

Operator's guides, also called user's guides, are written training materials for specific application procedures. Some vendors provide a single, all-encompassing guidebook. However, the documentation for a system with extensive application options might be segmented by job functions, with a separate user's guide for cashiers, another guide for front desk employees, and so on.

Technical manuals, also called systems manuals, focus on the engineering features of the technology application. These manuals typically include schematic diagrams of electronic circuitry and list trouble-shooting hints for service and repair workers. Managers of some businesses fail to request this kind of technical documentation because they do not foresee using it themselves. However, technical manuals can be valuable resources in times of emergency.

Technology application flowcharts may not be part of the standard documentation package; however, management should request them because they offer users insight into the operation of the application. System flowcharts illustrate the input-process-output logic, file structures, program sub-routines, inter-program relationships, and the level of program integration within the system. These flowcharts provide a way to analyze the effectiveness of the information system and prove invaluable when management contemplates software or hardware modifications to meet new information needs.

## Contingency Planning

The purpose of contingency planning is to define procedures that are to be followed when, for whatever reason, an automated application is not able to function properly. Contingency planning is an important aspect of technology implementation. This is especially true for the hospitality business that operates 24 hours a day, 7 days a week. There are four basic parts to an effective contingency plan.

The first part designates an emergency team. The systems manager (or supervisor) typically leads the emergency team, which is made up of representatives from various departments. Each team member is assigned specific duties and responsibilities that may range from being able to install spare parts to troubleshooting and carrying out somewhat sophisticated diagnostic routines.

The second part of a contingency plan identifies detailed information about hardware configuration, software design, supplier contact information, environmental requirements, and site considerations. This information is typically stored in a specific location and is made available to members of the contingency team.

The third part of the plan identifies technology backup sites (such as local service bureaus, web-hosted service providers, etc.) and sources of substitute equipment.

The final section of a contingency plan details procedures for recovering damaged files and for implementing temporary non-automated operations.

## ⚷ Key Terms

**direct costs**—In relation to the purchase of a technology system, the costs of individual system components.

**direct cutover conversion**—In relation to the implementation of a technology system, management chooses a date on which there is to be a complete switch from current procedures to new functions. Direct cutover is also called "going cold turkey" because it involves a complete withdrawal from the previous information system.

**flowchart**—In relation to technology systems, uses specifically designed symbols to diagram the flow of data and documents through an information system.

**hidden costs**—In relation to the purchase of technology equipment, costs associated with supplies, customized forms, training, overtime pay, and data conversion normally not included in the system purchase price.

**indirect costs**—In relation to the purchase of a technology system, these costs include taxes, insurance, shipping, and other costs that may result from: modifying the property's air conditioning, electrical, and telephone wiring systems; establishing contingency programs; installing uninterruptible power sources; and maintaining an inventory of spare parts.

**multi-vendor contract**—In relation to the purchase of a technology system, an agreement to purchase hardware and software from separate sources.

**other equipment manufacturer (OEM) contract**—In relation to the purchase of a technology system, a contract in which a business agrees to purchase hardware components and software packages from a single source, and this single source takes full responsibility for the performance of the system. An OEM contract generally involves purchasing turnkey packages.

**parallel conversion**—In relation to the implementation of a technology system, a property operates two different information systems simultaneously: the previous system and the new system. Both systems are maintained for at least one complete accounting period. Once comfortable with the new system's operation, management directs a complete conversion.

**property profile**—Compiles statistics about aspects of the current information system; useful when communicating information needs of the business to vendors of technology systems.

**request for proposal**—In relation to the purchase of a technology system, a three-part document prepared by management. The first section orients the vendor to management's business operations; the second section establishes bidding requirements for vendor proposals; and the third section deals specifically with user application requirements.

**single-vendor contract**—In relation to the purchase of a technology system, an agreement to purchase hardware and software from the same vendor. In most of these cases, the vendor makes the necessary hardware and software modifications before system implementation.

**site survey**—In relation to the purchase of a technology system, visits by vendors to identify important factors regarding specific business operations within a property that may affect system design.

**system conversion**—The process of switching from the current information system to the capabilities of a new system.

# Review Questions

1. How can management go about analyzing the current information needs of a hospitality operation? Explain how flowcharts can be used as a method of analysis.

2. What are some of the ways management can collect product literature regarding technology systems?

3. What factors must management take into account when determining system requirements?

4. What does the term "algorithm" mean? Explain how this term relates to management's task of determining system requirements.

5. What are the three major sections of a "request for proposal"? Explain why it is important for management to ask vendors to follow the same format when submitting proposals for review.

6. In relation to purchasing a technology system, what do the terms "direct costs," "indirect costs," and "hidden costs" mean? Give examples of each.

7. What are the three areas typically addressed in a contract for the purchase of a technology system?

8. What are the major differences between single-vendor, multi-vendor, and other equipment manufacturer contracts? Describe the advantages and disadvantages of each.

9. Upon completing contract negotiations, what factors must management officials address regarding the installation of a technology system?

10. Why is securing adequate documentation of each system component critical to the success of system operations beyond the installation period? Identify the three critical forms of documentation.

# Internet Sites

For more information, visit the following Internet sites. Remember that Internet addresses can change without notice. If the site is no longer there, you can use a search engine to look for additional sites.

### *Hospitality Organizations*

American Hotel & Lodging Association
http://www.ahla.com

Club Managers Association of America
http://www.cmaa.org

Educational Institute of the American Hotel & Lodging Association
http://www.ei-ahla.org

Hospitality Financial and Technology Professionals
http://www.hftp.org

Hospitality Industry Technology Exposition and Conference
http://www.hitecshow.org

National Restaurant Association
http://www.restaurant.org

## *Hotel Property Management Systems*

CMS Hospitality
http://www.cmshosp.com.au

Fidelio
http://www.micros.com

Resort Systems Incorporated
http://www.resortsystems.ca

## *Restaurant Technology Systems*

CMS Hospitality
http://www.cmshosp.com.au

Comtrex Systems Corporation
http://www.comtrex.com

Comus Restaurant Systems
http://www.comus.com

Eatec Corporation
http://www.eatec.com

System Concepts, Inc.
http://www.foodtrak.com

## *Point of Sale Systems*

InfoGenesis
http://www.infogenesis.com

NCR Corporation
http://www.ncr.com

## Chapter 12 Outline

## Competencies

1. Identify environmental threats to information systems and describe security precautions to take against them. (pp. 303–305)

2. Identify electronic threats to information systems and describe security precautions to take against them. (pp. 305–309)

3. Identify operational threats to information systems and describe security precautions to take against them. (pp. 309–311)

4. Explain procedures related to system and data backups. (pp. 311–314)

5. Describe the system documentation that should be kept covering hardware, software, and network equipment. (p. 314)

6. Explain the function of an information systems security audit. (pp. 314–315)

7. Outline areas covered by manual operations plans in the event of the failure of a property management system. (pp. 316–326)

# 12

# Systems and Security Maintenance

*From* The Fundamentals of Systems and Security Maintenance, *written by Jon Inge and produced by the Technology Committee of the American Hotel & Lodging Association, with a grant from the American Hotel & Lodging Foundation.*

MAINTAINING SYSTEMS SECURITY IS A THANKLESS, never-ending task, which, while essential, can never achieve perfect results. It takes constant work to keep the systems and their vital guest/operations data as safe as is reasonably practical without getting in the way of the day-to-day activities of operating the property. Even the best technical security will never be absolute, and everyone who uses any system must also keep a real-world sense of perspective and awareness about it, watching for the unexpected—and being prepared to handle it.

Detailed guest information and operational statistics are among the most valuable assets any property possesses, whether compiled manually or by computer. If these data are on a computer system, they will be more comprehensive, more accurate, and will allow for far more flexible reporting and data analysis than a manual operation can hope to achieve—and yet they are also more fragile. They are easily damaged or lost through user errors or deliberate attack, and the more we come to rely on them, the greater the disruption that follows such damage.

Paper and electronic records have always been subject to physical damage from fire, flood, and so forth. Electronic records are also vulnerable to threats that aren't as visible but that can be just as devastating. The very flexibility and interconnectedness that make modern systems so valuable and powerful also opens them up to outside threats, both deliberate and random, and any prudent organization must take measures to protect itself.

Of course, there's a balance to be struck between leaving systems wide open and implementing so many security precautions that the technology staff can't do its job. Nevertheless, the adoption of reasonable precautions to protect information is essential to maintain the efficiency of an operation.

The following chapter reviews the main threats to information and offers practical guidelines to making systems as secure as is reasonable without interfering with daily routines.

It's an old saying that the only completely secure system has no inputs or outputs, is encased in concrete, and lies at the bottom of the sea. All real systems interact with the outside world, accept information, process it, and send it back out in some other form.

The weakest security link in any system is human fallibility. The software programs that perform functions are written by people, and people handle the data going into them. People sometimes make mistakes. People aren't always honest, either, and may have their own reasons for deliberately corrupting or destroying your information—sometimes even when they work for you. The main threats to your systems information can be grouped into three categories:

- Environmental
- Electronic
- Operational

The following sections discuss each of these types of threats in detail and suggest suitable precautions. These threats overlap to some extent, of course, but these categories are nevertheless useful for general discussion. Each can be subdivided into accidental, random, or deliberate causes, but the end results are the same, and so are the precautions.

## Environmental Threats and Precautions

These are situations or events that threaten the very structure of the systems. Apart from the obvious effects of fire, flood, and earthquakes, there are less dramatic but still crippling effects from loss of power or external network connections. These threats are the most visible and have the most dramatic impacts.

Obviously, if there is extensive damage the property may have to close. In most cases, the impact will be localized, making it possible to continue at least to some extent with manual operations. Plans for manual operations should be in place for each aspect of the property. The priority (after ensuring the safety of the staff and guests) should be to protect the integrity of your data. A property cannot operate effectively without knowing which guests are in which rooms and which guests are due to arrive. Manual operations plans with clear control and coordination responsibilities are invaluable. Sample pages from a typical plan are included in the appendix at the end of this chapter.

On a periodic basis, during a relatively quiet time, practice manual operations—shut down the systems and run manually. Yes, it's a hassle, and it imposes extra work on the staff at the time, but the practice is worth it. When the power goes out for real, you'll be able to preserve the integrity of the data and keep running efficiently because the staff has learned what to do beforehand.

### Fire

Basic physical security—fire/smoke detectors, etc.—should be a given. Apart from the general property systems, the computer room (or area where the servers are located) should have its own fire suppression system. This needs to be one that doesn't use water (which damages the equipment unless used in a high-pressure mist) or halon (which damages the atmosphere and is banned in many areas).

### Flood

Make sure that the computer room is not located against an outside wall or in any area subject to flooding. This includes being aware of potential as well as existing hazards. Putting the computer room in the basement under the swimming pool is not recommended, even if "it's never leaked yet."

## Power Failure

Sudden power failures can corrupt data in the blink of an eye, so it's essential to have the key equipment protected. Most properties have a backup generator, but it's usually not large enough to drive every piece of equipment. All critical computer equipment—the servers, key workstations and report printers, and the network hubs/switches—should be on a dedicated power circuit.

The power needs to be clean, within definite voltage limits and free of "spikes." The critical-equipment circuit should therefore be filtered through line conditioners to ensure this, and each peripheral device (PC workstation, printer, scanner, etc.) should be plugged into a **surge protector**. The servers should have **uninterruptible power supplies** (UPSs) to cover the time until the generator comes on line and which allow for an orderly shutdown of the system if all power sources fail.

Complex properties that completely rely on their systems may want to investigate installing redundant power supplies, with feeds from different utility substations, so that a single exterior failure still leaves them with electricity.

## Network Connections

A network connection can be a lifeline. To those properties operating in a remote-server or **application service provider** (ASP) environment (where the main system server is located somewhere else), the connection to the server is clearly vital. Most properties today rely on a network connection to deliver reservations to them from some central source. In either case, having a secondary means of communication available as a fallback is often essential, even if it's the absolute minimum of a dial-up modem linking to the remote site.

# Electronic Threats and Precautions ─────────────

The data can become corrupted, either by accident or from viruses, hacker attacks, or other malicious acts spread electronically over the network. Attacks from the **Internet** or from programs attached to e-mails and documents receive a lot of publicity, but the majority of attackers aren't criminal geniuses concocting diabolical new ways to get into systems. Most successful attacks are made by pranksters trying to show off by using widely available tools to exploit known security holes in standard software, taking advantage of servers and PCs that have been left wide open and vulnerable.

The sad part is that the patches to fix these holes are also widely available, but they often haven't been installed. Systems administrators may feel too overloaded to keep up with them. Or, they may not have time to load all of them, even if they know they exist. However, tools are available to prevent the great majority of outside attempts at access from being successful. Keeping abreast of new developments isn't that hard, and implementing those tools that are most important to each property's situation is just a part of a professional approach to system maintenance.

The main precautions to take against electronic attacks are:

- Anti-virus software
- Firewalls
- Security patches

## Anti-Virus Software

Installing **anti-virus software** and keeping it up-to-date is an absolute requirement. There are far too many viruses in circulation, both attached to e-mail messages and embedded in common document formats (Word, Excel, etc.), for any organization to risk operating without protection. Some viruses are relatively benign, just displaying annoying messages and getting in the way of doing your work; others can wreak devastating damage to your system's data files.

New viruses will always appear unexpectedly, but the vast majority can be kept at bay simply by installing any of the current products from Norton, McAfee, Inoculan, and others, and by subscribing to their automatic-update services. It's simple, straightforward, and essential. The update files should be downloaded regularly: every two weeks is a good compromise between minimizing vulnerability and effort. The updates should be distributed automatically to all workstations via sign-on scripts.

There's some debate about whether anti-virus software should be loaded on an application server, since on older machines it can cause a performance slowdown. If this proves to be the case, the software can be removed as long as the server files are scanned at least once a week using the anti-virus software on a network-connected PC workstation. To make sure this is done, a policy must be established and scanning records must be kept.

Although not a real threat to the integrity of systems or data, there are a lot of "hoax" viruses circulating on the Internet that play off people's fears about genuine viruses. These hoax viruses are chain-letter-style e-mails that urge you, for example, to be on the alert for a particularly nasty virus, or to add your name to a petition to Congress to save NPR, or to participate in a Microsoft e-mail test program. These hoaxes don't contain codes that can be run by or damage a computer, but by encouraging people to "pass this urgent message on immediately to as many people as possible," they do clog up the system and are real time-wasters for both staff and the support team. A number of Web sites track these hoaxes and other urban myths; being aware of their typical characteristics (they're remarkably repetitive) will help focus attention on real threats.

## Firewalls

Firewalls are another essential. A **firewall** is a separate device or just a software program (depending on the complexity of your system) that sits between the property network and the Internet. It restricts the types of messages allowed to pass in and out of the network and restricts access to specified Web sites, according to parameters set by property management. It can also mask the availability of communications ports on the server and the Internet addresses of the PCs on your network, hiding them from potential attackers who search the Internet looking for vulnerable computers.

A firewall is needed even if you run a single-PC system, perhaps especially so, because you have a greater vulnerability with everything relying on one PC. Firewall settings cannot be absolute. Staff members need to communicate with people via the Internet, and there will always be exceptions to the access restrictions. With firewalls, just as with anti-virus software that will only catch 99 percent of the viruses out there, your staff must stay alert.

You may think that no one would be interested in a property's data files, and you'd pretty much be right. But hackers looking for a server for their own reasons don't care in the least who owns it or what's stored on it. All they're looking for is an opportunity to get into someone else's system—anyone else's system—just to prove that they can, or to use it as a launching pad for attacks on other systems. Any damage they might do to a property's operation in the process is completely irrelevant to them.

Some of the most powerful attacks that a firewall can help prevent are the so-called denial-of-service attacks. These involve small software programs downloaded by hackers to hundreds of unsuspecting companies' servers. These programs lie dormant until a trigger commands them all to activate at once and send messages to a single target system. This deluge of messages from so many different sources completely overloads the server and shuts it down.

Firewalls are especially important if you have staff (such as sales managers) who travel regularly and need to access your property systems from remote locations. At the very least, their access through the firewall must be subject to very specific authentication procedures, such as tightly controlled passwords, and physical keys plugged into their laptops, or other security measures.

If there is concern about sending valuable information over the Internet, such access should be made using a **virtual private network (VPN)**. This communications technique has software components loaded on both the mobile PC and the server, using any Internet access connection to link to your system but encrypting all messages. The downside to VPNs is that the coding and decoding process slows traffic noticeably, by up to 50 percent compared with unrestricted access, but the security of the data in transit is assured.

Firewalls can also allow you to track specific user activity, even down to the keystrokes typed. Few properties would have the time to monitor this potential mountain of data on any consistent basis, but if you suspect any staff member of wasting too much time on the Internet, or of attempting to access unauthorized software, or of fraudulent activity on his or her main system, these tools can provide you with key evidence. Just letting it be known that you have this tracking ability is often sufficient to keep people focused on their work.

## Security Patches

Security is a continual contest between hackers and those trying to keep them out. Hackers see every new precaution as a fresh challenge. They will try different combinations of messages, formats, and protocols to find and exploit potential weaknesses in the server operating systems. As these holes become known, the vendors issue **patches** to correct them, and these should usually be put in place as soon as possible, since word of any successful new attack methods spreads very quickly.

Occasionally a vendor will issue a fix that goes too far in imposing traffic restrictions. A past Microsoft patch to Outlook, for example, prevented any of the commonly used attachment formats from being received, even if they were uncontaminated. Fortunately, independent organizations issued patches to the Microsoft patch to restore a more useful level of functionality. This emphasizes the need to keep up with current developments in the security field.

**Routers** and other programmable network devices also often require their own security updates as potential holes in their software are discovered. Certainly neither they nor your system servers and PCs should ever be put into service with their default configurations and passwords unchanged; that's the first area hackers check.

## Other Precautions

There should be no local modems on individual workstations, for Internet access or for any other reason. All outside communications should go through a shared high-speed connection on the firewall, which will be both faster and more secure. The exceptions will be the laptops used by roaming managers and sales staff, which need modems for Internet access on the road, but their users must be made aware of (and accept responsibility for) the need for security procedures. With mobility and freedom of operation comes increased responsibility.

In larger properties, network management systems can help maintain security through their ability to control configurations remotely. There are also very useful network mapping software applications with auto-discovery routines that can be run to detect and record all parts of the networks, and to identify which PCs and servers are connected and the software they're running. It's been known for these to uncover an old server still in place but not properly secured—or even one deliberately left in place by a disgruntled ex-employee who used it to obtain access to his former employer's network.

Electronic security is a never-ending process. Keep up-to-date, monitor developments, prioritize them, and keep a sense of awareness about real versus spurious threats. Also, it's worth periodically investing in the services of a security consultant to attempt to break into property systems and give an honest, real-world view of the vulnerabilities, and to help set priorities for action. The peace of mind is worth it.

Security isn't just the administrator's job. Even if systems servers are patched to the most current levels, anti-virus software is kept consistently up-to-date, and individual PC browsers are set to identify attachments known to be risky, new attacks are constantly being developed, and their antidotes will always lag a little behind. Everyone who uses a computer still has to be trained to be aware and to exercise good judgment about security risks.

In the past it was good advice never to open an e-mail attachment from some-one you didn't know. Now it's not that simple; viruses commonly raid your address book for names to send themselves to. This makes it more important than ever to think carefully about whether any message you receive makes sense before opening it. How many copies of the ILOVEYOU virus were spread by people unthinkingly opening messages with that title from colleagues who would be highly unlikely to express that sentiment? How many received six copies and still opened it? If in doubt, call the apparent sender of the e-mail to verify that he or she sent it. And, save all attachments to a specific directory on your PC, scanning them with current anti-virus software before opening them. Yes, it's tedious, but it's not as time-consuming as the monumental effort required to clean up after a virus that has spread throughout the organization.

# Operational Threats and Precautions

The human element will always be a factor, through accidents such as making data entry errors, spilling drinks on computer hardware, or opening highly suspicious e-mail attachments, or deliberately in the form of attacks on the data system from disgruntled current or ex-employees.

Every staff member using the systems must understand that security is every-body's responsibility; they are all individually responsible to some extent for maintaining the integrity and usefulness of the data. Data integrity will always be subject to human error and impatience. There's no way to prevent all typing errors, but taking the time (for example) to check whether a caller already has a guest his-tory record instead of blindly creating a new one will always pay off in terms of better guest service and more repeat business. It's worth emphasizing to everyone that the more consistent and accurate they can make their data inputs, the more valuable the information gathered will be.

Education and reinforcement help staff members to understand the nature of the potential risks and to realize that there are good reasons for the procedures and policies put in place to minimize the risks. Because the issue is so pervasive, multi-ple levels of security have to be used.

## Restricted Access

In the same way that bank safety deposit boxes are locked, inside a locked vault, inside a locked building, users' access to data must be partitioned. Users must be required to sign in with passwords that are not obvious and that are changed regu-larly, and they must be restricted to those data areas and functions required for their work.

All good systems can be set to restrict individual users' access to various com-binations of menu functions, further divided into "read-only" or "modify" capa-bilities for each, combined with detailed audit trails to identify who made each significant change. Equally, the staff must have free and open access to all areas that do affect their work. If summary information from a restricted area would be useful to them, there are often ways of giving them a report based on—but without access to—the confidential detail behind it. It is a powerful inducement to use a system professionally when staff know that they can access anything they need, and also know that everything they do can be traced.

It clearly follows that the access privileges and passwords of any terminated staff member must be revoked immediately, and the main system passwords should be changed at the same time. If they have any systems knowledge or access to any sensitive data at all, they should be escorted off the premises as soon as they are terminated.

## Written Policies

Having written policies and procedures in place, and requiring all users to read and sign them before being given computer access, goes a long way toward raising security awareness. Typical policies address:

- Standard software

- Use of personal floppies or CDs

- E-mail and Internet use

- Passwords

- Computer room security

**Standard Software.** Limit applications to a clearly defined standard set, with no other software permitted on the PC workstations. Some operating systems allow this policy to be enforced through a **lock down** of the PC desktop configuration, and this is highly recommended. All users should understand that keeping the system as simple as possible will maximize both its performance and its maintainability. New applications can be added to the approved set as required, but only after review by the operations management to confirm their value and by the systems management to verify their compatibility with existing programs.

**Use of Personal Floppies or CDs.** Personal software should not be allowed on removable media such as floppy disks or CD-ROMs. The danger of contamination is too great; users may not take the time to scan disks for viruses before running any programs or copying data from them.

**E-mail and Internet Use.** Clear e-mail and Internet access policies are needed. Given modern work schedules, it's often realistic to permit staff a certain amount of latitude in conducting personal business at work. This includes a clear understanding of whether personal Internet access is permitted and under what circumstances, and on the degree of privacy allotted to all personal information kept on the property's computers, including e-mail. Management can decide whether to allow this and whether to retain the right to read all personal software and messages on any company PC, but whatever policy management sets, it must be in writing and signed by the employee.

**Passwords.** Passwords should be used responsibly. No writing them down on notes taped to the PC or kept under the mouse pad, no sharing them with other users or non-staff members. Passwords should be changed regularly (at no less than six-month intervals) and monitored by IT management. When key personnel leave the organization, their passwords should be immediately discontinued.

**Computer Room Security.** Computer room security must be maintained at all times. The room should be located away from heavy traffic areas (most definitely not in a through area), with access permitted only to those with a real need. It should have a self-closing, self-locking door with at least a combination lock or, preferably, an electronic lock opened with a magnetic-strip or other intelligent key-card.

# General Principles of System Security and Maintenance —

At the core of all security measures are three fundamentals, without which any other precautions will be far more difficult to undertake. These are:

- Regular system and data backups—stored off-site.

- Complete system documentation (what you have, who supports it) for the hardware, software, and network—reviewed no less than every six months to ensure that it is up-to-date.

- A security audit checklist—reviewed no less than annually, to ensure that your precautions are current.

The sample documents and schedules that follow are only guidelines. Some items won't apply to all operations, and many properties will have some areas not covered in the samples at all. Each property's needs and configuration are unique and must be uniquely documented to suit the particular circumstances.

## Regular System and Data Backups

Backups are absolutely key, both in the operational sense of having manual procedures to fall back on, and in terms of having duplicate copies of data and systems software.

Operationally, even without a system running, you can keep both guest and operations data up-to-date and accurate if you can fall back to pre-defined and tested manual procedures, with clearly defined responsibilities for control and coordination. It will also help if standby kits of the appropriate forms, materials, and supplies are kept handy and fully stocked. An example of manual operations guidelines is provided in the appendix at the end of this chapter.

The best insurance against system failure or data loss is having a good backup copy of the data and system files. Restoring from a backup is usually the only way of recovering lost data, apart from re-keying it all in from whatever paper receipts and records exist for each transaction. Even if you have to re-enter manually all changes since the last backup was run, that's still far preferable to losing it all.

Backups should be made on a regular basis, either on tape (cheapest) or CD-ROM (easiest to use if you need to restore a particular file). They must also be checked periodically to ensure that the information on them can be read if needed. Most properties use tape, which is inexpensive and proven to be reliable.

**Exhibit 1    Sample Tape Backup Log**

**Tape Backup Log**

Month:_____ Year:_____

| Day/Date | Time Started | Time Finished | Tape Used | Comments (errors/problems) |
|---|---|---|---|---|
| 1. | | | | |
| 2. | | | | |
| 3. | | | | |
| 4. | | | | |
| 5. | | | | |
| 6. | | | | |
| 7. | | | | |
| 8. | | | | |
| 9. | | | | |
| 10. | | | | |
| 11. | | | | |
| 12. | | | | |
| 13. | | | | |
| 14. | | | | |
| -------------------- | ------------ | ------------ | ------------ | ------------------------------------------------ |
| -------------------- | ------------ | ------------ | ------------ | ------------------------------------------------ |
| 29. | | | | |
| 30. | | | | |
| 31. | | | | |

**System Backup.** A full system backup of the network should be done on a weekly basis. As this will take more time than the daily data backup, schedule it for the least busy night of the week, and always do it on the same night every week for consistency.

**Data Backup.** Make a backup of the data every night, recording it in the backup log (see Exhibit 1). It's simplest and most secure to use 21 tapes (three weekly sets) for your nightly (including the FULL SYSTEM) backup, rotating through them in sequence. This assures that, if the first backup itself is bad, the previous backup is always available. Each tape should be labeled with the set ID (A, B, and C) and the day of the week, e.g., A-SUNDAY, A- MONDAY, etc., then B-SUNDAY, and so on. Keep blank tapes on hand to replace any that go bad, and store them in a location accessible to the person responsible for running the nightly backups.

Store all backup tapes, with date notation, in a secure fire- and heat-proof location somewhere away from the computer you are backing up, since in case of a fire or other catastrophe that damages a computer, tapes stored next to the computer also will be damaged. The night auditors will only need to access the tapes needed for the night the backup is being done.

One of the three sets of backup tapes should be secured off-site at all times. A designated person should take the most current set of backup tapes to an off-site storage location each Monday and bring the oldest set back to the hotel on

Tuesday, so there is always one set off-site. It could also be arranged for the tape backups to be picked up and traded with the service used for banking delivery, such as Wells Fargo or Brinks.

**Downtime Reports.** However essential backups are, they do take time to reload onto the system, and all transactions that have occurred since the backup was made still have to be re-entered to make the system data current again. To keep the hotel operating while this is happening, or to use when any minor interruption takes the system off-line for a short period, many properties print regular reports on key information at regular intervals during the day. These **downtime** reports cover such data as an in-house guest list, today's arrivals, folio balances, etc.

They are usually printed at regular intervals during the day, often scheduled around major changes such as the main check-out period. They consume a fair amount of paper, but if you ever need them, they are absolutely indispensable. To save paper, some properties copy the report data to files on a laptop computer instead of printing them, relying on the laptop's batteries to retrieve the information if the power fails. This can be a viable alternative for very small properties. For most hotels, however, it has the drawback that you have to find some way of printing multiple copies of the reports for staff use when the system is down.

Downtime reports should provide all essential hotel status and guest billing information. These reports should be run every two hours. If more than one department will need the same report to operate, make sure that sufficient copies are run, since you may not have access to a printer or copier at the time the reports are needed.

The specific reports run depend on the nature of the operation and the needs of management. The minimum suggested reports are:

- In-house guest list—in alphabetical order for the PBX and in numeric order for the front desk
- Availability—all available rooms for the front desk (with clean/dirty status); list of dirty rooms for housekeeping
- Arrivals—include arrivals for the next four days
- Guest ledger (current folio balances)
- Guest paying cash
- Expected departures
- Guest messages
- Room availability forecast for at least one month out
- Vacant rooms report

If you know in advance that the system will be down, also print guest folios for all occupied rooms, group masters, and house accounts. If time permits, housekeeping should run the following reports:

- Late check-outs
- Room change report

- Early departures

- Departures not checked out

- All room status (dirty and vacant rooms)

## Documentation

Documentation can be tedious to create and maintain (although automated tools can help with both functions), but it is also invaluable. Even in day-to-day operations, you gain both efficiency and peace of mind from having detailed and complete system documentation in place. This needs to cover hardware, software, and network equipment listing:

- What each item is

- Model and version/release number

- Name and phone number of whoever supports it

- Log of all changes made to it since installation

- Log of all service calls made

A system description summary sheet should be completed for each system at the property, including PBX, point of sale (POS), call accounting, voice mail, pay-per-view movies, etc. Exhibit 2 presents a sample form used to summarize a POS system. POS systems are electronic cash register systems that are used in food and beverage and retail outlets. Interfacing them to the property management system (PMS) enables the outlets to send charges to the appropriate guest folios. Various POS systems can also break out charges by packages and meal period. Exhibits 3 through 5 present additional helpful forms by which to document:

- Software license sites

- Equipment service and calls

- Equipment maintenance activities

Two network diagrams are especially useful. One is a physical schematic of how the hardware items (PCs, printers, etc.) are connected to the various network loops. This diagram would include all hardware on each network segment, with each item labeled with its make/model, IP address and any other key data. The other diagram is a software schematic that illustrates how the different applications interface and interact with each other. This can be especially useful when determining the impact of any particular system outage. The diagram should reflect the actual systems at a property, their interactions, and data transfer methods used.

## Security Audit

The **security audit** is the glue that ties all these precautions together, since it serves to check that every aspect of the operation is recognized and covered—backup

**Exhibit 2   Sample System Description Summary Sheet**

**POINT OF SALE (POS) SYSTEM AND PMS INTERFACE**

**System Description**

Vendor/Model:_____ Software Level:_____

Purchased from:_____ Contact Name: _____

Phone:_____ Fax: _____

Comments:   _____
_____
_____
_____
_____
_____
_____
_____

**Service Information**

Support Department Contact Name:_____ Phone:_____

Support Hours of Service:_____

Systems Engineer:_____ Phone: _____

Marketing Rep.:_____ Phone: _____

Comments:   _____
_____
_____
_____
_____
_____
_____
_____

procedures, documentation, physical access, password management, and so on. Exhibit 6 presents a sample checklist for an information systems audit.

It can be worthwhile to have a third party review the results of a security audit, system backup procedures, systems documentation, and your actual state of preparedness on a regular basis. If your property is part of a management group, each property can audit another one (to maintain objectivity, they shouldn't audit each other on a reciprocal basis); for independent properties, outside consultants can perform the same service.

**Exhibit 3   Summary of Software Licenses**

| Software Type, Vendor, Application Name/Version | Number of Licenses Purchased | Installed on Server (S) or PC (PC)? | If on Server, Number of Users with Access | If on PCs, Number Installed |
|---|---|---|---|---|
| | | | | |
| | | | | |
| | | | | |
| | | | | |
| | | | | |
| | | | | |
| | | | | |
| | | | | |
| | | | | |
| | | | | |
| | | | | |
| | | | | |
| Detailed lists to be kept separately. | | | | |

# Manual Operations Plans

The following plans and procedures are suggested as an outline for use whenever the property management system is down for any significant amount of time. Exhibit 7 outlines immediate actions to take when the system is down for any significant amount of time. The objective is to establish clear control and coordination responsibilities. Each property should prepare its own version based on its own operational needs and should prepare similar documents for all other critical systems (POS, sales and catering, etc.). All of these plans should be reviewed periodically to ensure that they stay current.

The key to running a hotel manually is good, organized communication between management and all operationally focused departments within the hotel, especially the front desk, reservations, and housekeeping. Most employees will never have worked in a manual environment and will be used to relying exclusively on the front office computer system. Consequently, all instructions to employees should be clear and precise, and the plans should be practiced regularly. Maintaining guest service is of utmost importance during this period.

## Management/Staff Roles

The following roles are suggested for the key management and operations staff. The task assignments should be customized to the nature of each hotel's operations. For example, while many properties may not have a systems manager, they should have one person who has responsibility for coordinating all support

**Exhibit 4    Sample Service and Support Call Log**

Before calling for hardware service, get approval from one of the following managers:
Name/Position:_____ Phone Extension:_____
Name/Position:_____ Phone Extension:_____
Name/Position:_____ Phone Extension:_____
Name/Position:_____ Phone Extension:_____
Name/Position:_____ Phone Extension:_____


**Hardware Maintenance Vendor**:_____
Contact Name: _____
Business Hours Phone:_____
Fax:_____
After Hours Phone:_____
Comments:    _____
            _____
            _____
            _____

**Critical Equipment**

The following key items are covered by a 24x7 maintenance contract:

| Equipment: | Location |
|---|---|
|  |  |
|  |  |
|  |  |
|  |  |

**Important Equipment**

The following hardware is on "normal hours" maintenance contract with service provided five days a week during business hours:

| Equipment: | Location |
|---|---|
|  |  |
|  |  |
|  |  |
|  |  |

**Low-Priority Equipment**

The following equipment is not on a maintenance contract. All service will be billed as incurred at a per call rate of _____:

| Equipment: | Location |
|---|---|
|  |  |
|  |  |
|  |  |
|  |  |

activity on the automated systems. It is most important that the responsibility for performing each task is clearly understood by all.

General Manager/Hotel Manager

• Authorizes notification of all management personnel.

**Exhibit 5    Sample Hardware Maintenance Summary**

Date/Time:_____ Reported by:_____ Reported to:_____

Equipment ID and Location:_____

Describe problem and any error messages:

_____
_____
_____
_____
_____
_____
_____

Resolution:

_____
_____
_____
_____
_____
_____
_____

Date Completed:_____ Hotel Person Closing Case:_____

- Receives status reports from the systems personnel.
- Makes/approves operational decisions regarding system downtime.

Systems Manager

- Determines magnitude of problem; estimates system downtime. Determines status of all correction activities in progress.
- Notifies response team on severity of problem and recommends degree of contingency to implement.
- Ensures all necessary functions and personnel are prepared to begin manual operations, if needed, and notifies appropriate service/vendor personnel.
- Keeps management updated regarding contingency status.
- Supervises repair, restoration, and replacement of data, components, systems, or entire computer room as needed.
- Prepares report for hotel management detailing the problems, causes and solutions, plan performance, and suggestions for modifications as needed.

Reception Manager

- Coordinates front office activity with the systems manager and reservations manager.

**Exhibit 6   Sample Information Systems Audit**

## Information Systems Audit
(Please comment on or explain any "No" responses.)

### A. Computer Room/Physical Systems

1. Is the computer room in a quiet area, not on an outside wall, and not where it might be subject to flooding?
2. Does it have a self-closing, self-locking door? What kind of lock is fitted?
3. Who has access?

4. Is there a separate air-conditioning unit for the computer room?
5. Are temperature and humidity measured on a periodic basis to confirm that they are within specified ranges?
   a. Who performs the measurements?
   b. Attach copy of most recent page of log.
6. Is there a fire alarm/smoke detector in the computer room?
7. Is it a local alarm system? If not, where else does the alarm get indicated?
8. When was it last tested?
9. Is there a local fire extinguishing system in the computer room?
   a. What type?
   b. When was it last inspected? (Attach copy of log.)

10. Is the power for all critical systems on a separate electrical circuit with clearly marked outlets?
11. Are all critical systems on UPSs with sufficient battery backup for at least 20 minutes?
    a. When was the last check of the backup's reliability under full load performed?
    b. Do the battery backup systems provide automatic shutdown of the computer after a specified length of time?
    c. When was this last tested?
12. Are all peripherals (PCs, printers, scanners, etc.) connected to surge-suppressing power strips?

13. Are preventive maintenance inspections being performed regularly? (This includes physical hardware—filter changes, etc.—and any software preventive maintenance such as NT server re-boots, re-booting the PMS to reclaim memory, etc.)

14. Is the computer room kept clean?
15. Is all cabling tidy and clearly labeled?
16. Is there a network diagram? (Attach copy.) Are procedures in place to keep it current?
17. Is there an inventory of all computer hardware?
    a. How often is it checked, and by whom?
    b. What is done if something is missing?

*(continued)*

**Exhibit 6 Sample Information Systems Audit** *(continued)*

18. Is there an inventory of all software applications and operating systems?
    a. How often is it checked, and by whom?
    b. Do proper licenses exist for all software?
    c. What is done if the number of copies in use exceeds the number of legal licenses?

19. Are there full, written descriptions of all computer systems and interfaces, including configuration, support information, current version level and modification history?

20. Are procedures with regard to fire, flood, or other emergencies posted in the computer room and understood by all who have access to the room and equipment?

21. Is there a disaster recovery plan? (Attach copy.)
    a. When was the last time it was tested?
    b. Where is the plan posted?

**B. Information Security**

1. When are full/partial backups done? (Attach copy of plan.)
   a. Who performs the backups?
   b. Attach copy of log.
2. Where are the backups stored?
   a. In what type of container?
   b. Who has access to the media?
   c. Where is the off-site storage location?

3. How are verifications done to ensure the backup is working properly?
4. When was the last verification done?

5. Are downtime reports run to a specific schedule? (Attach copy.)
6. Are obsolete reports destroyed?

7. What redundancy is there for the critical computer systems?
   a. Are there complete backup computers/hardware?
   b. When were the computer/software maintenance contracts last reviewed for all critical systems?
   c. Is there an action plan for failure of the backup?
   d. When was it last tested?

8. Are all support contact numbers posted by the equipment?
9. Are the trouble logs kept with the systems or in an accessible location? (Attach copy.)

10. Are written procedures for manual operations posted at all appropriate locations?
    a. When were they last practiced?

**Exhibit 6    Sample Information Systems Audit** *(continued)*

| |
|---|
| b.    Are "crash kits" of office supplies, pre-filled forms, etc., kept available and fully stocked? |
| **C.  Network Security** |
| 1.    How often are system and user passwords changed?<br>a.    Who determines the passwords?<br>b.    Are they secure? (At least 6 characters, mixed case and alpha/numberic, not easily connected with any specific user.)<br>2.    Is a procedure in place to ensure that employees leaving the company have no access to the systems?<br>3.    Does the current password list match the personnel list? |
| 4.    Are all operating system patches/fixes up to date?<br><br>5.    Is a network-wide anti-virus program installed?<br>a.    Are all the virus signatures/software updates current?<br>b.    How often are the servers scanned for viruses?<br>c.    Is there a written policy regarding the use of diskettes?<br><br>6.    Are there any outside connections to the Local Area Network?<br>a.    If the connections are made using a modem on an individual computer, who has control over the connection(s) and the account(s)?<br>b.    If it is a direct connection into the LAN by a router or other similar device, who maintains the connection, hardware configuration, and passwords for the device?<br>c.    Is there a firewall?<br>d.    Who maintains it?<br><br>7.    Have password cracking programs or external security consultants been employed to help determine the level of security?<br><br>**D.  Employee Security**<br>1.    Are new employees required to sign a written policy regarding computer usage and abuse?<br>2.    Are there written procedures and policies for access to the Internet, including e-mail and browsing?<br>3.    Are there written procedures for securing the computer systems when an employee is terminated?<br><br>(Attach copies of all such policies and procedures.) |

- Supervises the front office activity during downtime.
- Monitors controls and audit trails during downtime.
- Supervises in-house runners.
- Supplies food and beverage outlets with current guest list, no-post list, and cash guest list.

**Exhibit 7    Downtime Quick Response Checklist**

**Quick Response Checklist**

1. Alert managers.
2. If the system is down because of a power failure, *turn off all equipment imme-diately.* Failure to do so could result in further hardware damage. If the critical items are on uninterruptible power supplies (UPSs) with automated shutdown routines, monitor these to ensure that they are in fact closing down correctly.
3. Distribute the most recent downtime reports and destroy prior lists.
4. Designate a rack clerk, responsible for maintaining the room inventory and status, to begin to record all check-ins, check-outs, etc.
5. Designate a posting clerk, responsible for writing all charges on the guest folios.
6. Alert the outlets that the system is inoperable and that they must close checks to the manual key. All room charges must be taken to the front desk for manual posting.
7. Alert the audit staff members no later than four hours before their shift that the system is down and that they should report early to begin a manual audit.
8. Alert the central reservation help desk of the situation and estimated downtime, and arrange an alternative for continued delivery of reservations and feedback of hotel availability status.
9. The rooms division manager should write a letter to all in-house guests and arrivals notifying them of the situation.
10. Issue battery-operated radios to all key personnel, including PBX.

- Documents observed or perceived problems in plan operation for review and/or revision.
- Coordinates reconstruction of data, once system is restored.

Front Desk Supervisor

- Monitors and controls registration functions.
- Maintains room status control sheet.
- Maintains walk-in list.
- Communicates status changes to housekeeping.
- Maintains status change log.
- Supervises bucket clerk.
- Supervises re-entry of check-ins, check-outs, and moves once the system is restored.

Reception Agents

- Control filing of guest charges and maintenance of current balances. Supervise generation of source documents, vouchers/receipts, etc.

- Assist cashiers in balancing shift.
- Assist with posting of charges/payments once the system is restored.

Reservation Manager

- Distributes 30-day and 1-year room availability reports to all reservation agents.
- Supervises manual booking of reservations.
- Maintains manual reservations file.
- Maintains a manual room availability control chart.
- Supervises re-entry of reservations once the system is restored.

PBX Operator

- Notifies computer staff when the system is down.
- Maintains and updates telephone reference list with assistance of front office.

All Outlet Managers

- Coordinate food and beverage contingency plan with systems manager.
- Supervise execution of contingency plan in all food and beverage outlets.
- Supervise manual operation of outlets, including ordering, service, payment, and posting of all checks.
- Supervise entering of all information once system is restored.
- Assist in balancing process during downtime.

Cashiers

- Responsible for three-part check and check control sheet distribution to outlet cashiers.
- Monitor the manual tip control sheet and disbursement of charge tips.

Assistant Controller

- Coordinates accounting department activity with the systems manager.
- Supervises execution of the contingency plan in the accounting office.
- Supervises data reconstruction after the system is restored.

Accounts Receivable Manager

- Works with the front desk supervisor and bucket clerk on maintaining the manual guest ledger.
- Maintains manual banquet billings.
- Coordinates advance deposit refunds with accounts payable during extended downtime.
- Maintains manual credit card account balances.

**Exhibit 8    Items and Staff Needed for Manual Front Desk Operations**

| | |
|---|---|
| Forms: | Manual Room Rack |
| | Cash Guest Report |
| | House Count Sheet |
| | Registration Cards (handwritten or pre-printed) |
| | Guest Folios (handwritten or pre-printed) |
| | Reservations Forms (handwritten or pre-printed) |
| | Most recent downtime reports from system |
| | |
| Miscellaneous: | Index cards and alphabetical file |
| | Calculator with tape (battery operated) |
| | Pencil with eraser |
| | Credit card imprinters |

| | | |
|---|---|---|
| Personnel: | Posting Clerk: | Responsible for posting all charges to guest folios |
| | Rack Clerk: | Responsible for maintaining room inventory and current status |
| | Runners: | Responsible for communications between departments, insuring that departments are passing information correctly and that everyone is following the manual operating procedures |

- Monitors advance deposit activity.
- Supervises restoration of data.

Housekeeping

- Supervises manual room status controls.
- Establishes initial room status sheet (P.M.) housekeeping report.
- Supervises vacant room inspection.
- Supervises distribution of updated room status lists to front desk.
- Supervises manual assignment of room attendants.
- Maintains room status change log.

Night Reception Manager

- Performs regular audit functions when and where necessary.
- Helps generate manual reports during extended downtime.
- Supervises the night clerks during downtime.
- Assists in the restoration of data.
- Performs update and distribution of reports.
- Balances hotel accounts at the end of the day.

## Manual Front Desk Overview

Exhibit 8 lists items and staff needed to manually operate the front desk. Make sure that the room rack report (see Exhibit 9) and any other standard forms are already

**Exhibit 9    Sample Manual Room Rack Report**

**Manual Room Rack**

Floor Number _____        Section Number _____

| | | |
|---|---|---|
| Room #: _____ | Room Type: _____ |
| Status: _____ | Guest Name: _____ |
| Room Features: _____ | Check-Out: _____ |

| | |
|---|---|
| Room #: _____ | Room Type: _____ |
| Status: _____ | Guest Name: _____ |
| Room Features: _____ | Check-Out: _____ |

| | |
|---|---|
| Room #: _____ | Room Type: _____ |
| Status: _____ | Guest Name: _____ |
| Room Features: _____ | Check-Out: _____ |

| | |
|---|---|
| Room #: _____ | Room Type: _____ |
| Status: _____ | Guest Name: _____ |
| Room Features: _____ | Check-Out: _____ |

| | |
|---|---|
| Room #: _____ | Room Type: _____ |
| Status: _____ | Guest Name: _____ |
| Room Features: _____ | Check-Out: _____ |

| | |
|---|---|
| Room #: _____ | Room Type: _____ |
| Status: _____ | Guest Name: _____ |
| Room Features: _____ | Check-Out: _____ |

| | |
|---|---|
| Room #: _____ | Room Type: _____ |
| Status: _____ | Guest Name: _____ |
| Room Features: _____ | Check-Out: _____ |

| | |
|---|---|
| Room #: _____ | Room Type: _____ |
| Status: _____ | Guest Name: _____ |
| Room Features: _____ | Check-Out: _____ |

| | |
|---|---|
| Room #: _____ | Room Type: _____ |
| Status: _____ | Guest Name: _____ |
| Room Features: _____ | Check-Out: _____ |

| | |
|---|---|
| Room #: _____ | Room Type: _____ |
| Status: _____ | Guest Name: _____ |
| Room Features: _____ | Check-Out: _____ |

| | |
|---|---|
| Room #: _____ | Room Type: _____ |
| Status: _____ | Guest Name: _____ |
| Room Features: _____ | Check-Out: _____ |

filled out with the room numbers and other data that do not change. Prepare "crash kits" stocked with all necessary office supplies (pens, cards, pads, tape, etc.) and keep them in an area that is convenient to the front desk. The appendix at the end of the chapter contains steps outlining the basic manual operation of the front desk, followed by more detailed procedures for manual check-in, check-out, and other typical functions.

## Returning to Automated Operations

When the system is fully operational again, it won't know that anything has happened since it went down, and it must be brought up-to-date by manually entering all the transactions that occurred in the interim. This requires an organized effort on the part of all members of management to keep all users posting on the correct day. If all night audit work is organized into batches, all staff can concentrate on one day's activity at a time. A night audit must be run for each day that the system was down in order to bring the system up to the current date. Manual downtime procedures must be maintained until the system is running and its data has been verified as fully up to date. General steps to bringing the system up-to-date are:

1. Process the first day's work. Process all activity that was not posted on the day that the system went down, including check-ins, check-outs, all transactions, and room status changes.

2. Some systems (PBX, call accounting, mini bars, pay movies, etc.) that use an interface to post charges to guest folios may hold charges in a buffer. If these systems were operating during the time that the PMS was not, charges may post automatically when the interface is restored. This could result in charges being posted to the wrong accounts, double posting of charges, phones or mini bars being turned off or on inappropriately, and so on. Each of these systems should have a backup printer to report charges (including date, time, and room number) it was unable to send to the PMS. This is the information needed to post charges manually to the correct guests' folios, but the reports do not imply that charges are not still being held in a buffer. Check with the vendor for each of these systems to discuss how their systems work and how best to handle a situation where the PMS, the interface, or even the system in question is down. Add this information to this section of the manual instructions.

3. Perform a full rooms and financial audit for that day.

4. Run a night audit process on the computer system.

5. Once the above procedures are complete and the system is on the next day, process the remaining days' transactions in the same manner. Perform night audit and run a close-of-day for each day until the current day and time are reached.

 **Key Terms** ─────────────────────────────────────

**anti-virus software**—Programs that search for binary signatures (patterns) of known viruses that have attached themselves to executable programs. As new viruses are discovered, the signature database has to be updated in order for the anti-virus program to be effective. Vendors generally offer downloads via the Web in order to keep clients current.

**application service provider (ASP)**—A company that offers individuals or enterprises access over the Internet to applications and related services that would otherwise have to be located in their own personal or enterprise computers. Sometimes referred to as "apps-on-tap," ASP services are expected to become an important alternative, not only for smaller companies with low budgets for information technology, but also for larger companies as a form of outsourcing and for many services for individuals as well.

**documentation**—The narrative and graphical description of a system, including operating procedures, system documentation, and technical documentation.

**downtime**—The time during which a computer is not functioning due to hardware or system software failure.

**firewall**—A method for keeping a network secure from intruders. It can be a single router that filters out unwanted packets or may comprise a combination of routers and servers, each performing some type of firewall processing. Firewalls are widely used to give users secure access to the Internet as well as to separate a company's public Web server from its internal network. Firewalls are also used to keep internal network segments secure; for example, without a firewall the accounting network might be vulnerable to snooping from within the enterprise.

**Internet**—The interconnected system of networks that share standards and protocols connecting computers around the world.

**lock down**—An action designed to restrict the functionality of a system. For example, network administrators can lock down client desktops so that users can perform only certain operations.

**patch**—A temporary or quick fix to a program. Too many patches in a program make it difficult to maintain. The term is also used to refer to a general-purpose fix that does not actually patch a piece of the program, but is an entirely new executable module that replaces the old one.

**router**—A device that forwards data packets from one local area network (LAN) or wide area network (WAN) to another. Based on routing tables and routing protocols, routers read the network address in each transmitted frame and make a decision on how to send it based on the most expedient route (traffic load, line costs, speed, bad lines, etc.).

**security audit**—An examination of networks and computer systems to determine an organization's vulnerability to criminal invasion (crackers, viruses, arson, etc.) and natural disasters (fire, tornadoes, earthquakes, etc.), and other threats.

**surge protector**—A device that employs some method of surge suppression to protect electronic equipment from excessive voltage (spikes and power surges) in the power line.

**uninterruptible power supply (UPS)**—Backup power used when the electrical power fails or drops to an unacceptable voltage level. Small UPS systems provide battery power for a few minutes; enough to power down the computer in an orderly manner. Sophisticated systems are tied to electrical generators that can provide power for days. A surge protector filters out surges and spikes, and a voltage regulator maintains uniform voltage during a brownout, but a UPS keeps a computer running when there is no electrical power. UPS systems typically provide surge suppression and may also provide voltage regulation.

**virtual private network (VPN)**—A private network that is configured within a public network. VPNs enjoy the security of a private network via access control and encryption, while taking advantage of the economies of scale and built-in management facilities of large public networks.

# Chapter Appendix

## Manual Front Desk Operations

### Manual Room Rack

1. Establish a manual room rack on the rack sheets with an accurate and complete status of all rooms. Obtain as much information as possible about the status of each room from the downtime reports, the bucket, and the housekeeping reports. Use your staff (including security, bellpersons, and others if needed) to resolve any discrepancies.

2. Record the status of each room on the room rack sheets. Use the status codes most familiar to your hotel.

3. For each occupied room, complete the data on the room rack sheet.

### Posting Clerk

4. The posting clerk should create a folio for each registered guest and carry forward the last balance from the last occupancy report. A sample downtime guest folio is presented in Figure 1. Attach the folio to each registration card in the bucket. If manual posting becomes necessary, the posting clerk will post charges to this folio and will carry the balance forward as they post. If departure folios are relatively current, they may be filed in the bucket in lieu of manually preparing folios. Include the rate and tax on the folio. This process may take some time, and you may need to assign employees from other departments to assist with it.

### Housekeeping

5. The housekeeping floor supervisors update the executive housekeeper on room status.

6. Hourly, the executive housekeeper updates the front office manager and the reservation manager with the current status of the hotel rooms. The front office manager is responsible for updating the rack clerk. These four people are responsible for maintaining an accurate house count.

### Rack Clerk

The rack clerk generates an updated rack report that will be distributed to each department

7. Gather the registration cards for all arrivals and all departures since the time of the last backup list. Enter them on manual arrival and departure logs, and write "SYSTEM DOWN" after the last entries so that arrivals and departures before and after the downtime can be determined.

**Figure 1    Sample Downtime Guest Folio**

Date: _____

We're sorry, but we are unable to print a copy of your folio at this time. Please review the amounts listed below and note any corrections. A final folio will be mailed to you as soon as possible. Thank you!

Guest Name: _____   Room Number:_____

Mailing Address: _____

_____

_____

Balance as of: _____ at _____                    $_____
                                Date              Time

Room Charge for the night of: _____               $_____
                                           Date
Room Tax:                                                   $_____

Other Charges:

_____                $_____

_____                $_____

_____                $_____

_____                $_____

_____                $_____

_____                $_____

Total:            $_____

Amount Paid:      $_____

Balance:          $_____

Form of Settlement (circle):     Cash    Direct Bill    Amex    Visa/MC    Diners    Discover
                                                 (attach voucher for credit card settlement)

Time of Departure: _____        Charges Posted: ___    Clerk: _____

Clerk Number:      _____        Check-Out:      ___    Clerk: _____

                                     Folio Mailed:   ___    Clerk: _____

8. The rack clerk keeps track of the house count, including in-house guests, expected departures, 6 P.M. arrivals, etc.

## Check-In

9. At 5 P.M. the rack clerk, front desk manager, and executive housekeeper should compare their reports for discrepancies. These discrepant rooms should be rechecked manually; notify housekeeping once there is an accurate accounting of the house status.

10. For new check-ins, the front desk clerk handwrites a folio, attaches it immediately to the registration card, and passes it to the posting clerk for placement in the bucket.

11. Record cash-paying guests on the cash guest report and distribute this to the outlets on a regular basis.

## PBX

12. Fill out index cards for each occupied room for placement in an "in-house guest" accordion file for PBX operators. Include each guest's last name, first name, room number, check-out date, and credit status. The credit status is needed to determine if long-distance phone service should be allowed for this guest. Make note of any guest requiring accessible accommodations. Because this process may take some time, employees from other departments may be assigned to assist.

## Posting Clerk

13. At a time designated by management, the posting clerk should be stationed in the cashier/count-out room and begin posting all charges from the outlets. Information on the folio includes date, charge/outlet, reference number, and the amount.

## Shift Closing

14. At the end of the shift, the posting clerk totals all outlet charges by outlet, runs a tape, balances each stack of charges, and places all charges in the night audit basket.

## Check-Out

1. Pull the registration card and folio from the bucket. Make certain room and tax has been posted each night; if not, manually post the appropriate amount with date.

2. Post any adjustments or paid-outs manually using the appropriate form. Ensure that the type of adjustment, account code, date, and amount are recorded accurately on the folio.

3. Re-add all charges on the folio to ensure that the balance is correct and collect the payment. Attach a copy of the folio, credit card voucher, and any miscellaneous vouchers to the registration card, and file it with the appropriate method of payment in the shift work.

4.  Advise guests at check-out that all charges may not appear on the bill they've just been given and that a revised statement will be sent to them.

5.  Tell the rack clerk that this guest has checked out. The rack clerk will then change the status of the room on the rack sheet.

6.  The rack clerk notifies housekeeping and PBX of the status change.

7.  PBX removes the index card for that guest from their folder.

**Miscellaneous Posting**

Items needed: Pre-printed posting slips for miscellaneous charges, adjustments, and paid-outs. The posting clerk will post all guest charges manually.

1.  When charges are brought to the front desk from the outlets, the posting clerk will write the amount, time, date, and source of charge on the guest's folio.

2.  The posting clerk should initial the charge voucher.

3.  A copy of the charge voucher should be placed in the bucket along with the guest folio. If the copy machine is not functioning, make a manual copy and mark it as a copy.

4.  The posting clerk should set a copy of the charge voucher aside for end-of-shift balance.

**Paid-Out**

In hotels that routinely post charges from outlets that are not a part of the hotel (gift shop, etc.) as paid-outs, the following procedures should be followed:

1.  Fill out a paid-out voucher and attach it to the receipt that the outlet presented to you for posting.

2.  Present the receipt with the paid-out voucher to the posting clerk for posting to the guest folio.

3.  The posting clerk will include the copy of the receipt in the bucket with the folio.

4.  A copy of the receipt and the paid-out voucher will be included with the posting clerk's shift work.

**Shift Closing**

Shift closing will be conducted in the usual manner with the exception of balancing to the computer. Accounting personnel should be available to assist during shift closings.

1.  Complete the cash drop form and run a calculator tape to determine the total cash taken in.

2. Drop the correct amount of cash in the deposit envelope, leaving your bank at the correct starting amount.

3. Add each type of posting voucher you posted. This includes adjustments, miscellaneous vouchers, phone, restaurant, bar, etc.

4. Add each credit card payment by type (AX, VA, etc.).

5. Complete a shift-closing report.

6. Place the shift-closing packet in the night audit basket, including the shift closing report and the totaled posting vouchers by account and any miscellaneous notes.

### Night Audit

Each night, the night auditor and any additional personnel designated by the controller will perform an audit to ensure that revenue was posted properly. Special attention should be paid to each individual folio to ensure that they are all totaled correctly. Each morning the controller and designated representatives from the front office and accounting will record and audit all transactions that have been manually posted from the previous day, producing a manual revenue report. NOTE: The accounting department should create and attach additional documentation for this section describing specific functions to be performed by the audit staff and the posting clerks.

### Housekeeping

The housekeeping department will keep a manual record of the status of all rooms on a daily basis. It should generate manual section assignments, which could be implemented at any time. The following procedures should be followed once the rack and current house status have been completed:

1. In the morning, generate room assignments using the rack report prepared by the rack clerk.

2. Housekeeping floor supervisors will update the executive housekeeper on room status as rooms are cleaned.

3. Hourly, the executive housekeeper will update the front office manager and the reservation manager; the front office manager is responsible for updating the rack clerk. These four people are responsible for maintaining an accurate house count.

4. Report discrepancies immediately to the front office manager as they occur throughout the day.

5. The rack clerk will periodically generate an updated rack report for distribution to each department. At 1 P.M., housekeeping, the front office manager, and the rack clerk should verify the status of the expected departures. Conduct a physical check of the rooms expected to depart.

6. At 5 P.M., the rack clerk, front desk manager, and housekeeper should compare their reports for discrepancies. Discrepant rooms should be rechecked manually. Notify housekeeping once there is an accurate accounting of the house.

7. Begin filling out the manual assignment sheets for the next day's housekeeping assignments. Any minor changes due to late check-in should be passed by the rack clerk to housekeeping the next morning. Setting up the reports the evening before ensures prompt guest service and maintains housekeeping productivity.

**PBX and Call Accounting**

The systems that make up your phone system (PBX, call accounting, voice mail, and property management system interface) could fail individually or simultaneously.

If the PBX system fails, your phones will not function. To be prepared, the hotel should have several direct lines that do not go through the PBX that can be used if the PBX fails. Your PBX may also have specific power-failure phones that are designed to work when the PBX system loses power.

If the PBX interface to your property management system fails, phones and message lights must be turned on and off manually.

If the call accounting system fails, most PBX systems will buffer the phone call information until the call accounting system is restored. Back charges will then be processed automatically.

If the call accounting interface to your property management system fails, most call accounting systems will buffer the phone charge information until the call accounting interface is restored. Back charges will then be processed automatically. Most call accounting systems also have a backup printer that prints all charge information, which can be used should manual posting of guest folios be required. However, be wary of duplicating charges when the interface connection is restored.

Check to see if the voice mail system has also failed, by attempting to leave and retrieve a test message. If the system is not accepting messages, notify the PBX operators, and have them take manual messages. Check with your PBX, call accounting, and voice mail vendors to find out how your systems work and what backup and downtime procedures should be practiced by your hotel.

**Locating Guests**

Operators will create an index card for each in-house guest using the latest occupancy report, indicating the guest's name and room number. These cards will be filed alphabetically in the accordion file or file box for use in locating a guest.

**Manual Posting Calls**

If manual postings of call charges are necessary, the following steps should be taken:

1. The operator will fill out a telephone charge voucher for each call placed, indicating the room number, time, charge, and type of call (local or long distance), and will send it to the posting clerk for action.

2. The posting clerk will keep a manual ledger of postings so that the night audit can balance the phone charges that were posted during the day.

**Reservation Center**

Notify the central reservations help desk of the situation and estimated downtime. Arrange an alternative procedure for receiving reservations and passing back changes to availability.

**Manual Reservations**

All reservations should be taken on manual reservation forms, passed to the supervisor to modify future days' inventory, and placed in an accordion date file for later use. Reservations taken during this time should be filed by the date the reservation was made for proper entry into the system when it is back up and running. All requests for specialty rooms should be forwarded to a supervisor. If your hotel has the ability to transfer phone calls automatically to the reservation center, consider implementing this.

# Index